Tree With No Leaves

A Life Lived Through Infertility, IVF and Breast Cancer

SORJA REESE

 Published by Wild Weeds Press, December 2020 for the Katharine Susannah Prichard Foundation Inc.

© Sorja Reese. All rights reserved by the author.

Edited by Melinda Tognini. Typeset by Rebekah-Jane Sheedy. Cover design by Lisa Wolstenholme.

Cover images were painted by Sorja Reese.

This book is copyright. Apart from any fair dealing for the purpose of private study, research, criticism or review, as permitted under the Copyright Act, no part may be reproduced by any process without written permission from the publisher.

The author acknowledges the trademark status and trademark owners of various products referenced in this work which have been used without permission. The publication/use of these trademarks is not authorised, associated with, or sponsored by the trademark owners.

 A catalogue record for this work is available from the National Library of Australia

Printed by iPrintPlus

ISBN (sc): 978-0-6489210-6-6

ISBN (e): 978-0-6489210-7-3

'I'm in the middle of painting a tree trunk; it's not a 'normal' looking tree. The colours are more alive and vibrant than any tree you see out in nature. I am that tree. My journey through this physical life has slowly chopped away pieces of me. Like a barren and bare tree, I've learned to live without these leaves. Yet I am still here, standing tall and proud. The core of me is strong and sturdy like the trunk of the tree. My life force still pulses beneath the layers of bark and shines through, revealing a multitude of colours.'—Sorja Reese (Sunday 11 March 2012)

Contents

Acknowledgements	i
Preface	iii
Author's Note	v
Tree With No Leaves	1
Match Made on Paper	3
What's Wrong With Me?	7
Why Me? Why Such Pain?	9
Infertility Sucks Big Time	13
Hope Blossoms With IVF	20
Try, Try and Try Again	50
Rollercoaster of Emotions	69
Is It Time To Give Up?	75
Door Shut or Left Ajar?	80
New Focus, New Dreams	83
Out of Focus, Out of Mind	87
Decision Time	91
Door Firmly Shut	100
Life Goes On—Childless	118
What Now?	124
Time Heals All Wounds or Does It Just Cover Them Up?	129
Whispers of the Soul	137

Wake Up Call, Diagnosis of Breast Cancer	146
Perseverance, Patience and Pride	161
Cancer Sucks!	193
All Consuming Journey—Physical, Emotional, Mental and Spiritual	232
No Judgement—Life's Lessons	286
Onward and Upward	320
Learning To Forgive, To Love, To Hope and To Understand	341
Brave Face, Quivering Insides	357
Counsellor, Counsel Thyself!	372
Rediscovering Creativity	408
The Dreaded Four-Letter Word FEAR Versus Its Opponent LOVE	414
What's in a Word?	420
Cycles and Patterns	432
The Paint Strokes of My Life	448
Make a Wish on a Ladybug	454
Conclusion of Book, Not My Life	458

Acknowledgements

First and foremost, I want to acknowledge my darling husband, David, who has been through the worst of times and the best of times with me, often observing my pain and giving me his strength to last one more day. To our loving fur babies, past and present—Misha, Cheyenne, Krystal and Xena—thank you for loving us unconditionally and being my best friends, healers and support crew. Thanks go to my beloved family: my Pa Risto and my Ma Irja; my sisters Kirsti, Katri and Irma; and my brother Visa. Also, to my extended family, near and far: my mother-in-law, sisters-in-law and brothers-in-law, my nephews, nieces, aunts, uncles and cousins. I am grateful for my friends, some of whom have been with me for decades (you know who you are) and others who have joined me in a dance or two in this life before moving on. I thank each one of you for your love and support. I want to mention my general practitioner, Dr Patricia Moore, who has known me for years and has always been caring, patient and kind. To the numerous doctors, nurses and specialists in the medical profession, I sincerely thank you for helping to keep me here and very much alive. Also, to my Reiki Master, Carol Kirk, thank you for your years of teachings, meditations, readings and encouragement to share this memoir. A special mention to the three women who patiently helped me throughout this process of publishing my book: Lisa Wolstenholme, Rebekah Sheedy and Melinda Tognini. Finally, I thank the Spirit World, which includes my Spirit Guides, Angels, Archangels and Ancestors who have passed and yet are very much active in my life, as well as my dear family and friends who have passed through the veil of life and death. I love you and thank you for your continued presence in my life. I will strive to make you all proud of me.

Preface

A dear friend of mine asked me when did I decide to turn my journals and diaries into a memoir? Truth be told, I always instinctively knew I had to write down my experiences—as challenging as they were—as a form of healing for me, but also in the hope of being able to help others in the future. It's difficult to explain how I knew; I am a very spiritual person and it's as if a voice told me to make my words count.

In my lightest and darkest of hours, I found relief in expressing myself through words. I found meaning to everything I have lived through. I dissected, I analysed and I marvelled at human strength. I learned and I taught, I forgave and I loved.

From an early age, I found comfort in writing all of my thoughts, feelings and experiences down. I wrote during my teenage years of anguish and being bullied. On the flipside, I wrote during my travels interrailing around Europe, first in the company of my sister, and then later travelling solo in my late teens and early twenties. What strength I gathered from those experiences.

When I married my American pen pal David in Texas in 1995 at the age of 29, I really wanted my journal entries to reflect the quality of a romance novel and the subsequent happy ending. Let's just say life did not go quite as we had so romantically planned in our love letters.

It is through all my diaries and journals that this memoir has come into being. My book spans a period of twenty-five years of our life together. David and I have been challenged time and time again, yet our marriage has endured and we remain together in love 'in sickness and in health'.

The reason behind writing this book is to hopefully reach as many people as possible and help them realise how strong they are despite what life throws at them. The process of creation has proven to be very cathartic and an avenue to let my past roll away with my tears. I trust that my words can now help thousands of women and couples to realise that this human experience can repeatedly knock you backwards; however, with courage and a good dose of humour, you can keep getting back up, greet life with a smile and treat it as an adventure!

I hope that through reading my words you will feel as though you are walking in my footsteps and witnessing my growth from a young woman in my twenties to a mature, authentic Soul in my fifties. I have found my voice and my power. I believe that there is a purpose to all that has happened, and I am meant to help others, particularly women, to heal and to realise their own dreams.

Author's Note

I, Sorja, pronounced 'Sorry-A', was born in Finland in 1966. Translated from the Finnish language, *Sorja* means 'graceful and slender'. Well, I'd like to think I am fifty per cent true to the name, ha, ha, ha… My parents and four siblings immigrated to Australia when I was five. To this day it amazes me that my parents moved to a country halfway across the world with five children ranging from five to eleven, and without one word of English. I was born to a family that exemplified courage, perseverance and adaptability.

I have been quite the gypsy, as all our family have been, and over the years I have lived at numerous addresses in Finland, Australia and Texas USA. In Australia, I have lived in the states of Queensland, Tasmania, Victoria and Western Australia.

My whole life I have been a bit 'different' from the other children and, later, other adults. I have always had a fascination with all things spiritual or metaphysical and have had many psychic dreams since I was a child. Over the years I have amassed a large collection of books pertaining to many of these subjects. Due to my spiritual leanings, I have been open to seeing clairvoyants, mediums and psychics, either individually or in group settings. I have always wanted to learn more and read more and experience more. From my childhood onwards, I have been called an old Soul many times. I have dipped my feet into meditation on and off for as long as I can remember. I have also always had an affinity with animals of all kinds, often talking to them and being surprised by how easy it is to communicate with them, and how much they understand.

As a young child in Finland, I often had conversations with my imaginary friend whilst walking or riding my bike. I also made up songs to sing to myself as I created my own pastes and potions using whatever I found from the forest, such as mud, bark, berries and mushrooms. My mother was quick to ensure I never tasted my home-made products!

It is my firm belief that I chose to come into this incarnation knowing my spiritual strength would get me through the many physical challenges I have had since I was a child. As a five-year-old, I would scream with pain from horrible headaches and growing too fast. I know now that I have always been a 'sensitive' and react to other people's energies. I did not know how to protect myself from these energies at that time.

During puberty, my life became more complicated and painful. From the onset of menstruation, I never had a 'normal' cycle. After many years, due to the extreme pain and heaviness of my periods, my doctor prescribed the pill, even though I was not yet sexually active. I needed to experiment with many types before finding relief from my symptoms and side effects. At age twenty, when I was back living and working in Finland, I gave my body a break from the pill and actually went without having periods for a year. My body was very confused.

By the time I was thirty, having been married a year, David and I were ready to start a family. Unfortunately, my husband and I were not able to have children, either naturally or even after many IVF attempts. I have come to accept this over time and have learned that my fur babies bring me such joy, companionship and unconditional love. They have always been there for me during the most difficult times, healing me with their paws. There is no need for me to go through all the ailments of my life in this introduction. It is sufficient to say that my body is riddled with scars from surgeries and my life experiences.

I first met my Reiki Master, Carol Kirk, in 2009 when I was living in Safety Bay and actively sought out a meditation group to join. I had not heard of Reiki prior to this but noticed information about it during our meditation sessions. After many months of enjoying our meditation and spiritual conversation classes, where it felt normal to discuss my spiritual experiences and psychic messages, I courageously put my name down for Reiki I. I completed my Reiki I in October 2009 and subsequently my Reiki II in March 2010.

So what does it mean to experience the universal healing energy of Reiki? Reiki is translated as 'rei' meaning universal and 'ki' meaning life energy. A Reiki practitioner transmits healing energy through their hands by accessing the universal life energy, and it is quite a spiritual experience. Reiki is an ancient healing method originating in Tibet and dating back thousands of years. However, the Reiki practiced today can be traced back to the early 20th century in Japan and the spiritual teachings of Dr Mikao Usui.

Holistic in nature, Reiki is a very gentle, subtle, non-intrusive and effective form of energy healing which can bring about balance and healing on physical, emotional, mental and spiritual levels. Reiki practitioners seek to access this universal energy, allowing it to flow through them and their hands to reach the areas of the body (whether the physical body, the emotional body, the mental body or the spiritual body) and help facilitate this healing process. Often, we do not know which of these bodies is out of balance. Reiki taps into universal knowledge and can therefore direct the healing energy to where it is most needed at that particular time.

Everything happens for a reason. It is no coincidence that I became a Reiki Practitioner II in March 2010, with a full year of developing and honing my skills prior to the greatest challenge of my life. In February 2011, I received the life changing news that I had stage three Her2 Positive Breast Cancer. I knew I had to tackle this latest test with everything I had in my arsenal. Along with the surgeries, chemotherapy, radiation therapy, two years of Herceptin intravenous infusions every three weeks, and naturopathic help from my sister, I had my meditation and my special Reiki healing. Many a time, when the painkillers failed to work, I found relief in Reiki. Reiki has kept me going when I thought I could not take another breath. I am in remission and I will continue to be so. I give Reiki healing to myself every day; I've even woken up to discover I had been performing Reiki on myself while I was sleeping. Isn't that incredible?

Over many years, I have studied and qualified in numerous fields including an Associate Diploma of Business - Travel and Tourism (1991), Diploma of Professional Counselling (2006), Qualified Art Therapist (2007), Reiki I Practitioner (2009), Reiki II Practitioner (2010) and Reiki Master (2015). However, I am also an artist, writer and poet. I know that as long as I live, I will continue to study and to learn and to grow. Life is an adventure to be lived, not to be endured.

On a personal note to you who are reading this, please be curious. Read more, learn to listen to the guidance and messages you receive on a daily basis, but most importantly, learn to accept yourself, warts and all, and appreciate the miraculous being that you are. Once in a while, laugh as though there is no ending, let the tears of mirth run down your face without caring how you are gazed upon by others. You are enough. Self-love is the penultimate to self-healing.

I truly believe that each of my health challenges have occurred at a time in my life when I was out of balance, whether physically, emotionally, mentally or spiritually. Every time I have been stopped in my tracks by one health challenge or another, my higher self has recognised the bigger picture. One aspect of my body was out of kilter. Maybe I had not truly felt my emotions or grieved enough, or perhaps my self-talk was negative rather than positive. My message to you is to not bottle up your emotions and feelings, or just 'soldier on' through life and its many varied difficulties. Learn how to really feel and express your emotions. You never know—by allowing yourself the freedom to voice your feelings, you may cause a ripple effect and help others along the way.

x

Chapter 1

Tree With No Leaves

There are moments of time which are forever etched in your memory. No matter how many years pass, recollection of a particular moment, place and time comes easily to you. The suburb Glenorchy: a very ordinary suburb of Hobart, Tasmania, Australia. The house: an old, white-washed timber home surrounded by an overgrown garden, with a 'busy' and cluttered interior. The woman: a grey-haired, small but plump woman in her sixties, who radiated such a grandmotherly aura.

I was eager to hear what this so-called 'clairvoyant and medium' had to say to me, a twenty-something-year-old young woman. My sister Irma had recommended her to me after her own experience with the clairvoyant and medium. I was nervous but also excited to hear what my future possibilities and adventures in life would be…

My older sister Katri accompanied me to be my scribe, as no tape recorders were allowed in the session. I still have the notes from that day. I remember feeling optimistic and full of hope, as I had recently become involved with a wonderful man albeit through unusual circumstances. I was on such a high that I fully expected the clairvoyant to support all my dreams of marriage, children and 'happy ever after'.

I had visited other clairvoyants in the past, so I was wary about believing everything she said and the need to take it all 'with a grain of salt'. I know now, with the knowledge I have accumulated through years of my own studies, that a lot of what she told me was a combination of numerology, naturopathy and astrology.

The memory that is seared into my head and heart is the moment she spoke these words: 'You are like a tree with no leaves.' And she smiled with great sympathy and empathy. Of course, at the age of twenty-seven, those words made no sense to me whatsoever. *What tree?* I wondered. *What leaves? What are you talking about? OK, file it away for future reference and thought. Maybe this was a waste of money... this old woman is loopy...*

As the session ended, and following a short complimentary reading for my sister, this tiny lady gave me the biggest hug possible. I was bemused by her heartfelt hug and the expression on her face—such sadness, love and encouragement. She may or may no longer be on this earth, but I feel her imprint on my life.

Chapter 2

Match Made on Paper

For years I had been searching for my 'perfect match', my Soulmate, and after experiencing several disastrous relationships, I was beginning to give up hope of ever finding my 'other half'. I had an image of the type of man I would marry, but time after time I'd take a wrong turn and settle for a relationship that just didn't feel right. Tired of the merry-go-round courtship rituals and dating games, I consciously let go of the hunt for my perfect mate, so to speak, deciding instead to enjoy life as a single woman. Part of this choice was to broaden my interests and hobbies.

Around July 1993, an advertisement in the miscellaneous column of our local newspaper caught my eye. It read, *'American single men and women seek Aussies for friendship/romance',* followed by an address in the USA. I cut out the article and kept it in my purse for a few days before deciding to 'give it a go'. I had never been a pen pal before, so I thought it would be interesting to correspond with an American and find out what life was like in the USA.

After sending my address and a brief description of myself, I patiently waited for a reply. I really wasn't sure what would happen next. Would I receive an occasional letter from somewhere in the USA, or nothing at all? What I did *not* expect was a bulky letter containing a listing of approximately fifty single men from all around the United States of America!

My family and friends, who were used to my impulsiveness, were greatly amused. My mother and sisters shared a giggle or two as I poured over the descriptions of the various men. After much deliberation, and not wanting to appear greedy, I wrote to five of the men, thinking that maybe one or two of them would actually write back.

I did not foresee that just as I had received a list of men, I would in turn appear on a list of Aussie women. So, over a period of many months, not only did I hear from the five men I initially corresponded with, but I also received over forty other letters from single American men wishing to write to me. Needless to say, my badly bruised ego received a welcome lift!

I continued to write to three of the original five men; however, right from the start, one man in particular caught my interest and curiosity. I remember receiving his very first letter to me, and reading it with sweaty palms. I raced to my sisters and my mother in the kitchen, waved the letter in my hand and jokingly declared, 'This is the man I'm going to marry!'

After a couple of months of writing to each other, we exchanged phone numbers and photos. Although I still wrote to two other pen pals, I was becoming increasingly attracted to David. What had started as a hobby was slowly changing into a long-distance romance. Although we were yet to meet, we were falling in love. I found it so difficult to explain how I could fall in love with someone via paper and phone calls, but I did. My friends and family humoured my belief that I had found my Soulmate, but I could tell that they were sceptical.

Following approximately a year of corresponding, I took a one-month holiday from work and flew to Texas USA to finally meet my pen pal. This was the real test to see whether it was just wishful thinking, or whether I had found my future husband. We had both fantasised about our airport meeting for such a long time; however, probably due to nerves on both sides, it was a bit of an anti-climax. In fact, his first spoken words to me were, 'God, you're tall!'

And my first words to David were, 'I have to go use the Ladies.'

Despite the shaky start, I thoroughly enjoyed my month travelling with David. Not only that, but we did not disappoint each other. We decided we loved each other and wanted to get married. David even *hypothetically* proposed to me by asking, 'If I were to propose to you right now, what would your answer be?'

Leaving David and returning to Australia was one of the hardest things I've had to do, but both of us had numerous decisions and plans ahead of us. I decided to move to Texas, but it was another ten months before I finally received approval for my Fiancée Visa to the USA. The time apart was difficult, but we became pen pals once again and learned far more about each other than an ordinary couple would in a similar period of time. I always have found it easier to ask questions via letters rather than face-to-face.

On my twenty-ninth birthday, in September 1995, David and I married in Houston, Texas, and lived there for two years. After our first wedding anniversary, we made the decision to try and get pregnant. I happily threw my contraceptive pills into the rubbish bin and hoped for the best.

Although living in America was an excellent experience, I missed Australia, my family and my friends too much to be completely happy. Thankfully, David is an understanding husband and, after careful thought, he agreed to move to Australia with me. Once again, we found ourselves waiting for a visa. Finally, in August 1997,

David and I arrived in Australia to continue married life and expand our family. After a year of trying to conceive on our own, however, we knew we needed expert advice from a fertility doctor.

Chapter 3

What's Wrong With Me?

Sunday 31 August 1997 (Hobart, Tasmania, Australia)
I'm suffering from a horrible stomach ache, similar to the one I experienced in Texas one and a half years ago.

Tuesday 2 September 1997 (Family re-union at my sister Irma's house)
After meeting Ma and Pa's flight from Melbourne, we drove straight to Irma's place for coffee. By now, my stomach felt extremely swollen and I had repeatedly gone to the toilet for days. I couldn't stop crying because of the pain in my stomach and ovaries. This is where my 'fun' began. We left the rest of the family behind as Irma and David took me to Hopkins Street Clinic. The doctor there determined that I needed to be transferred to Royal Hobart Hospital to undergo further tests.

Thursday 4 September 1997
I've been poked and prodded so much. I'm tender all over and feel like a pin cushion from the morphine and pethidine painkiller shots injected into my thighs. They've taken urine, stool and blood samples. I've gone to the loo with diarrhoea approximately fifty times in the past eight days—not fun at all!

Yesterday, I went through a renaloscopy, which involved drinking a solution to enable doctors to see its passage through my intestines. Iodine was also injected to make it easier to scan my appendix scar area. In addition, I've had an ultrasound. It's always fun to be so full of wee that it feels like you're going to burst. The doctors are as baffled by it all as I am. They've checked my liver, kidneys, stomach, intestines, ovaries and uterus. I'm waiting to hear the latest results; so far, all they know for sure is that I'm a bit anaemic, and that my body is rejecting any type of food or liquid. I feel very weak and the painkillers make me light-headed, as though I'm tipsy. I hope something is worked out soon as David and I are supposed to be flying to Perth on the fifteenth.

Saturday 6 September 1997
The doctors released me yesterday evening, still unsure of what is wrong with me. However, I had been on solid foods all day and kept my fluid intake up. They couldn't conduct any further tests as my insides were too swollen and sore. I was given a referral letter to take with me to Perth, with an explanation of the tests performed and recommendations for future procedures. They advised me to go home and recover. David and I postponed our flight to Perth. Instead of the fifteenth, we go on the twenty-first. Hopefully, we still have enough time to find a rental house, before our freight arrives from Texas.

Tuesday 9 September 1997
Okay, my backache is gone and so are my headaches. The bruises on my thighs from the painkillers are fading, but the pain on my right side continues—persistent bugger!

Chapter 4

Why Me? Why Such Pain?

Sunday 12 October 1997

David and I have both settled into our new life in Perth, Western Australia. We've found a lovely rental property and have both managed to find jobs. I'm slowly adjusting to working again and I have seen the specialist gastroenterologist, who has referred me onwards for a colonoscopy on 12 November. The colonoscopy sounds terrible but maybe then they can help me with the ongoing excruciating pain. I feel so exhausted all of the time, tired from the pain. It feels like a fist of pain, raw and white hot, on my right side. I keep explaining it that way, like a mass of pain the size of my fist.

Tuesday 9 December 1997

Well, I guess I had wanted something different to happen—and it did! Way back on 15 November, I nearly missed undergoing my colonoscopy because of a stupid foul-up! My gastroenterologist hadn't tested me for some virus, so the hospital wasn't going to allow the procedure (Western Australia are the strictest in this regard) until I broke down. The matron took pity on me and went to see the hospital supervisor. Anyway, the colonoscopy finally took place at lunchtime. It was very uncomfortable despite the sedative.

Nothing showed up. I did not have Krohn's Disease, Irritable Bowel Disease or anything like that. It was back to square one.

I was home by 4pm and felt sleepy but okay. I ate a small portion of rice porridge in the evening. By 7pm, though, I was shivering uncontrollably and started a fever. Soon afterwards, I was sick as a dog—I ended up on the bathroom floor unable to move. David panicked and wanted to call the doctor. I told him to wait a while and I tried to rest on the floor. By 10pm, I was feeling so sick and weak that I knew it was serious. I told David to call the ambulance. The paramedics couldn't get the gurney near the bathroom and asked if I could stand. I tried but collapsed from the pain. The two of them half carried me to the gurney and then wheeled me to the waiting ambulance. David followed the ambulance to Fremantle Hospital. The trip was long, bumpy and painful. The paramedics wondered why we hadn't driven to the hospital ourselves. For one thing we didn't know where the closest hospital was. Besides, I couldn't sit up straight in a car seat!

At Fremantle Hospital, I told my history of tests already done and by 11pm I was admitted. I was kept under observation for twenty-four hours and they took more blood tests and X-rays. I nearly fainted from having to stand upright for the X-rays; the pain was killing me! After being given morphine, the pain lessened; however, I was mainly scared about what was happening inside my body. The next day, the doctors found an infection in my blood and decided the best thing to do was to perform a laparotomy to see what was going on.

At 8.15pm I closed my eyes and when I reopened them over an hour later, I had no right ovary. They had found the answer to my long-standing problem. Finally! I had a 10cm abscess growing on my right ovary. The ovary itself was abnormal and couldn't be saved. Was this the reason for ten years of hormonal problems? The next week included rounds of morphine, pethidine, drips, blood tests and major antibiotics to ensure the infection was gone. Apparently, they'd needed to remove a lot of pus as well as rearranging some of my organs back in to place. I had to learn how to breathe properly through my diaphragm, as it had been pushed and crushed for months! No wonder I was feeling light-headed all the time. They tell me my left ovary should take over for both of them and that I should be okay now. I pray so...

I was released from Fremantle Hospital after ten days to slowly recuperate at home. They gave me all sorts of medication to take because of my inability to keep food down. I kept having bad heartburn and diarrhoea. During the past month, I have lost so much weight and muscle mass that I'm nothing but skin and bone. I haven't been this skinny since I was fifteen or so! David wants me to fatten up.

Saturday 20 December 1997

So, it's been a couple of weeks and I'm eating again, sleeping well and walking longer each day, although it's embarrassing when little old ladies are passing me on the footpath as I hunch over and hobble along like a geriatric. I started back at work, although I am still suffering from stomach aches and tiredness, and my surgery scars make it difficult to sit for hours as I can't straighten up. I'm grateful I've got family in WA now that Irma and her family have moved here, as has Visa. We don't feel like it's just the two of us.

Yesterday, I had an appointment with my surgeon. He told me I was healing well, but he added that when they opened me up, my left ovary did not look healthy either; it had multiple little cysts on it. He said I would continue to have infertility problems and may have to consider IVF. He will refer me to a gynaecologist in January. So how do I feel? Very upset and fearful that we may be childless.

Chapter 5

Infertility Sucks Big Time

Monday 5 January 1998

My left ovary has been killing me lately! Please God, don't let me lose it, too! If I do, we'll never be able to have kids!

Thursday 15 January 1998

I was hospitalised again on the thirteenth for two and a half days. I hadn't slept much for two days because of the acute pain. After X-rays and an ultrasound, they found a 7cm cyst on my left ovary. The fallopian tube doesn't look good and there's a thick layer in the uterus lining as well. It does not look good at all! I have been referred to a specialist at King Edward Memorial Hospital in Subiaco. I will hopefully see them in two weeks' time. In the meantime, I have painkillers to help with the contractions and waves of pain. I feel depressed.

Saturday 24 January 1998

I'm feeling better than I have for months. My period started five days ago and I've had hardly any pain for three days. I'm also feeling more energetic and optimistic. The doctors at King Edward Memorial Hospital were down-to-earth and made me feel there is a chance of falling pregnant. Not only that, but our beautiful Keeshond puppy will be ready to come home in three weeks. I have hope again.

Monday 2 February 1998

Slowly but surely settling into our house. I hate work. Life seems so unfair sometimes. All I want is to become a mum. I don't want to go to work anymore and I want David to support me. Yes, I want to be selfish for once. Puppy Misha will arrive next week. I have a lot of love to give…

Friday 13 February 1998

The doctor pretty much confirmed my worst fears. We have only a minute chance of conceiving naturally. The infection I had most likely affected both fallopian tubes and the left ovary is most likely to be too damaged to allow fertility. He suggested IVF in six months' time. I ask myself, *Why does this have to happen to me? Why does this have to happen to us*? God, please help us to have a baby!

We have looked at our options:

1. remain childless
2. undergo IVF
3. investigate adoption.

We can't apply to adopt until we've been married for three years, so not yet. It's all a waiting game. At least we get our fur-ball Misha tomorrow.

Wednesday 11 March 1998

I can't believe how quickly time is passing. We've had Misha for nearly a month already. She's gorgeous and has brought a lot of joy into our lives. She makes us laugh a lot at her puppy antics. It's good to see David laugh and smile again.

Wednesday 22 April 1998

Shit! My health! My doctor has told me that I need to have another laparoscopy as soon as the Nurses' Strike is over. More surgery—will it never end? He said it could be dangerous because of my scars. For example, they could perforate my bowel. Bad news upon bad news. Our only joy is our Munchkin Misha.

Tuesday 12 May 1998

I went for my surgery on Wednesday 6 May and I've been sick ever since. The last few days I have had non-stop diarrhoea again. I want to crawl away and hide.

Wednesday 20 May 1998

I feel better though I'm continuing to bleed sporadically. What's a girl supposed to do? I don't want a hysterectomy, but will I have to suffer like this forever? What about my life? I'm thirty-one years old and I feel so old and spent sometimes. What kind of life am I leading? Should I resign myself to never having my own child? To pursue a career instead? Maybe buy a hobby farm or take up arts and crafts? That wouldn't be so bad, but how do I get out of this way of living now? The city stinks. I want to live in the country.

Sunday 14 June 1998

Here I go moaning again... sigh... I had diarrhoea for over nine days followed by haemorrhoids from the constant straining—that sounds like a comedy, doesn't it? But it wasn't funny. David is now sick with shingles caused by stress and being run-down. We are so broke at the moment. It's no wonder David is sick; we're being knocked down constantly. Is there an end in sight?

Misha is over six months old now and has a beautiful coat of hair and markings. Pat, the breeder, said that Misha would be a good show dog, but we won't put her through that. She's our child and companion.

I've been contemplating my life up to this point and wondering what all this suffering has been about? Have I been that bad? I'm stuck in a rut and I don't know how to get out. Reading back through this journal, I think the past year has been the worst year in my life! So much pain, so much suffering—the sheer futility of it all. My short-term memory has suffered so much from all the operations and anaesthesia that I'm starting to question my intelligence.

I've started writing short stories again for the mental stimulation. I wish I could start all over again. I wouldn't have pursued a travel career. Instead, I would have studied art, music and writing; they are my natural talents. Is it too late now? I'm nearly thirty-two. That's still young. I have to start liking and loving myself, and forgiving myself for all of the negative thoughts and actions. I have to learn from my mistakes and keep trying. I don't want to die without knowing who I really am or what purpose I have on this earth.

Wednesday 1 July 1998

I've been referred to the fertility clinic in September as, according to the doctors, we have nil chance of becoming pregnant by ourselves. IVF is our only option. I've shed so many tears and keep asking, *Why me?* Trying to stay strong is near impossible.

Wednesday 2 September 1998

An amazing occurrence has prompted me to write here—there's a hawk in our backyard. Only Munchkin Misha and I are home. I noticed it for the first time at 9.40am. It had killed another bird, a dove I think, and was plucking the feathers off and preparing to eat it. It's a striking bird of prey. It's been here for an hour so far and hasn't been bothered by Misha or by me. It's as if it feels safe here. I've talked to it, as the American Indians believe that a hawk is a messenger from the Spirit World. It's fascinating to watch. After an exceptionally long time, it flew away with its prize, leaving behind a scattering of feathers in our backyard. I'm still not sure what the message was supposed to be.

Sunday 27 September 1998

We have been added to a two-year waiting list for IVF, through the public hospital. There is no choice but to concentrate on work, paying our debts off, improving our fitness and having a life.

Sunday 7 November 1998

I'm on hormone tablets to help the regularity and length of my cycle. I've been feeling sick from period pain. The joys of being a woman. 1999 has to be a more upbeat year. I'm determined to be optimistic, to speak and act more positively.

Monday 25 January 1999

Well, that didn't last long. The positivism that is. I feel angry all the time and my stupid hormones are all over the place. Two weeks of having my period and then only two weeks' break before it happens all over again. I'm drained, literally, and tired. Shit! It isn't fair.

Sunday 14 February 1999

Happy Valentine's Day. I'm feeling better because I skipped the hormone tablets this month. I was sick of bleeding all the time. As a result, my moods have been more stable too. David and I are attending a symphony orchestra concert at Kings Park. We have a picnic ready with cheeses, veggies, dips, sausages, crackers, chocolate and wine. How romantic. It is important for us to have these dates and to remember that we are a family, even without children.

Monday 31 May 1999

It's funny how the older I get, the more I'm turning to God and spirituality, believing that there is life after death and power beyond our own existence. I never thought that after all the nasty business with my ex-boyfriend and religion I would turn to it now. It's weird how life twists and turns like it does. I'm older and I need more from life now.

I went to a 'healing' seminar with my sister Irma last night. We thought it would be about ourselves healing ourselves—our pains and diseases and so forth. It turned out to be a Christian healing, complete with two hymns and speaking about God, and the pastor's own healing stories. Those of us who felt they needed physical healing raised their hands and went up front for prayer.

I felt a great need for help and I guess I astonished Irma when I went up for healing. The pastor and his wife prayed for me. They placed their healing hands on my womb and asked for babies. I would not have believed the sensation had I not felt it myself. My whole body trembled with electricity. Even my eyelids zapped and snapped. My heart pounded hard and fast. I felt hot and then cold.

A very powerful experience. I even fell backwards into another man's hold, and then he lowered me to lie down on the floor. I thought it was a trick of television when I've witnessed it on television before, but I can honestly say I was touched by something unearthly, a spiritual force of some kind. David and I are considering going to some Sunday prayer meetings. Why not?

Tuesday 10 August 1999

I've been going to Tuesday prayer meetings. Even though I still find myself sceptical of some of the Church's showmanship, there definitely is something happening to me. The group of women are very supportive and friendly. Today, I found myself asking for their help of praying for me to fall pregnant and have a baby. I stood in the centre while they placed their hands on me and spoke out their visions and thoughts. To my total surprise, I started crying and shaking, and my hands were on fire. One of the women saw me as a little girl. She sensed God saying I was special and that He always loved me so much. He wanted me to be happy and have fun as I used to. My heart ached; it felt full, heavy and battered.

The woman added that He hadn't forgotten about me, that sometimes I doubted He was there for me when I called out and He didn't appear to listen. But I was to know that He was always there, sometimes carrying me. A couple of the women were also crying by this stage. It was all very emotional and I was amazed I let go. I cried so hard in front of people, something I rarely do. I felt like Sorja, the innocent seven-year-old.

Chapter 6

Hope Blossoms With IVF

Monday 1 November 1999

Life is so unpredictable. We moan about so many things for ages, but then the sun shines brighter and things start to work out better. Our social life has picked up and we've made friends.

Thursday 4 November 1999

I bought a new journal on Saturday 30 October. As my time for IVF treatment draws closer, I feel a need to start a record of my experiences, feelings, fears and joys. It's not only for my own personal benefit, but also possibly to help other women in the future.

I was in bed thinking about my upcoming adventure when I remembered how bombarded with statistics and details I felt when I first learned I would go through IVF. I wasn't interested in all of the medical mumbo-jumbo. Ultimately, I wanted to become a mum and hear of how other women coped with the stress of IVF. Anyone can access facts and figures through reading and researching, but there aren't many personal accounts to be read. That's when my idea hit me: I would keep this journal and write my story in it.

I must have had a premonition because two days after purchasing the journal, I called the Concept Fertility Centre, where I have been on a waiting list for over a year and a half. I had simply phoned to ask what details my GP should put on the referral letter for my first appointment at Concept Fertility Centre, only to find out that instead of seeing the IVF specialist Dr Mazzuchelli in February, my appointment will be next Tuesday. My time has been brought forward.

After being patient and waiting for so long, I'm now in shock that it is finally starting. I am feeling apprehensive and on tenterhooks but still one hundred per cent wanting to go through with it. I'm willing to suffer mood-swings, pain and whatever else it entails if the end result is a healthy baby or babies. I've had pain before, so that doesn't really scare me, but this time it is of my own choosing.

Many years ago, an older clairvoyant conducted a psychic reading and told me something that was to haunt me for years to come. She looked at my palm and said she saw the children line but that I was like *a tree with no leaves*. She didn't elaborate, but now I understand.

As women, we are brought up with the expectations of becoming mothers one day, as though it is our automatic right. As young girls, we don't ask, *What if I can't have children?* We make plans. We dream about our future husbands, children and home. No-one stops to think, *I might never find a man, never have a child and be homeless.*

So it was with me. I assumed that I would find and marry a man, which thankfully I did, but I also assumed we would have children by now. I am thirty-three years old and David is thirty-five. We have been married for four years and tried to conceive for three. I have been 'a tree with no leaves', like a winter-resting tree, waiting for the spring foliage. I refuse to believe I may be barren. I'm going to fight with all my spiritual, physical, emotional and mental powers to realise my dream of becoming a mother.

Today, I'm feeling very optimistic, a nice change from my pessimism of late. I used to be a far more positive person, until my health and my body betrayed me. I literally mean 'betrayed'. I felt my physical self was letting the rest of me down. For the longest time after my laparotomy to remove the right ovarian abscess, I couldn't believe my body's frailty or the pain I was experiencing. I prayed to God to heal me and take away the pain. My body disgusted me. I wanted a new model, believing the warranty on this one had run out.

Time itself healed me and, although my body shows the scars of battle, I feel fit and healthy and ready to go head to head in the ring with IVF. Even though the waiting has been exhausting and depressing, the time enabled me to improve my physical fitness to a level where I feel able to cope with the stress to come.

Friday 5 November 1999

Last night I dreamt of holding a two-week-old baby girl in my arms. It was such a beautiful dream that I woke up feeling optimistic again. I picked up the referral from my GP and I'm rearing to get going.

Monday 8 November 1999

Yesterday was a bad day. I called my mother to tell her the good news about my IVF being brought forward but instead of receiving support as I had hoped, everything she said was negative, for example, how bitter I would be if it didn't work out, the chance of having a handicapped child and the financial difficulties I'd face if I quit work. I was upset and angry for the rest of the day. Thank God for David and his bear hugs.

I feel better today because of a comforting dream. I was sitting on Jesus's lap, and although I can't remember our conversation, I know it was reassuring and gave me peace again.

Tuesday 9 November 1999

The Big Day. Our first appointment. So here we go. I was nervous all day. On first impressions, Dr Mazzuchelli is a caring older man in his fifties. As with any doctor, he asked questions of both of us first. He then explained the list of procedures, a checklist of what we would go through. He told us to be realistic—a woman of my age has about a twenty-five per cent chance of becoming pregnant per cycle with IVF. That leaves a seventy-five per cent failure rate. I know he was only trying to prepare us, but I still don't want to be a statistic. We will give it our best shot for a couple of years, and then move on if need be.

The ball started rolling—with a thick wad of material to read. We then had to go to Concept Fertility Centre to book appointments with the IVF coordinator and the counsellor, and to have David's sperm evaluated as to whether it can survive the petri dish solution. We also had our blood taken to test for HIV and Hepatitis, among other potential diseases. Of course, I had to have more blood taken than David. At least the nurse was a professional and had no trouble locating my deep veins. We now wait for our next step, an appointment with the counsellor and the IVF coordinator next Monday. I believe David was a bit shocked at how quickly things are happening now that we're not 'on hold' anymore. It's exciting but scary.

Thursday 11 November 1999

I've had two days to digest the information given to me. It is very comprehensive and detailed, and I had no trouble with it. It has posed a few questions though. For example, does having only one ovary make the process more difficult? When is it safe to have sex during the drug treatments? As public patients, what costs will we still incur? We will be able to ask the coordinator all these questions on Monday.

On Tuesday, David admitted that he was astonished at how things were on a roll now. I guess he was comfortable in the waiting zone, but now he is seriously thinking about the issues I have been contemplating for a long time. I guess we all prepare ourselves differently. I'm glad I'm not in limbo anymore. Sure, I'm scared of failing, but I've got to proceed thinking positively by praying for a successful pregnancy and a healthy baby.

Saturday 13 November 1999

Last night I had a frightening and unnerving dream. I was undergoing major surgery again and was having problems being anaesthetised. I have also been suffering tension headaches for days now. I guess it is starting to affect me. I have to learn to cope with stress, to calm down and relax. I have been listening to relaxation tapes at night before bed in an attempt of de-stressing. It doesn't seem to be affecting David as much, I guess because he won't actually have to go through as much as I. Men get off lightly!

We had my sister Irma and brother-in-law Grant and their two children Trent and Tory over yesterday. The kids swam and laughed freely and happily. I was envious of their family unit. Christmas is approaching soon, David and Sorja's fifth Christmas together. Every year, buying presents and setting up our tree and decorations has seemed so empty. To me, it isn't the same without a child's delight and excitement. Every year I think, *Maybe next year*...

Some days I wake up with so much anger and rage in me. I'm snappish with everyone and feel out of control. Is this anger about my infertility, or loneliness or lack of self-esteem? I'm not sure. It's as if a part of me steps back and watches this 'bitch' emerge to rant and rave, whilst shaking my head sadly inside. I've now been on progesterone (Provera) tablets for over a year to help control my cycle. Not that they have been particularly effective. I wonder whether these hormone tablets have something to do with my whacky moods.

I watched an episode of the *Oprah Winfrey Show*. It was about menopause and signs of perimenopause. I know I'm only thirty-three, but I swear I have suffered all of the symptoms mentioned: hot flushes, insomnia, forgetfulness, depression, formication (skin crawling), pins and needles, mood changes and irregular periods. Could it be because I have only one ovary left and my hormones have changed?

Monday 15 November 1999

We woke up bright and early, ready for our appointments. First, we saw the head counsellor (a friendly and comforting older woman) and she went over the three main stages of IVF:

1. hormone injections and nasal sprays
2. ultrasound and egg retrieval
3. embryo transfer and pregnancy.

We discussed our questions and concerns, and were relieved to find out that having only one ovary should not make a great difference as long as eggs are produced. Sex is safe until just prior to egg retrieval and four days after embryo transfer. This is because they don't want any free-floating sperm miraculously finding and fertilising an egg. Imagine having only two embryos placed in your uterus but ending up with triplets!

As public patients, we will still have to pay for some medications and injections. We may also have to pay for frozen embryo storage. I asked about the support groups and was given a list of contact numbers. Sometimes, having friends and family is not enough. It is better to be able to talk with couples who have undergone similar situations.

I was still a bit unsure of the 'six cycle rule', of how many attempts Medicare would cover. Thank God it is six 'egg retrieval' cycles and not just six embryo transfers as I first thought. As long as I'm able to produce numerous eggs per retrieval, I can have them frozen for later attempts if required.

My final concern was about my irregular but long periods, and how they would affect the regime of hormones. Apparently, the nasal spray halts normal hormonal activity so that the injectable medications can control when ovulation occurs; therefore, my cycle won't be the same anyway.

The counselling session was a lot less intimidating than I thought it would be. I had an upset stomach all morning because of nerves. She suggested we try not to disrupt our lives unduly, to stay busy and to keep our minds off the treatment. I can continue working until embryo transfer, at which point I will need to give up my current physically taxing job. If I had a desk job, the situation would be different. I definitely don't want to take a chance and risk losing a baby. I will need to tone down my exercise routine but not totally give it up. As my body is used to being active, I can continue walks and light swimming but not weightlifting or riding.

David was pretty much silent most of the time. I guess that, like a typical female, I talked enough for the both of us. It must be hard on men, having to watch their women undergoing so much. The counsellor said I would need to be sympathetic and understand that it won't be easy on David either. I will receive a lot of support from the medical staff, but David will feel left out of the circle.

She suggested we treat ourselves in some way after each stage—surviving each phase I should say—for example, going out to a restaurant or theatre or picnic. To celebrate or commiserate as need be. It's a very good idea. I know that if I ever have any questions or fears, I can call Concept and talk to either a counsellor or a coordinator.

Once we finished with the counsellor, we moved on to see the sister in charge of co-ordinating our IVF. She clarified a few more points, but our detailed drug treatment will be discussed next Tuesday after seeing Dr Mazzuchelli again.

Finally, David had to go into a special fathers-to-be room to produce a sperm sample. I took the opportunity to sit quietly and drink a cup of tea. Afterwards, he told me of the 'wonderful' room. It was as small as a bathroom, with a bed, a sink and a couple of magazines of the erogenous kind...

Tuesday 23 November 1999

We had our appointment with our doctor to hear our results from all the blood and sperm tests. We are both negative for HIV, Hepatitis B and Hepatitis C. My Rubella antibodies are still effective; therefore, I am immune. David and I are both O positive blood group and, thankfully, David's sperm test was fine with healthy swimming sperm. Now we have the full go ahead. Dr Mazzuchelli has decided to try the quick method, beginning when my period starts.

We were given our drug list and treatment scenario and, basically, we don't see him until either the ultrasound or egg retrieval stage. It was a very quick visit, about five minutes. I must say, he was a bit abrupt, but I guess he sees hundreds of couples, and he is human and can't always be patient.

We then had an appointment with one of the coordinators again. We were given our various drugs. My program will include Synarel nasal spray daily from day two of periods, initially two sniffs morning and night for seven days, and then decrease to one sniff morning and night until theatre for egg retrieval. I will also need Puregon injections daily from day three at 100iu dose (HMG injections). Blood tests will commence on day eight of my cycle to determine how hormones and egg development are progressing. I think I will feel like a farmed chicken expected to lay numerous eggs! At a further stage, I will have vaginal ultrasounds to picture the egg progress.

Our coordinator was once again very helpful and explained things in detail, for example, how to use the Synarel spray. At this point, we were also required to sign all of the legal consent forms for theatre and so forth. I was given detailed instruction sheets, and other paperwork to complete at home (always paperwork and red tape).

Our only upsetting news was the fact that, as public patients, we will have to go back on the year-long waiting list should our first cycle not succeed. In other words, once egg retrieval in theatre has taken place and pregnancy has not occurred through embryo replacements. This was news to us. No-one had told us that before and it wasn't written anywhere in the paperwork either.

We just have to pray that I am successful in producing numerous eggs and that a number of them will survive when injected with sperm. In that way, the embryos may be frozen for future attempts. Please God, don't let me have to go through all of this, and then have to wait yet again. I don't know if my sanity can handle it.

Now I wait for my period to start. It's funny, but I've never been so eager for it to begin before. I'm not so eager to start jabbing my thighs with daily injections though. I'll go to the Concept Clinic for the first time and let them talk me through it.

Wednesday 24 November 1999

It's crazy, but I'm anxiously waiting for my period to start (a first!). It is day twenty-eight, and still no sign. For the last six months I've started on day twenty-six, so this is late for me. Just typical. When you don't want them they come early and when you do… nothing. How frustrating. It's my mind sabotaging my body. I have to try and not stress out but I don't want to miss out before the hospital closes for Christmas and New Year.

Sunday 28 November 1999

Still no sign of my period. I felt bloated, irritable and headachy. I had the munchies, as usual, but that went away after a couple of days. Now my breasts have been tender for about four or five days. Of course, both David and I have had our hopes raised that we may be pregnant, but I think I should be having other symptoms by now if I were. My body has betrayed me so many times in my life that I'm trying very hard not to get too excited.

I've been praying to God continuously, asking for some helpful signs that my wishes have been granted and I am pregnant without having to go through IVF. But—and it's a big but—if I'm not, the time is ticking away and we may not make it to start our cycle before Christmas. We would have to wait until next month. I'm feeling very angry, frustrated and sorry for myself.

Monday 29 November 1999

I just called one of the coordinating sisters at Concept to ask about the lateness of my period. I explained about being six days late and being on Provera which normally regulates me. She was very reassuring and suggested I come in tomorrow morning for a blood test to find out what my hormone levels are. She said there are drugs to make me bleed, but unfortunately it would be too late to start our cycle this month.

Tuesday 30 November 1999

I woke up early to go and get my blood test taken. This time, I didn't even feel the needle go in. I had to call back for the results at two. I have just rung and my hormone levels are really low, which means my period should start in the next few days. I am not pregnant. How devastating to hear that over and over. If they start by Friday, we can start the cycle. If not...

Wednesday 1 December 1999

What an emotional rollercoaster! Such highs and lows. I feel exhausted already. I'm going to buy some natural herbs such as hypericum (St John's Wort) and valerian to help me calm down and relax. My internal chatter is keeping me awake at night. I think I've been my own worst enemy as my thoughts have been responsible for affecting my body cycle. Stress is answerable to so many complaints. My period finally started at the last hour. I called Concept and I have the go-ahead to start the Synarel spray tomorrow, followed by the injections on Friday. We made it just in time as they close from 24 December until 3 January.

Thursday 2 December 1999

I am only bleeding lightly, but I don't think that will make much difference since my hormone levels were low, indicating my menstrual cycle. Anyway, I whiffed in my first dose of nasal spray. Even with the instructions, I am nervous I didn't do it right. It's supposed to be all controlled—the dose in the pump that is. I wish I could stop worrying about every single thing. It didn't taste too bad, except for a chemical after taste in the back of my throat. A soother soon fixed that. The evening dose was more difficult as I couldn't get the spray to pump up right. I had to try it twice.

Friday 3 December 1999

Well, my p's are at a standstill. I'll have to ask them about that... The sister assured me that Synarel can sometimes delay periods or make them act weird, so that's a relief. I was taught how to inject myself. Actually, the hardest part was getting the Puregon ready. When I broke open the top part of the ampules, I managed to fling one across the room. I then mixed together the tablet and saline solution with a longer mixing needle. The actual injecting part of the process was easy. I'll try and do it myself at home, but I can always go to them if I really stress out trying to get it all right.

Sniffing the Synarel was easier today; I'm getting the hang of it.

So far, I feel okay, only a bit funny in the stomach. I must say I felt a bit furtive walking around town carrying a brown paper bag full of drugs and needles as though I was some kind of junkie rushing my stash home.

Saturday 4 December 1999

I'm so proud of myself. I did it! Only slip up was that I broke the top of the ampule into tiny pieces and cut myself as it's made of glass. I managed to remove the syringe cap off better this time. There certainly is a technique to it: rock it back and forward a little. Inserting the needle was as easy as yesterday. David had to look away even though I told him it wasn't too bad, only a little stinging sensation. For a treat, I went to the bakery to buy breakfast; I deserved it for overcoming that milestone.

Now, I've got to go and take a sniff again (that sounds so strange). I must be getting used to the spray as I hardly noticed any chemical smell or taste anymore, only a tingling sensation in the nostrils. So far, I haven't had any major mood swings, thank God. David is expecting some kind of super-bitch to emerge... Today, I feel a bit fuller, as in my breasts feel larger than usual. Also, I'm so tired and lethargic that I need to take an afternoon nap.

Monday 6 December 1999

The injections and nasal spray are getting easier with practise, although the glass ampule shattered again yesterday. Today, I found an easier way to do it. I hold a kitchen towel over my index finger and still use my thumb to break open the glass. This way, the towel provides support and my index finger does not get cut. My left ovary is starting to throb, which means something is happening with the follicles. I hope they are starting to develop uniformly and perfectly. I also have lower pelvic pressure. But I'll survive this.

Tuesday 7 December 1999

Those damn ampules! Why do they have to be made of glass? I shattered another one. I'm midway through my drug treatment but, thank God, I feel okay. No hot flushes or mood swings only continued pelvic pressure. I'm still continuing to work and will continue to do so unless I feel worse.

Wednesday 8 December 1999

I've had a fair bit of pain in my ovary. Something must be happening. I hope several egg follicles are growing uniformly and perfect in shape and strength. At least if it doesn't work out this time, I'll know what to expect next time. I'm getting used to sniffing and jabbing. I still feel funny about taking my spray and disappearing to the bathroom to take my snort...

David said that I'm so brave. I guess I am. If you can get past the thought or fear, you can do anything. It's the mind you have to battle with. I've come up with a saying: *If a fat man in a tutu can do it, so can I*. It's referring to a story of a fat man who always wanted to learn how to be a ballet dancer. He did, with an instructor who said he was actually very dedicated and professional. He even chose to wear a tutu.

Thursday 9 December 1999

I am so angry. I went for my scheduled day nine blood test and had my injection there. After spending an enjoyable day shopping, I called up at 2.30pm for the blood test results. Apparently, when I thought my period had started last week, they had not in fact. I had my usual two days of menstrual pain and I had a discharge, but they're telling me I didn't. So all of this has been a waste. We have to cancel this cycle and start again, probably in January. I have an appointment with Dr Mazzuchelli on Tuesday again; he better not accuse me of lying about my period. As if I wanted to start injecting myself. As you can see, I'm still fuming. At the moment I hate my body for doing this to me. I tried to warn the doctor about my erratic stop and start cycle, but he didn't want to know about it. Perhaps now he will listen...

After the storm of fury came the flood of tears. Bucket loads of them. I don't usually cry so easily, but my sisters rang for support and I broke down. Of course, I pretended to be strong when I told my husband, although I was snappish. When he came home, I apologised. He understood. He believes we were rushed into it because of Christmas and the office closing for holidays. I guess we were. My mind panicked and my hormones went crazy.

My dog, Misha, hovered over me while I cried. She was very concerned and loving. What would I do without her? The bright shining spot in my life.

What a kaleidoscope of emotions. No wonder couples can separate over IVF. It's so stressful. The only thought keeping me sane is that either my Soul chose this journey or God wants me to go through this for some reason. Maybe so I can help others?

Friday 10 December 1999

Last night I had extreme hot flushes/night sweats and a really dry throat. Must have been because I stopped the Synarel spray. My body is now withdrawing from the hormones, so it will probably act up a bit again. Today, I feel very tired and sleepy, but also more fatalistic. Like, round one is over, onto the next phase. I feel I should contact a support group but I am grieving and I don't want to talk to anyone. In a strange way, I even missed jabbing myself this morning because doing so meant I was actually doing something…

Sunday 12 December 1999

I've felt edgy and snappish the last two days. I started bleeding and having bad period cramps today. I feel angry at this because I thought I had already had my period. Also, it's a reminder of no pregnancy.

Tuesday 14 December 1999

My period has been very heavy this time around. I had an appointment with Dr Mazzuchelli at 3pm today. I was all nervous again, expecting to be told I had done something wrong and it was my fault this cycle didn't work. I was afraid he would be uncaring and wouldn't listen. I was wrong. He rang up the clinic to clarify my results and the sister told him exactly what she had told me. I said I was confused because I'd had signs of cramping and bleeding, but that it all stopped with the Synarel use. I also explained to him that my periods have always been erratic unless controlled by drugs such as the pill, sometimes not having periods for a couple of months and other times twice in one month.

He was obviously listening this time and was concerned. I said I would find it impossible to tell when 'Day One' of my period was. I asked him if it was possible to control my entire cycle either with drugs or hormones. He said it was but not in this case because it would upset my internal rhythms even more. He was trying not to disrupt it too much.

I felt more at ease with him because he listened. We are going to try something different this time. A slower method, not rushed, and it is actually fine by me. Hopefully it won't scare my body as much as last time. We are going to wait until 29 December and have a blood test to see if I have ovulated by then. If I haven't, I'll have to wait another week and have another blood test and so on. If I have ovulated, I will restart the Synarel spray until my next period. The Wednesday after my period has started, I will commence the injections at the same dose. So, trial and error… In the meantime, I have to stop thinking about it and give myself a break.

Monday 20 December 1999

I wish I could say that I've got on with my life, keeping active and not giving IVF a thought, but I can't. It was in the back of my mind even while having fun in the pool, and seeing my brother-in-law Grant playing with his children Trent and Tory. My mother rang and made her usual noises of concern for me. She says I have had enough pain and she hurts thinking about what I'm experiencing. But as I said to my husband, pain is no stranger to me.

I just rang Concept to clarify something that was bothering me. I have always had a feeling that I ovulate earlier than day fourteen as expected. As I'm going to get my blood tested on the twenty-ninth, I wanted to know whether it would show if I ovulated early as I wasn't sure how the hormones fluctuate. The sister reassured me that the test would show that I have ovulated, regardless of where in the cycle. What frustrated me was the fact that she said ovulating earlier was very unlikely. I said there were always exceptions to the rule.

Surely in their long medical careers they have seen women who don't fall into the 'normal' patterns and hormonal cycles!

Wednesday 29 December 1999

I've been very blasé about it all for the last week, not stressing about IVF and maintaining an 'I don't care' attitude about what the blood test would reveal today. It was probably self-protection, but it worked. I went this morning, first for the blood test and then for the instructions for my next trial. I also asked the sister a few questions about the Synarel spray. Was it safe to take if, by some miracle, I had fallen pregnant naturally in the meantime? The answer was yes. It had happened in the past and because it was taken for such as short time, it showed no negative effects on a pregnancy. I also asked whether it would stop periods from starting. Apparently, it can delay them for a couple of days but not stop them. It was a short visit again. There were a lot of women waiting…

I phoned for my results in the afternoon and received a surprise. My blood test showed that not only had I ovulated, but my hormones were at base level, as if today is day one of my period when in fact I'm not even bleeding. I told them I was not a 'normal' woman with predictable readings. The sister rang Dr Mazzuchelli and now they've decided to use the flare up regime as per the first attempt. I'm to start the Synarel tomorrow and the injections on Friday (New Year's Eve). I was right about ovulating early. I knew it. Listen to your own body. You know best and sometimes better than the medical profession.

Saturday 1 January 2000

It's strange writing 01/01/00 for the first time. You know my wish for the New Year. Well, I've been sniffing and injecting again. At least this time it's a lot easier as I know what I'm doing. Breaking the ampules is easier, too, by using the rocking back and forwards method the sister told me about. I've taken a more relaxed approach this time around. I don't want to suffer the levels of stress I experienced last attempt. I even allowed myself a couple of glasses of champagne to bring in the Millennium. I pray for success every day.

Sunday 2 January 2000

This time, I've been suffering from headaches every day. The pelvic pressure and ovary ache are back. Today, we went to a friend's barbeque. She is five months pregnant and two other women with babies were there also. I tried not to let it affect me, but it was difficult. When meeting new people, I always tense up for the question, 'Do you have children?' Thankfully, it didn't come today, but there have been many times in the past when someone has carelessly and hurtfully said that wasn't it time I had children and I wasn't getting any younger. That's when I plaster a fake smile on my face and pretend it doesn't bother me. I feel I should be wearing a plaque stating why I don't have children. Something like *I am childless, but it is not my choice*.

Wednesday 5 January 2000

The last two days I've been having really bad nausea, not vomiting but a 'pukey' feeling. The pressure on my stomach, pelvis and ovary was so bad at work that I had to leave early. Of course, the hormones were making me feel all teary and emotional as well. Another bad night of insomnia left me very tired and absentminded. Probably too stressed out. I nearly got run over by a turning car as I crossed the street. In my befuddled state, I just didn't see it. Pretty scary.

I had my blood test and injection at Concept again and waited on tenterhooks for the results. I braced myself for phoning back, with tissues handy in case of bad news again. But fortunately, my hormone levels have increased to 8,500 which is apparently good news. This time my body has responded accordingly. However, they need to keep a close eye on the levels. If the oestradiol levels reach 12,000pm/l, it's considered to be close to the risk level of Ovarian Hyper Stimulation Syndrome (OHSS). I'm to have a blood test and ultrasound on Friday morning. Pray, pray, pray. Oh God, let me have a dozen healthy, perfect eggs and not suffer OHSS.

Friday 7 January 2000

Oh, where do I start? I went in for my usual blood test and shot, and then for my vaginal ultrasound. I've had one before, so I wasn't anxious, just nervous about the results. Well, Dr Mazzuchelli physically jumped when he saw how many growing follicles I had on the screen. At least twenty-five! Can you believe it? I prayed for twelve; I got twenty-five. He asked me how I felt and I told him of my tiredness and nausea. I wasn't too bloated today or in pain. He was concerned about the number of follicles and whether I was going into the danger zone. He told me to call back at 2pm for my hormone levels and blood test results. The ultrasound showed numerous follicles of a good size and shape. I remember the nurse telling me that they liked to aim for six or eight and here I've got twenty-five...

Anyway, I prayed the whole way home for them not to cancel the cycle on me and for me to be able to survive the whole procedure.

I was so tired I needed a nap again. It's no wonder I have felt out of sorts. Preparing myself for a cancellation, I called at two on the dot, but I was in for a surprise. Although my oestradiol levels were now at 16,000pm/l, I am scheduled for egg retrieval on Sunday 9 January. They probably decided to go ahead with it because I wasn't feeling so bad, vomiting, diarrhoea or kidney pain. I'm to rest, rest and rest at home, and to drink a lot of fluids for the next few days.

I have to go in at 9pm tonight for my HCG injection, thirty-six hours prior to ovum pick-up. It's to be administered at the Emergency Night Department because Concept is closed. Apparently, it's given on the butt and is quite painful. Just great, eh? I'm to stop the nasal spray and Puregon injections now. Tomorrow, bed rest before taking my first antibiotics in the evening. Fast from midnight Saturday, ready for theatre on Sunday. I have instructions to be at Concept by 8am in preparation for theatre at 9am. David will be there, ready to produce his sperm when required, probably a couple of hours later. I'm to skip my morning antibiotics, but restart Sunday evening.

As Dr Mazzuchelli won't be in, Dr Thomas will perform the procedure. I've met him before. If all goes well, they will retrieve many eggs and hopefully a portion of them will survive to the embryonic stage. I will be required to stay at the hospital for six hours to monitor my post-anaesthetic response, and then rest at home again. They will then decide whether to transfer the embryos on Tuesday or freeze them for later cycles. It all depends on my physical state. I won't mind as long as we get through this successfully. The embryo transfer is the least painful and invasive part. Wish me luck, Universe.

Saturday 8 January 2000

Last night's injection wasn't as bad as I had been told to expect by others who have gone through it. Sure, it stung, but only for a short time. I felt a bit bruised but not overly so. Today, I've felt so tired, with continual nausea that won't go away with food or anything else. I'm just bearing it as I know it won't last forever. Nervous about tomorrow, of course.

Sunday 9 January 2000

In theatre and too groggy and not-with-it to write in this journal.

Monday 10 January 2000

Okay, I can write about it now. With my day bag packed with a book, toiletries and nightie, I arrived nice and early at 7.15am. At 7.30 I went to my ward, where I was given a pleasant single room to myself for the day. As it was Sunday, it was pretty quiet, and the nurses were very cheerful and helpful.

David and I waited patiently for things to happen. I changed into the wonderful backless gown—such a fashion statement. The anaesthetist visited me to ask questions about my health and reactions to anaesthetics in the past. An orderly wheeled me down to theatre at 8.30am and David accompanied us. The orderly had a great sense of humour and kept us chuckling the whole way. I could have walked but it was hospital regulations to be wheeled in. Before theatre, the embryologist spoke to us about the procedure and what to expect afterwards. Both David and I had to sign forms stating how many embryos we wanted to have implanted later. We had only two choices: one embryo or two. We chose two for better odds of one succeeding, although I would love twins.

After ensuring I had emptied my bladder and that all my wrist and ankle bands, and heart monitor stickers were on, I said, 'See you,' to David and was wheeled into theatre.

I transferred myself onto the theatre table and let the nurses prepare my blood pressure monitor, heart monitor and arm ready for the anaesthetist and the IV. As I have deep veins, I always dread this part: the prodding and poking until finally finding a good vein. I just gritted my teeth and prayed for a safe ovum collection.

Dr Thomas asked me about my ovaries, and I reminded him that he only had to head in one direction, as I don't have a right ovary. He then jokingly stated that because I only had one ovary, everything would be half-priced. We all laughed. I was injected with an anaesthetic and given oxygen, and I knew no more.

It only took about half an hour, as I was already in recovery at 9.45am. I stayed there until the nurses checked my vital signs and ensured I was okay. Over the next four hours, I was given one litre of serum albumen (albumex) intravenously to prevent OHSS from developing. I was also given progesterone pessaries to insert into the vagina three times daily to help line the uterus for pregnancy. As my hormones have been messed around with so much, my body would not be producing sufficient progesterone. Basically, from 10.30am until 4pm, I rested in my room on the ward by reading and talking to David. I was able to eat lunch, thank God, as by this stage I was starving. David disappeared to do his part at midday and I told him to have erotic thoughts about me.

'Not the way you look right now,' he replied.

Gee, thanks hubby.

Out of the twenty-five follicles shown on the ultrasound, only fifteen were the right shape and size for pick-up, meaning fifteen ova. This was a good result from one poor, over-worked ovary. I went home with David feeling tired and a bit bloated but optimistic. It was up to the embryologist now. As the evening progressed, my stomach and ovary became more tender. I didn't want to take painkillers to mess up the antibiotics, but I found an icepack to help numb the pain.

Today, I felt no more nausea, thank goodness, but the tenderness remains. I called for the results at 2pm and was told that six have fertilised. Apparently, they are still incubating the others hoping for further eggs to fertilise. The embryologist said they can't understand why only six out of the fifteen fertilised, as both my ova and David's sperm is above average quality.

I'm to go at 7.30am tomorrow to have two embryos implanted. Oh, please God, Jesus Christ, Guardian Angels, Mother Nature, Powers That Be, Universe, please let these two embryos, or even one, latch on to my uterus with a fierce survival, determination and fight to live! I'll do my best to nourish you and take care of you, if you only give me the chance.

Tuesday 11 January 2000

The Big Day. I woke up after a night of broken sleep and have had an upset stomach all morning. David has taken the day off work to be with me. We arrived at 7.20am and I was admitted to the Day Surgery unit at about 8am. After taking my vital signs again, the clinical nurse gave me a sedative in tablet form. I was glad because I was too nervous. At 9.30am, I was wheeled to the Concept theatre area to wait my turn.

The embryologist confirmed that unfortunately no other embryos had formed overnight, but the two to be implanted looked promising. One was already a four-cell division and the other a two-cell. I mentioned to her that my stomach had been aching for days. She replied that Dr Thomas had observed my left ovary was enlarged, and he believed I wasn't suffering from OHSS. The pain was most likely caused by the fact that Dr Thomas had punctured all twenty-six follicles even though only fifteen contained ova. After everything my poor body has been through, no wonder my abdomen feels bruised.

Anyway, at 10.10am it was my turn for embryo transfer. It took about ten minutes and was very similar to a pap smear. Legs up, knees bent and bottom up a little. After opening my cervix with a speculum, Dr Mazzuchelli made the transfer. He said that my uterus looked very prepared and lined. He had to wash away some of the mucous so that he could reach the entrance of my womb. When he was ready, the embryologist handed him a thin tube containing the embryos.

Apparently, the cervix has to be forced open gently but firmly, as it is a very protective layer of skin and muscle, preventing bacteria from entering. This caused no discomfort to me and after a couple more minutes, it was done. I felt like a turkey being basted.

I had to put my legs down and lie still for a minimum of half an hour. Now it was just a matter of time for the results to show. I was wheeled back to Day Surgery to listen to my relaxation tape, take a nap and have a bite to eat. At 11am, I was allowed to change back into my clothes and sit in a recliner. I left the hospital at 12.30pm. I've spent the rest of today pretty much doing nothing but resting, apart from a little bit of activity such as washing dishes.

I asked about going to the toilet after the procedure, and the nurse reassured me that the wondrous human body allows the urethra to do its job without causing the cervix to relax and let the embryos fall. Evidently, a lot of women have the same fear. So, I can do light housework and walks, but shouldn't do anything that raises my heart rate or body temperature for at least the next two weeks. Wish us luck. Positive thinking, positive talking and don't stress.

Thursday 13 January 2000

I've been talking to my two little embryos for the last two days, telling them I love them, to feel safe and grow healthily inside my womb. I've told them we've been waiting for them for so long and they are very welcome…

I'm not going to allow myself to think negatively and to give up. No. I'm tired of being afraid all the time. I have asked God for my wish—the healthy birth of my twins—and now I shall receive this precious gift from Him. The answer to my prayers. *Ask and you shall receive.* I am grateful to God and the Universe for hearing my pleas. By now, the cells will have divided and divided again, and hopefully attached to the nutritious endometrium. Hang on, little ones, hang on. My stomach ache has eased and the left ovary is less tender. All is well in my body…

Friday 14 January 2000

How are my little ones doing? Just fine. My abdomen is less bloated, my ovary is only a little tender and I have no nausea. I phoned Concept; it was on my instruction sheet to call day five after egg collection to assure them that OHSS hadn't set in. I have only tomorrow to go with the antibiotics, but I still need to insert the progesterone pessaries three times a day until told otherwise. I am convinced I am pregnant carrying twins. I know its early days still but

I have faith. I also believe one is a girl.

Sunday 16 January 2000

It's very difficult to keep positive when family and friends tell me not to get my hopes up. I know they mean well but I need encouragement now. Deep down, I'm realistic about my chances but I can't let myself think negative. I'll think I'm pregnant until proved otherwise. One week to go. Try and keep busy.

No more ovary or stomach ache, but my breasts have been really tender for days. I also seem to have a keener sense of smell and taste, hopefully signs of pregnancy. Although my hay fever is bothering me, I won't take my tablets because they may be harmful to the babies. I have the sweet food munchies and I'm a bit cranky; I hope I'm not pre-menstrual. Please God, don't let my period come. I don't know how I will cope with the disappointment again.

Monday 17 January 2000

A funny thing happened yesterday afternoon. I was praying for a sign of reassurance, peace and positivity from God. As I looked up and out of my bedroom window, I saw two doves fly into the yard directly in front of me. They proceeded to kiss and exchange titbits of food, before the male jumped up onto the female's back and—say no more. Afterwards, the male flew away and the female looked straight at me as if to say, 'See, nothing to it!'

I chuckled and said, 'Is that your answer, God?'

Today, I woke up feeling energetic, with no pain anywhere. I pray this is a good sign. However, the suspense is killing me. I'm trying not to think about it but it's impossible not to dwell on it. To fill in time, I've decided to visit Grant and Irma's place in the country for a few days. Once I told David of my plans, we got into an argument, no doubt a result of stress. He felt I was abandoning him or that he had done something wrong. I explained I needed to escape for a while, not from him, but this house of waiting. I said that his support alone wasn't enough, and I needed my family too. Eventually, he understood. I know it's difficult for him too, but he has less time to think and to worry than I do. Sitting in the sun in the country, with nature, is just what I need at this moment.

Tuesday 18 January 2000

Time is getting closer and closer. Today went really fast, full of activity with my sister and talking as per usual. At least it kept my mind busy and free from obsessing about Sunday (D-Day). Apparently, David spoke to a woman who had undergone IVF, who told him that if you haven't bled within seven days of implanting the embryos, it's a very good sign. She had had three attempts before success and each time she bled after three days. So hopefully we've done it.

Wednesday 19 January 2000

Another day sped by and we hardly talked about my 'possible' pregnancy. I'm feeling tired and more easily puffed out. Not sure whether it's because I haven't exercised as I usually do or because of? We'll see... I'm glad I came here—less time to think, think and think.

Friday 21 January 2000

My life has been revolving around IVF. I haven't been to work for two weeks because of having the embryos implanted. I now wait for Sunday's pregnancy test. Well, I have done everything in my power to make this pregnancy work. I've rested, eaten healthily, avoided taking any risks and thought positively every single day—chanting, praying and believing. If, God forbid, it hasn't happened, I'm definitely not to blame for it and I'm not going to question my actions. Despite all of this, I still feel optimistic and positive.

Saturday 22 January 2000

I'm anxious and I've had a stomach ache today; I hope it's only a digestive problem. Got a bit of a scare during the day, as I was spotting a little. I know that shouldn't worry me but it's hard. God, please grant us the miracle of life growing inside of me. This time tomorrow we will know...

Sunday 23 January 2000

It's in God's hands now. Blood test was taken at 8am and we get the results at 2pm. Wait, wait and wait. We saw a rainbow; that must be good luck. How can five minutes be so nerve racking? It's five minutes until I have to call. My heart is thumping, my stomach is churning, here we go...

NEGATIVE. The sister calmly informed me that unfortunately no pregnancy hormone was detected. I should stop the progesterone pessaries and my period should come within a few days. She told me to make an appointment with Dr Mazzuchelli to discuss our next step. I shook my head at my husband sitting next to me, and he looked understandably devastated and upset.

After the phone call, we sat quietly, not crying, just in shock. I was too emotionally spent to even shed tears. I felt numb, drained physically, emotionally, mentally and spiritually. I knew it wasn't my fault and that I had done everything I could. It just was not meant to be. I was sure I had been pregnant for a while but, for some unknown reason, the embryos didn't implant.

David and I took a walk with our beautiful furry four-legged baby and talked about it all. I need to have a couple of months break. We have been on such a stressful Ferris-wheel since November. I just want to live without it for a while. Our three remaining frozen embryos will be there when we're ready again.

I'm getting strong period cramps again, another reminder I don't need. I'm surprised I haven't sunk into a severe depression. It's strange, but I feel fatalistic, as if it was to be expected. In a way, I get the feeling I haven't nurtured myself enough in order to nurture children. Although I was physically ready, I don't think I was spiritually ready. I feel a need to find my own balance first, though the big question is how?

Chapter 7

Try, Try and Try Again

Friday 28 January 2000

I've simply been existing for the last few days. My depression sunk in as soon as my period started fully. Somehow that was more indicative that I wasn't pregnant. I was in severe pain, with stomach cramps and a backache for three days, more so than usual. I'm sure this was because of being over-stimulated with the hormones. All I wanted to do was dwell in my misery, sleep a lot, eat more and not caring about anything. Even my prayers became a brief, monotone mumble before bed. I asked my husband whether he had prayed since Sunday, and he said, 'No.' I guess we both feel betrayed and fed up.

To be on a high and then come crashing down was a terrible experience for both of us. Since Sunday, David has suffered from twisting his back, having headaches and being lethargic. He is definitely suffering as much as I am. I've been having progressively worse nightmares every night. Last night, I woke up screaming, 'No. No!'

David had to comfort me. I've been taking my chamomile teas, valerian and hypericum to calm me down, but it hasn't exactly helped me have a calm and peaceful night's sleep.

I'm disgusted with myself for falling into old bad habits of not eating healthily or exercising. So back to it. It is understandable to grieve, but I'll feel better if I look after myself.

Monday 7 February 2000

I've been so depressed lately; I can't seem to shake myself out of it. I've got back into fitness and I exercise; it doesn't help. I sleep—I'm sleeping at least ten hours every night—and I still feel lethargic. I read. Nothing is working. How do I get myself out of this dark pit? I don't see a point to anything. If I'm not to be a mother in this life, what is my Soul's purpose here on earth?

Unfortunately, David has borne the brunt of my mood swings. It's as if I'm questioning everything because of my depression, my marriage included. I'm crying out for help; is anybody listening?

Monday 14 February 2000

We went to a Valentine's concert on Saturday and not even that cheered me up much. My body is really pissing me off. I've been spotting mid-cycle again. Ever since I started menstruating at age fourteen, I've never known a 'normal' cycle without being on the contraceptive pill. If we aren't able to have children, I have to do something about my cycle for my own sanity's sake. I may even go through an early menopause; the signs are all there and I'm so scared. Can't the doctors listen to me and really help me?

Friday 18 February 2000

I've decided to start volunteer work. I need to stop feeling sorry for myself and helping others will take my mind off my problems. I've been drowning in my own negativity; it's time to swim out.

Tuesday 22 February 2000

I had my appointment with Dr Mazzuchelli today. He is less intimidating than when we first met, and is more 'human', empathic and caring. He was puzzled that only six out of fifteen eggs fertilised. I wonder what went wrong. He asked about my cycle and how I was feeling. The next attempt will be different—no drugs or hormones whatsoever. They will use my natural cycle to implant the embryo three days after I ovulate. The problem will be to find out when I ovulate, which means blood tests again. Once more, I had to explain that my cycle was not a predictable one and the timing was erratic. However, they will not control my cycle with drugs because they have more success with using a woman's own cycle. Oh well, here we go again.

As we only have three embryos left, Dr Mazzuchelli wanted us to consider the choices we have regarding the number to implant: one by three attempts, two and one, or one and two. For women under thirty-two, it is the preferred method to use one at a time because of the extra chance of multiple pregnancy. But as I am thirty-three—thirty-four this year—he suggests they implant two at one time again. I don't know. I guess I'm afraid of using up the three and then having to go back on the waiting list. That's being negative I know.

Dr Mazzuchelli also assured us that we had done nothing wrong. My levels were fine but once the embryos are in the womb, it's out of our hands, so to speak—within reason, of course. I told him I did not feel guilty because I know I had done everything right. He asked whether we were ready to start now and I said, 'No, we need a little break.'

So we'll continue next month, with blood tests starting from day twelve of my cycle to check oestrogen, progesterone and ovulation. He said we had to keep plugging away at it and not to give up.

Wednesday 15 March 2000

Although I haven't written for a month, it's not to say I haven't thought about our childlessness. It's as if I'm on automatic pilot doing tasks I'm meant to be doing, and watching the days go by. Irma's best friend, Angelea, just had a baby boy through IVF and sent some photos. I'm happy for her but still jealous and sad for me.

I've been doing a lot of Soul searching, trying to find my niche in life. Every day I hear of the dangers of the world and I ask myself whether it's wise to bring another child into this world. There's no guarantee our child couldn't turn against us. It's really scary hearing how a six-year-old boy shot a girl he didn't like! What is this world coming to? I understand that a lot depends on the way parents bring up their children, which makes me worry whether I have what it takes to be a good mother. I guess it's normal to have doubts.

Saturday 25 March 2000

I've gone to see a naturopath. I feel lethargic most of the time and I know I have been depleted in nutrients. She's started me on some herbs and minerals to help balance my digestive system and hormones. My goal is to make sure I'm getting sufficient vitamins and minerals, not only for myself, but also to ensure a baby could exist in a nutritious environment, that being my womb. Once I feel healthier, I will continue with the program. I've been on the regime for three weeks and I haven't suffered from PMT as badly. Slowly but surely I will gain more energy.

We've got ourselves a new addition to our family. A nine-week-old puppy, a long-haired German Shepherd named Cheyenne. She's absolutely gorgeous and Misha loves her new playmate. We are now a family of four. Also, I start my Red Cross Volunteer work at

Fremantle Hospital on Monday. Life has changed a bit—by my own choosing.

Wednesday 12 April 2000

It's been three and a half months since our last attempt and I feel it's time to give it another shot. I feel ready emotionally and physically. I had a blood test on Monday (Day 12) to check my hormone levels. It is important to align the implanting of the embryos with my natural cycle. I'm to have another blood test tomorrow to see if I'm any closer to ovulation.

I called the embryologist today to find out at what stage our embryos were frozen. Two were frozen at the two-cell stage and one at the four-cell stage. There's only a seventy per cent success rate of thawing frozen embryos, so hopefully at least two of the three will survive. It's all a gamble, isn't it? I asked whether it was possible to let the embryos multiply to six or eight cells before transferring them into my womb, but apparently that places them at greater risk of contamination. I will trust their years of experience and place the life of 'my children' in their hands. It's a scary thought knowing I don't have much control of the situation, my body or my future children.

Friday 14 April 2000

Okay. I'm feeling like a pin cushion or a blood donor. I had to go back on Thursday and again today for a blood test (The levels were at 210 on Monday, 500 on Thursday, and 800 on Friday). Close but not yet. Guess what? Back again tomorrow morning. Obviously, I haven't ovulated yet on day sixteen. None of this typical day fourteen ovulation for me, no. Maybe that's been half our problem... not having intercourse at the right time? We'll wait and see what happens tomorrow.

I had a talk with the nurse on Thursday and she commended me for taking a break from it all. She said that so many women push themselves and persevere until they burn out from the stress. She gave me ten points for being 'in tune' with myself and recognising when to pause. I collected my antibiotics and folic acid as well.

About six weeks ago, I bought myself Maybe Baby, an ovulation indicator which is basically a tiny microscope that measures the level of oestrogen in your saliva. When you are close to ovulating, fern like structures appear, and when your levels are low, only dots appear. Out of my own curiosity, and to see if it will help me find out when and if I ovulate, I've been dutifully 'spitting' every morning. So far, I haven't really seen a pattern. Some mornings there has been a slight fern pattern but then the next it's back to dots. I've yet to see a fully fern like pattern. I'll keep charting it over the months; it can't hurt.

Sunday 16 April 2000

Ugghh! More blood tests on Saturday (levels at 1,000) and also this morning. My poor veins were not impressed. Maybe Baby is showing swirling clumped ferns today. I was out to lunch with a group for my sister's birthday when I had to call for my results. It was funny going outside and using my mobile phone to find out what my levels were like. We joked around, saying it was like I was checking the stock exchange... Anyway, I have finally ovulated today, at day eighteen, not day fourteen as always stated! There are exceptions to the rule, and I am one of them. I'm to call on Tuesday afternoon to find out whether our embryos have survived the thawing process. Pray to God they do. If all goes well, embryo transfer will take place on

Wednesday. I have to rest and de-stress because I have been a wreck the last few days and have caught a cold. Relax. I surrender all.

Tuesday 18 April 2000

I've been drinking plenty of orange juice and eating fruit and veggies to get well. I've also managed two good nights' sleep and I feel rested. I phoned at 4pm to find out that only two of the three frozen embryos survived the thawing out process. So, only one chance at this before we will have to go back on the waiting list. We're to go to the hospital tomorrow at 10am. I had to take an antibiotic tonight and take two a day for three days afterwards. I also have to insert a pessary every night for two weeks. I surrender all.

Wednesday 19 April 2000

It's my mother's birthday today and hopefully the beginning of our pregnancy. We went in at 10am and waited for half an hour before I put on my fabulous hospital gown again. I accepted a sedative to calm my nerves, although I wasn't as nervous as last time. David went away until it was time to be wheeled into Concept. Embryo transfer occurred at 11.40am. It was painless and quick. Dr Mazzuchelli was friendly and wished us luck. I was wheeled back to Day Surgery to rest quietly for an hour. I listened to my relaxation tape and felt calm.

After lunch, I was allowed to sit in a recliner chair until my release at 2pm. David went for a walk to Kings Park. I guess it was pretty boring to hang around at home. The sedative was still making me sleepy, so I took a nap. I've got a stomach ache, but I think it may be because of the antibiotics I need to take.

I'm a lot more philosophical this time around; I'm not going to obsess like I did before. Of course, I still pray for a positive outcome, but if it really isn't meant to be, no amount of kicking and screaming or chanting will help. I surrender all. Now, I'll take care of myself, relax, eat well and wait patiently for twelve days until our pregnancy test.

Friday 21 April 2000

Happy Easter. Stomach ache and left ovary tenderness persists. I hope it's just the antibiotics—only two more tablets to go. It's hard taking it easy when I'm normally an active person.

Tuesday 25 April 2000

Today, we visited a winery for Irma's birthday. It was very peaceful and my brother Visa insisted on shouting us lunch. Cheyenne's grown so much; she's nearly as tall as Misha now. She had a bit of a setback when she caught Coccidia, a bowel virus that affects dogs, but now she's healthy. I'm having a much needed break from work.

Days have passed by quickly. My stomach ache and ovary pain have disappeared and my breasts are no longer tender. I don't know what that means. Oh well, I'm very calm and fatalistic. If it happens, it happens. In fact, I've forgotten about it a few times until someone asks me how I feel. *Whatever will be, will be...*

Friday 28 April 2000

I really don't feel positive about this. As days go by and it's closer to the pregnancy test, I'm getting a stronger sense that it isn't meant to be. Not yet and maybe not ever. I've thought of ways to have a fulfilling life without children. I adore animals and I would love to own and run a hobby farm. I intend to study animal care so that I won't always have to call a vet for minor problems. It will be a different kind of happiness, but we can still be happy. Our animals can be our children. My lower back and ovary have been aching. Not a good sign. I feel tired and heavy.

Sunday 30 April 2000

I'm spotting again. That's it then. Tomorrow's blood test will confirm I'm not pregnant.

Monday 1 May 2000

Not pregnant. Nothing to say. Seeing the doctor next Tuesday to put ourselves back on the waiting list.

Wednesday 17 May 2000

I haven't felt enthusiastic about anything lately. I can't seem to shake my lethargy and depression. We saw the doctor and it was pretty much a waste of time. We didn't have any more frozen embryos, so back on the year/year-and-a-half waiting list. They will send a letter advising us of the date. If we were rich, we wouldn't have to wait. Who knows whether we'll go through it all again? Time will tell. One day I'm okay with it all, the next I'm morbidly sad. My two dogs are my best medicine; I treat them like children anyway.

Tuesday 6 June 2000

Well, got some more excitement we didn't need. Our car broke down and we have been evicted from our rental house because of Cheyenne! The owners didn't like a German Shepherd on their property. We're packing and moving again to another rental property, blah... here we go again.

Wednesday 28 June 2000

Two weeks ago, I received a surprise letter from Concept which read, *Due to vacancies occurring, you are now able to come through earlier on the IVF program.* What an incredible shock. Believing I would need to wait at least a year, I had put it all out of my head. Now, I have to go back into IVF mode. I made an appointment with Dr Mazzuchelli for 3 July to discuss when to start the process all over again. It's funny that when you let go, positive things can happen.

Monday 3 July 2000

I've been in low spirits again—major PMT mode combined with bad sleeping habits and eating lots of goodies. The thought of going through everything all over again overwhelms me and scares me. I'm praying for strength and courage. I feel disillusioned with my doctor as well. Although he did answer all of my questions, I could feel his impatience emanating from him. I think he is a 'results' and 'facts and figures' doctor who would like all his patients to just passively follow his plan. I wanted reassurance we're doing the right thing and I left there feeling miffed!

Anyway, I found out that it is safe for me to take a Blackmore's Pregnancy and Breastfeeding capsule which contains 200mcg of folic acid. I was concerned I was overdosing on folic acid because of ingesting Concept's 5mg folic acid. You can't overdose on folic acid; it's safe.

I also asked about using the ICSI procedure (Intracytoplasmic Sperm Injection) to increase our fertilisation chances, but Dr

Mazzuchelli said no. Six out of fifteen was quite an adequate result. He said we would do exactly the same as we did last time. So, blood test day twenty-five to check ovulation and then back to Synarel spray and Puregon injections. Now, I'll just wait again for a change…

Tuesday 18 July 2000

Yesterday, I rang Concept to let them know that it is day forty-one and my period still hasn't started. The sister asked me to come in for a blood test to check hormone levels and also to sign paperwork for the new IVF cycle. As I waited, two mothers with their IVF babies visited Concept. You could see their love and pride in their achievements. I think they were going through IVF for a second child. In a way, it was both optimistic and pessimistic for me to see a success story.

After my blood test, I collected all my new 'supplies' and asked to borrow a video entitled *Why Me?* It deals with real life cases of couples handling their infertility, and explores their range of emotions from anger to resentment to frustration and so forth.

On my way to and from Concept, I saw people less fortunate than me: a man in a wheelchair raging at another man on a bicycle; an old man who was knocked down and hit his head but stubbornly refused to go to a doctor; and a young teenager overdosing on drugs on the train station steps. It was as if the Universe was showing me that my life isn't that bad.

Thursday 20 July 2000

Today, I found out that my sister Irma is pregnant. Needless to say that, although I was happy for her, I balled my eyes out. I'm due for my period which is another slap in the face. My husband comforted me and told me not to give up hope.

I don't think I can go through IVF attempt after IVF attempt. I think I need help, maybe see a counsellor. My emotions are veering from *no big deal* being childless to *I can't live without children*. I feel I'm losing control over my life. Sometimes I'm filled with such rage I feel I could physically hurt myself or someone else, and I'm scared about the depth of that emotion. I need someone to talk to. Not my family, but someone who can assure me I'm not losing my mind. I came up with a quote of my own: *Like one part of my heart stopped beating*.

Friday 21 July 2000

Irma's pregnant. I can't shake my depression. My emotions range from severe depression to rage. I'm breaking apart. I have insomnia at night and lethargy throughout the day. And I feel snappish at little things. A loss of control. A nervous breakdown. I need help. God help me, please!

Sunday 23 July 2000

Went for another blood test. My period started yesterday, but I wanted to make sure it was the right time to start Synarel. Yes, I'm to start Synarel tonight and injections tomorrow. Let the fun begin again.

Tuesday 25 July 2000

Knowing what to do has made it a lot easier this time around. Also, they have finally made it simpler to administer the Puregon injection. The solution is already pre-mixed, so no breaking of ampules and no cuts. Just simply flip off the cap and withdraw the solution with the needle, change over to a smaller injecting needle and go for it. The Synarel spray is still disgusting, but I just pop a soother or lolly into my mouth afterwards.

My mood is more upbeat. My body seems to like these hormones, as I feel more energetic and positive, and my period has stopped after four days. Yeah! I'll go for a blood test on Saturday to check whether I'm producing eggs (yep, a chicken again).

Thursday 27 July 2000

One word of advice: never inject yourself into your thigh muscle… ouch! For some reason, I've jabbed myself in the muscle rather than fat for two days in a row and, let me tell you, it hurts. You don't know whether to continue or pull it out and try again. I didn't want to risk contaminating the needle, so I plugged on with it. I don't have a phobia with needles, but I can understand how easily it could develop. Better luck tomorrow? I'm feeling fine, only slight discomfort and nausea.

Saturday 29 July 2000

Blood test yet again. The sister gave me my Puregon injection in my upper thigh. Ooooh, how it stung! Why these needles are hurting more this time, I just don't know. Anyway, my results were at 3,200pm/l oestradiol. They want me to return for an ultrasound tomorrow to check how many follicles are growing. They don't normally do ultrasounds on a Sunday, except on special occasions. I guess they want to be careful I don't develop OHSS. Dr Thomas will do the ultrasound at 9am.

Sunday 30 July 2000

I've been having insomnia for the last few nights, either from stress or my body being 'revved up' by hormones. The result is that I'm exhausted. After my blood test and injection, Dr Thomas performed the always interesting vaginal ultrasound. He asked if I had a normal pelvis and I said yes. He then joked that he didn't want to find three ovaries! I said that no, I only had one. I guess that was what he was really asking and I misunderstood. Anyway, the ultrasound showed my left ovary doing extremely well and producing numerous follicles, approximately seventeen this time. He also checked my right side because sometimes the hormones produce a residual reaction in the leftover tissue. Sure enough, it looked like one follicle. They'll have to keep an eye on it so that it doesn't develop into a painful cyst. My results showed my level at 5,600pm/l. I can skip the doctor's tomorrow but will need to go back for a repeat performance on Tuesday. Maybe the follicles will have reached maturity by then. I'm constantly nauseous whether I eat or not. It's like having morning sickness without being pregnant. Great, huh? The nurse took 20ml of blood today in preparation for egg retrieval and storage.

Anyway, I'll try to rest and nap when I can. I saw a notice on Concept's billboard asking for sperm and egg donors. For five 'donations' of sperm, a man is paid $250. The money would come in handy, but I feel funny thinking that David could have biological children somewhere out there when we don't have any together. I haven't seen the counsellor; it's as if speaking to someone about how difficult this all is would be admitting to a weakness of spirit. I'm holding it all together for now, but who knows how I will be if it doesn't succeed this cycle?

Tuesday 1 August 2000

The ultrasound showed numerous good-sized follicles and my levels are at 12,000pm/l now, so it's a go-ahead. I can stop Synarel and my Puregon injections now. I have to go in at 9.30pm tonight for my HCG injection in the butt. I start antibiotics tomorrow and then must fast from midnight. The egg retrieval will take place on Thursday morning and I'll have to stay at the hospital for about six hours. All going well, embryo transfer will occur on Saturday. David will leave me at the Day Surgery as no visitors are allowed, and they will call him when his sample is required. How romantic...

My levels are high, so I'll probably feel more bloated and sick tomorrow after my injection tonight. I have to drink a lot of water and rest again. Looks like I'm prone to OHSS if I'm not careful. I feel sick enough already. Oh well, what can I do but go ahead now?

Friday 4 August 2000

Egg retrieval went well yesterday, with fourteen out of the eighteen follicles containing ova. I didn't need a drip this time, as I didn't have as many follicles as last time, but I will have an extra blood test on Tuesday to ensure I haven't developed OHSS. My stomach has been extremely sore and bloated, although most of my nausea has disappeared. I've tried to take it easy but it's difficult with normal life chores to do.

I rang at 2pm for my results and good news: nine embryos have formed. Nine out of fourteen is good! Tomorrow, I need to be there at 8am for my embryo implant procedure. Then I can rest again...

I spoke to the embryologist yesterday and apparently last time nine out of the sixteen actually fertilised, but three of them over-fertilised and would not have been genetically acceptable for embryo transfer.

Sunday 6 August 2000

Boy was it busy at Concept yesterday, the busiest I have seen it. I was allocated a bed in Ward Five as Day Surgery is closed during the weekends. In the beds opposite me were two very pregnant women, and next to me was a woman who had just undergone egg retrieval (eighteen for her). I was whisked in early to wait at Concept. There wasn't time to give me a sedative on this occasion.

Dr O'Neill performed the embryo transfer this time, two by four-cells. Dr O'Neill had a different technique to Dr Mazzuchelli. I had to have my legs suspended uncomfortably in stirrups; I was sloshed down and a cover with only a hole in it was put over me. He also made small talk the whole time. It's disconcerting to have someone chatting away between your spread thighs. For example, he asked, 'What does your husband do for a living?'

Whaaattt? I thought. *Is he for real? Asking me that when his head is in between my legs inserting our embryos?*

I guess every doctor has their own methods…

I wanted to make sure that last Thursday they actually pierced the follicle shown on the right-hand side of the ultrasound. When the embryologist came to tell us that one out of the nine embryos was not good for freezing, I took the opportunity of asking her. In November 1997, I had what I was told was an oophorectomy, the removal of my right ovary and partial removal of my tube. Now, this is what stumped us: at egg retrieval, they removed eight out of my right side and six from my left. This sounds impossible, as the ultrasound previously showed seventeen follicles on my left and only one on my right. Even if there was scar tissue remaining, surely there wasn't enough to produce so many eggs from my right side? I'll have to double check the information. She said I should investigate further with my GP. If I still have a partial ovary on my right, it would explain why I continue to suffer pain there during my cycle. It would therefore be real pain, not phantom pain as I believed! Anyway, I'll think positive and eat healthily for the next few weeks, with some heavy duty praying too…

Tuesday 8 August 2000

Partial blood test today. Results were 35pvc. This apparently means everything looks good and I'm not likely to suffer from OHSS. Another nine days until my pregnancy test. Yesterday, I had bad hayfever. I always fear it will cause the embryos to bounce about and not attach, but I've been assured they are well protected inside the womb. Today, I've felt queasy all day. Nerves or something else?

Friday 11 August 2000

Wavering from optimism to pessimism one hundred times a day. No pelvic or ovary pain but breasts a little tender. The progesterone pessaries are making my skin waxy and I'm breaking out much more. We got our form for frozen embryo storage. Seven have been frozen and that's good. My other sister Katri and her daughter, Nikiita, are arriving in Western Australia next Tuesday.

Irma is constantly complaining about her pregnancy and morning sickness. I just feel like slapping her! I would gladly endure feeling sick just to know I had a baby growing inside of me.

Tuesday 15 August 2000

A couple more days to go… no spotting. I pray to God I won't have my period. Please let the test be positive. I've had occasional ovary ache and my breasts are still a bit tender. No carbohydrate food attacks as usually happens before my periods. I have to just wait and see…

Wednesday 16 August 2000

I spoke too soon. Period cramps, pain, bleeding. I can't stop crying.

Thursday 17 August 2000

Negative pregnancy test. The sister suggested counselling. I've thought about it; we'll see… I feel angry, sad, upset, drained, jealous of my sister, fatalistic and slightly crazy all in the one go. We have seven embryos frozen but I'm not ready yet. It's too difficult.

Tuesday 29 August 2000

I've made an appointment with the counsellor for tomorrow at 1.30pm. I thought it was time since my emotions have been all haywire; I have an underlying, uncontrollable rage inside of me. I've been swaying from a carefree *I don't care* to unexpected anger and loss of control with my husband, my family and my dogs. I haven't felt very supported. I guess people are too wrapped up in their own lives and dramas. I also had a mini breakdown—I couldn't stop crying for one and a half hours. I feel very much alone.

Friday 1 September 2000

I'm not losing my mind. The counsellor was great. It's good to have someone neutral and impartial listen to your concerns. Basically, every emotion I have experienced, and am still going through, is quite normal. They are the different stages of grief and mourning for, in fact, I am dealing with death. Death of a possible baby each time it fails as well as death of a dream. To be angry is justified, but I have to find ways of dealing effectively with the anger rather than shouting at others. For example, punch a pillow, go for a walk or find other constructive avenues of letting go. It isn't helpful to suppress your emotions; it's important to allow time to feel, to heal and to renew. I was with the counsellor for forty-five minutes and it did help. She was caring but also realistic. We have to concentrate on a plan B in case I never get pregnant, such as investigate ways to start a hobby farm. For the time being, I'm to keep away from people who upset me. It's okay to acknowledge I'm not coping. It's okay to cry.

Chapter 8

Rollercoaster of Emotions

Saturday 30 September 2000

My thirty-fourth birthday. It sounds better than thirty-three for some reason. It's going to be a good year for me. I can feel it. I'm going to regain my confidence, get motivated and *shine*. Let myself become who I'm meant to be.

Irma and I had a fight more than five weeks ago and we haven't spoken since. It's the longest time ever in our lives. I guess time will heal wounds, even spoken wounding words. Katri and I have spent a little time together. It's hard with David and I living here and all of them living up an hour away. We're going out to dinner tomorrow night with Katri and my brother, Visa. I've got my period and am not feeling particularly upbeat, but it should be okay. We're spending the night at Katri's new place.

Oh yeah, guess what? I got myself a tattoo for my birthday. It's a dove, a heart and a flower—it's very pretty. I wanted to bring peace, love and beauty into my life, and that's what I felt the tattoo represented. It wasn't too painful, as I applied some emla numbing cream before having it done. Now it stings a little but they said it should heal in about four days' time. I like it, and so do David and Katri.

Monday 30 October 2000

Time has passed and time has healed. I feel better able to cope emotionally. I no longer have severe mood swings, only the normal highs and lows of PMT. It took a couple of months of silent treatment, but I've 'made up' with Irma. It's still difficult watching her pregnancy develop and her belly grow, but I'm not so angry. I think she is trying to make more of an effort too. She's not complaining so much about the side effects and the unexpectedness of it all.

I've made an appointment to see Dr Mazzuchelli next Monday, although I need my GP to renew my referral first. We've got seven embryos. We only need one to survive, but I'm making other plans for next year if all fail. I want to complete this IVF chapter of my life before starting another, for example, studying, an apprenticeship or full-time work.

Wednesday 8 November 2000

Well, here we go again... I saw Dr Mazzuchelli and finally he is coming to the same conclusion I've had for a long time: I'm pre-menopausal. My periods are getting further apart again, every seven to eight weeks now. It saves on pads and tampons, I guess, but it's still not a good sign. We will now try something different yet again. I feel like a lab rat! I've got instructions for FET (Frozen Embryo Transfer) using Progynova, an oestrogen based drug used by pre-menopausal or menopausal women.

I had a blood test yesterday to confirm that I had ovulated. Now I'm back on Synarel spray to stop my body from producing its whacky hormones. When my period starts, I'll commence taking the Progynova tablets. The regime is as follows:

- days 2 to 8—one 2mg Progynova tablet

- days 9 to 15—two 2mg Progynova tablets (morning and night)
- day 12—Blood test (20mls)
- day 13—commence progesterone pessaries (twice a day) and antibiotics (twice a day)
- day 15—embryo transfer
- day 16—continue Progynova tablet (once a day), pessaries and antibiotics.

Hopefully, this will ensure that the 'right' quantities of hormones are circulating in my body to sustain an embryo. If I fall pregnant, I will have to continue to take the tablets for ten weeks, until the placenta commences producing sufficient hormones on its own. So wish me luck; I don't know how all of these new hormones will affect me.

Friday 17 November 2000

I've taken Synarel for ten days. Uggghhhh! I was spotting for six days before my period finally came. I was in agony. The worst cramps I've had in a long time. I guess the fact I haven't had a period for two months has made my body want to make up for it, as they were very heavy and clotty. I began Progynova on Wednesday. So far, no huge side effects, just slight headaches and tiredness. I have my blood test and ultrasound next Friday with Dr Mazzuchelli.

Friday 24 November 2000

Blood taken (20mls). Ouch! I had to press the needle entry point for five minutes afterwards because the nurse got a good bleeder vein. The ultrasound showed my uterus lining at 9mm, which is a promising sign. A couple more days and it should be optimum thickness. I'm to stop Synarel spray now, continue with Progynova and start progesterone pessaries on Sunday. I'm to call on Tuesday to find out about the survival of embryos as well as the embryo transfer time for Wednesday. Antibiotics to commence on Tuesday. Drugs, drugs and more drugs...

They've rearranged the Concept waiting area to be cosier and to promote interaction between patients. It encouraged me to start a conversation with another woman and we compared our needle experiences.

On the train ride home, a friendly young lady noticed I was reading the Genesis Support Group Newsletter and began a conversation about her mum's endometriosis and her own pregnancy problems. She even gave me a card for an acupuncturist who has helped with her medical problems. I believe things don't just happen; I was meant to meet her. She wished me luck and squeezed my shoulder in support as she left. How heart-warming to feel a total stranger cared.

Tuesday 28 November 2000

Tomorrow morning is D-Day... again...

Two embryos were thawed and both survived. We have five left frozen, which hopefully we won't need. I feel fine and positive, although a bit snappish today from the stress of it all. I'll listen to my relaxation tape at bedtime. My husband doesn't seem too fazed—typical male behaviour—and I'm irritated because of it. So, let the Universe and God speak...

Wednesday 29 November 2000

I arrived two hours early, as David dropped me off before heading to work. I enjoyed a cup of coffee and then sat in the sunshine. I went to Day Surgery at 9.30am and had the usual blood pressure, temperature and pulse check before changing into my 'bootifull' gown. A nurse gave me a sedative because my nerves and stomach were a bit jumpy. At 11.40am I went in for my FET and whilst waiting, I chatted to some of the other women.

Dr Mazzuchelli was in a joking mood and the procedure went well. One of the thawed embryos didn't divide any further, so they let it 'succumb' and thawed out another one. I had a two-cell and a six-cell go in. I rested back in Day Surgery with three other IVF patients until 1.30pm when I could sit in the lounge. I started a conversation with a woman next to me and we compared our history with IVF. We exchanged numbers and we'll keep in touch and support each other. At home, I rested and cooked a little. I feel optimistic. Maybe baby...

Tuesday 5 December 2000

I'm only on one Progynova and two pessaries now. I've felt great for days, no pain anywhere and so full of energy. These hormones are exactly what I've needed. I feel so good. Blood test next Monday and I'm having coffee with one of the women I met at Concept.

Thursday 7 December 2000

Still feeling great. Optimistic. No pains. No breast tenderness nor any ovary, stomach or back ache. Looking good...

Monday 18 December 2000

I haven't written because it has been too difficult to write. I started spotting and bleeding late Thursday 7 December, and it continued through to Monday's test. Pregnancy test negative yet again. I had coffee with my fellow IVF traveller on that Monday, and we commiserated with each other. It was good to share thoughts and fears with someone who knew what I was going through. I stopped all drugs on Tuesday and my period came on fully. I've kept myself busy with Christmas preparations and spending lots of money. It helps for a little while but then reality sinks in: no gifts for our children for another year. Year after year. I'm seeing my doctor this afternoon to discuss next options, if any are left... I want to tell him that the oestrogen helped keep me balanced and feeling good.

Tuesday 19 December 2000

Why is it that every time I see Dr Mazzuchelli, I feel like such a failure as a woman? I must say, he isn't always the most encouraging person to hang around. He told me he can't keep me on the oestrogen permanently; it's only for IVF purposes. However, if all else fails, I can look into Hormone Replacement Therapy later on. I'll find an empathetic female doctor who will listen and try to help me.

For the past couple of weeks, I've been stuffing my face full of food in my misery. Same bad habit I've had for years after emotional turmoil and heartbreak.

After New Year, we'll start the same regime as last time. I've been having major doubts about going through everything again. I am afraid. This will be the last time; I've had enough. I want to close this door and open one to another future I have in mind. I am tired.

Chapter 9

Is It Time To Give Up?

Wednesday 3 January 2001

Sounds so futuristic, 2001. Happy New Year! After Christmas, we travelled down south to Walpole and camped in a group for New Year. Such beautiful national parks and countryside scenery. We swam at Greens Pool and the Circular Pool. We explored the 'city' of Denmark, went on a cruise, cycled, fished and walked a lot, including the Tree Top Walk in the Valley of the Giants. What an active and very busy six days.

It was such a nice break from the city and all this IVF stuff. I can't believe how long we have been pursuing this dream. Now that I'm back, I feel stressed and depressed again. You can only run away from your problems for so long. I've been wavering every day. Yes, go through it again. No, quit now. I've decided yes but only one more time. I'll go for a blood test tomorrow and so it begins…

Thursday 4 January 2001

Yes! Ovulated. Synarel tomorrow…

Wednesday 10 January 2001

A few headaches and mood swings, probably due to the Synarel. I'm going to Concept tomorrow to pick up my supplies of Synarel,

Progynova and antibiotics. I'm quite out of sorts, feeling stressed and depressed again. My consolation is that this is the last time. One way or another, life will change for me!

Thursday 18 January 2001

Two weeks on Synarel and finally my period decides to make an appearance. Last time it was within one week of taking Synarel. Even the sister at Concept was ringing me up to ask whether they had started. Anyway, déjà vu, same program as last time. I can't wait for the 'feel good' drugs. Progynova made me feel balanced last time. Tomorrow, I can start them again and hopefully my mood will lift. I'm tired of feeling so down all of the time. I guess stress doesn't help. A lot is happening in our work lives as well. On with the battle.

Saturday 27 January 2001

I don't know if it's the continued use of drugs or what, but my nails and gums are suffering. My nails are chipping and peeling, and my gums are bleeding and sore. I guess I have been on Synarel for over three weeks, which can't be good. Like last time, my mouth is dry. My blood test and ultrasound are on Monday. I haven't felt enthusiastic at all this time, just going through the motions. IVF is a strain all round: physically, mentally, emotionally and spiritually.

I've had more energy again with the Progynova, but I'm not as bouncy with optimism. Our dog Cheyenne gave us a scare when she accidentally swallowed five of my Progynova tablets. We took her to the vet to help her empty her stomach contents. I don't know how harmful they could have been for her. Menopausal drugs for a spayed dog!

I've had questions floating around in my mind of late, for others contemplating IVF:

- How important is having a child?
- Is it worth the strain of IVF?
- Is your marriage strong enough to survive the pressure?
- How can you have a fulfilling life without children?

In some strange way, I enjoy being different and not like everyone else who can just fall pregnant and have a baby. The doctors and nurses make you feel special during every embryo transfer, a little like a 'delicate' person. It's as though it's become my identity. And you get instant sympathy from strangers. *Poor woman. She can't have children.* Does this make me a bad person or is this normal?

Tuesday 30 January 2001

I had my ultrasound and blood withdrawal yesterday. When I rang the sister, she wasn't one hundred per cent sure of the doctor's instructions, so I had to call back. Of course, this made me all nervous and worried. Apparently, the uterus lining is only at 7mm, so not thick enough yet. I have to increase my Progynova to three a day for four days and have another ultrasound on Friday. Boy oh boy, is the Universe stretching this suffering by making me take more drugs. I don't like it. The Synarel is giving me a horrible dry throat during the night. I feel headachy, sluggish and fed up with life.

Friday 2 February 2001

My ultrasound was at 8am. It was quite funny. Dr O'Neill calmly placed a finger of a rubber glove over the vaginal ultrasound probe, the assistant applied lubricant to it and in it went. After a pause, he announced, 'What a wonderful looking endometrium, simply wonderful!' He then added, 'Hopefully, you'll get pregnant this time.'

I had to keep a straight face; he just looked so delighted with my 9mm endometrium. I will finally stop the Synarel tomorrow, start pessaries twice a day and reduce Progynova to once a day. I'll phone on Sunday to get a time for Monday's transfer.

Monday 5 February 2001

Yesterday, when I rang Concept, I reminded them to thaw out all four frozen embryos and it was just as well. One didn't survive the thawing out process and another didn't divide. The remaining two healthy embryos went in, a four-cell and a two-cell. The staff know me by name by now and everyone was kind. I had to go to Ward Five because Day Surgery was closed today. Anyway, I was pretty dopey all day because of the sedative and slept a lot. Blood test on Saturday 17 February. Countdown begins… This is peculiar: the blue pen I have been writing with throughout my IVF journey finally ran out of ink. Does this mean my story is complete?

Wednesday 14 February 2001

Happy Valentine's Day. My hubby surprised me by arranging flowers, chocolates and a lovely card on the dining table while I was away. What a nice surprise when I got home. Well, so far, I've felt fine. I've been wavering from hope to resignation. A couple more days to go…

Saturday 17 February 2001

Well, that's that then. The end of my dream of being a mother. No go. The cursed period started again, with spotting from Thursday.

I've cried, grieved, raged and finally given up. I need a referral from Dr Mazzuchelli to see a female gynaecologist to help me now.

Monday 26 February 2001

I had to make an appointment with my GP instead, as Dr Mazzuchelli is a gynaecologist and doesn't write referrals to see other gynaecologists. Seeing my GP was no problem, but getting an appointment with a female specialist is practically impossible, as there are only a few around Perth. I've made an appointment with one for 21 May. Oh well, I'll have to cope the best I can.

Chapter 10

Door Shut or Left Ajar?

Sunday 18 March 2001

I have moved on with my life after IVF. I tried singing in a choir for a few weeks in Fremantle, and it was great fun, but I had to give it up because I found myself a new job and the times clashed. I'm now a weight loss consultant with Jenny Craig. Isn't that funny? Life has turned full circle. Once a client and now a consultant. I've finished my training and tomorrow is my first official day. It's scary but I'm sure I'll enjoy helping people through my job. Irma gave birth to her third child, Khan, on 13 March.

Monday 18 June 2001

Time has just flown. Half the year gone already. I saw a specialist and unfortunately the only way I can combat my menstrual and skin problems is to go back on the pill. She recommended Diane 35. I started them today and we shall see what happens over the next few months. I'm enjoying my work. It keeps me very busy and my mind off my childlessness. David and I have planned a getaway to Sydney for my friend Samantha's wedding in September. David and I have joined a gym and have seen some great results in our fitness and weight loss. Although we've had a few rough patches, our marriage is still strong and our four-legged children, Misha and Cheyenne, keep us entertained on a daily basis.

TREE WITH NO LEAVES

Saturday 15 September 2001

Sydney in less than two weeks, yeah! It's been a scary, sick world lately and we need a bit of fun. Terrorists bombed the US (New York Twin Towers and Washington Pentagon) and approximately 4,000 people were killed on 11 September. I don't know whether this will cause WW3 or not. I pray not! Katri and I had a huge argument, but all this trouble put things into perspective. Too short a time on this Earth to spend time arguing.

Tuesday 2 October 2001

I've got to say that our Sydney trip was the best holiday we've had in years. We loved the cosmopolitan atmosphere. We had a fantastic time meeting up with Samantha and John. The wedding was wonderful. Samantha looked beautiful and I looked great in my new evening gown, if I do say so myself. David and I did heaps of sightseeing and we walked for hours every day. We visited the Sydney Aquarium, Chinese Gardens, Darling Harbour, Circular Quay, Opera House, The Rocks, Paddy's Markets, Spanish Festival, Botanical Gardens and the Northern Territory Aboriginal Show. We ate many different cuisines such as Spanish, Indian, Mexican, German, Continental and Australian, of course. What a time we had. It's always hard to slot back into your home life after holidays, isn't it?

Monday 12 November 2001

Okay, time to move out. A car crashed into our front bedroom wall, knocking our letterbox down and leaving our garden in a mess in the process! Thank God we were alright as well as the female driver, who we suspect was intoxicated. We're looking for a rental house in the Perth hills area, which will be great, as I will see my sisters and my brother more frequently if I'm living closer to them.

Wednesday 23 January 2002

On 10 December, we moved to a quiet no through road location in Mundaring. It's a large four-bedroom, two-bathroom house on about an acre of land. The only complaint we have is that the yard is full of grass seeds and prickles, and our poor girls, Misha and Cheyenne, had to be shaved totally bald! Misha looks like a Blue Heeler instead of a Keeshond, and Cheyenne looks like a Greyhound mixed with German Shepherd. We have to control ourselves around them and not laugh so much, as their feelings are already hurt by their own reflections.

Monday 23 September 2002

Goodness, this diary doesn't seem to be a priority does it? I'm still working for Jenny Craig but asked for a transfer to a closer location. We've been to a few social functions, such as *The Man From Snowy River Arena Spectacular* at Burswood and a cocktail party at Katri's. Mum and Dad visited for a few weeks during their usual around Oz trip, and David and I went on a camping trip. Life goes on. I'm sure we've done other things, but I've forgotten the rest. Nothing soul-shattering. I wish I could say I've moved on from desiring to become a mother, but a small part of me still wishes for an absolute miracle to occur, for Mother Nature to change her mind and grant me a pregnancy…

Chapter 11

New Focus, New Dreams

Friday 21 February 2003

We have moved again (sigh), back down south of the river to Port Kennedy. David changed jobs and the drive from Mundaring was both time consuming and expensive, so it made sense to move closer to his job at Henderson near Fremantle. I quit my job at Jenny Craig to allow time to focus on my new goal of becoming a professional counsellor. I've enrolled in a two-year Diploma of Professional Counselling which is home study based in conjunction with attending practical seminars at Mt Lawley. I've had many people suggest I become a counsellor, and I believe that my own life experiences will enable me to empathise with, and hopefully help, a lot of people.

The beach is five minutes away by car and we take our girls to the doggy beach regularly. We are all happier. Irma visits every weekend and spends the night because her own courses in Naturopathy, Homeopathy, Bowen Therapy and Flower Essences are only half an hour away from us instead of the longer distance from the hills. We are determined that 2003 is going to be a great year for us.

Sunday 9 March 2003

I've spent the last week reading all my diaries and journals. It has been a real eye-opener. What arrogance and childishness in my twenties and so much pain in my thirties. As I get closer to forty, I wonder how I'll react to what I write now? We do change and evolve over time.

I love my studies; they are very challenging, good for the grey matter, and I keep getting signs that I am doing the right thing. I am meant to help people. I am meant to really listen and care. I know I have it in me to be a great Grief and Loss Counsellor. I really appreciate David letting me concentrate on my studies for the next two years. He is working long hours but is so much happier. In fact, we are both happier here. The downside of being a student at home is having the munchies on a regular basis. The weight is creeping back on and I need to work my butt instead of just sitting on it.

Monday 12 May 2003

I've started a fitness workout at last; David put a program together for me. I've made a few trips up to the hills for a break from my studies. I have days where I feel really down and unmotivated, but I give myself a pep talk and get back into gear so that I don't fall behind in my studies. I've been on progesterone cream for five months now and the periods are becoming more regular, once a month. I've found that when I'm on the cream, I feel more balanced and positive. Yoga is helping me as well.

Monday 21 July 2003

Well, halfway through Unit 5 already (twenty-two units all together). Most of it is interesting, though some of it is a bit dry for my taste. I'm finding winter a bit depressing and the cold mornings make it so hard to get out of bed. I've made some new friends through my course, and it's good to get to know people on my own wavelength, not only in the course, but also on the spiritual side of life. I'm feeling the need to read more psychic stuff, for example, books by John Edward and James Van Praagh. I even bought a six CD set on how to develop your psychic powers.

Overall, David and I are happier than we have been in a long while. We have friends visiting us from interstate in November, and I'm planning a trip to Queensland to visit my eldest sister, Kirsti, and her family in January next year. It's exciting to have lots of plans.

Thursday 1 January 2004

Christmas and New Year have come and gone for another year. At least this year we went all out with the Christmas decorations and presents, and we had everyone over. There were activities such as hat decorating and face-painting for the young kids, and Piñata for all of us.

I've just finished Unit 10. Nearly halfway through the course already and the hard work is paying off. I can start volunteer work soon, and I've decided to put my name down for work at Jenny Craig again. The money will come in handy for our camping trips, and we want to visit Tasmania for Christmas. It's always good to have something to look forward to in life and holidays are good for the Soul.

I'm feeling a bit blah in myself and with my marriage lately. There's got to be more to life than this. I've accepted the fact of no children, so what else is in store for me? The beginning of a new year always starts me thinking about my life and where it is heading. I'm trying out another progesterone cream (Profeme), as the other one is not working anymore. I'm enduring horrific periods. I'm considering a hysterectomy if things don't improve soon.

Monday 28 June 2004

Half a year gone again. Oh well. I had a lovely three-week holiday in Queensland catching up with Kirsti, Steve and their sons Rainer, Kester, Jarrin and Kailum. I used my new video camera for capturing memories. I've been working for Jenny Craig for four months again and also volunteering. I've made some really lovely friends through work. It all became too much with my studies (onto Unit 14), work and volunteering, so I gave up my volunteer work. I'm seeing another specialist. He is a GP and a naturopath who also uses Chinese medicine and kinesiology. Hopefully some relief and help are on its way…

Monday 14 February 2005

Happy Valentine's Day for another year. Let's put this succinctly. I changed jobs again and am now a receptionist at a Day Spa in Fremantle, together with Julie, a new friend I met through Jenny Craig (we both left). At the present time I'm onto Unit 17, yay! I haven't been able to study as much due to work and health problems. I'm continuing to see my specialist, and he has put me on a new set of Chinese herbs. He is as stumped as the rest of them. David and I are celebrating our tenth wedding anniversary in September this year. We still have some issues as a couple but we are trying to work through them. Both Mum and Dad are having some health problems, which are being investigated. The years of alcohol abuse are catching up, I think. I'm right into numerology at the moment. It's absolutely fascinating stuff and I'm learning a lot from the two books I've purchased.

Chapter 12

Out of Focus, Out of Mind

Sunday 24 July 2005

For years you hold it all together. You are strong. People admire your courage and perseverance. You congratulate yourself on how well you have coped, and your husband and family are proud of the progress you have made in your life. Suddenly your life comes to an abrupt halt with six simple words. Your four-year-old nephew utters, 'You're a mum; where's your kids?'

You smile and say, 'What kids? Do you see any kids?' You pretend it's all funny, but you shrivel up inside and wait...

It's close to midnight, your sister has collected her children hours before, and you've indulged in a few whiskey and cokes and finally let go. You break down as you haven't broken down in years. You realise that you aren't so strong. Your front breaks down and you shatter into a thousand pieces of heartache and pain.

Where are my kids? I'm thirty-nine years old and I still haven't come to terms with my infertility. Will I ever? As I sob in my husband's arms, I yell, 'Will it ever stop? I want it to stop! I want the dreams to stop! I dream of babies still and breastfeeding. I need it all to stop!'

I have to let it go. I don't want to be in my eighties and still grieving for the children I never had. How I've fooled myself into believing I'm over it. I've grieved, I've raged, I've cried, and I've buried my dreams, only to let it surface with a child's innocent words.

It's as if I want a shutter to close off a portion of my heart, the portion devoted to my offspring, to enable me to get on with my life. Not the life I dreamed of and fantasised about but an alternative, fulfilling in its own way. I want my heart to be able to brush off insensitive queries from friends and acquaintances, to not let another woman's pregnancy upset me ever again, to be able to rejoice in their happiness without having resentment, envy and jealousy eat away at me. To feel 'full' as opposed to 'empty'. To not try and fill this empty space with food or alcohol.

I have spent the last few years studying to become a counsellor in order to help others cope with their loss and grief. The irony is that I have not nurtured myself as much as I have wanted to nurture others.

It's okay to cry.

It's okay to rant and rave.

It's okay to be a drama queen.

It's okay to lash out.

It's okay to wallow.

It's okay to act strong.

It's okay to pretend.

All emotions, all feelings, all of these states of being are okay. Don't let anyone tell you how long you can grieve, how long until you 'let go' or 'move on'. There are no limits or stages. Only you can live your life the best you can, feel what you can, be what you can be... It's your life and it's your time.

Sunday 9 July 2006

One year on... Time certainly is a healer as 'they' say. Well, to a degree anyway. I feel sane again. It's taken me years to start feeling a bit like the 'old Sorja' with her sense of humour and sense of 'why not?' I've completed my studies and am now a fully-fledged counsellor. It is strange how you think you're going to go in one direction, for example, motherhood, and then end up heading in a completely new direction. 'They' also say that enduring heartache can make you a stronger person and enable you to use your experience to help others in need. I have found I am more understanding of others and can empathise with them.

At present I am a Drug and Alcohol Addiction Counsellor working at a Rehabilitation Centre. I have seen so many people in pain and heard so many horrifying life stories. I understand how easy it would be to want oblivion or to escape from a harsh life. I know that using alcohol or drugs is one form of escapism, a temporary release from having to feel and from having to grieve.

I remember spending days in bed, trying to escape through sleep, almost willing myself to die. I also remember how upset my husband was and how he himself was helpless to help me. Looking back, I was so consumed by my own sense of loss and grief that I didn't have anything left to give him, including the time to notice he was grieving in his own way. I now understand that men and women grieve differently. As women, we cannot assume they are coping with it any better than us. I think I wore my grief so openly and so raw, that I expected my husband to display it in the same way, not silently and internally as he did and still does.

A few months ago, Katri and Irma commented that I was becoming the 'Sorja' they had always known. I suppose they are right to some extent. I'll never be the same carefree, cheeky girl I was, but I've certainly found some of me again. I was lost in a kind of limbo for many years. Yes, I did suffer from depression though I never sought help for it. Ironic now that I am a counsellor… Studying grief and loss counselling has certainly helped me understand why I went through such extreme ranges of emotion, anywhere from apathy to rage.

Chapter 13

Decision Time

Sunday 6 August 2006

Yes, it's that time again. The dreaded p's. Every time it makes me feel down and depressed, all these bodily functions for nothing. Why do I have to go through such agony every five weeks or so? Yes, my cycle is that whacky. Sometimes three weeks and sometimes seven. There is no rhythm and so much pain lasting the entire period—up to five or six days of cramps, back ache, headache, leg ache and such heavy blood loss.

I just don't see the point of all of this suffering without the reward of a baby. I've tried just about everything: gynaecologists, specialists, and naturopaths—so many lotions, potions, pills, suppositories and pain killers. I gave myself until I turned forty to try every possible avenue before finally giving in and having a hysterectomy.

I turn forty next month.

I can honestly say that I am fed up with my periods ruining so many vacations, one being our tenth wedding anniversary last year. Imagine my husband and I planning a romantic getaway to a country cabin for five days. Lovely restaurants, walks and drinking wine in front of the fireplace... Wrong! I spent most of the time in bed, clutching a heat pack against my swollen stomach. We even had to leave the restaurant early, as I had to unbutton my jeans under my jumper due to the discomfort. The next morning was no better, as I woke up having flooded my night gown and bedding. Talk about romantic.

I can think back to so many moments revolving around my periods and the accompanying pain, and I know that life is not meant to be like this. I wonder how many women try to predict when their periods will fall and whether they will ruin holiday plans with family or friends? I joke with my sisters about needing to buy adult nappies to avoid any more 'accidents', but it is no joking matter. When 'super' is no longer 'super' enough, what does a girl do?

I understand the French term *petit mort* as meaning *little death*. It is a little death each time I have my period. No matter how much I say I have 'let go', a portion of my Soul still holds on to the tiniest hope that a miracle could occur for us. I can consciously give myself a good talking to, but that tiny voice still whispers, 'What if this time?' I guess the only way to stop that voice is to physically have my uterus and remaining ovary removed from me. I am hopeful that then I can have some internal peace. In the meantime, 'they' say *make pain your friend*—are 'they' men? Would I mourn the loss of pain from periods? I seriously doubt it!

Monday 6 November 2006

Well, here begins another chapter of my life. I went to see the gynaecologist Dr Patton on 20 October, and he agrees that my best option is to have a hysterectomy. I did tell everyone that I would wait until after my fortieth birthday and that is now.

I had prepared myself to plead my case to him. I had written and typed out a brief medical history just to show him how much I had already endured. He read it and made little noises of sympathy when he got to some of the 'juicy bits', such as the benign tumour in my right ovary. He then asked me what I thought I should do and my answer was, 'Hysterectomy'.

He said he had to hear it from me and that the decision was mine to make. He then conducted a pelvic exam and pap smear before ordering blood tests. And, of course, there was the lovely full bladder ultrasound again. I remember that one well, as I'm sure most women do!

Unfortunately, the ultrasound revealed that my left ovary has once again twisted around to rest behind my uterus, with the fallopian tube also kinked. It also revealed numerous little cysts inside it. In other words, it is unhealthy. It would be unwise to leave it in, as I would have to face surgery again later. So full abdominal surgery faces me again on 30 November. Before, I had a countdown to D-Day with the IVF implant days. Now, it's on again for a very different reason. I am torn between elation and depression, relating to the end of a dream versus hopefully the end of pain and liberation from periods.

The surgeon will most likely remove my uterus, cervix and remaining ovary and tube. I will have to go on HRT due to surgical menopause being induced and as I am only forty, I will need oestrogen to prevent heart disease and osteoporosis. I will also get a rapid onset of menopause instead of a gradual one. Just greeeeaaaattttt!

Monday 7 November 2006

My boobs are killing me! They always feel huge, bulging, uncomfortable and oh so tender two weeks prior to my periods. If I were a chicken, this would be the perfect time for breast fillets. I wonder what being on HRT will do. Will I still have painful breasts?

Time will tell.

Friday 10 November 2006

Today, I felt furious about my childlessness again. Everywhere I go, I see mums with babies or dads with toddlers. Every other woman on this planet seems to be able to fall pregnant except for me. So what did I do with this fury? Firstly, I tried to drown it with food and when that made me feel worse, I punched the shit out of the punching bag during my one-and-a-half hour circuit workout at home. That certainly helped me release some of that fury in a healthier way.

Monday 20 November 2006

What an emotional rollercoaster this past week has been—I'm becoming an expert. Last Wednesday, I took a call from my doctor saying surgery would have to be postponed, as my blood tests revealed I had a blood disorder which is dangerous during surgery. Apparently, my blood has difficulty clotting and therefore there is a risk I could bleed to death! As I had received the call during work hours, I tried to remain strong but then broke down from shock and fear. Very emotionally, I tried to explain the situation to my colleagues and they understood I needed to go home. Of course, my period started on the Thursday, and all I could do was to wait until the Friday appointment with my doctor to find out more about this blood disorder. I was afraid I would bleed out with my period, as I had many clots and flooded again.

On Friday, I found out that I have Von Willebrand's Disease (VWD), which primarily affects the blood. VWD is due to a deficiency in certain clotting factors in the blood. This deficiency is of a protein in the blood called the 'Von Willebrand factor' and it affects the clotting mechanism. Not only that, but the doctor also said I have endometriosis! All these years and no-one has picked up on that? I've been reading up on the symptoms, including pain, adhesions of organs and heavy periods. I've been furious that I could have been helped years ago and avoided such agony. Also, all this time I thought I had a chance of getting pregnant, but now I know the odds were stacked against me. I feel foolish that I wasted so many years continuing to think I had a chance when I really didn't.

Today, I feel saner than yesterday. Yesterday, I felt D E F E A T E D. Now I'm telling myself to stop being such a drama queen and get on with life. I'm seeing a haematologist this Friday to do more tests with regard to VWD, which will hopefully help prepare me for the new surgery date, 18 December 2006. I know I have a lot of support from my family, friends and work colleagues, and surgery is the best option for me.

Sunday 26 November 2006

The haematologist I saw on Friday was such a lovely man. He took the time to explain what Von Willebrand's Disease is in terms I could understand, and the consequences of having this disorder. I have Von Willebrand's Factor levels of forty per cent and type 1, which is the most common form of VWD. I need to be concerned when I undergo major dental work or surgery, as I have an increased bleeding risk. Also during periods, which explains so much! He said I need to let others know in case of an emergency, for example, a car accident, so that the emergency department can administer DDAVP (Desmopressin), which helps with blood clotting. I must also avoid Aspirin and NSAIDS (Non-steroidal anti-inflammatory drugs) because they can lead to increased internal bleeding. Since VWD is familial, he recommended that my father, mother, sisters and brother get tested as well.

As for my surgery, I first have to go to the Day Surgery on 5 December, for a DDAVP trial, administered intravenously. This can have side effects such as a headache, flushed skin, increased blood pressure and fluid retention—just great. If this is successful, they can administer DDAVP before my surgery on the eighteenth to prevent me bleeding out. Fingers crossed...

Monday 4 December 2006

On Friday, I had a doctor's appointment to get back my results and sign the paperwork for my surgery. My pap smear was fine and the haematologist's tests confirmed Von Willebrand's Disease. Within the next two weeks, I have to see the anaesthetist as well as go for a pre-admissions interview. On the Saturday night prior to Monday's surgery, I have to stop eating. On the Sunday, I have to take some horrible stuff to empty out my bowels, and drink fluids and eat jellies only. This is because of my scar tissue being so close to my intestines and there is a greater danger of being 'nicked'. Oh joy, once again. They will administer the DDAVP on the Monday morning before my surgery, which will take place sometime after lunch. I'll see what that's about tomorrow when I go along for the DDAVP trial.

Friday 8 December 2006

On Tuesday, I was at the Day Surgery by 8am. David dropped me off and went 'gallivanting' at the shopping centre whilst I had the DDAVP trial. The nurse put an IV line into both my arms, but unfortunately my veins were being difficult, and I had to get jabbed in five different spots. The Desmopressin was allowed to drip slowly into my right hand (below thumb, near wrist—ouch!) and bloods were taken from my left arm. They took blood for readings and blood work before DDAVP commenced, then half hour after it had gone through, then one hour and, finally, after three hours. Within an hour it looked as though it was working because the nurse had a really hard time extracting blood out of my veins despite trying many spots. I also went cold; my hands and feet felt like ice. After a blanket and some heating gel packs, my body warmed up enough to enable the nurse to draw blood. I did get a few of the side effects—a headache, fluid retention and fatigue—but these disappeared after a couple of days. I was also told to watch my fluid intake for that day and not exceed one to one-and-a-half litres, which was hard, as I normally drink a lot of fluids! So, now I know what to expect on the morning of the surgery.

Friday 15 December 2006

I'm exhausted! I've been preparing for a siege. Lots of shopping, preparing food stocks, cleaning, gardening and paperwork. I know my husband is quite capable of doing everything during my recovery, but at least I feel better for being as organised as possible. Yesterday was my last day at work and I am incredibly grateful for their good wishes and prayers that my surgery will go well. I am receiving a lot of support from family, friends, work colleagues and clients. I do feel loved.

On Tuesday, I had my appointment with my anaesthetist, who seems pleasant. He had to do some research into what I can have for pain management post-surgery, due to my having VWD. I can't have an epidural, so I will have a personal pain control IV pump that administers morphine when I push a button. I cannot have NSAIDS either, so I will have alternative infection controlling drugs. During surgery they will monitor my conscious state with sensors on my forehead, which is a relief as I've heard of the nightmare stories of people being aware during operations. I also had my pre-admissions appointment at the hospital. Although the nurse was a little abrupt, she was thorough, conducting a heart monitor test, urine and blood tests, and measuring height and weight. She systematically completed the accompanying mountain of paperwork. So all systems go. Now I have the information I need, for example, what to bring to the hospital, how to use the oral fleet on Sunday, the clear liquid diet all day Sunday, and post-operative physiotherapy exercises such as deep breathing exercises, coughing, circulatory exercises and walking.

I have been making the most of *life* these past few weeks. Enjoying little, simple things and being grateful for them. I have also thought about death and mortality. I'm not ready to die but should it happen then I have reflected upon what I have achieved, how I have connected with some people and not with others. Most of the time, I have been a good person or, as one client said to me yesterday, 'Sorja, you are a good woman.' I know there is room for improvement, but I have tried to keep level-headed and grounded. I'm still willing to learn more about myself as well as those around me. One way or another, I feel I'm not done yet, whether here on Earth or when I have crossed over.

Saturday 16 December 2006

I'm getting nervous thinking about all of the *what ifs?* We went boogie boarding today. I floated on my board and looked up at the sky, just trying to *be* in the moment. I've prepared as much as possible; now I have to let go and trust in my Guardian Angels and all those sending me positive energy.

Chapter 14

Door Firmly Shut

Sunday 17 December 2006

Ooohhh... my stomach! Firstly, I had to consume nothing but clear fluids all day such as apple juice, sprite, black coffee or tea, and a bit of jelly or clear soup (yuck). Then I had to take oral fleet to empty my bowels out over and over again. Well, the hunger has gone, only to be replaced by nausea and stomach cramps. Lovely. Now to try and sleep before my big day tomorrow. I'll write later when I'm able to.

Monday 25 December 2006

It took me longer than I thought to be able to write about my progress. What remains prominent in my mind about the last week? PAIN, PAIN, PAIN. I never knew there were so many ways of experiencing excruciating pain! Let's go back to what I can remember. I arrived at the hospital at 10am and was directed to the admissions department. David and I went into the administration officer's room to fill in the usual paperwork and sign forms. We were then shown to my allocated room. I was told it would be quite a wait. David perched on the end of the bed for about half an hour and I could see he was getting restless, so I told him it was okay for him to go. Hospitals aren't that entertaining, I know. My roommate turned out to be an elderly lady who had been there for three weeks, poor woman. She'd had a hip replacement and needed skin grafts on her lower leg as well. She was in a sorry state as she suffered incontinence, had what sounded like the flu and goodness knows what else. All in all, a very vocal roommate.

Then, oh joy, it was time to shave my pubic hair in preparation for the surgery (luckily the nurse finished before the doctor came). Just after midday, it was time for my DDAVP to be administered. Dr Patton 'tsk-tsked' over my deep veins and I had the 'fortune' of having the IV in the most painful spot again. Lucky me. This time I did become all flushed in the face as the doctor so kindly pointed out. At about 1.30pm, it was time to be transferred onto a gurney and wheeled down to surgery. What a pleasant surprise to find myself placed under a ceiling painted with all the characters from Snoopy. There I was, with my lovely hairnet on, staring at Snoopy dancing away, waiting for my Desmopressin to finish doing its job in my blood.

At 2pm, it was show time. I had to move myself onto the metal operating table. At least they let me keep the pillow under my head while I was still awake, although I'm sure they whipped it out after I was unconscious! The anaesthetist attached a monitor on my forehead and placed my arm securely onto an arm rest. A nurse tied my arm to it. I looked at the clock, which read 2.13pm, and then Dr Woo said, 'Okay, time to go to sleep now.'

He injected me, I looked briefly at the lights and then yup, sleep time…

Two hours later, I woke up screaming in pain. They obviously hadn't administered any painkillers yet, and I felt my entire body ripped apart; it was shocking! They had to make sure I came out of the anaesthesia well first before assessing my pain levels. Duh, I had been sliced open and stapled back together. How much pain did they think I would be in? They asked me how much pain I was in on a scale of one to ten and I screamed out, 'Eight or nine!'

For the next hour, they observed me in recovery and ensured I was as comfortable as possible. All I remember about that time is whimpering in pain, and a sensation of burning and tightness in my lower abdomen. When I was returned to my room, I had to let them lift me onto my bed, as it was automatic for me to try and move myself instead of just lying there. By this stage, they had provided me with a personal pain control pump, which I could press any time I felt pain. It was attached to the same IV into which my DDAVP had been given, so there I was with all manner of tubes attached. I had a catheter, as I was obviously not in any condition to go to the toilet. On the left side of my stomach were three drains, one under the skin, one under the fat and one under the muscle. These were to drain the excess fluid from my internal wounds. Then there was an IV to administer fluid, as I was not able to drink or eat anything yet. Being so encumbered made moving about on the bed extremely tricky. It was not a pretty sight. Oh yes, I also had an oxygen mask to get that oh-so-needed oxygen back in. My poor husband visited me that evening and must have been shocked at the sight of me. The next day, the nurse told me that I had been quite yellow in the face.

Wednesday 27 December 2006

I needed to take a break from writing, as I was too tired and had a short attention span—must be the painkillers I'm on. So, back to my first night in hospital… I don't know how they expect patients to rest and recover when the nurse comes to check your blood pressure, temperature, drains and wound site every hour or so. The machine administering my painkillers kept beeping any time my arm bent the wrong way. My IV fluid made regular clicking sounds, too, so you can imagine how restful it all was. When I did manage to drop off to sleep, my roommate was violently ill and lost control of her bowels. I felt sorry for the nurses on duty who had to clean up in the middle of the night. I was almost glad when morning arrived so the horror night was over.

On that Tuesday morning, a nurse, who had experience in physiotherapy, suggested 'we' try and get out of bed and possibly take a shower. She told me to roll like a log to my side, push with my elbows and hands, and let her help me the rest of the way up. I felt woozy and dizzy, and had to take numerous deep breaths. She then asked me to stand with her help; I did, and nearly passed out. I heard a roaring in my ears and said I felt faint. So much for me making it to the shower. Oh well, she quickly settled me back down and said never mind, she would give me a facecloth wash in bed. I guess it *had* been less than twenty-four hours since my surgery. I tell you, all my inhibitions, shyness and modesty just had to be thrown out the window. When you're as helpless as a kitten, you have to swallow your pride and let strangers do things for you that would normally seem embarrassing. Thank God for nurses and caretakers.

I did cheer up at the lovely flowers that arrived over the course of the day. I felt loved, that's for sure. My husband visited a few times and took away my blood stained nighties, caused by the seepage of the drains. Poor Darling, not a nice thing to have to see let alone wash. Tuesday night was not good either, as my roommate snored all night and my ear plugs just dulled the sound.

Thursday 28 December 2006

Took a little break again from writing... On Wednesday 20 December, I felt a little stronger and was so happy to have the catheter removed in the morning. By this stage I was able to slowly get up without passing out. Yeah! When I had to visit the toilet, I was able to shuffle my way across the hall to the main bathroom. Yeah! Even though I still had my drains, this felt like such an achievement. The nurse asked me if I felt strong enough to have a shower sitting down and I was happy to give it a go. It was an interesting experience, keeping my drainage bottles from getting in the way, but I managed it all on my own. I felt so proud.

That afternoon, the drains finally came out, and I was able to drink and nibble on a tiny bit of food. My IV fluids were removed as well. What progress. I had visitors that evening; I was really happy to be alive and having normal conversations. I could also 'walk' the corridor a little.

Oh, I forgot. Dr Patton visited me the morning after surgery to take a look at my surgical site and to say the results of the tissue tests were not in yet. A trainee doctor took more blood to test my platelets, white cell and red cell count. I'm assuming that everything was good, as nobody bothered telling me the results. Patients are often kept in the dark about their own bodies and it is very frustrating. I was told that if everything went well, I would be released the next day. A nurse from Hospital in the Home (HITH) would visit to check on my progress for a further three days at home.

Due to my lack of sleep, my husband asked the nursing staff whether I could be wheeled to another room for that last night. No offence to the elderly lady, but I really needed some rest. Luckily, the room next door was free for the night only, as it was used for day surgery patients during the day. I happily watched a movie on my rented television and settled down for some sleep… not! The downside of being able to eat a little is that it produces gas. When you are lying horizontally for long periods of time, it has a habit of not moving and, as a consequence, producing strong colic pains. The night duty nurse tried to help with a lovely concoction of warm water, Mylanta and two dissolved Panadol. Ugghh! Apparently, she kept checking up on me throughout the night, only to find me restless, feverish and clutching a pillow. What do they say about best laid plans? So much for sleep…

When I 'woke' up and staggered to the toilet, it was as though a truck had hit me overnight. I felt bruised from head to toe. It was a relief to move about a bit and attempt to get my circulation going. I was surprised to have a bowel movement that morning—how funny it is to be happy about that. However, I wasn't quite prepared, and my stomach took a beating, as I didn't support my wound enough. It was a sensation of lifting and dropping very fast—Ouch! I was relieved I didn't have a colostomy bag and that I was able to go normally. Yahoo. Life's simple pleasures, ha, ha, ha.

I moved back to my original room as day patients began arriving. David came to see how long it would be until I was allowed home, and we were told Dr Patton had to visit me first sometime that day. The morning nurse was a lovely woman who took the time to clarify everything for us. She explained that it was no wonder I felt bruised all over, as I would have been on a metal table, upside down, legs in the air, for nearly two hours of surgery. She also said that surgeons work hard and fast to get the job done, meaning they are not always gentle when they know you are unconscious. My poor body has a right to feel bruised for a while.

One thing I have not discussed yet. When I arrived at the hospital,

I was dismayed to discover the surgical ward was right next to the maternity ward. I tried not to look at the nursery as we walked past, but closing my ears to babies crying at night or in the mornings was very difficult. True, straight after the surgery I didn't care as I was in too much pain, but as I grew a little stronger, the baby wails became too hard to ignore. I think it's pretty insensitive to force a childless woman undergoing a hysterectomy to see women who have just given birth. I had no choice but to pretend it wasn't painful for me emotionally.

About lunchtime, I was given pain medication to take home and my home visiting nurse came to speak to me. Then Dr Patton signed me fit for home. I mentioned my abdominal pain and he said that it was normal as was the low grade fevers. He was in his usual rush, but I quickly enquired whether he noticed endometriosis when he opened me up. He said it was all definitely inflamed and my left ovary had to be removed because it was so bad, but he was still waiting on other results. He added that he would discuss all this at my six-week check-up on the 2 February 2007. He also hoped the little nub left of my right ovary would produce enough hormones so that I wouldn't require HRT. Only time will tell.

Pretty soon after that, my sisters came to pick me up, as David had left earlier to do chores. It was all such a rush that I didn't get to wish my roommate good luck or thank my nurses. An attendant wheeled me out as my sisters, niece and nephew carried my belongings. Ooohhh... so nice to see my own home again, to be in my own bed, my own toilet and my own shower. Hubby had the house clean and tidy with the beautiful bouquets of flowers everywhere. Irma decided to stay a couple of days to help me out alongside David, whilst Katri took the kids back home to the hills.

In the past week—oh my God, it's been one week at home

already—I have been through quite a process of recovery. Hmmm, let's see... continued colic pain whenever I eat or drink, afternoon and evening temperature spikes, two days of migraines, sore back muscles from lying down so much, and one day of burning up from my abdomen to my head. I don't think it was a hot flush, as it just didn't stop for a whole day. I had to cool myself with a facecloth and ice cubes all over my face, neck and chest. That must have been a funny sight. Also, I had a fair bit of discharge, which is to be expected for a few weeks.

I ran out of my painkillers after three days. It was only a supply of twenty tablets, and boy was it difficult to get more. I guess it didn't help being Christmas time. Finally, David was able to persuade the HITH nurse that my pain was for real and simple over the counter medication wasn't enough. What did they expect? Me to be fighting fit and pain free after one week? I know I'm strong, but I'm not Superwoman! Because of my Von Willebrand's Disease, I was not able to take any NSAIDs so all I had was Paradex (or Dextropropoxyphene Hydrochloride and Paracetamol). The Dextropropoxyphene affects the body's feeling and response to pain by acting on certain nerve receptors, while the paracetamol reacts with certain chemicals in the nerves and blocks pain impulses as well as reducing fever. All I know is that it works. I have been able to reduce the painkillers from between four and six hours down to every eight hours and, in fact, I survived ten hours without taking anything last night. Now I know I'm making progress.

Irma, who is a qualified naturopath, homeopath, herbalist and Bowen therapist, has been an immense help. Prior to surgery, she helped me prepare my body for the upcoming trauma of surgery through, for example, Homeopathic Arnica. Then, after my surgery, she has been helping me deal with various complaints and symptoms. As the hospital didn't give me anything other than the painkillers, she has advised me about how to help my body recover through natural anti-inflammatory tablets and other healing formulas. I am immensely grateful to her, as without her help and that of my husband and other family members, I would be in a much worse condition than I am now.

The male HITH nurse, who came to remove my clamps (I call them staples) on Christmas Eve, was surprised at how quickly and cleanly my wound was healing, with no sign of swelling or redness. I attribute that to the Arnica and Traumeel (natural anti-inflammatory tablets) I have been taking every day. By the way, removal of the twenty or so clamps wasn't as painful as I thought it would be, only a little pinching feeling. Speaking of my stomach, it's a strange sensation still. The wound site of the cut feels tight and a little hot sometimes, and above it, a band of about two inches feels numb, as though it doesn't really belong to me—the flesh I mean. I wonder if this will disappear.

Friday 29 December 2006

Who would have thought that simple activities such as showering on a plastic chair, going to the toilet and walking around slowly would make me so breathless, as if I had run a marathon! I know this will get better... the danger is that now I'm back to taking all of my vitamins and supplements, I feel so much more energetic and want to do more. The problem is that after half an hour of just pottering around with no heavy lifting, as instructed, I suffer pain for the next hour or so. Not fair! David is constantly telling me off for overdoing it, but I'm supposed to do light exercise from now on. Oh well, I'll find the balance somehow...

Oh yes, how could I forget? This morning, I woke up in the middle of a raunchy, sexy dream with its usual sensations! Yay! Some of my hormones must still be working, as the week after my period would have been my usual time to feel horny. I happily divulged this to my husband and he said maybe I won't need HRT after all. Fingers crossed.

Saturday 30 December 2006

Sometimes it's one step forward, two steps back. I had a rotten night with a lot of colic pain again. Isn't it funny how we revert to a rocking motion when we don't feel well? I felt myself rocking all night long, even when half asleep. I guess it is soothing to be in gentle motion. Today, I feel bruised, as though someone punched me in the kidneys. I hope it's not an accumulation of painkillers, but it's just as well I am weaning myself off them (I lasted fourteen hours without anything). I may need to take a bit more, as I just don't feel right. I have a headache, backache and stomach ache. I'm trying to remember that it's still less than two weeks since my operation.

Monday 1 January 2007

Happy New Year! Well, I had planned to allow myself a glass of wine with David last night, but I had such a bad day with fever and pain that I thought I'd better forego the wine and stick to the painkillers. My colic pains have been relentless and my temperature spiked further. I was a bit concerned because my discharge smelt a bit funny, but I didn't want to panic and rush to the hospital. So, I'm monitoring my temperature for now, and keeping my fingers crossed that I haven't developed an infection. My scar looks good though and not inflamed at all, but what is happening internally? Oh yes, the numbness on my stomach, which was making it feel as though it didn't belong to me, has gone. Now I feel the tightness and bruising that I didn't before. I don't know which one was preferable: the numbness or the pain.

Tuesday 2 January 2007

My hubby went back to work today. He's worried that I'm on my own but I'm okay. My fever spiked again last night but seems to be behaving itself today. I think I have to be careful about what I eat and avoid foods that are too rich, as it is hard enough to digest any food at the moment. So porridge, fruit and light meals it is. I guess it wasn't smart of me to eat liquorice a couple of days ago (I paid for it and I don't mean money ha, ha, ha). I'm just trying to take it easy today and do light, gentle movement, for example, a slow walk in the backyard. On the positive side, I have lost six kilos in two weeks! That's a bit too rapid but it hasn't been my choice. I don't know how much will stay off once I feel better and am eating normally. My skin also seems clearer. I hope I don't jinx it by gloating about it. For now, I look forward to the moments in my day when I feel calm and without pain, when I manage to remain in a comfortable position. My headache keeps returning, though it could be the unsettled weather we're having.

I had a flashback of being in recovery and having one nurse say to another, 'This woman has had a total hysterectomy with bilateral salpingo-oophorectomy.' In layman's terms it means the complete removal of the cervix, uterus, ovaries and fallopian tubes. Funny how memories come out of the blue. I also remember a theatre nurse looking at my chart whilst we were waiting for the operating theatre to be ready, and the way she exclaimed that I'd gone through a lot of surgeries: appendectomy, laparotomy, oophorectomy and, of course, my IVF procedures. She asked me if the IVF had been successful and I said, 'No.'

She asked me if I had any children and again I said, 'No.'

She squeezed my shoulder sympathetically. I'm glad she didn't offer me any platitudes. Silence was better. Reminds me of a song about silence being golden.

Wednesday 3 January 2007

Progress! I've been able to eat more normally. I actually managed to shower standing upright for the first time in over two and a half weeks, and I shaved my legs. Although I had to sit down, it's still progress. I continue to experience wind pain every time I eat or drink but because I'm able to move about more, it shifts more quickly, and I have more strength in my stomach to push it out. Who would have thought that I would be so pleased to be able to fart and to write about it?

I watched a movie, read a book and munched on some chockies. I must be getting better to want to eat chocolates again. Emotionally, I felt 'blue' today. I hear about the rest of my family partying and socialising during this busy time of the year, and I feel distinctly left out and sorry for myself. I know I just have to *be* for now and get stronger, but there's nothing wrong with my mind, only my body. I know I have to maintain a positive attitude for my recovery and avoid letting all those negative thoughts and emotions spiral me down into depression. I only need time and then I can go out like everyone else. I'm looking forward to being physically stronger, as I can then sit up straight and make good use of David's Christmas present: my new easel, canvas and paints. That will be a creative outlet for me, a very therapeutic way to be expressive.

Friday 5 January 2007

My temperature has been normal, or nearly normal, for the past two days. That's a good sign. I actually slept on my side and it didn't hurt. I still had the pillow there, but I didn't have to have a death grip on it anymore. I've been doing light housework such as dishes and laundry, one item at a time, without too many side effects. My back is sore today but I could have just slept wrong. Last night, I dreamt about playing basketball and preparing to go out dancing. My mind is very willing but my body has to catch up still. My only complaints are my colic pain and my discharge. I'm sure the inner bruising will take time to heal. Okay, time for some pampering. I've got my face mask on and I put some fake tan on. The better I look, the more likely that I will feel better, too.

Saturday 6 January 2007

I was able to do more today than I have for weeks. I hope I didn't overdo it; I just had energy again, probably because I'm having proper nutrients. I've been living in sarongs and loose t-shirts, so it was a nice change to be able to wear my loose shorts. I certainly noticed my weight loss in them. Irma gave me some more homeopathic remedies to help with my recovery process.

I've had to have daytime naps for the past two days and then I'm awake late into the night. It's past midnight now as I write this. Never mind. I'll get back into some kind of rhythm soon enough. I'm going away to Katri's place for a few days. It'll give David a break and provide me with a change of scenery. I've been going stir-crazy, as I haven't gone anywhere since returning from hospital over two weeks ago.

Saturday 13 January 2007

The five days at Katri's were quite active compared to at home. I was determined to start walking for at least fifteen minutes a day, even if it was a slow shuffle around the countryside. We also went visiting, so I put on full make-up for the first time in weeks and felt more normal. Sitting upright for longer periods than normal didn't help my healing. Even though Katri picked me up from home and drove me back, I found it uncomfortable sitting for the hour's journey.

I had a fever again and ached all over. However, I've been able to cope with taking painkillers only once a day, twenty-four hours apart. I also enjoyed some wine with my sisters without any nasty side effects. My sleep was a bit erratic. I slept on a single bed whilst still needing pillows either side of me to support my stomach when I rolled over in the night.

David and I just went for a walk with Misha and Cheyenne. The walk that normally takes twenty minutes took thirty minutes due to my slow gait, but I did it. I took my measurements to see where I had lost weight; silly me forgot how swollen my stomach still is. Straight after my surgery, my stomach was as round and hard as a basketball. Although it has reduced considerably, it is still much bigger than normal. The sad and ironic thing is that people seeing me walking funny with a round tummy could quite naturally assume I am pregnant. It would be so upsetting if someone actually asked me that.

Anyhow, onto something more humorous. I feel as though I'm in a different parallel universe, where my time is much slower than others. The other day, Katri said she was going to put her car back into the carport whilst I changed into tracksuit pants. I was putting one leg into the pants when my sister came back. She was already finished and yet I was still changing. I did a double take and blinked as happens in a comedy.

I had a scare back at home last night. Since I was feeling so much better and David didn't feel like cooking, we ordered takeaway consisting of saffron rice and spicy beef curry. Although I only ate half of mine, and fairly early in the evening, I was in agony in the middle of the night. I tried antacids, my Buscopan for stomach cramps, a pot of fennel tea and, finally, some Panadeine Forte. I guess my stomach didn't appreciate too much protein or spices. For two hours, I writhed in pain, worse than I could remember experiencing before. No position was comfortable. Kneeling on the floor, lying flat or with knees bent, sitting up or walking hunched over in pain—nothing helped.

It's the first time since the surgery that I actually balled my eyes out. 'Please stop, no more, please stop!' I cried out. 'Please God help me!'

My husband has been sleeping in the other room to give me space and peace and quiet, so he didn't witness it. I tried to keep quiet, but at one point I screamed out loud. It's lucky he's a deep sleeper and didn't hear me at all, as I'm sure he would have called an ambulance if he had seen me. About 3am the pain eased, and I was finally able to calm down and sleep. Needless to say, I have been back to eating fruit, porridge and salad today.

Tuesday 16 January 2007

The great progress continues. I drove my car for the first time in a month yesterday. Sure, it was only to the post office and coffee shop and back, but still I did it. I didn't realise that pushing your foot onto the brake and accelerator tugs at your stomach muscles, so yes, it pinched a bit, but not so bad. I have also been able to do more about the house, for example, light housework and cooking dinner. Of course, I'm exhausted afterwards, but feel a sense of being alive. I keep chanting to myself, silently most of the time, *I am getting better. Every day I feel stronger and healthier.* The bleeding and discharge has also stopped after one month, yeah! I feel more able to see people; however, I keep receiving strange looks from people when they see me holding my stomach and walking slowly. Oh well, that'll get better soon, too.

Wednesday 17 January 2007

Oops, I did it again! Four hours out and about paying bills, shopping and drinking coffee with a girlfriend meant I was on my feet too much. I paid for it with pain; it feels like I've pulled a muscle in my stomach. Tsk, tsk, I'd better take it easy tomorrow.

Monday 22 January 2007

I'm pushing myself to do more 'little by little' and 'slowly but surely'. My body lets me know quite clearly when I've done too much and then I rest. I've visited girlfriends; contacted work for updates on what's been happening 'in the real world'; started painting pictures again; and continued with my grief and loss studies, which is so appropriate at this stage. I still read and watch movies when it all becomes too much, but I certainly feel as though I'm getting back to living again instead of just recovering. What a journey! I still have my digestive problems and headaches, but I refuse to let them win.

Friday 2 February 2007

My six-week post-op check-up was today. As per usual, my doctor and surgeon, Dr Patton, was a man of many words (not). He looked at my file and said, 'Well, that's good isn't it?'

'What? That everything's out?' I asked.

'Yes,' he replied.

If it wasn't for my questions, he would have just conducted the physical post-op exam and let me go. He was pleased with my surface scar, as it has healed up so well. My internal examination was a bit painful, what with him using the speculum and then taking some tissue samples for laboratory tests. He said it still looked a bit inflamed but otherwise all good. My questions were answered as follows:

- There is no need for blood tests unless menopausal symptoms appear.
- The headaches are most likely caused by the anaesthesia and hormonal fluctuations.
- My digestion and constipation will take a while to settle down.
- I can try the natural Promensil tablets if symptoms of menopause occur, such as hot flushes and night sweats.
- Last week I had symptoms that reminded me of PMS, for example, headache, backache, stomach ache, irritability and tiredness. This is apparently a good sign that my nub of a right ovary is still producing hormones.
- I'm to see my GP if any symptoms develop and then blood tests can be done; I can always get another referral to see him if necessary.
- The pain I've had on my lower right-hand side is most likely wound healing or a strain, not a hernia.
- He found no current sign of endometriosis; however, he said

there were lots of adhesions from my previous surgery, and they could have been as a result from burnt endometriosis. When I commented that I would probably develop more now, he said, 'Not necessarily.'

I guess I've been given the all-clear to resume normal activities. Since his poking and prodding, I've been bleeding all day again, not heavily, but annoyingly enough. I'm not ready to go back to work yet. In fact, I am a bit depressed and feeling my losses, as there are so many of them: loss of dreams and plans, loss of children and grandchildren, loss of youth and time, loss of body parts, loss of identity, loss of hope and loss of 'family' occasions and celebrations.

Chapter 15

Life Goes On-Childless

Wednesday 7 February 2007
I can't shake my 'blues'. I'm not laughing at comedy DVDs. I'm just reading and escaping into the fantasy worlds of novels. I feel that at seven-and-a-half weeks post-op I should be able to do more. I can still only sit upright for a couple of hours at a time before I ache. I walk a little faster but not for long distances at all. My painting is enjoyable at least. I guess studying grief and loss is bringing a lot of my depression to the surface. I tried my vibrator yesterday for the first time post-op and it just wasn't the same. It still hurt a little and the orgasm wasn't as intense. I guess time will tell how that, and making love again, works out in the future. Overall, I'm feeling blah and isolated in my loss. Like the majority of men, my husband isn't a good communicator and doesn't have much to say to me. Words of reassurance would help.

Monday 26 February 2007
I'd say I'm three-quarters there. I've gone back to work and as long as I don't go crazy with doing too much physical activity, I'm doing fine. I have had an annoying immune problem with my lips and the corners of my mouth. The chemist said it was lack of vitamin B but after three weeks of taking everything, my lips still aren't back to normal. It's embarrassing because it is visible even with make-up.

Oh well, I'm sure that too shall pass. I felt I needed to return to work and think about other people's problems to stop focusing on my own too much. Enough self-pity! Time to move on with the rest of my life. I keep expecting to have my period and it is an odd feeling that I won't have another one. My bladder seems stronger as well, which is a great development.

I know I will have some grief coming up now and again, but who doesn't? I'll just take each day as it comes but keep on moving forward. That's the main thing. We still haven't had sex. It's been ten weeks since the surgery, but I'm too scared to have my husband's weight on top of me, as my lower stomach can't handle any pressure as yet. Time keeps a-ticking...

Monday 23 April 2007

I saw my GP four months post-op due to numerous distressing menopausal symptoms over the last couple of months, such as irregular body temperature, night long chills then sweats, hot flushes, waking up repeatedly during the night, insomnia, lethargy, tiredness, irritability, mood swings, depression, itchy skin, dryness, some hair falling out, heart palpitations, tingles in my arm and memory loss.

I tried Promensil for over a month and it didn't help. Dr Patricia Moore heard me out, before saying that it sounded as though my poor remaining ovary tissue has fizzled out and I've been thrown into full-blown menopause. She read the letter from Dr Patton, in which he had written what a tedious job it had been to release my scar tissue and adhesions before he could even operate. Tedious! Huh! So sorry for boring you.

I spoke about how painful intercourse had been on the few times we attempted it, even with lubrication. She recommended I tested out Premarin (oestrogen hormone therapy) for six months. Following this, I should go without Premarin for six months and see what happens. This should help with all of the menopausal symptoms and should start to help within two weeks. Sex should also improve with the Premarin and more healing time.

Tuesday 25 September 2007

It's time to stop this chapter of my life. The hormone therapy has worked wonders and I feel healthy. What a relief to be free from pain after so many years. It's time to let go, leave the past behind and begin a new, exciting, happy and fun life. So *au revoir*, diary. Thank you for listening. My next journal will be a gratitude journal. After all, isn't it great to be alive!

Thursday 27 September 2007

This is my gratitude journal. Today, I am grateful for my health and I feel fit. I am grateful for the company of my sisters, nephews and nieces. I am grateful for a good night's sleep. I am grateful for the warm weather. I am grateful for David's love for me. I am grateful for having loving pets. I am grateful for colour and art in my life.

Wednesday 3 October 2007

I am grateful for a fun day with family at Seaworld on the Gold Coast in Queensland. I am grateful for Ma and Pa arriving here safe and sound from Tasmania. I am grateful for so much laughter. I am grateful for my energy. I am grateful for abundance in all areas of my life.

Friday 5 October 2007

I am grateful for peace and quiet. I am grateful for my home. I am grateful for such an understanding husband. I am grateful for my music. I am grateful for creating my acrylic paintings. I am grateful for Ma's cooking. I am grateful for serenity.

Wednesday 10 October 2007

Happy seventieth Birthday, Pa! I am grateful for a good night's sleep. I am grateful for all the laughter over these Queensland holidays. I am grateful for all my sisters. I am grateful for my health and fitness. I am grateful for my lifestyle. I am grateful for this rain. I am grateful for money in my wallet. I am grateful for Josh Groban tickets and a concert to look forward to.

Thursday 11 October 2007

I had an amazing dream. *I was digging in the soil and found a shoebox that was full of treasure. An old mouse had been collecting bits and pieces for years, old books and antiques et cetera. His skeleton was in the box and we gave him a proper burial. I dug deep and found a large green emerald the size of my palm, uncut but dazzling.* My message from the dream was that if you dig deep enough, you will find the treasure within.

Monday 29 October 2007

I am grateful for having all this time to heal physically, emotionally, mentally and spiritually. I am now ready to start living again rather than simply existing day to day. I am grateful for being able to help people. I am grateful for a balanced life, one that is not too lazy but not too stressful either. I am grateful for a fulfilling life. Thank you for financial abundance. Thank you for health abundance. Thank you for love and for making love.

Sunday 11 November 2007

Thank you for my being *alive*. Thank you for such an active weekend. I'm feeling so grateful for Pilates, walking, boogie boarding and painting. What an abundant life. I also astral travelled last night. I was so free. No body, just my Soul flying, swimming, dancing and twirling in the sea and the sky. It was fantastic! I was having such a good time that I didn't want to come back to my body. I had to convince myself, *Sorja, you are on your bed. Go back. You're in bed, open your eyes, Sorja, open your eyes!* I was fighting with myself, as I wanted to keep being free, weightless and happy. I opened my eyes, coughed and tried to reorient myself by drinking water and visiting the bathroom. Wow, what an experience.

Tuesday 18 December 2007

Today is the one-year anniversary of my hysterectomy. I feel fantastic. I am so grateful to be alive. I am so grateful to be free from pain. I am so grateful for having all this energy. I feel fit and healthy and at peace with myself. I have let go. I have learned to trust and have faith in life again. I feel motivated. I am grateful for my social life and supportive friends. I am grateful for my improved relationship with David. I am grateful for better communication with Mum and Dad and my brother and sisters. I am grateful about learning to love and forgive myself. I am grateful for finding a community rich with like-minded people. Life is good.

Monday 31 December 2007

My year in summary: surgery, recovery, quit my job at Serenity Lodge due to burnout, discovered my love of art and painting again, started my own business in counselling, travelled to Queensland for Pa's seventieth birthday, attended the Josh Groban concert in Perth, started a new job with a pharmacy as a weight management consultant for Betty Baxter, and participated in a community art project.

I am happy to let 2007 go, and start a new and exciting 2008. It's time for new beginnings. My power words for this *new* year are faith, courage, love, patience, energy, vibrancy, happiness, joy, fun, social life and activity, physical fitness, passion, colour, lots of money, and high self-esteem from being able to help others. Thank you for my physical, emotional, mental and spiritual abundance.

Chapter 16

What Now?

Wednesday 31 December 2008

Well it's been a year since I wrote in this journal and for good reason. I went off track in 2008 and did something I thought was expected of me by everyone—and was miserable because of it. I have to be honest and say I did not enjoy 2008; I am glad it's over. I worked in a job I did not like and was always far too tired to paint. I spent a lot of time driving to and from work, which made those days even longer. David and I have grown further apart due to added stress, and we have both spent a lot of money to deceptively make ourselves feel better. I did get my fifteen minutes of fame on television this year by appearing on *Mornings with Kerri-Anne* in October. The Betty Baxter commercial aired on television in November with my client (who had lost an incredible thirty-three kilos with my support) and me as his Weight Management Consultant. It's ironic that, as a result of my own depression and unhappiness, I am the heaviest I have been in twelve years. I lost touch with my own dreams, desires and needs this last year, and now it is time to reclaim myself!

My wish list for 2009 is to become healthy, fit and energetic, happy with my one and only body; to enjoy my new job at Tall Poppy Art Framers and Art Gallery; to experiment with my art and trust myself and my difference; for David and I to become husband and wife again, with a marriage that is intimate, close, sexy and passionate; to make new friends and new social contacts with emotional connections; to experience lots of love and happy times with my family; and for continued health for my girls, Misha and Cheyenne.

Thursday 31 December 2009

Another year on—what actually happened? I did enjoy my first year at both Tall Poppy Art Framers and Art Gallery, and Sea Sirens Art Framers and Gallery. David and I had a lovely camping trip to Honeymoon Pool in February/March, and Katri and Nikiita joined us for an Easter holiday in Albany. In April, we bought a treadmill which has been fantastic. I joined a weekly meditation class in June with like-minded people, which I thoroughly enjoyed. I went to visit Irma, who had moved to Queensland, in July/August for two weeks, and Irma and I travelled all the way to Rockhampton. David became an Australian citizen on 4 August. Later that month, Ma and Pa visited Western Australia. David and I went with a few friends to see the fantastic Il Divo concert in October. I studied Reiki I (Level 1) and became a Reiki I practitioner in October. David and I had a camping trip to Esperance at Christmas time.

Since joining Carol's meditation group in June, I have become more spiritual. I am fascinated by all things metaphysical. I bought myself a pack of animal tarot cards and am getting comfortable using them for myself at this stage. I am continuing to keep a dream journal and have noticed that I have many psychic and predictive dreams. It is very spooky sometimes! I have been able to see animal and human auras on occasion, and find the colours fascinating to observe. I have learned to pay more attention to signs from my Spirit

Guides and from the Universe. This knowledge will continue to grow and, given time, my psychic powers will increase. I have to get balance back in my life and allow my body to reflect my spiritual learning. I want to learn to truly love and accept myself and to let go of fear.

Tuesday 5 January 2010

Okay, I'm back on track with doing Pilates, yoga, boxing, light weights, playing some Wii games and jogging on the treadmill. We even went boogie boarding for over an hour today. Last night, I dreamt that my guides told me to stand tall and straight, and to smile.

Wednesday 13 January 2010

During my meditation class tonight, I was told by my Spirit Guides to *make my words count*. I'm not sure if they mean verbally or written. They also told me that I need to continue with my painting and my Reiki.

Wednesday 10 February 2010

OMG! I woke up at 4.45am to David screaming out, 'Cheyenne!'

She was having an epileptic fit with major convulsions and foaming at the mouth for about two minutes. It was frightening to see! David took the day off work and drove her to the vet. The toxicology results showed no poisons in her blood and that she seemed to be in perfect health. The vet said that it could be epilepsy or a brain tumour. Cheyenne seemed fine by the evening and all we can do is to wait and see if it happens again.

Sunday 14 February 2010

Woohoo! I jogged and fast walked ten kilometres in ninety minutes. My personal best record so far.

Tuesday 16 February 2010

Happy Birthday, David. We took both our girls to the groomers today and Cheyenne had another fit that lasted about two minutes. We left Misha at the groomers to be picked up later but brought Cheyenne home. We think the high-pitched noise of the poodles there set her off! We rang the vet clinic and they are recommending that we put her on medication to stop the seizures.

Monday 22 February 2010

Poor Cheyenne, or Ratbag as we call her. The medication is making her dopey and sleepy all the time. Not the same bright-eyed girl we are used to having around us. Both our girls are becoming noticeably older. When we take the girls for a walk along the beach, they can't run the way they used to or even handle long walks anymore. It's so sad. I, on the other hand, am getting stronger by working out and it feels great. Exercise can be so addictive.

Sunday 28 March 2010

I've just spent the past two days qualifying as a Reiki II practitioner (second degree). It's all very fascinating and I have learned a lot. I intend to continue Reiki healing energy on myself, my pets, my loved ones and friends if they are open to it and request it. I have bought myself a professional massage table with all the accessories so that I am able to offer Reiki and am able to be mobile.

Saturday 3 April 2010

We had a fabulous family reunion at Katri's house today. Irma and Khan have arrived back in Western Australia and we were all there to celebrate. As with all family gatherings, there was a mixture of laughter and personality clashes served up alongside the food and alcohol.

Chapter 17

Time Heals All Wounds or Does It Just Cover Them Up?

Wednesday 21 April 2010

I'm learning so much through my meditation classes. Tonight, I received messages about setting personal emotional boundaries with people. I was also told by my Spirit Guides to have more fun and joy in life, to learn unconditional self-love and to be self-luminous (which means generating and emitting my own visible light) without always expecting others to fill the void or need in me. I've been chanting, *I forgive myself*, *I love myself* and *I honour and respect myself*.

Saturday 15 May 2010

David and I booked a cabin down south for five days. It's a cabin with a spa and a fireplace to ward off the cold. We took the girls to the kennel and poor Cheyenne suffered another seizure. The kennel owner was confident in being able to take care of her and had seen epileptic seizures before, so we trusted her to handle anything that arose. We have been using the same kennel for many years and the girls liked it there.

Thursday 20 May 2010

What a cosy cabin in Beyondarup Falls in Nannup. The getaway was just what we needed. We walked in the rain, had a spa on the outside veranda, snuggled together and watched the birdlife, as well as listening to the motorbike frogs at night. We did the typical tourist thing and explored the towns of Nannup, Bridgetown and Balingup. We walked through lovely gardens with trees resplendent in their autumn foliage as well as through the gorgeous Golden Valley Tree Park. What beautiful colours to drink in with our eyes.

We found an amazing antiques museum and could have stayed there for ages, as every 'nook and cranny' was filled with memorabilia from days gone by. The music playing was awesome songs from the 1920s and 1930s. On the second night in the cabin, I heard some weird noises coming from the rooftop, like scratching feet on the tin roof, as well as weird mewling sounds like those from a cat or a baby. We later found out from the owners that they were made by the miniature bats living there! So hard to leave our country escape and return...

Monday 31 May 2010

I've got to be honest and say that sometimes I feel so disconnected from everyone, including David. I've started re-reading the book *The Secret* by Rhonda Byrne. My life is my choice and my thoughts are my own. If I want things to change, I alone am responsible.

Saturday 5 June 2010

I woke up to an amazing experience at 6am. This is what I wrote in my dream journal: *I felt and heard such powerful voices speaking to me, a male and a female Spirit Guide. They were giving me numerous instructions and were going through my life. They said, 'Yes, we understand all of the misfortunes you have gone through, and that you couldn't have a baby, but you have to take better care of yourself and you're not listening'.* I guess I'm just a stubborn person. We all have free will and I acknowledge that I don't always act in my own best interests...

Thursday 10 June 2010

I choose from a basis of love not fear! Thank you, Universe, for my abundance of health, wealth and happiness. I've noticed that my dreams have been so accurate lately. I have to trust them and listen to my inner guidance.

Monday 14 June 2010

I need to stop judging myself so harshly. I love and accept myself unconditionally for who I am. I had my mammogram today. No change since the one two years ago, thank God. I had a fabulous dream. *A man was showing me how to paint a huge canvas. There were lots of splotches of colour and I was told to let go and be crazier with colour.* In another dream last night, *I saw a huge mountain in the distance and was told that I would have to climb it one day.* What? For real or figuratively?

Tuesday 15 June 2010

I heard these words in my dream: *Healing comes in many forms.*

Wednesday 23 June 2010

Isn't it funny how some people become so excited by things, objects and stuff, whereas others become excited by experiences and the emotions attached to those experiences, for example, travelling to distant places and interacting with other nationalities? I know which category I belong to. You can't take stuff with you to the grave, but I believe that learning from experiences and relationships does linger within your Soul.

Sunday 4 July 2010

Woohoo! Irma, Katri and I booked the flights, accommodation and car hire for our trip to Tasmania today. I can't wait for our joint holiday in December. Three sisters running amok!

Friday 9 July 2010

Oh, what lessons we need to learn in this life in order to help ourselves, and to love and make ourselves happy...

Tuesday 20 July 2010

I don't know why I feel so tired all of the time. I exercise, I sleep and I take care of my nutritional needs, yet I feel tired. I don't know if it is a physical or spiritual tiredness.

Wednesday 28 July 2010

I've had a rash on my lip for months. If you believe in the mind and body connection, what am I not speaking about? At meditation tonight, I received a message about being true to, and honest with, myself. What am I hiding from myself, I wonder?

Thursday 29 July 2010

I love my girls, Misha and Cheyenne, so much. I know I have to accept them going, but please not yet! They're our children. They have been our support and our joy for so many years that I cannot imagine a life without them.

Friday 6 August 2010

David heard the fabulous news that he's got a new job as a mechanical supervisor at Australian Submarine Cooperation. Of course, this is more responsibility and a larger salary; however, I just hope that David will be happy. I also received the good news that my painting of a seal has been accepted into an art exhibition.

Monday 9 August 2010

Okay, Sorja, it's time to shine and start afresh! With that in mind, I started going to Zumba classes. Oh, what fun to learn the new steps and exercise in time to upbeat music. This is a great way to kick start a healthier lifestyle and fitness. Life is good.

Thursday 12 August 2010

Wow. I've been able to stop my nightmares from progressing or continuing. In the dream, I have been able to say, *Stop! I don't want to see that!*

Monday 23 August 2010

You know what? I respect myself more when I take care of myself and don't have such self-hatred due to drinking alcohol, eating too much and thinking negatively!

Monday 30 August 2010

I heard these words last night in a dream: *If it is to be, it is up to me.* Today was a strange day. I watched television shows and cried all day. I tried to make myself feel better by having a beauty day: dyeing my hair, applying a face mask, shaving and plucking unwanted hairs and so forth. Throughout all of this, I felt maudlin. What is wrong with me? Why can't I feel happy?

Monday 6 September 2010

A couple of established artists were very complimentary about my seal painting—'One Fish Too Many' (July 2010). They said that my use of tones and colour blending was excellent. It warms my heart to hear such compliments. I have a hard time stopping my inner critic and am often frustrated with my paintings. In my mind's eye, I see such beautiful colours and creations and then when I can't transfer the images onto canvas I get upset. I have to learn to just enjoy the process and not always focus on the end product.

Saturday 18 September 2010

David and I decided to explore South Yunderup after work today and what do you know? Impulsively, we put our name down on a block of land we found! The timing feels right to build our own home now that our finances have improved. We spent ages looking at display homes, house designs and dreaming about living in our own home. Wow! It's exciting but also nerve-racking. Next step is to speak to a broker. I know that it's going to be a long process, but we have started the ball rolling…

Thursday 30 September 2010

Happy birthday to me, happy birthday to me… la, la, la… Forty-four today or two by twenty-two, ha, ha, ha. It ended up being quite an emotional day for me. Even though I got birthday calls from my family, most of the day was spent patiently listening to them download their problems onto me. In the evening, I burst out crying in front of Katri and Irma and ran into my bedroom, as I couldn't take it anymore. I have to learn not to keep things bottled up so much, acknowledge that I am not Superwoman, and show my vulnerability. I also have to learn to assert myself and speak up about my feelings instead of pushing them down with food and wine. As my guides have told me in my dreams, *We give you guidance, but you have free will.*

Wednesday 10 November 2010

I've been doing Reiki energy healing on myself lately and it has helped me release a lot, for example, feelings of guilt over my not-so-perfect behaviour. I just have to get on with life and let go of my negative emotions. A lot of the time I expect so much from myself and from others. My goal is to listen with love and accept everyone without trying to change them. My male Spirit Guide told me, *to listen and hear, look and see, sense and feel, trust your senses to guide you.*

Thursday 18 November 2010

I'm feeling so much better now that I have lost weight and have been consistent with my exercise. Irma, David and I are going to a party on the weekend. I feel more confident about my appearance and have bought myself a lovely dress. I'm so looking forward to dancing and having fun. I saw a shooting star last night. What does that mean? A good sign or a warning?

21 November 2010

Irma and I danced for over two and a half hours at Julie and John's party last night. It was so much fun until someone trod on my toe with their high heels (I had thrown my shoes off to dance more freely). Eek, I think my little toe is broken, as it's turning a nasty colour and my right foot is swollen. The price you pay for fun, sigh.

Friday 26 November 2010

Okay, now it's getting strange. I've seen a couple more shooting stars in the past week. It's unusual for me to see so many. I don't have a good feeling and, in fact, I've felt blue for days now. My foot, or rather my toe, is so sore that I haven't been able to jog or go to Zumba, as it hurts to wear closed shoes at the moment. I feel so tired all the time. I'm having a hard time getting excited about our new house next year as most of it is paperwork at this stage. I'm sure once it all starts and we have to make our choices, for example, tile selection, it'll become more real to me.

Sunday 12 December 2010

Today, we gleefully took a photo of our block of land sign with its 'sold' sticker on it. We celebrated with a lovely lunch at Ravenswood Hotel. It feels good to have a goal to work towards as a couple. Moving forward in life...

Tuesday 21 December 2010

Another milestone! We signed our home building contract today. Woohoo! What a lovely Christmas present for us. We'll have Christmas at Visa's this year and then Katri, Irma and I will be off to Tasmania on 27 December. Roll on good times...

Chapter 18

Whispers of the Soul

Wednesday 29 December 2010

We got up at 3am on Monday to catch a taxi by 4.30am, big yawn... We finally arrived in Hobart at 6pm, exhausted after such a long day travelling or in transit, with a three-and-a-half-hour stopover in Melbourne. When we collected our rental car, I was assertive and insisted on driving to Orford, as I was the only one who had slept. Nikiita (Katri's daughter) flew over to Tassie with us and was spending the first part of her holiday at Orford too. Needless to say, Mum and Dad were overjoyed to see all of us, and Mum had prepared a feast with a variety of Finnish cuisine.

Yesterday, Irma, Katri, Nikiita and I worked off a few calories by taking a trip down memory lane. We walked for over one and a half hours exploring our favourite spots, including the Quarry and Spring Beach. We got back to another delicious lunch of smoked fish courtesy of Pa, and Ma's salad. Irma and Katri drove Nikiita to her Nan's place, whilst I kept Ma and Pa busy showing them David's and my house plans. Mum showed me lots of old photos and letters revealing our own heritage and family tree background. I listened to Ma for hours and hopefully helped her to feel less lonely and unheard. I also watched Pa make a couple of 'vihtas' for our enjoyment in the sauna. It is a tradition in Finland to make a 'vihta'— a bundle of fresh birch twigs with leaves that you gently whip yourself with in the sauna. This promotes circulation and releases toxins from your skin. It sounds weird, I know, but your skin feels so soft afterwards.

Last night we three sisters proceeded to have a sauna, drink wine, sing, read the old sauna book—a record of all those who have appreciated our hospitality and who wanted to leave a comment about their sauna experience—and reminisce. Ma and Pa had fun listening to us. Pa got all teary and said how much he loved us; it was so sweet. After our sauna, we attacked the Christmas food with gusto. Two Christmas feasts this year—how lucky!

Today was another busy day. Katri and Irma stayed at Orford, whilst I drove Ma and Pa to Hobart to take care of business. Now it's late, after 11pm, as I am writing this. Everyone is asleep. I'm tired physically, mentally from speaking Finnish all day long, emotionally from listening and taking on all of their energy, and spiritually, even though I've been doing Reiki on myself each night. Please, Universe, help me sleep well and without nightmares tonight, so that I feel rested for our trip to Hobart for a few days for New Year's Eve celebrations.

Saturday 1 January 2011

Happy 2011! What a busy few days catching up with all our friends: Penny, Astrid and Roger, Robyn and Gary. The weather has been behaving itself, with temperatures ranging from 20ºC to 25ºC. We braved the thousands of people who turned up for the famous Taste of Tasmania and even met up with more of our friends by accident. Yesterday, it was just as well we had 'nanna naps' in the afternoon in preparation for our New Year's Eve partying, as we ended up staying up until 4.30am. Not bad for us old chooks, eh? What a fun night. We walked around looking at the yachts from the Sydney to Hobart Yacht Race, drank at our old favourite pubs and chatted to locals. We each ate a pie at a bakery at 3am, which was doing booming business because of the half-drunk, or fully-drunk, starving hordes of people. Food seems to be a main theme for us on our holiday. Today, we have munched our way through pastries, chicken kebabs and salad, berries and ice cream in a waffle basket, not to mention the McDonalds for dinner. Ugghh and aarrgghh, my poor stomach! The Salamanca markets have grown to be huge now and we had to park a long way away, so at least we got to walk a fair distance to counter-act some of those calories. The next few days are booked out for more luncheons and parties with friends.

Monday 3 January 2011

Holidays don't always go smoothly when family is concerned. We all have very different personalities and, as much as you love each other, spending too much time together can cause friction. For me, I recognise when I need 'time out' and am learning to choose to spend a day on my own to re-energise and refocus. In this instance, I let my sisters visit more friends whilst I indulged in some serious retail therapy after Christmas and New Year sales. Woohoo!

Wednesday 5 January 2011

I'm shaking as I write this. My mother has been on one of her drinking binges. She's into her second day and has cursed me over and over again in Finnish. We drove back yesterday, unsure of our reception. Last night, we all had a sauna again, along with a few wines. The difference is that we know when to stop, but Mum and Dad keep going with only light naps or, more accurately, passing out in between. What an emotional night for all of us. Dad poured his heart out to us; we three sisters tried to soothe the atmosphere. We were the adults and our parents were the children this time around. I thought we were making some progress, as Irma counselled Dad in his room whilst I performed a bit of Reiki on Mum in the living room. However, later in the evening it was my turn for an emotional breakdown when Mum actually slapped me—although not hard—across my face and yelled at me for not having children! What kind of mother does that to her own child? I ran outside, still in my swimsuit from the sauna. Irma and Katri found me balling my eyes out in the light rain. They comforted me when I screamed that it wasn't my fault I couldn't have children. Irma gave me a homeopathic remedy, which calmed me down relatively quickly. Talk about a highly charged and emotional night! These verbal cuts run deep and may take a long while to heal.

Today, we ran away for a few hours, or more precisely, we walked for over two and a half hours, as it was obvious that the drinking binge had yet to run its course. Is it any wonder that we avoid visiting our parents when faced with repeat performances year in and year out? In the afternoon, we drove away for another few hours' respite until receiving a distress call from Dad. We had a 'fun' time taking it in turns to calm Mum down that evening. I even sang and whistled to her to help her sleep. Who is the parent here? They are both behaving like teenagers! We love them, of course, but it does severely try our patience. Mum and Dad went to so much trouble with Christmas preparations, but then Ma frets in advance of us leaving again and not spending all of our time with them, which then becomes a good excuse to drink.

Sunday 9 January 2011

On the road again... it was time for us to make a road trip to visit more friends in the northern parts of Tasmania, including Sophie, Steve and their kids. It's hard to switch back to 'normal' behaviour with friends after the ordeal we've been through with our parents. We did manage to have a great time catching up and laughing with our friends, as well as amongst ourselves during the hours in the car. It was a relief to have a few days break to gather our emotional energy. We tried not to think about what would happen when we returned to our parents' place. It's the same patterns of behaviour and repetitive conversations that wear you down...

Last night, everyone else had gone to bed (all was peaceful at the 'front') and Irma and I were talking quietly in the kitchen when we heard a ruckus outside. I opened the kitchen door carefully and, to my delight, found a possum happily perched on a wooden ledge. I chopped up an apple for his night snack. I wasn't scared of him at all even though possums have very sharp claws. I patted his furry back as he climbed into a better position. He was quite happy to stay there, munching away and posing for our cameras. We took some fabulous action photos of him reaching out for a piece of apple. Then his cheeks puffed out before he swallowed the apple wedges. Obviously, he had a sweet tooth. It was one of the highlights of this trip as I'm such an animal lover.

Monday 10 January 2011

We've had a lovely time reminiscing over old photo albums, hours of fun and laughter over our fashion sense. It was nice to have a peaceful day for a change, with everyone behaving themselves. When Mum and Dad don't drink alcohol, we all sigh with relief and are able to find moments where we enjoy their conversations and unique sense of humour. We can *see* them as our parents again rather than destructive, misbehaving teenagers. I also decided to go through my old suitcase stored here at my parents' and look through all my memorabilia. Amazing the way an item can take you right back to the time and place you got it from; all of the memories come cascading down from some deep recess of your mind. It's time to go home tomorrow…

Tuesday 11 January 2011

We dropped off our hire car and checked in our luggage at the airport early in the morning. As our flight wasn't until late, Katri and I spent the final day of our holidays gallivanting around shops with Mum and Dad whilst Irma spent some more time with Angelea. The flight ended up being late due to lousy weather, but we were okay chatting at the airport food and beverage area. We cracked up laughing when I said that if they asked us the question, 'Do you have anything to declare?' at customs, my reply would be, 'Yes, we're idiots!'

Friday 14 January 2011

I appreciate my life so much more after spending time away from my home life. My hubby was very smoochy and huggy (yes, they are real words) and my girls were very happy to see Mummy home again. So nice to be back in my own bed, use my own shower and enjoy all of the other comforts of my own home. Yes, of course there are all of the chores to do, but somehow it's comforting to be back into the usual routine after such a tumultuous holiday. I've been going to bed early, as I've been so jet-lagged and tired from all of the Tassie drama.

Monday 17 January 2011

Saturday the fifteenth was absolutely hectic and tiring. We left home early to meet our broker in the city and spent two hours working through the paperwork for our house. It's out of our hands now; fingers crossed we receive some good news this week. Then we spent time re-looking at carpets, bricks, vinyl, taps, handles and so forth, ready for prestart. After lunch, we had another appointment to select our phone, data, television points and their locations in our house. We arrived home after 5pm and, following a quick rest, I got stuck into some gardening for a couple of hours. No wonder I felt worn out by the end of the day.

Yesterday, we had a family fun day, which included boogie boarding and a late lunch at our place. I wasn't much company, as I still felt exhausted and bone-weary. Something doesn't feel right…

In early December last year, David and I were sitting on the couch watching television when I ran my right hand over my left breast and felt a lump. I asked David to check it for me and he felt it too. I'd just had a mammogram in June, so we both assumed it wouldn't be anything sinister, with the lump most likely being a cyst or something similar. I didn't want to book a doctor's appointment during the crazy Christmas holiday period and, after all, we were heading off to Tasmania for our holiday. I told David that I would deal with it when I got back from Tassie. Whilst on holiday, I asked my sisters to feel the lump too. They agreed that I should book in to see my GP when we got home. In Tassie, I tried not to worry and avoided mentioning it to my parents or friends; however, my hand kept straying to the lump and a part of me whispered, *Sorja, get David to make an appointment for you ASAP.*

My appointment is booked for this Saturday. The large lump, about two centimetres in width, has been there for over a month now. I have to be honest and say that it has played on my mind a lot. My left armpit has been sore for ages as well, and I don't think it's from a sporting injury.

Wednesday 26 January 2011

The doctor I saw on Saturday 22 January was not my usual GP. Instead, I saw a very brusque male doctor who took all of two minutes with me. He shoved his hand down my bra to feel the lump, tearing my bra in the process! Well! At least I managed to persuade him to write me a referral to see a specialist for a mammogram and an ultrasound for Tuesday next week. Just wait and see now...

I had a powerful dream on Saturday 22/01/11—a very spiritual date according to numerology. In the dream, *I was getting into a lift and I wanted to go only a few floors up, but a huge, tall male Archangel pushed the lift button to go up to the top at very high speed!* I think this means that my spiritual growth is about to be accelerated whether I'm ready or not.

Irma and Khan came over to spend a few nights with us and one night we had an amusing episode to do with a cockroach. We were having a late night with Irma (surprise, surprise) when she noticed a huge flying cockroach on the ceiling. It dropped onto the floor and I quickly placed a plastic container over it. The cockroach started running around inside of the container in attack mode and we acted so much like little girls. Anyhow, this is the note I left for David for the next morning:

David, morning Hon. Can you please take care of big cockroach under container, with ornament dog on top, under the massage table? Xxxooo

Irma and I giggled so much and we hadn't even been drinking.

Chapter 19

Wake Up Call, Diagnosis of Breast Cancer

Sunday 30 January 2011

I woke up early this morning to a very vivid dream that I immediately had to record down in my dream journal. This is what I wrote: *I'm in a competition having to traverse across miles and miles of chasms and valleys with huge drops. I'm holding onto cables or wires and suspension ropes and I have a small backpack. There are long stretches where I couldn't stop to drink or go to the toilet or anything. I just had to keep putting one hand in front of the other and not look down. My feet were suspended and only occasionally could I rest them on more rope. I lost track of other competitors, and some didn't make it! I was fighting for my life! I had a small dog that kept me company from time to time, but mostly it was just me and the elements of nature. I finally found a point where I could jump off without killing or hurting myself. I ran the rest of the way to the checkpoint. Someone asked me whether I knew of those competing and I said, 'Yes, I'm one of them.'*

I staggered to an older woman at a table and gave her my photo identification card with my name clearly written on it and she couldn't believe that I was the first one to finish the race. I had won! I collapsed onto a chair and got water. I was given gold coins, a plaque and other badges. When I went in search of a toilet I was accosted by some dark men. They wanted my winnings but I fought them and yelled at the top of my voice and then used my strength to run and run and run. The angry men gave chase, but I wasn't going to give them what I had fought so hard for!

Tuesday 1 February 2011

This morning I had a mammogram of both breasts and they found the suspicious lump. They did an ultrasound and Dr Robey decided to take fine needle biopsies straight away. I think there were six samples in all, which he would send off to the lab marked as URGENT. Although he used an anaesthetic, it still hurt when he poked around and juggled the tissue to get a good sample. Dr Robey was probably one of the nicest doctors I've come across over the years. He explained everything and was kind to me. He even arranged an appointment with my GP when I said it was usually hard to get in to see her, as she was booked out for weeks. I'm to see Dr Patricia Moore on Thursday at 8.30am for the results and the next step…

Of course, I broke down in the car because the way they were reacting made it seem unlikely that my lump is a cyst or calcification of the breast tissue. I also remembered the dream about fighting for my life. I called my workplace to request a replacement for my shift on Thursday, and I broke down again over the phone. I held it together for the phone call to David but then broke down yet again on the call to my sister Irma. I met her for coffee before her work shift and I bought some tablets for stress and anxiety. By 3pm, I had a splitting headache and my breast was hurting, so I came home. Thankfully, David will be home soon…

I drew my daily indicator card from *The Animal-Wise Tarot* deck of cards by Ted Andrews—and two cards flipped out, one on top of the other. The Queen of Winged Ones (Scarlet Macaw), which is my

Significator card, was upright on top of the Five of Ancients (Gecko) card which was upside down. According to my Tarot book, the explanation of The Five of Ancients card is, *Do what you must in struggles*. My interpretation is that I have to do what it takes, whatever the news is...

Wednesday 2 February 2011

Today, I knew I had to keep busy to keep my mind off tomorrow. In the afternoon, Irma and I picked up my X-rays and they definitely show a huge lump that wasn't there seven months ago.

Thursday 3 February 2011

I woke up early and got ready to see Dr Moore with David. No easy way to write this. I have been diagnosed with breast cancer. I was calm at the doctor's but David wasn't... Patricia has referred me onto Royal Perth Hospital for the next stage: further biopsies and treatment options. Of course, we both fell apart in the car and once we got home, we continued to cry bucket loads! I texted my family and friends, and received replies and calls all day long. I rang Irma, who will support me in my fight with all of her knowledge. Patricia said that I should do whatever is necessary— prayer, meditation, diet, exercise— and not to be too proud to ask for help and support. I have been overwhelmed by the response from people and the way everyone has offered help.

I rang Ma and Pa, as I thought that they should hear it from me and not my sisters. Ma was very supportive. I received calls from my girlfriends, one who said I sounded so calm. I guess I had cried so much already and had moved back into a frozen state of shock. By the end of the day, I was tired of talking about it and just wanted to shut down for a while.

I am going to work tomorrow, as I don't want to stay at home moping—too much doom and gloom. I have to focus on my marriage, my family, my girls, our house, my art, the present and the future, my life. I want to *live*, so I have to fight with all of my strength, focus on positive thoughts and a positive outcome. There will be good and bad days. This is not a death sentence. They have come a long way with so many high-profile celebrities supporting Breast Cancer Research. It is one of the 'better' cancers to get. Like my good friend Sophie said to me, change the word 'cancer' to 'measles' and if I lose my hair, buy a red wig and try to have some fun with it. I need to watch comedies and take lots of walks on the beach, like David and I did tonight.

I have between fifty and a hundred people praying for me, meditation groups have put my name on their healing lists, and Sophie said she has a direct line with the man upstairs and knows that I will be okay. My work friend Margaret said that I'm a strong character, and if I have to have parts of my boob removed, it's just fat and it doesn't make me. They have all sent their love which is very much appreciated. Even my niece Nikiita sent a text, *I love you Aunty Sorja*. Irma gave me some Rescue Remedy to help me cope with the stress and anxiety.

We tried to nap in the afternoon. David managed but I couldn't stop thinking. It's late now; I'm feeling shock, denial and grief, all in one big jumble. Katri rang earlier in the day, so upset that she couldn't teach and offering to come over tomorrow, but I need to go to work (my choice).

It's okay for me to be assertive and tell people when I need time out. My left armpit has been sore for weeks and I see a bruise there.

I pray that it hasn't spread to my lymph nodes and that it's only an infection. I keep icing it to numb the pain. Please let the public hospital specialist team contact me soon to arrange the next step. Please, Universe, be kind to me.

Saturday 5 February 2011

Yesterday, the Universe arranged for me to be kept busy at work. I had visitors, too, and my Tall Poppy work friends gave me lovely bunches of flowers. Ma and Pa rang to check up on me; however, it was obvious that they were 'on the bottle' as a coping mechanism. My lovely hubby also dropped by on his way from Garden Island to Henderson, and he rang a few times later in the day. By the end of the day, I was totally stuffed, especially as I didn't get home until 6pm! David went to buy us dinner whilst I sat outside with the girls, throwing the ball to Ratbag Cheyenne and drinking wine. I have had a break from wine since Sunday, but I just wanted to feel normal, and it is normal to have wine on a Friday night, the end of the working week.

I'm praying we get the formal loan approval paperwork soon, so that the house building can commence. I need to focus on something positive and good: our future dreams. Tomorrow, my brother, Visa, and his fiancée Susie, are coming over to see our block of land and look at our plans on the site. We will go out to lunch, too. Today is a normal Saturday, doing housework and laundry at home. These tasks don't stop even when your world feels like it has.

Well, I just found out my appointment date for Royal Perth Hospital is for 8 March. What? I have to wait one month? Ugghh, I'm so angry! I'm pissed off that I have to wait again. What do I do for a whole month? Get on with my life, try not to give up and get fit. I've got to get stronger to prepare my body for the fight. This is all planned by the powers that be, and I don't mean the hospital. I guess prestart on 14 February won't be cancelled, which is good, and the loan approval and the paperwork will be done by then.

Focus on what is important, Sorja! I will work like normal, get back on the treadmill, eat healthier and prepare myself as much as possible. Positive thinking, Sorja. Words from random (or not so random) songs keep going around in my head, all relating to being a survivor and a winner, about not giving up and what a battle there is ahead.

Dr Patricia Moore rang and said she's not happy with 8 March. 'That's not good enough.' She will call them on Monday or Tuesday and 'jump up and down' to get an earlier date. They may need more information to be sent to them and more tests. The next step is a core biopsy, but they can only do that there in Perth. Thank you, Patricia, for your help and your fight for me.

Monday 7 February 2011

I had a dream last night (surprise, surprise, as I always dream). *There was a big, burly and aggressive neighbour in our yard, and I told David to just throw him over the fence, but he couldn't. So, I got fed up and picked the man up with both of my hands and held him horizontally over my head and tossed him over the fence into his own yard. I looked at David and said, 'See, that's how you do it!'* I think this dream means that I am stronger than David in all of this battle ahead...

My niece Tory takes after me in some ways, such as having very vivid and detailed dreams. She sent me this text today:

Morning Sorja, I hope you're doing ok. I had a dream last night of you in a field of pink flowers in a white flowy dress smiling and laughing running toward your painting stuff which faced a massive oak tree that had various different coloured birds in it. It was a very pretty sight... I'm not sure what it means though.

I asked her how she felt about it when she woke up, whether it made her feel happy or sad. She replied, *Yer, I did feel happy about it, love lots as well Tory xxx.*

I interpret the dream as follows: the pink flowers denote all of the love and support I will receive; the white dress is purity, spiritual support and protection; the oak tree symbolizes powerful strength and steady progress; and birds are generally regarded as symbols of freedom and messengers from the Spirit World. All in all, a very uplifting and positive dream.

Tuesday 8 February 2011

Last Saturday went downhill after David came home depressed. He had a right to be, having asked 'what if' questions all day long. Then, when I went to buy Emla numbing cream for my armpit and breast, the pharmacist was so serious and 'real' about how tough cancer is. It was all too much for me! I tried a one hour walk on the beach but it didn't calm me enough, so I got stuck into the wine again. It's not the solution, I know, but I reacted in a self-medicating way. I put on my new headphones and listened to Josh Groban, watched photos on the photo frame and balled my eyes out. Ratbag startled me as she crept up on me. I screamed, waking David up and scaring him. Cheyenne jumped away in fright. Poor old girl. She was just curious as to why Mummy was sitting in the dark by herself. She couldn't hear the music from my headphones. Anyway, there is no right or wrong way to deal with any of this.

TREE WITH NO LEAVES

Needless to say, Sunday morning was a shaky start for me. Visa, Susie and Susie's daughter, Alex, came over about 9.30am and, although it was a bit awkward at times, we managed to have an okay day. We checked out our block of land, then the rest of South Yunderup, followed by a lovely lunch at Ravenswood Hotel. A raven's constant cawing stressed me out some, but it was Ravenswood after all. We drove to Mandurah for a coffee and by then we were all tired so went our separate ways. My brother was obviously upset on my behalf and told me to remember that I am a 'lucky duck'. All of us kids grew up with animal nicknames and mine has always been Duck. My house is full of duck ornaments and stuffed duck toys, given as gifts over the years. I came home to rest and gave myself Reiki healing and felt much better in the evening.

Since then, my moods have been a twirly mix, up and down, up and down, flat, up and down, flat and so forth. I have to take it one day, one hour and sometimes one minute at a time. I'm keeping myself as occupied as possible.

I received my appointment letter for the Royal Perth Hospital Breast Clinic yesterday, and I called them to talk about my concerns over the delay. What would happen in the next month, since my cancer had appeared so quickly? A lovely nurse rang me back and, after reviewing my results, she has managed to swap appointments so that I can see the surgeon earlier, on 22 February instead of in March. I now have only a two week wait instead of a month, thank God.

We received some excellent news yesterday; our loan has been officially and finally approved and the proof documents arrived today. Yeah! Thank you, Universe, for some good news. Prestart is next Monday and the bank loan paperwork should arrive soon.

Instead of moping at home today, I swam twenty laps of a fifty-metre pool and then spent time in the sauna and spa. I treated myself to coffee and lunch as a reward for my efforts. I'm trying to focus on drawing in the positive, expecting the positive, finding laughter and fun, and bringing joy into my life.

Thursday 10 February 2011

Eleven reasons to live:

1. my family relationships
2. my husband, David
3. my Misha and Cheyenne
4. my learning ahead—assertiveness, kindness, human connections, love of self and others, patience and trust in myself and others
5. learning coping mechanisms and healthy, rather than self-destructive, habits
6. future house together with David
7. continuing my passion for art
8. mediumship and spiritual learning, and growth to use in this lifetime
9. learning the strength of my body and to love my body
10. learning the balance between the mental, physical, emotional and spiritual
11. perseverance—learning to never give up and learning to forgive.

Friday 11 February 2011

I had another powerful dream last night. *I was speaking to one of my male Spirit Guides (a tall and skinny man with dark hair; standing on my left side). He was explaining why I've got breast cancer. Actually, it was more like a discussion, as he asked me if I knew why and I replied that I understood it was because of relationship issues, and it was more about unresolved conflict than any physical things that I have done to myself—right or wrong—for example, my diet et cetera. I asked him if I was going to survive and live, and he said I knew that he couldn't answer the question—it wasn't up to him; it was my choice and my journey.* Harrumph!

Tonight, I went to a spiritual workshop. It was a good turnout of about fifty to sixty people. We were guided through a very effective meditation. At first, we lit up the chakras through colour meditation. We then visualised an apple, asking ourselves what colour it was, what it looked like, where it was and in what setting. Finally, we had a conversation with it by asking questions and listening to the answers. It sounds weird, but it proved to be very enlightening.

I saw a shiny red apple with a green leaf still attached, close to an apple tree full of other apples. However, I also saw a worm inside the apple and this upset me. I knew the worm was my cancer eating me and that I needed to remove it. No matter how many bites were taken from the apple (me), I would still be a shiny red apple, as it wouldn't change my essence. I also knew I would have to accept help from all those other apples (people) and that I would gather strength from that tree! The red symbolised the red chakra characteristics of life energy and vitality. The base chakra also refers to physical and emotional strength, will power and sexuality. The woman who led us through the meditation also said that the worm represented holding back, holding things in and not saying the things I really wanted to say.

Tuesday 15 February 2011

I went to see a very spiritual movie called *Hereafter*. It really made me think about weightlessness, peace and quiet, the comfort of other Souls and my Spirit Guides. It does sound so tempting, but I really don't think my time is up.

Thursday 17 February 2011

Today was difficult. Not only was it a stifling hot day at work, but my left armpit, arm and breast were so sore and weak with shooting pains all day long that it was hard to complete my work tasks. I was very short-tempered when I got home. I feel as though everyone expects me to be so strong all the time. Everyone tells me how strong I am, that I will beat this cancer, and I must stay positive. It is so hard. I'm human and vulnerable. I can let go and cry. I have to write to my cancer and tell it my feelings, since no-one else wants the truth of how I feel and how much I hurt!

Sunday 20 February 2011

Dear Cancer, this really sucks! My emotions are all over the place. At work on Friday, an acquaintance dropped by and once again made light of my breast cancer. She commented that it's so common these days and then launched into her own health problems. I understand she's going through her own stuff, but really! Listen to me for a change and take all of this seriously. Breast cancer is not a topic to brush over. It makes me so angry.

In fact, a lot of things are making me angry at the moment. I'm angry at myself, I'm angry at David for not taking care of himself physically, I'm angry at having to do stupid house chores, and I'm angry about being angry! David said, 'I'm so busy with work worries, new house worries and you, that I'm not thinking about myself.'

I got angry with him because I want him to look after himself, so that I don't have to worry about him and his stress levels. He said that I have been sick all of our married life. Well, all of our married life he has been overweight. I truly believe that this breast cancer on my left side, which is the feminine side, is a lack of female nurturing, linked to my relationships (mother-daughter, father-daughter and husband-wife as well as girlfriend to girlfriend), unspoken words and unexpressed feelings. This also includes the lack of nurturing I have given myself. I have denied the female aspects of myself and shut myself down in so many ways. Years of hating my body size, my periods, my infertility, my womb for not being able to carry a child, and now my breasts and hatred of the invasion of cancer.

So, Cancer, hating you is not beneficial. You are in my breast and therefore a part of me, so as a part of me, I have to accept you and forgive you and love you. You are a manifestation of my disassociation from my femininity, and my left spiritual side. Ultimately, it is my choice and decision whether to fight or give up. The balancing of my life scales. Libra is my star sign, and bringing my life back into balance is my goal.

Wednesday 23 February 2011

Wow, I just re-read what I last wrote in my journal. Phew, what anger. Some of the stuff I wrote is 'for my eyes only' and I was obviously in a really dark place to spew forth such vitriol. I guess it's better to let it all out, even if only to yourself, eh? I've received lots of supportive messages and texts, for example, *Dear Sorja, I was devastated to hear your news. You have a big fight ahead but fight you must. Listen to your body and take one day at a time. You and David will be in my thoughts and prayers. Look after yourself and each other.*

On Monday, I went for a solitary walk at the beach and sat on the sand. It was still hot, even at 6.30pm, but it was nice to listen to my music, watch the waves and see people enjoying themselves, their families and their dogs. I have to admit I've thought about the 'what ifs'. I've even talked to Irma about my desire to be cremated as opposed to burial, as well as where I would like my ashes scattered. Morbid I know, but it's natural for your mind to drift towards things like that when you are given such a diagnosis.

Yesterday was 22/02/2011—significant numbers in numerology. After a sleepless night for me as I was worried and thinking too much, David and I left home early to go to Royal Perth Hospital. Even after taking one and a half hours due to morning peak hour traffic, we were still half an hour early for our appointment at the Breast Clinic. Irma dropped Khan off at school and caught a train to Perth to support us. As we sat in the waiting room, news of an earthquake in Christchurch, New Zealand, came onto the television screen. Many dead or missing in the rubble—what a disaster! We all wondered out loud, *what the hell is going on this year, 2011?* Major cyclones and floods in Queensland, bushfires and loss of houses in Western Australia, and now an earthquake in New Zealand. What kind of spiritual shake-up are we experiencing? It put things into perspective, as we are all still alive and, in my case, I still have a fighting chance to remain that way, unlike all those who have died in the floods and earthquake.

The staff at the Breast Clinic were fabulous and spent a lot of time explaining what will happen to me over the next few weeks and months. I met my surgeon, Mr. Jose Sid Fernandez, who is such an empathetic man and really put all of us at ease. He said that he will aim for a conservative breast surgery to retain a lot of my breast. He asked what size bra I wore and I honestly answered 14DD. He asked me whether I minded going smaller, more like a C cup. Fine by me. I nearly giggled when I saw him struggle with how to word it in front of David, Irma and the nurse, Glenys, that I was rather, errr... (What? Large? Ample? Well-endowed? Just pick a word; it's okay) and that the nip and tuck would fix the droop of the breast. Well, I never! Ha, ha, ha. He said that down the track, he could lift the other breast so they matched, and I would have a good cosmetic result. Honestly, at this stage, all I want is the cancer out...

Unfortunately, during the exam, he felt a lump in my armpit, which then had to have a biopsy, or fine needle aspiration (FNA). The doctor who did that was very nice, too, and used a lot of anaesthetic, so it didn't hurt.

David, Irma and I went out to lunch whilst we waited for the biopsy results. We got back at 1pm and the lovely Glenys explained more. She gave me a heap of information booklets to take home to read as well as a nice pillow with a shoulder strap that tucks under my armpit to offer relief from the pain. She also fitted me for a post-operation bra. I was getting brain overload and I could see that by this stage of the day, both David and Irma were, too.

I saw my surgeon again once the results came back from the laboratory. More bad news: the cancer was detected in the lymph nodes too! (Whilst we were waiting, both Irma and I had a really bad feeling that it had spread.) So, to cut a long story short, next week I have a pre-operation appointment, a physiotherapist appointment on Monday, a CT scan on Tuesday and a bone scan on Wednesday to make sure it hasn't spread anywhere else. Please, Universe, no! My operation is booked for Friday 11 March and I'll have to see a haematologist prior to this to check on my Von Willebrand's and

Desmopressin use prior to surgery. Following surgery, I'll have a drip in my armpit for a week, with a Silver Chain nurse visiting every day to check my temperature, blood pressure, dressings and drainage. My follow-up appointment is on 22 March to discuss the next phase, chemotherapy followed by radiotherapy later in the year.

Oh, what fun... not! I have one hell of a fight on my hands. I had blood tests and received my schedule of appointments, and then we all drove home in an absolute daze. It was all too much. I drank wine and cried my eyes out. By this time, David was in bed, as he had to wake up early for work the next day.

Chapter 20

Perseverance, Patience and Pride

Thursday 24 February 2011

Irma had a call from Mum. Now Mum and Dad are planning to arrive in WA in three or four weeks' time for Visa's wedding to Susie, and to help us through this difficult time. David is angry about them coming, as he doesn't think it will be in my best interests. I am torn. I will appreciate the physical help, but I hope Ma and Pa don't have any drinking binges, leading to fights and abuse. David will tell them to piss off or worse if I'm hurt more, which I understand. I also understand that Mum and Dad want to be here with their youngest child. So, the whole family, or most of us, will be together for the wedding. Oh dear, families...

I'm wondering what my illness will not only teach me but teach all those around me: work colleagues, family members and friends. Massive lessons, no doubt. Irma has been upset and crying, and I have found myself trying to keep a strong face in front of everyone, but it is very tiring. I called work to explain that I felt too overwhelmed by all of this to work for a couple of weeks, and they were very understanding. I'll go and see them in person in a few days to catch them up on what's happening. I'm seriously considering resigning so that I can put all my energy into living and recovering.

Saturday 26 February 2011

Today, I woke up with a massive headache, probably from the continuous heat wave as well as reading all the information in the pamphlets and booklets. I decided enough is enough for now, so I made myself a cappuccino and watched *The Secret* on DVD. This got me all fired up, so I jogged five kilometres on the treadmill and did some stretches. After a shower and a beautifying session, David and I went to the cinema and dinner out. So I walked the talk today to 'feel good'.

I wish David would get fired up too and acknowledge that 'we were born to be alive'. Sometimes I feel so frustrated by how flat he is most of the time. I've got to realise that it is not my job to lift up his spirits all the time; he has to do it himself. I need to focus on keeping myself positive. If anyone drags me down, I need to learn how to walk away and spend time with more positive people or animals, whatever makes me feel better, like nature always does for me. I am grateful for these: love and support from my family, my husband, my friends and of course my girls; good health, strength and fitness; my healing; the building of our new house on our block of land; my painting and my art; passion in my life; and nature, both flora and fauna.

Monday 28 February 2011

For the life of me I couldn't sleep last night. I was so tired, but my mind wouldn't shut down. I tried sleeping on the bed, then the couch under the air conditioner, then back on the bed with frequent trips to the toilet amidst the tossing and turning. I think I finally slept from 3.30am to 6.30am, when the alarm went off. Not happy!

I had to catch the train into Perth by 8am for my appointment at the Outpatients Clinic at 9am. I ended up spending from 9am to 12.30pm there. First, I saw a nurse to fill out lots of forms. She measured my height, weight and blood pressure (which at 131/91 was the highest I've seen it for me). Then I saw a lovely doctor, the head of Anaesthetics, and he said that since 2008, all major hospitals have brain monitors to ensure that patients don't wake up during surgery. That's a huge relief! I kept having to sit in the waiting room in between consultations, and they forgot about me for a couple of hours. Everyone else had come and gone and I was left there. Chirp, chirp, chirp (cricket sounds). Finally, one of the surgeons and his student saw me; the student gave me another breast exam, as it is a teaching hospital.

I had two and three-quarter hours to 'kill' before my next appointment with the physiotherapist, so I walked back to the city centre and had another coffee, looked at some shops and then ate lunch. Back at the Breast Clinic, I met my physiotherapist, Emma, who is just lovely and went through my post-operation exercises. I also found out that I can ask to have my chemotherapy at Rockingham Hospital rather than Royal Perth, which will be much easier access for me. Emma also mentioned that the Cancer Council offer yoga classes in Mandurah and meditation in Rockingham.

I didn't get home until after 6pm. I had been honest with the doctors about my level of drinking, and they didn't seem too concerned, so I decided to have a few white wines. It's now 11pm and I'm still awake. I'm so sick of these headaches all of the time. Probably stress headaches.

David has a friend whose wife went through breast cancer a few years back. David's friend has been preparing David for what he will go through. Unfortunately, David keeps coming home saying his friend told him this and that and she went through this and that and the same thing... I keep saying that I am not her, and my life has been totally different. I wasn't able to have children. I've gone through so many illnesses and surgeries and IVF. There is no point in comparing me to anyone else or vice versa. We all are different people going through some similar experiences, but we may react differently. There is no 'one size fits all' rule applied here! Of course, I reacted in anger when he spoke to me in such a tone of voice. I said I would gladly change places if he thinks he's going to have it tough. I swear, choose words carefully because they may be insensitive at times.

After surgery, I won't be allowed to do much housework or shopping for a couple of weeks. David said that he'd better get used to it when he hung my hand washing on the clothesline, I really don't get his humour at times... I guess that my anger is really coming to the surface in my writing tonight. *Ok, Sorja, you are tired; go to sleep.*

Hey, on a positive note, our land settled today. Next will be the mortgage documents and then they can start to build. Irma will keep me company tomorrow; we won't have to leave too early as my CT scans aren't until 1.45pm in the city.

Tuesday 1 March 2011

Yay, I had eight hours of sleep. Thank you, Universe. Irma and I caught the train into the city again. I wasn't allowed to eat anything and could only have water after 9.45am, four hours prior to my scan. As soon as we arrived at the hospital after walking from the city centre, I was given the contrast solution to drink (three cups) and it didn't taste too bad, as it had a nice liquorice flavour added to it. I had a cannula inserted into my right arm so they could later inject a dye to 'light me up inside'.

There was a funny scene when I had to remove my bra and shirt, and put on a gown. I was about to do it right there in the reception area without giving it a thought; the nurse stopped me and directed me to a change room. Oh, Sorja! I guess I am so used to whipping off my bra in front of medical staff that I didn't even worry about where I was. The same nurse had trouble finding a good vein and had to let a senior nurse do it. Apparently, I have deep veins but they are also small.

In the middle of all of this, David rang me in a panic, saying I had to sign an extension of the land settlement form and fax it back to either him or the settlement place within the next hour and a half! Irma and I were both furious, as I was stressed out enough without any added pressure. Thankfully, the nurses and office staff were so kind to me when I explained my dilemma and allowed me to use their fax. All okay in the end, sigh...

Pretty quickly it was time for my scan. I left Irma stuffing her face with cookies (ha, ha, ha) while I went for my chest and abdominal scan. It was a bit scary because while I was lying down in the CT (Computed Tomography) machine, the nurse shouted, 'Oh, Shit! Stop the scan!'.

She left the room, and I lay still for ages until she returned. She explained that she had pressed the red button which switched off the machine and now it would have to warm up again. Phew, talk about scaring me! The scan was paused again when they realised I had a zipper on my pants. Apparently, metal affects the reading, so I wriggled out of my pants and we were off again...

'Take a deep breath,' said an automated voice. 'Hold.' Later it told me, 'Breathe.'

This happened several times before it was over. At least it only took about ten minutes all together inside the CT machine. When they injected the dye, I felt hot all over, with a horrible chemical taste in my mouth and a sensation of hot pee coming out of my bladder. I didn't really pee; it just felt that way. All normal side effects, so I'm told. The yucky chemical taste hasn't left my mouth totally, and it's 7pm now.

The whole thing only took just over an hour. Irma and I slowly walked back in the heat (35°C) and I was finally able to have a bite to eat. As we were looking at clothes stores, I had to rush to the toilet due to a totally upset stomach from the contrast and dye solutions. I felt so sick that I told Irma that it would be best if we caught a train home. I experienced wonderful Reiki self-healing once I got home. I saw a beautiful white light and felt comfortable and at peace. It was just so beautiful. Thank you, Universal Reiki Energy. I'm sitting outside as I write in my journal and thinking, *okay, I'm halfway through my tests for this week.* Tomorrow, I have another early start, with a bone scan at 10am in Perth. Oh well...

People keep texting me. This is also stressful at times, as I feel obligated to reply to everyone even though I feel like shit!

Wednesday 2 March 2011

One day at a time... I had a bad night of pain in my armpit, despite a few wines and a couple of painkillers. My lymph nodes are sore and inflamed, and there is nothing I can do to alleviate the discomfort. I arrived at my appointment early. At 10.15am, the technician inserted a needle into my left arm—my right arm was too sore from yesterday—and put a couple of tubes of the radioactive dye in. Of course, she also had to comment on my veins. Hey, I was born this way, it's not my fault! I was told I could eat and drink as per normal and go for a walk and return at 2.15pm.

I occupied myself by having a cuppa and reading, buying button-up pyjamas for after my surgery, and eating lunch. Then, for some strange reason, I felt compelled to sit inside St Mary's Cathedral opposite the hospital. Hearing the chanting and being in such an atmosphere of peace and love brought tears to my eyes, and I had to hurry outside before I totally broke down in public. I'm sure the people there would have understood, but I have spent so many years pushing my tears down and showing a brave face to everyone that it is now difficult to break down the walls in order to let my vulnerable self out.

At 2pm, I was back at the Nuclear Department. I changed into a gown and the technician strapped my legs and my arms onto the bed. I felt like a psychiatric patient being strapped in! The full body scan took thirty-five minutes and I was told not to move a muscle. The camera started at my head and face. I closed my eyes because I felt scared and claustrophobic as the machine came right down on me. I felt as though I was in a sandwich press. The only way I kept calm and still was by meditating and pretending I was at the beach. I felt the buzzing and the light, the vibrations and the occasional pressure on, for example, my kneecaps.

I was relieved when she said we were done after my chest, both sides of my lungs and ribcage. I was concerned when the chatter in the other room stopped and there was quiet and seriousness. I hoped they were just concentrating and didn't see anything of concern. I don't sense that it has spread anywhere else apart from the lymph nodes. Please, Universe, let it be so.

I dragged myself out of there and caught the train back to my car at Rockingham Station. I stopped to buy groceries and treated myself to some rental DVDs to watch over the weekend. I deserve it, that's for sure. David told me how proud he is of me and that I have done so well this week. I think so too. Tomorrow, I have the thrombosis and haematology appointment at 11am in Perth. It's Katri's turn to keep me company.

Thursday 3 of March 2011

Today in a nutshell:

- Fuckety computer acted up and I couldn't print my list of medicines for my appointment.
- Got to Rockingham railway station and the car park was full. Fuck!
- Warnbro railway station full. Fuck!
- Realised by 10.15am that I had to drive into Perth city. Fuck!
- Got to Perth at 11am and parked at Mc Giver Street Hospital car park.
- Raced to my appointment (I had arranged for Katri to meet me there) and there was some mix-up with my appointment date; my letter stated today but their computer said it was booked for the seventeenth. Fuck! Luckily, my sister was there to argue my case and the nurse sorted it out.
- Counsellor talked to me and persuaded me to have a cup of tea. She calmed me down and said not to worry.
- Haematologist saw me and said I wouldn't need re-testing if Desmopressin worked for me four years ago with my

hysterectomy. The blood tests would check my levels and that would suffice.
- Two women—a nurse and a counsellor—spent a good half hour chatting to me about making myself a priority and to be selfish for a change. The counsellor, Claire, said she understood I was also a trained counsellor; however, this was about me, not others. Claire mentioned that my 'bucket' was empty and I had to find ways of refilling it by walking on the beach, painting, doing yoga and meditation, my Reiki and watching funny movies. Women were renowned for caring about others and not themselves, and Claire encouraged me not to feel guilty, to let things go in the house and that it didn't really matter. I am so tired and it would have been so easy to just let go and cry, but I didn't. I wanted to run from Claire and pretend I was so strong. It was as if she could see right through me. I could tell she saw my vulnerability, as she kept touching me. I'm not used to that.
- Finally, we left after I had eight vials of blood taken.
- Coffee, lunch, and then a hunt for the perfect outfit for my brother's wedding. No luck—too hard, too hot, too tired. Fuck!
- The drive home in peak hour traffic took longer than normal. Fuck!
- House chores, shower, call to Irma, wine and food, tears, tiredness, pain, depression. Fuck!

Sunday 6 March 2011

Well, I've been in a lot better mood the past few days, thank God. I even found my outfit for Visa's wedding. We three sisters spent a fun-filled day at the shops yesterday. After visiting many boutiques and almost giving up, we found a gorgeous red and black combination for me: black pants; black shirt; sheer, flowing red wrap; and red shoes. It looked stunning all together and I was happy with my choice.

Tuesday 8 March 2011

Yesterday, I went berserk with the cleaning. I took out my rage on the dusting, sweeping and vacuuming. I must have cleaned for five hours. David became concerned, not understanding that this was my way of coping and something I could control. After cooking dinner, I sat, exhausted, drinking wine and watching a DVD.

Today, my muscles were sore, however, I felt more even keeled. I had a dream. *Irma told me to drive—the steering wheel was on the left-hand side instead of the right—I didn't want to, but Irma made me drive. We drove up this vertical incline and I knew the car couldn't get to the top. The tyres were losing their grip and we tumbled backwards all the way down. We didn't die; we just ended up at the bottom of the hill again.* I guess I feel a bit out of control at the moment...

Thursday 10 March 2011

I was a bit overwhelmed by the calls, texts and visits at work yesterday, as well as having to say the same thing over and over again. It was my last day at work and by the end I was drained from spending so much time talking to people. In a spare moment I felt the urge to write this down at work on 9 March 2011.

'I think I understand why I've got breast cancer. I think I chose to go through this journey for my growth as a Soul. All the learning and experiences I have gone through has led me to this moment in time. It is a culmination of all of my Soul strength, my knowledge and my perseverance. My current challenge will help me to help other women. I have gained knowledge and experience through courses, reading, employment and life:

- business—travel and tourism
- customer service
- weight loss and self-esteem
- health and nutrition
- importance of pampering yourself, for example, at day spas
- counselling—grief and loss
- counselling—addictions
- art therapy
- spiritual books and numerology
- practising Reiki healing
- meditation and relaxation.

My goodness! Putting all of that together makes me a perfect candidate to run women's groups, perhaps a breast cancer support group? Universe, what do you think? This is something I can see myself getting excited about and actually doing… using my skills to feel useful and needed, and to be of help to mankind so that my life is not wasted. Of course, I know I need to take one step at a time. I am not to rush through my recovery and stress out about the future'.

Today, I am accepting all the love the Universe is sending to me. My good friend Samantha sent me a lovely package containing a dream sack, soap and shower gel, and a book by Doreen Virtue titled *Daily Guidance from Your Angels*. It was beautiful and appropriate, and I am grateful. I am very blessed for having such support from family and friends. Thank you, Universe and God. It's funny how something like this makes me feel more connected to people, to God and to myself.

I have an early start for my surgery tomorrow. I have to wake up at 4am to shower and shave and be at the hospital by 6am. I'll write in this when I am back from the hospital—and I will be back! The surgery will be successful and all will go perfectly. A song keeps going around in my head: 'Love is All Around' by the band Wet Wet Wet.

Monday 14 March 2011

I arrived at the hospital at 6.15am on Friday 11 March. David stayed with me until I was shown to the Day Surgery unit at 7am. I waited in a numbered chair—mine was green three—and watched as numerous people were moved through like a production line. I saw people move from chairs to beds and then, after being prepped, they were wheeled away to their respective surgeries. I listened to my music and I wasn't seen until 8.30am, when I filled in the usual paperwork, had my BP and temperature taken, and endured the 'fun' of finding a good vein for the cannula to go in. The breast surgeon had a few attempts and finally succeeded with the third try on the left hand. Then, it was back to waiting until 10.30am when I was asked to go on a clinical trial for anti-nausea steroidal or non-steroidal drugs administered during anaesthesia. I declined, as I would have had to make trips into the city for further blood tests during my recovery. No, thank you. It was optional anyway.

I waited some more until I was finally seen by the haematologist at 2.30pm. I called David at midday so he wouldn't worry. A nurse gave me my DDAVP infusion through the IV and then I was wheeled into the pre-operation room at 3.30pm. What a long wait! That's eight hours in a chair with no food, water or bed rest, just my iPod and magazine, and trying to snooze in a chair. What a nightmare.

I chatted to the operating theatre nurse for about twenty minutes about all manner of things, such as coffee, wine and my upbringing in Finland. This helped the time go faster and I was able to relax a little as they prepared the operating theatre for my surgery. I was wheeled in at 3.50pm. After a quick chat, my heart rate and blood pressure monitors were strapped in—I had Velcro style dots put on my forehead to monitor brain activity during my surgery as well—and whilst I was distracted, the anaesthetist knocked me out.

The next thing I knew was my surgeon Mr Jose Sid Fernandez waking me up and saying that it all went well, they had removed quite a few lymph nodes and I would be sore. He would see me at my follow-up appointment on 22 March. This was at 7.30pm meaning that surgery had lasted for over three hours.

I experienced severe chills after that and I needed lots of extra blankets, including a heated one for my head. I kept saying, 'Ccccccold' over and over. It took me a couple of hours to feel warm again, as I shook from the shock and trauma of surgery. The night was spent with numerous interruptions by nurses checking my BP on my leg, my temperature and my drain and wound sites. At one point, the nurse woke me from a deep sleep by touching my foot and I screamed, 'Oh, my God!' It woke up the other women in the room.

The Tramal tablets, which I had been given for the pain, made me feel nauseous and I also had a migraine in the middle of the night. I drank heaps of water and took more anti-nausea drugs. A weird side effect of taking Tramal was time distortion. I looked at the clock at midnight, fell asleep and then thought I had been asleep for hours. I looked at the clock again and found it was five past midnight. What? Five minutes only? How weird.

I met a lovely lady next to me in the room. She'd had a breast reconstruction after a botched job during her double mastectomy operation. She talked to me for half an hour about her journey and asked about mine. She offered me bits of advice, which I appreciated.

I was released to home care after less than twenty-four hours post-surgery, which I found staggering. At midday, after receiving my medication to take home, David bought us a proper coffee, and I finally felt okay to eat a little bit before our drive.

A Silver Chain nurse has come to see me every day to check my progress, and I have had my darling David and my sisters taking turns to spend time with me. I've received heaps of calls and texts, and when I told my brother about the weird Tramal side effects, his response was, 'Oh, so Duck's tripping.'

(Ha, ha, ha and yep this Duck sure felt like she was tripping!) My response was that at least these psychedelic drugs were legal…

Today, I've been watching a TV special called *My Breasts Could Kill Me*, an English program featuring the Dawn Porter story. OMG! It showed breast surgery, lymph node removal, chemotherapy, hair loss, MRI and mammograms, breast reconstructions and so forth. It is very confronting but also informative. Apparently, most breast cancers take five to ten years to be detected as a lump. That means that the *single cell* started going whacky five to ten years ago! It's now 2011, so that was the years 2000 to 2005. My IVF was in 2000 to 2001, when I pumped myself full of hormones. However, being childless and not breast feeding also increases your risk as does drinking alcohol. I can't help wondering what caused this. Irma also said that Mum tried so many pills to avoid getting pregnant all the time that perhaps I was born with defective genes? Who knows? Other forms of cancer, such as leukaemia and prostate cancer, run in the family too. It's driving me crazy trying to figure out why me?

I guess Tuesday 22 March will be important to find out what type of cancer it is, whether it's hormone driven, what grade and, God forbid, if it has spread elsewhere besides the lymph nodes. Okay, I'm stressing out again. I need to perform some Reiki on myself and then sleep.

Tuesday 15 March 2011

I woke up to the mobile phone scaring me. It was Sandy, the Silver Chain nurse, saying she was on her way to see me. It was a scramble to get decent, brush my teeth and hair, and tidy up the bed in time. She changed my dressings but left the drainage container even though it's at 250mls already. Oh, yuck! Apparently, it's vacuum sealed and it's better off leaving it rather than risk exposing the tube to air and germs. I've got one clean one there if and when this gets too full.

After a few phone conversations and a visit from a friend, I walked round and round the backyard and front yard in an attempt to get my bowels going, as I haven't gone since last Thursday. I've taken laxative powders but so far, nada…

Oohh, I just showered—it feels good to be clean. The plastic cover supplied to wrap over my breast is certainly not waterproof. Each time I've tried cling-wrap, and the plastic cover over the patch, blah nothing has worked. I've had to pat dry the dressings as much as I could and then use the hairdryer on cool setting to dry it further.

Also, to my embarrassment, I got stuck in my clothing. Just when I thought I was so clever getting my arm movement and range back, I tried to put my buttonless PJ tank top on, and I got caught up in it. Proud Duck had to yell to David, 'Help, I'm stuck!'

Sheeze! Now I hope my wound isn't oozing, as my armpit is still wet. Damn, it sure is... Oh, Sorja. Nurse to the rescue tomorrow...

Thursday 17 March 2011

Phew, successful number twos finally. Okay, otherwise not the best couple of days as the drain in my armpit had been leaking onto my clothes and the bed sheets but not into the drain container as it was supposed to do! The Silver Chain nurse, Paula, changed the bottle and dressings yesterday morning. Later in the afternoon, I noticed that the connection tube to the bottle had snapped. We called Silver Chain, but as it was already 7pm, no-one could come out to see me. We ended up at the Rockingham Hospital Emergency Department from 9pm until 11pm. The doctor there was unsure and didn't want to take the drain out even though I wanted it out and the nurse there was fighting hard for me. She managed to re-dress the wound and attach another new drain container, which thankfully worked last night. Now it's 5pm and it's been leaking again all afternoon. I'm going through numerous small towels under my breast and arm to catch the yellowish fluid draining from my wounds. Sigh. I called the Breast Clinic and Glenys said that the drain can come out tomorrow anyway, with it being day seven post-surgery. I can tell Silver Chain to take it out, so one more night of this... David has had to attend a course these two days (Thursday and Friday) even though he didn't get to bed until midnight and had to wake up at five. Poor thing is so exhausted.

Friday 18 March 2011

According to the radio, my morning stars for the day are to 'Keep positive and upbeat today'. I just woke up from a dream. *I was dressed up in high heels and ready to go out with the family, but I was really down and depressed. I was in the study or library of an old house and Shane, an old friend who died years ago, stopped me and asked me to chat with him for a bit. He was mature looking, well dressed and serious. He looked at me with kindness and understanding. I didn't want to sit down, so I leaned against a wall and played with my high heels, flipping them on and off. We were chatting about this and that before he stopped me mid-sentence and asked about me. He said that I'm always talking about others, but he wanted to focus on me.*

I said, 'Oh, are you like a counsellor?'

I was being sarcastic, but he was still kind and smiled and replied 'Yes.' I was taken aback. He asked me 'What do you want from your life?'

I stumbled to find an answer. He said I needed to find something worthwhile for me, something I would get excited about. I answered truthfully that sometimes I just wanted to give up and that I was just so tired of all of this, meaning my ill health and pain. He just nodded in empathy and total understanding. That was when my alarm went off and I woke up. Amazing dream!

Yeah! Sandy took my drain out today. So much more freedom of movement without having to hold onto the drain tube and container, and it didn't hurt much when it came out. Funny thing happened. Within minutes of pulling the drain out, I got a splitting headache. Was it something to do with the lymph nodes? Sandy left us heaps of dressings to use for the ooze that will continue to drain out of the wound over the weekend. We won't need the nurse, as David can do it for me.

After Sandy left, I asked Irma if she, Khan and I could go for a walk at the beach. Irma and I strolled in the balmy ocean as Khan played and dived in the water. We sat and chatted for a while before walking most of the way back to the car. I had to stop in the shade and asked Irma to get the car, as I had a headache by this stage, and my breast and arm ached. We ate a delicious lunch before heading home. I was proud of myself for managing the walk and I so enjoyed the fresh air.

Claire, the counsellor, rang for a chat, and even she was shocked that I had been released from hospital after less than twenty-four hours. She asked how I was doing emotionally and I told her that I had woken up in a low mood; however, after our walk in the sun, getting vitamin D and having my drain out, I felt heaps better.

Now it's nearly 5pm. I need to lie down and stop being such a superwoman. I spoke to Visa and he will visit on Sunday. I told him I am free from the drain and he called me a cordless Duck, ha, ha, ha… a sense of humour sure does run in our family.

Sunday 20 March 2011

It's so much easier to move around without the drain. It's not leaking much anymore, though the inner bruising was stirred up by the removal of the tube. I've had very impressive outside bruising, many brilliant colours as the bruises heal with the help of Arnica cream. I'm sure the doctors will be very impressed at how quickly the bruises are fading. It's the internal ones that have bothered me more, as it's been hard to lie on my side at all, even with my soft pillow. Oh well, this too shall pass, as they say.

Yesterday, my nephew Khan and I looked after each other whilst both David and Irma worked. We watched the movie *The Dark Knight* and there was a moment when someone said things get worse before they get better. Khan said that was with me too. He said, 'You were worse, you had surgery and now you're all better.'

I explained that the journey wasn't quite over and I had further treatments to go. It's no use lying to children, as they will see the truth for themselves, for example, when my hair falls out due to chemotherapy.

Today, Visa visited for about four hours. Mum and Dad arrived in the afternoon and Mum cooked dinner whilst I gave myself Reiki healing and napped again.

Monday 21 March 2011

Sandy discharged me from Silver Chain today. Mum, Dad, Irma and I had a busy day. We walked from Irma's place along the beach and in the water to Pengo's Café near Penguin Island. We drank coffee and slowly walked back in the 32°C heat, phew. After some painkillers and five minutes' rest, we all went to the shopping centre to run various errands. By the afternoon I was exhausted and happily went to lie down whilst Mum cooked up a storm. Thank you, Ma.

Tuesday 22 March 2011

We had a lovely time last night sitting outside in the balmy weather (Ma, Pa, Irma, Trent, Khan, David and I). I drank a few wines because I was starting to feel really scared about my mortality again. Ma and Pa were reminiscing about when we were children. Apparently, when we were coming over from Finland to Australia for the first time, I was standing at the ship's railing, singing in Finnish in my sweet five-year-old's lisping voice. I sang a song about a new life ahead of us once again. I had made up the words. Wow, what an old Soul. I don't remember the song, but I do remember parts of the sea voyage over to Australia.

I was in bed by 11pm last night and slept in until 10.30am. Must have needed the sleep. Mum and Dad had left by 8am to drive to Katri's place in the hills. David and I had a leisurely morning and decided to head into Perth a little earlier and have a coffee before our 2.55pm appointment. David and I chatted, trying to stay positive and calm. We saw a different nurse and a different doctor than those present at my surgery. He gave us the devastating results: forty-five lymph nodes removed with forty-four being cancerous! Type of breast cancer: Duct. Two tumours were removed, one being 24mm and the other 7mm. Tumour Grade: three. Oestrogen and Progesterone receptor status were both negative. HER2 status: 3+ positive. HER2 derives from a protein called human epidermal growth factor receptor 2. This protein promotes the growth of cancer cells. Ugghh!

The doctor then examined me before Mr Fernandez was able to join us. They drained a bit of the fluid build-up with a needle from my armpit (60ml), but as it was numb, it didn't hurt that much.

I had physiotherapy with Emma for forty-five minutes afterwards and it really helped my pain. We were home by 6pm, both of us in shock.

Thursday 24 March 2011

I've laid low for the past two days. I sent a text to everyone and have received lots of encouraging replies back. I haven't felt like being positive and chirpy for anyone. David and I took the girls for a walk at the school oval yesterday evening. I've been reading information, watching television and now I've got a face mask on trying to act normal at least.

Pa left a message on my mobile saying Ma had taken three bottles of beer and her handbag, and gone walkabouts again. I've got enough on my plate without having to respond to Pa's plea again. I always try to give advice and listen... I'm too tired and spent to be able to offer anything at the moment. Universe, please forgive me for not jumping in to help and rescue them yet again. They are responsible for their own lives and Soul journeys. I am responsible for my own actions, feelings and thoughts.

I have been doing my arm exercises and massaging all the sore spots. It feels like there's broken glass all over my upper arm and elbow area, but I do feel it's getting better and stronger! *Good girl; keep it up, Sorja.* Another positive is that the land is ours now. We've approved our final house plans and the next step is the concrete slab down, hopefully soon. Life keeps on chugging along...

I must say that I am proud of myself. I watered the plants all by myself. I washed the dishes, put clothes away and, just now, I completed one kilometre of walking on speed three on the treadmill. Good girl, Sorja.

Friday 25 March 2011

What a hullabaloo kind of day! My eldest sister, Kirsti, and her family came over. They had arrived from Queensland yesterday for Visa and Susie's wedding and, after many changed plans, fifteen of us ended up having lunch together at the Rockingham foreshore. I asked Irma to drop me home at 2.30pm, as it was too taxing on me to join them in their afternoon pursuits. Tomorrow is the big day—

my brother's wedding day.

Monday 28 March 2011

On Saturday morning I was chilling and feeling pretty good until David and I had a huge fight before getting ready for the wedding. I was sick and tired of him moping around all woe-is-me like... Admittedly, he's had days of stress headaches, and he's not looking after himself, so he's gained weight again. Consequently, he's snoring like a trooper! This is making me as mad as hell, if you can't tell. He argued, 'My wife has breast cancer; what do you expect?' He said he was too busy looking after me to look after himself. Bullshit!

'No, you are not looking after me; the best way to look after me is to take care of yourself,' I said. 'Take your tablets, watch your diet and exercise.' I am so worried about him dying of a heart attack because of his weight and the amount of stress he is under, and I don't need to have that concern on top of everything else.

'I have a feeling Ma and Pa will ruin the wedding,' he added at one point. 'Maybe the wedding will be cancelled.'

I was furious. Of course, I just lost it! As a result of our full-blown yelling match, I was running late to shower and get ready. As normally happens in the frame of mind I was in, everything appeared to go wrong after that. My skin flared up, my armpit wounds were festering, and I had a hard time making the two suture sites stop bleeding... on and on and on... We were fifteen minutes late leaving the house. When we were finally in the car, I put on my iPod and tried to ignore David until he tapped me to ask me about directions to the wedding. Are you kidding me? We had months to sort it out and he was leaving it to the last minute. Unbelievable! Men!

As you can imagine, I was not at all in party mode. We still arrived in plenty of time, thank God. Apparently, I looked better than I felt. After greeting Nikiita, Katri, Ma and Pa and, of course, Visa the groom, I started to calm down. The champagne helped too, ha, ha, ha…

When Visa and Susie exchanged their vows, I started crying. It was all too much. I took lots of wonderful photos, and the rest of the ceremony, including the drinks and nibblies, went fabulously. I tried to keep Ma and Pa company, as they looked so lonely. And yes, they behaved and did not ruin the wedding! We wrapped up at the venue at 8.30pm and continued on to Visa and Susie's place. Katri dropped Ma and Pa back to her place before joining us. A bunch of us continued chatting, drinking and taking photos until David and I left at midnight. We arrived home after 1am. By this time, David and I had kissed and made up after our fight. David apologised—we both did—and he said that his behaviour did not help me. I said that I smiled even when I didn't feel like it and that you couldn't always drag people down. Sometimes, you had to pretend instead of acting 'woe-is-me'.

On Sunday, after a very restless night on my part, David made me breakfast in bed—thanks, Love—and later Irma, Khan and I went to see the movie *Rango*. It's amazing how many people don't laugh in this life. We laughed so much while other adults just sat like zombies with no expressions on their faces.

I went to bed at 10.30pm, which is early for me, but woke up feeling fearful and in pain at 4am. My wound has become infected and my breast is very red and hot, probably a staph infection. Because of my concerns, I called up the breast care nurse today and she said she was happy to see me before my oncologist appointment at Royal Perth Hospital.

Irma and I left at 1.45pm and reached the city at 2.30pm; we grabbed a coffee and then went to the clinic. It was definitely a staph infection! The breast care nurse told me to keep it dry and to ask my Perth oncologist, Dr Andrew Redfern, to prescribe antibiotics and painkillers. Irma and I spent from 4pm until 5.30pm with the oncologist. He looked at my wound, agreed it was infected, and gave me my required prescriptions. Dr Redfern kindly and thoroughly answered our multitude of questions. In essence, my IVF did not cause this cancer. In fact, contrary to my beliefs, I am not at fault. The genes or chromosomes just went haywire very aggressively and now we have to treat them just as aggressively! He went through the process of chemotherapy, the many different drugs I will be on and the side effects. He went through the length of time of treatment: about four to six cycles of chemotherapy and then, after my first four cycles, Herceptin every three weeks for a full year. The information was so involved that, according to Irma, I went all bug-eyed, with red veins sticking out of my eyes. By the end of the session, I was exhausted and hungry, as I had skipped lunch. A stale sandwich soon fixed that. We caught the 6pm train. We went via a chemist to get my scripts filled, arriving home by 7.15pm.

I am overwhelmed. Why is it that when I feel this way, I hit the wine to numb myself even further? It's most likely because I have seen my parents react to everything by drinking alcohol; they have been my role models of resorting to unhealthy coping mechanisms. I know wine is not systematically good for me, but emotionally it helps sometimes. I keep getting told these words by my Spirit Guides: *Healing comes in many forms.* I'm not sure whether they approve or disapprove of my particular methods; however, I do know that we always have free will in our lives. I am so tired of these extremes of emotion. I know this is all a part of the journey I agreed upon before incarnating into this body and this life. I have to accept all of it, not just the good bits.

Irma wants me to read the *Conversations With God* series of books by Neale Donald Walsch. I know she means well and doesn't want me to give up and die. Nobody does. They all keep saying how well I look and how strong I am. I feel like I am doing this for them sometimes, all of the pain and disappointments over and over and over again. Please help me, Universe, my Guardian Angels, my Reiki Masters and my Spirit Guides. I need all your combined strength and prayers. No, I am *not* being a drama queen; I am just human.

Earlier today, my hairdresser, Alison, cut my shoulder length hair to a short, pixie style again, as there is a ninety-five per cent chance of hair loss with my chemotherapy regime. I wanted some control and say in when it comes off—or most of it anyway. It took me two years to grow it to this length and half an hour to chop it off. It's unfair and it sucks!

David says I am focusing too much on my tests and treatments and I need to switch off. So easy for him to say and so bloody hard for me to do. Prime example, it is now 1am and David is sleeping peacefully while I am wide awake. I have physio tomorrow at 2pm, and I have a friend who is coming to keep me company, which I appreciate.

It's so hard. I'm crying again. I did nothing wrong to cause this. It wasn't my diet, my drinking, my exercise or even my IVF. The oncologist did say, however, that my recovery and the chance of reoccurrence is affected by obesity, exercise, vitamin D, fruit and vegetables and, to a lesser extent, alcohol intake. I am able to continue all of my natural therapies, but I am to cease three days prior to my chemo. I am able to recommence four days after my chemo. In between, my antioxidants and ProFeme cream are all okay. What a relief. So f------ tired. Bed or music?

P.S. There are two lymph nodes they will have to keep an eye on as the scans showed small signs of inflammation under the clavicular and in the middle of my chest. Chemotherapy will shrink them and Herceptin will stop the growth. They will be monitored throughout my treatment as will my heart because Herceptin has been known to damage the heart muscle. Oh, bloody great.

Wednesday 30 March 2011

I woke up to the song 'Human' by The Killers in my mind. Isn't it funny how words can stay in your head? Yesterday, I had one hour of gruelling physio on my arm, mostly the upper arm and elbow area. My physiotherapist, Emma, did not want to go anywhere near my inflammation so as not to aggravate it even further. Oooh, it was so painful but, like she said, it's one step forward and two steps back, and you sometimes feel more pain before it gets better. She complimented me on my hairstyle and said short hair suited me.

I had a fever and chills last night. I think all the massaging forced the inflamed lymph vessels to work harder but, on the positive side, my arm is a lot straighter now. I slept with my arm on a pillow, keeping it straight most of the time. Today, I was spent, so I mixed my household chores with periods of rest. My energy levels waver so much. The inflammation is still very red but not as sore as it was, and the antibiotics are slowly kicking in. Dr Andy Redfern called to say my treatment will commence in two weeks' time, at Royal Perth Hospital for the first few cycles and then later I'll be transferred to Rockingham. My heart scan will happen in the next week.

Sunday 3 April 2011

All of these bloody family conflicts, dramas and miscommunication! I am so angry. This is a time in my life when I need the support of all of my family. Unfortunately, Ma and Pa felt unwelcome, as if they were intruding, partly due to David being protective of me. That is apparently the reason they left our place early. Argh! It was all another case of miscommunication, this time David being misunderstood.

After discovering the reason Mum and Dad left, I had an argument with David last night. Poor David copped it once again! I didn't yell at him, but I told him how angry I was at him. As with any argument, they can easily sidetrack into other unresolved conflicts. I said that I showed interest in the house plans, and the least he could do is to show interest in my cancer! Oh dear… He replied that he had read all the pamphlets and information packs but only when I was in the shower or napping. I asked him why he had to keep it such a secret and why he didn't do it in the open. I thought he had been putting his blinkers on and pretending it was not happening. If any good came out of this argument, it was the clearing of the air and being honest with each other. I said that Irma was on his side too and was able to see it from his perspective: his new job and the stress that goes with it; our new house and dreams; and his wife who's been ill for most of his married life. David said that he didn't think of me that way. It gave us both 'food for thought' anyway…

Today, Katri came for the day and we had a cuppa before picking Irma up for a walk at Pt Peron. It was a gorgeous day of 31ºC. We soaked our feet in the warm ocean and thoroughly enjoyed our walk. Later, Katri and I looked at the wedding photos before she had to drive home. David had the day to himself to catch up on his chores and much needed sleep, as he'd had a restless night after our spat. He looked so sad and tired all day. He must get so fed up with having to explain himself to us. I'm sorry, David. I do love you.

My range of arm movement has improved, but the arm and breast are still bright red and hot to the touch. I'll have to call the doctor to see about more antibiotics. I also have to call the Crawford Lodge Wig Service and see about a new hairdo...

Tuesday 5 April 2011

It's nice to be able to drive again after three and a half weeks of not driving and relying on others. Today, I left at 11am, found Rockingham train station car park full yet again and so drove to Kwinana station. Oh well, go with the flow. Dr Redfern had been kind enough to organise an appointment with a doctor at the Breast Clinic at short notice when I rang him yesterday. The doctor and breast care nurse both looked concerned over how red my skin was after one week of antibiotics, and Mr Fernandez came to look at it as well. He was happy with the scar healing so well but agreed that I needed another week of antibiotics for the infection. If it wasn't any better after that, he would recommend that my chemotherapy be postponed. I believe that it will all be clear by the weekend.

As I was late for my appointment with Emma, and she had another client booked after me, we just chatted for a few minutes. Emma couldn't work on my armpit area anyway, so she said for me to allow the healing process and to keep doing my arm exercises but not to force the movement.

Friday 8 April 2011

Wow, one month since my surgery. I was just able to hang some clothes on the line outside for the first time since then. Woohoo, progress. The second round of antibiotics is working, and the soreness and redness is finally going away slowly but surely, thank God.

On Wednesday, I had a bad night's sleep so I was already sluggish but I pushed myself to get ready. I met Katri in Perth for a coffee and cookie before we caught a train to Nedlands. We walked a little distance to Crawford Lodge Wig Service. We spent less than an hour there and it did feel a bit rushed, as I couldn't try on all of the wigs I wanted to. I found the experienced volunteer to be less helpful than the younger trainee. It was as if she wanted me to hurry up and choose a wig my own natural colour. Luckily, Katri and I were assertive enough to ask for red wigs to try on. The lady had to eat her words when she saw that the red colours actually suited me and my complexion. Why stick to my normal hair colour when what I'm going through is anything but normal?

I was only allowed to borrow one wig, so we settled on a shoulder length red wig with highlights, but I was also able to choose three turbans and a couple of bright scarves. Katri helped steer them away from colours that just weren't me, such as pukey pastels. I look like a totally different woman with the red hair. David, Katri and Irma liked it a lot.

Katri and I had lunch and a glass of wine at an Italian restaurant before catching a bus back to Perth. I bought a large black shoulder bag for my hospital visits, as I'm struggling to carry everything in my normal handbag. I was thoroughly exhausted when I got home and napped a little again. I seem to be doing a lot of that lately. *Oh well, go with the flow, Sorja.*

On Thursday, Khan was sick with a stomach bug and Irma was

stuck, so I let Khan stay with me for the day. I can't do that after I've had chemo. I told Irma that and she knows she'll have to make other arrangements when she is working. He watched television in the living room, and I stayed on the futon in the other room watching movies. I also listened to the CD for men whose partners are going through breast cancer; it was excellent and made me teary but also helped me to look at it from David's perspective.

Later that night, after Irma had collected Khan and David had gone to bed, I really let go and cried and cried and cried. I had put on a brave face when modelling my red wig for them all, but reality hit me hard in the face when I was alone. I even felt guilty asking David to take another day off for my physio and radiology appointments on 21 April. I can't catch a train as I'm too scared of how I will be feeling and looking. I need someone to take me and be with me. I can't do this on my own. I know David can take carer's leave, as the company he works for is very supportive and his bosses are very understanding.

Today, I slept in until 11am (OMG) after my very emotional night sitting outside on the bricks at midnight just bawling my eyes out. Anyway, no rest for the wicked. I have a lot to do today, such as house chores, food shopping and errands to run at the shopping centre.

Monday 11 April 2011

Yesterday, David and I drove to our block of land in South Yunderup. The sand had been levelled out, and there were outlines of where the concrete slab is to go down, as well as a water tap and a porta-loo! Progress, hee hee hee... Afterwards, we explored the surroundings a bit more—the display homes and the town of Pinjarra where we couldn't pass up coffee and pancakes at Dome

Café. We drove home via the chemist for more painkillers and some haemorrhoid cream, as unfortunately I've had them for over six weeks. Even though I'm going to the toilet regularly, my body is rejecting this regime of antibiotics and painkillers. On a positive note, my armpit staph infection is almost gone. It is only pink now instead of angrily red and inflamed.

I was restless watching television in the evening and decided to take my glass of wine into my painting room and start a new painting. Oh, what fun. I only managed one hour before I grew tired, but that was a good start and I will continue…

Today, I tried calling to see if there is a *breast cancer* support group in this area of Safety Bay but no, the closest is Attadale or Armadale. OMG! As if any woman is going to drive that far when she's not feeling one hundred per cent. There are more generalised cancer support groups here; I may check them out, but I don't know. There is a need for a breast cancer support group here in the Rockingham/Mandurah area, so… more reason for me to set one up when I have recovered. I got chills in my entire body the other day when I was thinking about running my own group.

I had my heart scan in the city this afternoon. The trip there went smoothly this time and I had plenty of time to walk from the train station to the hospital, have a bite to eat and drink a cup of tea. At 2pm, I went to the Nuclear Medicine department for my injection of dye. I had to wait one hour for it to travel to my heart and around. I went to the cafeteria to read whilst it did its job. I didn't have to take my clothes or jewellery off for this scan, just drink copious amounts of water to push my stomach out of the way before the scan.

Once again, I meditated for half an hour, thinking of beaches, sunsets, waterfalls, puppies, my girls—anything but the machine hovering over me, making noises and creating a slight pressure against me. It was weird to have a picture of a waterfall pop into my head, but after the scan finished and I waited for them to make sure they didn't need to repeat the procedure, I looked into a room behind me. There were posters of four different waterfalls! Maybe I had astral travelled?

Thankfully, I was told I could leave and I didn't waste any time in walking back to the train station. I was so tired that I listened to music the whole journey back and then drowsily drove home from the station. Tomorrow is my first cycle of chemotherapy. Universe, wish me luck. No side effects, please, and let me cruise through it all...

Chapter 21

Cancer Sucks!

Thursday 14 April 2011

In a nutshell, because I'm too sick and tired to go into every detail… We left home at 7.45am, driving through peak hour traffic so that we arrived at 9.10am. (So much for the nutshell, eh?) We waited from 9.30am until 10.30am in a dingy, old waiting room full of other patients waiting for their oncology appointments or treatments. After speaking to Allison, a co-worker of Andy's, I found out my heart is strong and they now have a baseline for future scans. We waited for another half an hour for the meds to be ordered.

The treatment room was chocker block full of cancer patients and their support people, young and old, male and female. The woman next to me was also going through her first chemo for breast cancer (she even has HER2). We chatted a bit and her daughter was there too. Their husband and father had gone through chemo last year but had sadly passed away in November. Now the mother was seeing the same nurses for her own treatment. This is some kind of life, eh?

My saline solution had gone through before midday, and by this time I had shooed David away. He was so nervous and frustrated about the waiting time that his restlessness was stressing me out. Thank God the nurses know what they are doing, applying a heating pack to my right arm and hand to get the veins to stick out; the fluid pumping in also helped with my hydration. Thankfully, they provided lunch and I listened to my iPod to keep me calm and centred. David returned in time to hear at least half of the nurse's instructions about the side-effects, what to do and what not to do, what to avoid and so forth.

At 12.11pm, I was infused with Doxorubicin, also known as Adriamycin, three tubes of bright red solution. I felt an odd chemical taste in my mouth like you do when you have an anaesthetic. David looked quite pale and asked me how I felt. I flippantly said, 'What, do you expect? My head to rotate three hundred and sixty degrees and for me to spew green vomit all over the place like in *The Exorcist*?'

The nurse smiled and said, 'Oh, please, I hope you don't.'

David went to buy lunch for himself and escape for a bit, which was totally understandable.

After my saline was finished, my next drug, Cyclophosphamide, was infused intravenously; this was a clear coloured fluid in a small bag. I felt a little nauseous and the cannula site stung and pinched. The nurse was able to apply a heating pack on it to relieve that sensation. Finally, one bag of saline to flush the vein and then we could go.

It was 1.45pm by now. David and I took the opportunity for a coffee and cookie break—I had a 2pm appointment at the Breast Clinic to check on my staph infection. Glennys called me in to have a quick look and, as she wasn't one hundred per cent happy, Mr Fernandez came to check it. He was so funny. He was so impressed by his handiwork on my breast (no pun intended) that he nodded to himself happily and asked what Glennys thought. How funny to have two people looking at your breasts and comparing the results. I really believe that the Arnica 6c helped it heal and shape up much quicker than they expected. He was okay for me to stop taking the antibiotics, especially as I had begun my chemotherapy.

While we waited in the Breast Clinic, I spoke to two other women going through similar treatments. They talked about problems with their drains, and they'd both had repeated seromas, one of them six times, the other three. I was lucky that I only had one. I know I have worked hard on my rehabilitation exercises on my arm and just moving and doing chores. You've got to keep moving, Sorja, it really helps! I asked one of the women if she did her exercises and she assured me she did, but she is morbidly obese and I think that she may not be moving quite enough. Anyway, who am I to judge? We all have our own journeys…

We went home via the shops and got back before 5pm. I rested, as by this stage I was feeling some side effects: body aches, muscle spasms and twitching, headache, nausea, dry eyes and a dry mouth. We made a very unwise choice for dinner—takeaway Indian beef curry. It took me forty-five minutes to slowly eat it, as it was hard for me to swallow the solid food. This also contributed to me feeling ill all night. I had to take anti-nausea drugs and painkillers to help me through the night. Lessons learned the hard way, eh? Sticking to easily digestible foods and drinks is the way to go.

On Wednesday, I still felt pretty crappy but I didn't want to mope at home. Irma came to the rescue. We went for a lovely walk on the beach for forty-five minutes and picked up Khan from school, with a detour to the shops to buy colloidal silver, as my staph infection looked like it was inflamed and rearing its ugly head again! I spoke to Dr Redfern first. I didn't want to go on antibiotics again, so I wanted to give the colloidal silver a chance, and he said I could give it a go and see what happened.

We then went to buy ingredients for Irma's healing soup. I'd asked her to make it for me as it is easier to digest and full of good nutrients. I tried to nap whilst Irma cooked, and Khan watched television. I listened to calming American Indian music, but I couldn't sleep because of severe indigestion and colic-like pains. I decided to move a bit by watering the plants. I managed to shower and eat a bit of the soup even though I felt very nauseous.

This morning, I didn't crawl out of bed until 11am, as I had frequent trips to the toilet during the night, with all of my fluid retention being released thanks to the soup and the chemo, and being back on my progesterone cream. I've managed some porridge and coffee. I feel better, just a bit queasy and headachy still. This will all pass with time. I think I have enough energy for a bit of housework.

Oh yes, how could I forget? One other side effect for the first twenty-four hours is that your pee is a pinky red from the chemo, not actual blood, just the colour. It's now after 5pm and I am proud of myself. I managed two hours of housework. It helped to keep my mind off how I feel. A good distraction... not sure it is advised, but it worked for me...

Saturday 16 April 2011

Happy forty-seventh birthday, Irma. Well, yesterday was a total write-off! I woke up feeling so yucky that I kept dozing throughout the day. I had absolutely no energy and everything seemed like such an effort, even reading on the sunlounge outside. I've been having so many nightmares every night that I know my body is in turmoil and battling my inner demons while I sleep. My headaches and nausea have continued, and I've had a hard time distracting myself from it this time.

I received a call from Irma in the afternoon—the family drama continues. Mum and Dad have headed off to Queensland already! Some misunderstanding again I bet, such as not feeling welcome—who knows the truth? Ma and Pa are obviously deteriorating in their mental faculties, and their alcoholism leads them to see or hear things that aren't necessarily true.

I'm just in survival mode and not able to say the right things to everyone. I can't be their counsellor all the bloody time, and I have the right to not get as involved in my family dramas. I think that I have enough on my plate! Pa's brother in Finland is in intensive care after suffering a fall and an aneurism in the brain. I think my parents' modus operandi is to react to bad news by escaping. Thinking that his brother and youngest daughter are both suffering is all too much for Pa.

David was lovely and supportive when he got home. We took the girls for a walk and I was able to talk to him about it all. He said that he wasn't going anywhere and was in it for the long haul. We had to focus on good things such as our house and our winter escape holiday at the end of May.

Today, I feel better and I'm going to try without the anti-nausea tablets. I've been able to go back on the purple carrot juice and other vitamins, which is good because I've got visitors coming over later, and I would like to feel semi-normal.

Monday 18 April 2011

Julie's visit was good but I became tired towards the end. She was confused as to why I still had my breast, so I explained the breast conservation surgery process, my HER2 cancer and so forth. I only had a ten-minute break before Visa, Susie and, later, Irma arrived. Susie gave me a foot massage on the couch; it was kind and loving of her. I was able to sit up on a chair for a while, but then my back was killing me, so I lay on the couch. I tried to drink a glass of white wine; it took me two and a half hours and it wasn't even a full glass. It tasted like vinegar, just like my coffees... so unfair! It's only temporary, I'm sure. I feel like I'm being forced into a major detox and cleanse through all of this (apart from the chemo, ha, ha, ha). Julie said that my skin glowed. That's one good thing, eh? They stayed for three hours and I was stuffed by the time everyone left. It was nice to have company and family time, though.

I've been thinking... this is a second chance for me, a renewal. All my cells will be re-born through this treatment. I'll have new hair, new skin and new cells. I will not waste this opportunity for re-birth into a stronger and healthier human being. Drinking too much wine as a coping mechanism for stress, disappointment and sadness has been my downfall. I think, to a degree, it is a huge issue with most members of my family. It's not healthy and it's destructive to all of our relationships.

On Sunday, Katri came over for the day. David went to check on our house and found progress; the wire mesh was down ready for the concrete. After a cuppa and biscotti, Katri and I went for an hour's walk. I pushed myself hard, probably too much too soon, but I loved the sea air in my face. I nearly fainted towards the end, but I was stubborn (so not like me!) and wanted to walk all the way back to the car—practising the idiom of 'mind over matter'. I was proud of myself. I must admit I had to eat something really quickly when we got home as I felt faint.

On the evening of Sunday 17 April, I heard some tragic news via a text from Katri. In Finland, our cousin Sari had died from heart problems and was buried three days ago. Our uncle Rauno (Pa's brother) had also died and was buried today! Apparently, our other uncle (Sari's father, Mauri) called Pa today. We were all aware of Rauno's ill health and expecting his death, but our cousin was only thirty-nine. What a shock! I remember her tagging along in Finland when I was ten and she was only five. Sari followed me everywhere and I thought her a pest. I also remember going back to Finland at nineteen years of age; she was fourteen and going through a punk rock phase. I didn't know her as an adult and that is sad. My aunt Ritva must be absolutely devastated to bury her daughter and her brother in the space of one week. Poor Pa must be heartbroken, and I pray he doesn't do anything stupid to himself out of anger and grief.

I didn't sleep well last night, always during full moon, but I kept chanting to myself. *I feel better. Thank you for my healing. I am safe. I am at peace. I am calm.* Today, I have felt better, not one hundred per cent, but improving every day. Irma visited and we chatted about life, us, family and the importance of feeling grateful to be ALIVE.

During meditation, I have had a vision of my body being covered with ladybugs and birds, a sign of good luck. I had another vision of hundreds of people holding a large python. Everyone stood in a row and held a part of it. The python represents my kundalini life force energy. I have lots of love, support and prayer around me. I am very grateful. I am a SURVIVOR. I am going to get through this one day at a time.

Good Friday 22 April 2011

I've had a recurring dream of washing loads of dishes for other family members. My conclusion is that I don't have to clean up other people's messes. I'm also dreaming of eating foods with blueberries; I need to eat blueberries for the antioxidants. Over the last few days, I've resumed normal activities. I even contacted the Cancer Council to find out what's available in the Rockingham region as far as support is concerned. There is a 'Look Good, Feel Better' program happening right here in Rockingham in early May, as well as yoga, meditation and Reiki through the Cancer Council.

Yesterday, David and I went to Perth. We bought scarves for me, ate lunch and then I attended my physio appointment, not with Emma who was on holidays, but another lady, Chris. She was pleased with my progress and now I just have to work on my range of movement, as the cording is gone, thanks to God and all of my own hard work. Also, the staph infection has finally gone, with only pink skin remaining now.

At 3pm, I saw the Radiology Oncology department oncologist. It was hard to hear that I am at 'high risk' due to the number of cancerous lymph nodes. She also said that the node in my chest is most likely cancerous, and that is why the chemo will be so important in reducing the size and killing it! My radiation won't start until my chemo has finished and will involve five to six weeks, Monday to Friday, of treatment that takes about twenty minutes each time. I will have to have scans to ensure they zap the right spots and I will have small tattoos to mark the field.

More and more heart scans and body scans to check if lymph nodes reduce in size over the course of treatment, blah, blah and blah... A year or more of this? It's hard not to feel overwhelmed by it all. Heavy sigh. I have to focus on the positives, such as going to check out our house; the concrete slab is down. Woo hoo!

Saturday 23 April 2011

David has been quite out of sorts for the past two days, and it is good for us to have a break from each other when I go up to the hills for a few days tomorrow. I understand his stress levels, what with work, the house and, of course, me... It's only normal for him to snap a little. He did apologise tonight, saying that with all I'm going through, he's supposed to be supportive and not short-tempered. I explained that I'm trying to have fun with my sisters and my friends on the days I feel good to make up for the days I feel rotten. I told him that he was human and it was okay for him not to be perfect.

Wednesday 27 April 2011

Another challenge, or should I say milestone. After my blood test at the hospital, I was on the toilet at home and noticed that my pubic hair was falling out after wiping. I plucked a few to test them and it all started to come off in my hand! It was so bizarre and felt unreal. It didn't take any effort to pluck them, and it was making such a mess that I just went ahead and shaved it all off. I am not wasting time having clumps coming off each toilet visit. I shed a few tears afterwards as I realised that my scalp hair wasn't going to remain for long either because it was already thinning out.

I'd better go on the treadmill so that I don't get too upset and so I gain some energy. Even if I just walk, it's better than nothing. Just bloody great! Half of my back tooth came off when I had my lunch. Another letdown by my physical body!

I went to meditation tonight for a bit of spiritual equilibrium to balance out the physical. I was restless, as I had back pain while sitting in the chair at meditation, therefore I was grateful to feel healing energy emanating from multiple unseen spiritual hands. In my visualisation I saw darkness and lightness in turns. I also got an image of my Spirit Guide, White Horse, followed by a vulture eating dead meat, then a spotted baby deer.

I analysed this as the vulture eating my cancer away, and renewal afterward represented by Bambi. Carol, who runs the meditation, saw Pac men just like I visualise during chemotherapy. She saw rebirth for me, with some very exciting times and experiences in the future—in meditations, in Reiki and in life. Some good will come from this period of my life. Carol also gave me a gift, a CD called *Getting Ready* by Dr Bernie Siegel. It's to do with how you approach therapies, ways to help you to live and not die. Your thoughts travel all the way to each cell, so it's important to think of it all as *rebirth*.

Thursday 28 April 2011

Today, I felt depressed because when I shower, my hair falls out in clumps so easily. I already have to do a comb over so that my scalp doesn't show through my thinning hair. My tooth has a temporary filling, as the dentist said she wasn't allowed to drill or give needles during chemotherapy treatment. It'll last until I can have it replaced with a permanent one once chemo finishes but before radiation starts, as they can't do anything during radiation treatment either. I'm having some champagne (why the bloody hell not?) whilst I cook meatballs and vegetables for dinner.

Sunday 1 May 2011

Highs and lows... On Friday, I watched the fairy tale wedding of Prince William and Catherine. Yesterday, Katri came over for the weekend and we went for coffee and to the cinema which was nice. Last night, I had a breakdown when I showered and the hair was falling off and onto my face, sticking to my face and feeling creepy like something from a horror movie! I cried and cried and cried in the shower, but no-one heard, as they were asleep. Afterwards, I lay on the couch and listened to Josh Groban on my iPod and let the tears flow on... David woke up when he rolled over and realised I wasn't in the bed. He found me on the couch and, after talking a little and comforting me, he persuaded me to go to bed, where I tossed and turned the rest of the night.

Today, David was very gentle with me. He suggested we go to Pinjarra for breakfast then visit our block of land and house. I managed to feel semi-normal by spiking up my remaining hair, applying some make-up and dressing in nice clothes. Katri, David and I had a delicious breakfast at Dome Café, then we went to admire our slab of concrete and the power box.

Afterwards, Katri and I walked along the beach for nearly an hour. We then sat watching the many pelicans catching the warm air currents, so free and loving life. Of course, we had to enjoy an ice-cream after all of that exercise, hee hee hee... My taste buds are back to normal and food tastes good again, just in time for the next round of chemotherapy...

Now to the downside of things... I went into the shower and this time I wanted to just scream and scream and scream! My hair was coming off all over my face, chest and down my back. It was such a horrific, creepy feeling: slimy from the shampoo, itchy and so alien it felt like it was not mine at all. I kept plucking the clumps out of the drain so that it wouldn't block up the whole system. *It'll grow back, it'll grow back*, I chanted to myself. *I let go, I let God.*

Feeling as though I was going to crack up and go totally insane, I heaved with cries and screams from deep inside my Soul. By the time I exited the shower, dried myself and looked in the mirror, I think I did go a bit insane. As I ran my comb and hands through my hair, it just would not stop shedding in clumps from my scalp. I balled my eyes out and could not stop myself from plucking out my hair until I was half bald. I was sick of it coming off in strips and strands upon my pillow at night or whenever I combed it. I wanted to take some of the anger out on my hair, thinking, *Fuck it! If you want to come out, then fucking come out then!* Does that make sense?

There is no way I can walk out the door without a scarf or turban or wig now. It was obvious to David how upset I was when I came out and quickly walked into the laundry with my dirty clothes. He followed me there, looked at me, looked at my scalp and just took me in his arms. We both cried and cried, and he shushed me to try and calm my hysterical sobbing. After a long time, we ate dinner. David went to shower and I put on my woollen cap. David asked me if it was for his benefit and I replied, 'No, it's so that I can't see my remaining hair and scalp in my reflection.'

I feel like I've been in fear for so long. I was so afraid of my hair falling out and now that most of it has, I realise that I'm still here, still alive, just more vulnerable. I look like a newborn with my few wisps of hair left. I know that I am loved and I have to keep going on, no matter what. I can't give up! Never, ever give up! This is my life; I have to live for me, not for anybody else.

Monday 2 May 2011

Boy, the tears are a-flowing... I gazed in the mirror and I looked like a cancer patient; I couldn't deny it any longer. Just to make my morning, Misha had diarrhoea all over the living room mat and carpet. Oh, what joy to clean it up first thing in the morning before brekkie.

I sat outside drinking my coffee and trying to cheer up with the gorgeous weather—sunny and 25°C. I got the mail, which included a card from Ma and Pa... Can you believe Ma sent me a 'Congratulations' card! WTF? It has funny pictures of a cat and two dogs with big googly eyes and reads, *A special message just to say...* It was supposed to be a sound card when you open it up, but the battery was dead and it just makes a gurgling woofing and meowing noise. The rest of the card says, *Congrats to you and have a great day!*

Congratulations for what? My cancer?

Then Ma has written, *Hai, paranehan nopeasti ja iloista tulevaisuutta. Rakkaudella Ma, Pa, Gipsy ja Bussicat.* It translates as *Hi, Get well soon and a happy future. With love Ma, Pa, Gipsy and Bussicat.* That's caused me to have conflicting feelings and emotions: anger, hurt, upset, confusion and resignation but tolerance also. They are not quite in their right minds and her twisted humour hurts and inflicts pain. I don't even think they understand why we get upset. I mean, who sends a congrats card to a person at their lowest point in life?

They have let me down so often in the past and when I need sympathy, encouragement, pure love and support, what do I get from them? Alcoholic insanity. Another message for us to reduce our alcohol consumption. I've been doing a lot of emotional eating and drinking as a coping mechanism in the past week. At least I'm feeling my emotions with tears and righteous anger. I think I'll go and punch my boxing bag to get rid of this rage in a healthy way... Who knows? Maybe Ma meant the house construction and the card was supposed to cheer me up? I'm unsettled at the moment. I've got my second chemo tomorrow—well, physio at 9.45am, bloods at 10.30am, doctor's at 11am and then chemo afterwards. Another big day for me. Whoopee, I ended up doing forty-five minutes of boxing, dancing, resistance bands and stretches; I feel better for it.

Wednesday 4 May 2011

Well that's two down. We arrived in the city by 9.15am for my appointment with Emma. She had another PT trainee with her and I was okay with that. I told her about my accomplishments, and she looked a bit shocked and concerned that I was doing too much. Emma told me that my limit should be ten to fifteen minutes of light boxing or band work, certainly not my workout session of forty-five minutes. I was being a 'stuperduck' again—a stupid super Duck. On the positive side, my improvement has happened in 'leaps and bounds'. She said that a lot of people have the cording last for months and months. I told her that I had done what she told me to do. I'd also pushed myself with housework and food shopping. Emma advised me to take it more slowly with heavy bags as the cording could return as a result. My breast had some fluid build-up, protein and water, so she massaged it and showed me how to do it myself while lying down if David wasn't comfortable doing it for me. I have to be less impatient with my progress and gentler on myself. Emma recommended the exercise classes but they are held in Mandurah. I'll see…

I had my bloods taken and then went up to see Dr Alison White in Medical Oncology. The waiting room was fairly empty, as most people had come earlier in the day and were in the treatment room already. When we saw Dr White, I told her about my symptoms from the last chemo and she said that they all sounded like normal reactions. I also asked about the safety of using Recktinol—for my haemorrhoids—longer than the package recommended. She said that after my treatment was complete, I could have them banded. Although a simple procedure, I can't have any surgery now; as the cancer treatment is priority. Oh well… I've been using colloidal silver for the past few days and it feels less sore, so I will alternate between the two for relief. I went red with embarrassment talking about it, which is funny because after my comfort in showing my breasts all the time, what's my bum but another piece of anatomy? No shame in that. Just like the English show *Embarrassing Bodies*.

I told David to get himself lunch as I was munching on a sandwich, apple juice and custard provided by the hospital whilst I waited for my drugs to be ready. He looked so pale, uncomfortable and stressed. I wanted him to have a break and he wanted to check out some camping stuff in the mall anyway.

This time the chemo took from 12.30pm to 1.45pm… heat pack, anti-nausea medication, IV fluid, red Pac men (ha, ha, ha) and the white Pac men. David came back for the last half an hour. The treatment room had mostly cleared by then and only a few of us were left. I was the last to leave.

The nurse gave me a cute blue cooler bag with my take home drugs and also an immune booster injection that I have to give myself. Unfortunately, my white blood cell count had dropped too low, so I have to inject a Filgrastim Pegulated 6mg/0.6ml Prefilled Syringe twenty-four hours after my chemo session. This will boost my system so that I don't catch any germs. I can start on my natural immune boosters on Saturday again: my purple carrot juice or blueberry juice, a high concentrate antioxidant that makes you feel energetic and stronger.

It's a combined effort of natural therapies and man-made

medicines as well as my Reiki, meditation and relaxation music that will get me through this. Talking to my body, telling all my cells that I love them and don't resent or hate them, will heal me. I don't think it is helpful to think of it as a battle or a fight, more a rebirth.

Last night, I had a dream. *A man was shooting everybody and I thought that I would distract him and that I would get away, but he found me and pointed the gun at me but before he could shoot me and kill me too, I shouted, 'Stop, I love you!' He was so dumbfounded that he put the gun down.* See? Love is the answer. I think the gunman was the cancer!

I also dreamt of a woman showing me how to fold my scarves to fit my head properly. I had trouble with it in real life, so my female Spirit Guide showed me how to do it in my dream life. Isn't that amazing? Ask and you shall receive answers…

Walking through the hospital with my turban and scarf was an experience. How people looked at me different from normal. I'm used to people looking at my height and my blonde hair, but this was dissimilar. Some were curious, others sympathetic… it's like I have a big sign saying, *Yes, I have cancer.* I walked tall and proud anyway.

Friday 6 May 2011

For the last few days, there have been moments of feeling yuck and then not too bad. I have had a headache for three days though… Yesterday, I spent a few hours outside—or was it Wednesday? The days blend into one. I did walk on the treadmill for half an hour, I remember that. I also slouched on the couch watching movies.

Today, I decided to be brave. I would put on my face and red wig, and go to Rockingham City for lunch, visit Irma and buy PJs from Target. I was nervous before getting out of my car, but then I took a deep breath and just got on with it. You know what? Less people stare at me than when I walk with my normal 'old' blonde hair. I blended in more which surprised me; it was a huge relief. Irma couldn't even find me easily at the food court. She had to search through every red haired woman there. Ha, ha, ha.

After my shopping trip and visiting former work mates at Tall Poppy, Irma, Khan and I went for a short walk by the beach. We looked at the *Castaways* entries for this year—Castaways is the City of Rockingham's signature arts and cultural event, celebrating environmental awareness through artistic innovation; the outdoor sculptural exhibition showcases artworks from Western Australian artists, created from repurposed materials. A lot of them had a dark and sombre quality about them, reflecting the state of many people's minds. The sun was too much for me and by this stage it was nearly 4.30pm, so I was glad to go home. I did so well being away from home for four hours and it was only Friday after having chemo on Tuesday.

I'm finding that the hats, wigs and scarves still put a lot of pressure on my temples as do the glasses. With most of my hair gone, there's no cushioning effect. How do I resolve that, Guides? These pressure headaches are tiring.

Saturday 7 May 2011

David left before 6am for a one-night trial of his solo camping trip to Lane Poole Reserve. It'll do him wonders and I am glad he did it. Have fun, David. I occupied myself with the usual household chores. As I folded the dry clothes off the line, an amazing sight and sound stopped me: five kookaburras landed on our pine tree in the backyard, laughing loudly. I looked at them and their laughter was so contagious that I laughed and laughed with them. They left soon after that. How unusual. I guess they were telling me to laugh and not be so serious all the time.

Thursday 12 May 2011

Five days have gone by so quickly. We have been living with this diagnosis for four months already. On Sunday, Katri and I tried to go for a walk on the beach but, with it being a very hot day, neither one of us could cope with the sun beating down on our heads. So we sat on a bench under a pine tree to watch the world go by instead. Hundreds of white cockatoos fed off the pine trees and gorgeous pelicans flew, or more appropriately glided, over our heads in the bright blue sky. It was just lovely to *feel alive* and appreciate the sun, the sea, the birds and the trees… sounds like a song…

    On Monday, Irma accompanied me to my appointment with my new oncologist, Dr Albert Gan, at Rockingham Hospital. I met Marla, one of the clinical nurses, and she is just lovely. She took my height (taller than normal because of the turban, hee hee hee) and weight (more than my scales at home). Dr Gan was pleasant, too, and very thorough, which is excellent. He asked me what my side effects were. I hadn't mentioned my repeated heartburn and acid reflux to anyone until he asked me that question. Thank God he did, because the tablets he has put me on have helped tremendously, and now I do not have heartburn. He also changed my anti-nausea medication, as the previous one wasn't one hundred per cent effective. He said that it is trial and error as to what works with each different person. The best news is that he is happy to take me on as his patient and my treatments can be done at Rockingham Hospital—so much more convenient for us.

After lunch, Irma and I finished our 'to do list' at the shops. People certainly stared more with me in my turban and scarf; it was pretty obvious. I guess when you think about it, how many people walk around on a warm day wearing what I was wearing? Oh well, I looked quite artistic… a bit like a gypsy or a fortune teller.

I had my *Look Good, Feel Better* day at Rockingham Hospital on Tuesday for two and a half hours. There were about twenty to twenty-five women there including the six volunteers. I shouldn't have bothered putting on 'my face' because I had to remove my make-up to do the workshop, step by step, starting with skincare—cleanse, tone, sun block and moisturise. Then the cosmetologist showed all of us how to build the face—foundation, cover up, powder, eye shadow, eye liner, rouge, eyebrow pencil to sketch in eyebrows (if lost), mascara (if you had eyelashes left), then lip liner and lipstick. We were all gifted with a fabulous assortment of skin products and cosmetics generously donated by a range of cosmetic companies without singling out any particular brand, which was good. It was like Christmas. We were all so spoiled. It felt nice to be pampered and cared for, and I found the whole workshop very uplifting.

We also watched a DVD which demonstrated how to choose a wig and wear it, as well as different ways to tie turbans and scarves. I was the only participant wearing a turban with a scarf; most of the women who had lost their hair wore wigs or scarves alone. The age of the women ranged from forties to seventies, I think. I was surprised to see that a lot of the women were very overweight or obese; I guess some of the cancers are driven by oestrogen, which is found in fat cells. I'm sure not all of the women there had breast cancer; it didn't matter as we had a lot in common, and you could see the fragility underneath the laughter. I got a bit teary myself when we watched the DVD, and I felt all the pain and fear in the room.

Maxine, who is in charge of the chemotherapy treatment room, showed a few of us the facilities. Wow! The treatment room was brand new in October or November 2010 and there are only ten chairs, all of which look very comfy, and each with their own television. There is also space for a few people to accompany you if you wish. The clinical nurses were all very nice and friendly, and I felt so much more at peace with the thought of having my chemotherapy here instead of all that way in Perth. Thank God Dr Gan approved me into his clinic with the referral from Dr Redfern.

I wanted to show off my stash of freebie goodies to Irma so, with a quick detour home to grab some lunch and my anti-nausea tablets as I felt queasy, I drove to her place. Irma was duly impressed. Trent and Khan arrived later, and I showed them my wispy locks of hair. One thing the workshop convinced me to do: shave off the ridiculous comb over I had going on. The few women with shaved heads looked better and more adjusted to their hair loss, so I was going to, too.

Irma was able to buzz cut me right there and then, and Trent and Khan were amazed by the outcome. I've actually got a nice shaped skull under my hair. I felt so much better. No more waking up with hair strands all over my pillowcase. So there!

David got a bit of a shock when I got home but was happy I wasn't as distraught as when chunks of hair were falling out. No siree, I kinda embrace my baldness for now... but, brrrr... it's cold without a scarf or turban or hat! You never realise how much your hair keeps the warmth in, and I totally empathise with bald men and women now.

I'm sitting outside in the sun, under the sunshade, writing this journal. How often do people just STOP, WATCH, LISTEN and FEEL? I see white butterflies dancing with each other, flowers blooming in the warmth of the sun and birds doing aeronautical manoeuvres or balancing acts to suck out the nectar from flowers or to drink from our bird bath. I see our two furry daughters, Misha and Cheyenne, eating goodness knows what from the lawn. I hear a neighbour chain-sawing wood for the coming winter, another neighbour's canary singing joyfully, and a football match being played in the local school sports field in the distance. I hear the gentle wind stirring the leaves and, now and again, a domestic occurring within a flock of small birds, no doubt squabbling over territorial rights.

I feel at peace. I feel comfortable. I feel the warmth of the sun, the slightly cool breeze of autumn blowing my scarf against my face. I feel satiated by the tasty lunch I just consumed outside, not from the lawn like our girls, ha, ha, ha. I feel loved by the world at this very moment.

Last night, I felt compelled to go to meditation, despite the continual back, kidney pain and headache I've had for a week. It ended up being very worthwhile. I received a lot of healing from invisible hands in the Spirit World, as well as numerous messages. I drew the 'snake' card from the deck which read, *Transmute all poisons. Shed the skin of the past. Honour the change in progress.*

I was told by my Spirit Guides that I need to write my book and include all my journal entries and thoughts from my past IVF journey as well as the one I am going through at present. However, I must also include photographs from my transitions, for example, my hair loss, and my paintings—as these represent me, my Soul and my life. I am to be honest and real when I write and publish this book so that

I can help other women to feel less alone, to hopefully talk and share with others about their individual challenges. It's okay not to always show a brave front; I'm learning through this every single day.

I used to spend hours worrying about silly things, such as whether my skin had broken out or if I looked fat in some outfit. Now, I've gone out with no make-up (and lived), worn daggy outfits (so what?) and I worry about losing too much weight through chemotherapy. What a turnaround eh? I don't check my face in the mirror as often as I used to (vain, I know) because I'm too busy with going to the toilet or making sure I'm drinking enough water and eating healthy foods seventy-five per cent of the time (a girl's got to have some treats after all).

Earlier today, Christine Gillies (Cancer support coordinator) visited me at home. I found out about all the free Cancer Council funded services available in the Rockingham/Peel region. These include yoga, meditation, exercise classes, Reiki, reflexology, and counselling sessions. She was another lovely lady and we happily chatted for an hour. I am definitely going to access these services, as they will help balance out the mind, body and Soul.

Saturday 14 May 2011

What a cold day. I watched a couple of medical shows. I didn't know that my grade of cancer, grade three, can sometimes turn into grade four and be the worst-case scenario as it is harder to control. Please, Universe, No! I've been in such a good head space lately, but that news was sobering.

I completed one hour of gardening and weeding for the rental inspection on Thursday. My left hand told me when I had done enough, as it felt bruised, so I have to take it slowly. We went to a friend's birthday drinks, and I dressed up in dramatic red and black to make an artistic statement. It was the first time that they'd seen me in my scarf and turban. It was a good evening, with about ten of us, and I offered to be the designated driver since David was having a good time with the guys and drank more than he normally does. They all commented on how good I looked. I am glad the focus wasn't on me, though, as they talked about other normal stuff. At one point, it was all a bit too much for me; my headache was bothering me again and the sound of their voices was getting to me. I had to try really hard to concentrate on one person at a time.

Monday 16 May 2011

Yesterday, we went to check on our house and the bricks were two thirds done. We took a lot of progress photos and it's all looking so real now—our own house. We then went to our new haunt, the Pinjarra Dome Café, to indulge in pancakes, berries and ice-cream with coffee. This gave us the energy to tackle the rest of the weeding when we got home. Two hours of weeding, yanking grass and raking left me sore and tired but proud of my hard work. After one hour, David told me that he can do more during the week and that I shouldn't overdo it, but I went into my stubborn mode and just wanted it finished. I joked that I wouldn't kill myself with weeding and how bad would that look? Coroner's report: Death by weeding. Ha, ha, ha (sick humour, I know).

Last night, David and I had an argument over his weight gain. He said he was so stressed out with me, my cancer and work, and I told him that he was using it as an excuse! I said that I loved him but how could I respect him when he didn't respect himself? He was always talking about looking after himself and getting fit but not putting any action to his words. I told him that others rolled their eyes whenever I mentioned he had started a fitness regime. They had heard it all before over the past sixteen years, as had I. I argued that the way he was going, I would be burying or cremating him long before I died and was cremated. Harsh but true. His obesity, his stress levels, eating and drinking too many fatty foods and sugary drinks, not taking his vitamins/minerals/supplements or exercising is a recipe for an early death. We've both been using my ill health as a poor excuse for not changing our ways and habits. This is not healthy behaviour and it has got to stop! I may not be obese, but this behaviour is not helping me to fight and win this health challenge.

It's a cloudy day today. I again woke up with a headache, which has been non-stop for weeks. I feel flat and unmotivated to do the required housework for the rental inspection. I even declined a visit from Irma when she rang. She told me about a 'wonder' cancer-curing 'gunk' that draws out the cancer and gave me the name of a website to go on to read real-life stories. I don't think she realises that sometimes it's just too much hearing about all of these miracle cures. It's not that I don't believe them; I just don't have the mental energy to research them. It's sometimes hard enough to just get out of bed and do everyday chores like the laundry and dishes. I find that I can only read a little at a time, especially with this headache.

Wednesday 18 May 2011

The Universe is kind. Yesterday, I found Modern Techniques (Wigs) with no problems and easy car parking. The lady there was nice enough to see me early as I got there before my appointment time. I saw a 'wheat mist' short, blonde wig on a stand and I loved it straight away. We tried on lots of others, but we both agreed this one suited me the best and made me look younger, not older like the darker wigs did. I bought it using my $180 voucher from oncology. I also bought shampoo and conditioner for washing the wig, a wig stand and a night cap, and was happy to pay the extra $115. Well, it was worth it to feel better.

I wore my new wig to my physiotherapist appointment at the Breast Clinic afterwards, and Emma loved it. She said it looked 'au naturale' and really suited me. Emma gave me a bit of physio on my arm, under arm and left breast. I am at ninety-five per cent and have made excellent progress. She said that there was no need for me to continue with physio because the missing five per cent may or may not return over time with continued exercises. I can call her anytime if I have concerns about lymphoedema or what exercises I can and cannot do. I have a tendency to over-do it, such as doing push ups on a fit ball, which is not good at this stage. My arm will be my indicator as to when it's had enough, as it will have a heavy, tired and achy feeling. She also said that unfortunately, as they had removed so many of my lymph nodes, I can't go into spas or saunas again. My body won't be able to cool down efficiently or drain the fluid build-up. That sucks! I love spas and saunas. I'm to avoid swimming pools for now due to chemotherapy and infection risk. Sigh. At least that's only short term. I left at 3.30pm but due to rain and heavy traffic, I didn't get home until 5pm. I did manage to go on the treadmill for forty-five minutes whilst watching the Eurovision Song Contest.

Today, nearly four hours of cleaning for rental inspection tomorrow. I got a break when Irma and Khan visited and we watched the Eurovision Finale. I woke up this morning to a song going around in my head: 'Running Scared' by Ell & Nikki, one of the finalists from Azerbaijan. Wouldn't you know it? It's the country and the song that won! How spooky is that? It's like my Spirit Guides are playing with me and giving me hints to future events. If only some lottery numbers...

Thursday 19 May 2011

My eldest sister, Kirsti, sent me a cute little 'devil duck' with horns to help me fight during my darkest times. Wahoo! The rental inspection was excellent and now no more until we move out. I feel so tired after only about four hours of sleep. I've got to go food shopping and pack for our mini trip away to Pemberton. David has taken the girls to the kennel for five days. I am so looking forward to just getting away and walking on the bush tracks, gazing at the fire, snuggling in bed and doing a bit of sightseeing. Being elderly, the girls are allowed to stay in the newer kennels, which are normally for smaller dogs. They are smaller inside, but they have their own little back yard. *White light* my girls—sending protective, spiritual white light to encompass my girls.

I wore my new 'do' to the shops and was looked at by a few men for the right kind of reason, not out of pity. It's a nice 24°C today, but it's going to drop down to 6°C overnight. Definitely going to be colder down in Pemberton but more reason to be cosy inside and snuggle.

Saturday 21 May 2011

We left after 8am yesterday morning for our escape to Pemberton. We went via our new house and it looks like most of the brickwork is done. It was pouring rain, so we didn't spend a helluva lot of time there. The water was pooling on the concrete floor and our feet were getting wet, as there was no roof yet. We decided to just grab a takeaway coffee and pastry from Pinjarra Dome Café as we wanted to get going 'on the road again'.

Most of the drive we were happy to listen to country music. I gazed at the countryside as David drove. We stopped a couple of times for pee breaks. I had a strange spasm in my back and kidney area, which bruised me so much that I had to put deep heat cream on and swallow strong painkillers. These made me very drowsy but at least the pain dulled.

We both got a huge fright when an hour or so from our destination, around midday, a large red kangaroo jumped out from the dense forest on our right, crossed in front of an oncoming car and then in front of us, before disappearing into bush to our left. It was raining and the roads were slippery; David slammed on the brakes but also did defensive driving and, thank God, we missed the kangaroo. It was taller than our car and would have done a lot of damage to us and the car! Luckily it didn't change its mind and double back to where it came from like they sometimes do. I was nervous the rest of the way to our cottage.

We arrived at Treenbrook Cottages just before 1pm. The older couple seem kindly and very helpful. The cottage is so cosy. It has two bedrooms, a bathroom, toilet, kitchen and lounge with comfy couches and a fireplace. The first thing we did was to unload the car and then David lit the fire, as the rammed earth cottage was decidedly nippy. It's in a lovely tucked away part past Pemberton, amongst trees and fields full of tiny birds and a few smaller kangaroos.

I was so tired that I didn't want to go anywhere else, so I watched some of the DVDs that had been provided whilst David had a nap. Later on, I napped too. It went dark before 6pm and we went for a little stroll to collect more logs for the fire to make the cottage nice and toasty. A few drinks before we cooked dinner together. It was nearly midnight before we went to bed.

I got up after 9am following an okay kind of night. The morning was loud with birdsong, kookaburras cackling away and the dripping sound of raindrops on the tin roof from the trees above. After a breakfast of pancakes and berries, we leisurely got ready to go sightseeing. We first drove to Pemberton and walked around the town. The houses were mostly made of old timber and situated amongst gently rolling hills. The air was brisk and cut through my wig. I felt very self-conscious and kept adjusting it, as I was afraid it would fall off or move to make it obvious that it was a wig.

I found a frog mug for Katri and a smoochy, soft, pink beanie for me to wear in the evenings. My wig is so scratchy and although I can handle it for a couple of hours, it bothers my scalp after that. We found a gorgeous wood gallery full of beautiful artwork. However, the prices were way too high, especially in this economic climate. It was sad to see so many houses and small businesses for sale. We proceeded onto a few wineries for wine tasting, and we bought a bottle of a nice, fruity red, which was more like an aperitif or dessert wine.

David and I had a very late lunch after visiting the Gloucester Tree. We couldn't believe some of the parents allowed their very young children to climb the rungs of the tree. They looked to be very slippery and dangerous from the rain. What a magnificent tall tree! I felt sorry for it, with all these people climbing it and all those iron spikes hammered into it. There were so many beautiful, colourful birds all over the forest floor and they were so tame. I took some great photos of them. Lunch was at Hidden River Winery and it was delicious. We ate in an old railway carriage. Good food, good wine and good dessert. Ugh, we were so full afterwards. We drove to the

Cascades and Big Brook Dam to walk a little, work off a few calories and stretch our legs. A quick visit to the local shop and it was time to collapse at our 'home away from home', to stare at the fire and relax.

It's been a relief not thinking about the Big C every minute. It has also been wonderful to be more romantic with David, holding hands, kissing and smiling at each other. I found a bird book in the cottage which helped me identify some of the birds we have been seeing here, such as Western Rosella, White-breasted Robin, Grey Fantail and, of course, the sparrows eating our toast crumbs. We found a dunnart inside our cottage. The owners had put a live trap behind the fridge and one got caught inside. We released it outside and it scampered away very quickly. It looked very similar to a mouse, but the nose was different, and the owners explained that it was a small marsupial called a dunnart.

Sunday 22 May 2011

What a soul enriching day today despite a shaky start... I slept in until 10am as I didn't fall asleep until after 3am. I slept in the other room as David snored and I had an upset stomach all night. David made us a brunch of scrambled eggs, tomato, mushrooms, capsicum, bacon, cheese and toast. This was pure energy food for our planned day of walking and hiking. We left at 12.30pm and got back at 4.30pm. We walked the Cascades for half an hour, up and down the forest tracks. We walked to the Bicentennial Tree (fifteen minutes) in the Warren National Park, and we walked for another half an hour up and down stairs to Beedelup Falls at Beedelup National Park. I got some amazing photos of an adolescent kookaburra.

We had afternoon tea of coffee and scones at the Pemberton

Lavender and Berry Farm, and strolled around their serene grounds. We said hello to their miniature horses, ducks, chickens and alpacas. Apparently, alpacas don't like to be eye-balled for long, and they will spit at you if they feel threatened by your gaze. I took a funny photo of one of them and it certainly looked quite intimidating or a bit mad. I just laughed when I looked at their brochure. Quite wisely, the owners put the evil looking one behind the friendlier looking alpaca. The evil looking one was white but with a steely blue gaze, whilst the friendlier looking alpaca was chocolate brown with a bit of white on his face and kind brown eyes.

When we got back in the late afternoon, we decided to do one more walk along the track as recommended by the owners of Treenbrook Cottages. It was another half an hour in quite overgrown forest, but the track was easy to follow. It was growing darker already and was a bit spooky in places. My hips, knees, legs and the rest of my body started to seize up and complain, especially going up the little hills. The sights were worth it though, as we came across an amazing range of mushrooms and fungi glowing in the evening light. There were so many different colours of them, some orange, some white, some yellow, some green, some brown and some beige. The air was fresh, and it felt so good to be alive with all of my senses tuned in. It's the opposite to what it will feel like in a few days' time—my third chemotherapy is on Wednesday.

I'll have to mentally, emotionally and spiritually transport myself to one of the walking tracks again when that IV goes in! I'll picture myself breathing in that crisp air and hearing that birdsong or drip of water off the leaves… Now, back in the cottage, I hear the pinging of the fireplace as the metal heats up or cools down. It is so cosy and it will be sad to pack up and go in the morning…

Tuesday 24 May 2011

We had a lovely romantic evening on our last night in the cottage. Yesterday, we got up early and were on the road before 9am. The long drive home from Pemberton was filled with a feast for my eyes. As we left, the eerie foggy morning changed the landscape and it was a fitting farewell; we both were sad to leave our autumn escape. It was fulfilling to gaze at the beautiful green vista, the rolling hills and rocky outcrops dotted with sheep, cows, horses and goats. The man-made pine plantations added to the glorious views. At one point, I burst out laughing when I saw two emus racing each other alongside the barbwire fence. Wow, could they run! I never knew they could move so fast.

We reached our new house by lunchtime, as it was a lot quicker going via Bunbury. The house is certainly taking shape and we can visualise living there. I stood in our kitchen with the gorgeous sunshine pouring in through the window frames.

After madly unloading the car, unpacking and freshening up, David went to pick up the girls from the kennel. I went to get my bloods taken and then on to see Dr Gan. Talk about holiday over. My blood tests showed that I have developed anaemia on top of a low white blood count... sigh... No wonder my heart has been racing so much lately. It was harder to pump oxygen through my body and is why I've been feeling extra tired. I put my body through a lot on those walks. Okay, so I overdid it again. The doctor and nurse were amazed I did so much, considering what I am going through. I guess it's just my tenacity or stubbornness. They said that half an hour walks are okay but two hours is way too much. I have to listen to my body and let it recover properly in between treatments, otherwise I could go backwards. Dr Gan reassured me that the pounding of my heartbeat in my ear is common with chemo; however, my anaemia has made it worse. He advised stronger iron tablets and taking better care of my diet, for example, eating more red meat and spinach.

He wants me to monitor my headaches and if they continue or worsen, he would like a brain scan to be performed. To help with my restless nights, he prescribed a mild sleeping tablet to be taken only if nothing else works. For the next blood tests, he wants a full blood count (FBP, UEC, LFT, iron studies, vit B12, red cell, folate, vit D and calcium). I spent a good hour talking to Marla afterwards. I was the last patient for the day, so we had time to chat which was lovely. It was very comforting, especially her compliments about my appearance with the blonde wig on.

Today, I was so tired and sore that I was quite happy to just do a few chores, such as laundry, and lounge on the couch watching some recorded shows. Irma came over in the late afternoon, and we caught up on the gossip and the latest family drama. It's so hard for me to distance myself from the conflict around me, as it goes against my nature. I've always been a mediator and counsellor, but this is not doing my health any good! I'm in between my two squabbling sisters who are like chalk and cheese. I see everyone's viewpoint, but unfortunately the members of our family are all stubborn, and it will take a long time for this latest conflict to blow over. I honestly don't have the mental, emotional, physical or spiritual energy at this point in time. I have to step back and look after *numero uno*. Irma and I reverted to our old habits and drank too much wine. David was worried because of my chemo the next day. I guess I had all of these emotions twirling around me and, rather than dealing with them in a healthy way, I drank to push down the fear, worry and pain. I knew what was ahead of me and I used it as my coping mechanism. What's that saying? 'To err is to be human'? Again, I forgive myself.

Thursday 26 May 2011

Well, yesterday was my first time in the Rockingham Chemotherapy Unit. It is so new and clean, and the nurses give me more one-to-one time. David only stayed a few minutes, and it was just as well. Whether it was too cold, or I was too dehydrated from drinking alcohol, or I was just too nervous, my veins did not behave! It took over half an hour for three nurses and four attempts at different vein sites to have success. David would have passed out for sure, as even I couldn't look after a while. And bloody hell it hurt! I had to bite my lip, breathe deeply and pray for assistance. It was very traumatic this time around. My right hand is badly bruised, but luckily the Arnica pilules and Arnica paste are helping. I listened to my iPod to calm down and let the Pac men and women do their job again. I had a sandwich and lemonade when I could. David picked me up in the afternoon (I was there from 10.45am until 1.30pm) and I was so drained that I went straight onto the bed and crashed for two hours. Unsurprisingly, the evening was very low key as well. Last night, I had night sweats, chills and was very restless. The extra nausea infusion and tablets are working well at least.

Today, I have been a couch potato and then an outside lounge lizard in the sun writing in this journal. I've been able to eat okay. I gave myself the immune boosting injection again, although I had to seriously psych myself into it. Well, I'm halfway there: three chemos down and three to go... looking on the bright side of life.

Saturday 28 May 2011

Yesterday and today blended together, a mixture of restless sleep, watching television on the couch and trying to sit outside for a bit of vitamin D. David and I took the girls for a walk yesterday evening. I conquered my mental and physical fatigue, put on my wig, cap and face, and went for a half hour walk by the beach. I listened to a blend of my music and the waves crashing on the shore. I must admit it was a struggle keeping one foot in front of the other, but it was worth getting out of the house and into the 24°C sunshine, and observe life happening around me. There was a couple with a dog on the beach, two grown men flying their remote-controlled airplanes and a brave family swimming in the water… brrr… I've had a lot of indigestion and heartburn today, which is very frustrating, as the tablets are obviously not working.

Sunday 29 May 2011

Katri visited for the day and we had a yummy lunch of fish, chips and salad in Mandurah. We checked on our house but, although the timber had been delivered, nothing else had progressed. Afterwards we went to Irma's (no showdowns thank goodness) and Katri told us that Alison, another friend of ours, has just been diagnosed with breast cancer. She hasn't had surgery or anything as yet, so a long journey ahead for her… I've said okay to Katri giving her my phone number for chatting, but I'm nowhere near healed enough to offer counselling as such.

Monday 30 May 2011

I had a very restless night with hot flushes and continuously having to pee all night! We had torrents of rain all night long. Today, I stayed more positive. I sat in the brief sunshine in between the rainstorms and I cooked our dinner early. I walked on the treadmill for half an hour and we also took the girls to the park. I meditated on my Reiki table for half an hour and felt so much better for it. Good girl, Sorja, you can do this. Don't be ruled by fear; let love guide you.

Tuesday 31 May 2011

I had a day out visiting friends from work. I was happy to be out of the house for a while, so it doesn't feel like a tomb! David has been working so hard, including all weekend. I feel guilty for not working. I honestly cannot see myself having the strength yet. I need time to recover and sleep and heal.

Our relationship has become much stronger through all of this and I've come to realise how much I do love him. I was overcome by fear the last few days and have had numerous nightmares as well. Fear of dying, fear of living, fear of the treatments, fear of it coming back, fear of being alone, and fear of not mattering... on and on and on. I have to accept this fear and let it go, not bury it deep down again, to acknowledge it but not let it consume me! I am protected. I am loved. I am safe.

Wednesday 1 June 2011

The first day of winter and it has rained for the past few days, which is great because we need it. I woke up feeling so much better; I sang and whistled all morning. I've been having a lot of dreams that have been working on my feelings and emotions. I think that an important part of this whole process is to work on my emotional, mental and spiritual aspects as well as the physical. During my dream state, I am able to sort through a lot of my emotional baggage, whether re-living past events or facing my fears about my future. I'm allowing myself to feel now instead of pushing everything down with food or alcohol. I don't hate myself anymore and I am beginning to treasure myself, which is pretty amazing. I am glad and grateful to be ALIVE. Thank you, Universe, and thank you, God.

Late in the day, I went into work to hand in my official letter of resignation. This was no surprise, as it was pretty obvious I wasn't returning to work any time soon. After a lovely chat and catch-up, I went to rent some comedy DVDs and then still had enough energy to do food shopping. David made us yummy tacos for dinner. He said I was doing so well that he forgot what I was going through. This was after a little tiff over a stupid shopping item and I had lost my temper. I'd had such a good day and I was so proud of myself for achieving so much—laundry, dishes, shopping—and I was tired. My legs were depleted and the muscles ached, so when David questioned my choice, I got angry. It's okay to be angry and let it show. After getting angry with David in the past, I would pour myself a glass of wine to stifle those feelings of resentment, anger and hurt. Now, I went to my bed, put on my relaxation music and calmed my mind for half an hour whist David cooked dinner.

Afterwards, David apologised for hurting me. I guess I was too sensitive and flared up quickly, forgetting to take his comment 'with a pinch of salt'. He told me he was extremely proud of me and commented how well I'm doing. Everyone keeps on saying that I look good and I say thank you. Look good, feel good. Sometimes camouflaging yourself with make-up, wig and nice clothes helps you believe that you are cured and healed and whole and good, already on the other side of treatment, already healthy, fit and happy. I look in the mirror and say, *Looking good!* That lifts my mood. I chant to myself, *Thank you for my healing, thank you for my new body, new skin, new hair, new breasts, new attitude and new me.*

Thursday 2 June 2011

How we measure the passing of years through the milestone birthdays of our family. Nikiita sixteen, Tory eighteen and Katri fifty this year... wow! I woke up after yet another restless night (waking up every one or two hours, so unfair) and got out of bed at 9.30am—better than 11am anyway. I didn't let it spoil my day. I ate brekkie outside in the brief sunshine. I ate lunch outside, too, after watching a suspense movie. I washed my wig... my hair... and let it dry on its stand. Then I baked pepita, pumpkin and current scones. I'd forgotten how much work was involved, but I thoroughly enjoyed the sensation of rubbing the butter through the silky flour with my fingers and later using the cookie cutter shapes to make different kind of scones, love hearts, four leaf clovers and spades. I had fun and they tasted good too.

Before it got dark, I sat outside on my camp chair and looked at the sun highlighting the flowers and leaves against the blue sky mottled with fluffy clouds. I felt at peace and admired nature's beauty. I also felt immensely proud of myself for making the most of my day and feeling stronger. As I thought this, a majestic hawk flew directly over me—about three metres above me—and landed in the pine tree in our backyard. I knew that the Universe was signalling to me that I was on the right track with my thoughts and actions.

When David got home, I shared this experience with him. I also shared my thoughts and the fact that I've been doing a lot of soul searching lately. Out of a catastrophe or curse can come a blessing in disguise. I'm taking responsibility for my actions. I am as much to blame for our marital problems as David. My insecurity led me to suspect David of cheating on me and it was compounded by drinking alcohol. I imagined things that were not there and my distorted thinking created distorted images in my head. Now that I'm not drinking as much—nothing for the past nine days—I'm actually able to think more clearly and accept my part in our relationship difficulties. I also see others more clearly, no longer through 'rose-coloured glasses'. I'm learning to trust my instincts and acknowledge my strengths, not only my weaknesses.

Saturday 4 June 2011

Two fantastic days full of laughter and rest. Three times now, I've had a recurring dream about finding a bright red crystal rock, the size of a fist, a treasure. I know red is the colour of energy, vitality, chi, passion and life force. I am finding it repeatedly, so I feel that this is a good sign.

Monday 6 June 2011

Another two great days have passed, apart from having very painful mouth ulcers. Yesterday, David and I checked on the house again. The roof beams were up and it looked larger and more like a house. We didn't realise Pinjarra was having a festival and there were hundreds of people everywhere! We found a nice place for afternoon coffee and scones near the Peel Zoo. It was a restaurant and café next to the Murray River called Redcliffe on the Murray and apparently they have live music on Sundays. We walked over the suspension bridge, sat on the bench in the sun and enjoyed a smooch. It was a lovely day. In the evening, I completed half an hour on the treadmill and even managed to jog at a light pace on level six. It felt good and my breast didn't hurt.

After a rather slow start to the morning, Irma texted to see if I wanted to go for a walk outside today. It felt like the right thing to do. We ended up walking for over one and a half hours in the brisk winter sunshine and fresh air. We sat on an upturned boat in a secluded section of the beach and just enjoyed our talk and the pelicans around us. We had ice cream as our treat and it tasted delicious. We spent a good four hours outside and it was healthy, rather than sitting on the couch watching television all day.

When we drove back from the beach, a hawk sat in the middle of the road, holding on to a dove by its claw, obviously the hawk's dinner. It was weird as it refused to move from the road. It just kept staring at us and Irma had to stop for a minute until it finally flew off. We both commented on the unusualness of it all, like another message from Spirit. That's twice in a week. Maybe the Universe or Spirit was acknowledging our healthy choices, our fit-for-life activity and sunshine therapy?

Chapter 22

All Consuming Journey-Physical, Emotional, Mental and Spiritual

Thursday 9 June 2011

Tuesday was a day of rest, which I needed as my chest area was pinching for a couple of hours. I wasn't sure if it was indigestion, a cramp in my chest muscle or my heart. David and I took the girls for a short walk as they were struggling in the icy cold wind too.

Yesterday, I had my very first appointment with my counsellor, Marie. It was interesting to sit as a client instead of as the counsellor. Yes, I did do a lot of talking for just over an hour. What I liked about Marie was the fact that she didn't just listen to me prattle on, but she made her own observations and shared them with me. For example, she asked me how I got to be so incredibly strong. None of us like to praise ourselves, so it was a shock hearing it from a total stranger at first. I then allowed myself to acknowledge it within myself. I've had to be. Ultimately, what has got me through all life's challenges has been me: my skills, my strengths, my will, my 'sisu' or perseverance and my Soul. The help and support from family and friends certainly plays an important part of recovery from anything. However, it's our own inner power that, time and time again, lifts us out of our own despair, frustration, pain or depression. If we let it.

Marie also asked about what gifts the cancer could bring to my life. I had no trouble answering that as I have thought about this a lot:

1. The gift of better relationships—more open and honest and from the heart and Soul, not just empty words but better communication.
2. The gift of realisation that I do want to live well into my eighties. Before, I was undecided and depressed and questioned the point of living. Now, I accept that it's my choice how I live with whatever time I have left on this earth, whether a couple of years or decades.
3. The gift of having future goals—moving into our new house, writing my book, running a women's group, having fun and laughing more, travelling and entertainment.
4. The gift of learning healthy boundaries, my knowing when to step back from conflict between friends or family members. It is not my role to be the mediator or counsellor for my family.
5. The gift of learning that it's okay to be self-centred, not to be confused with being selfish. To focus on self is healthy and part of our growth here on the physical plane. Our needs have to be met.

After my session of 'chatting', I went to Irma's and we walked by the beach for forty-five minutes, even though it was a cold and windy day. The hot cuppa was much appreciated back at Irma's. I got home before dark and took the clothes off the line, washed the dishes, cooked a quick dinner and wondered why I felt so bone weary, ha, ha, ha. I shared bits of the counselling session with both David and Irma.

This cancer challenge hits you from so many different angles and it is exhausting!

- *Physically*—the treatments, the appointments, the exercise and healthy eating, the calming of the body.
- *Emotionally*—bringing up such a range of feelings daily, hourly, minute by minute, dredging up buried emotions and airing them out for analysis and re-feeling and re-hashing.
- *Mentally*—thoughts tumble over each other, dreams and nightmares, post-traumatic stress disorder, re-living the medical procedures in your mind, reading up on the latest research of causes of cancer, cures and treatment options.
- *Spiritually*—whoa! Why did I choose this Soul journey? What is the cancer telling me about my life? What is out of balance? Step back from my body, my physical self, and look at my Soul growth or Soul lessons to be learned. Looking for clues and signs from the Universe. Am I on the right track?

No wonder there's this fatigue. My mind raced so much last night that I couldn't sleep, and I had to resort to a sleeping tablet in order to make myself rest. Today, I am driving up to the hills for a bit of R and R with Katri and Nikiita.

Friday 10 June 2011

Earlier this week, I was cheeky and sent Kirsti a birthday card to Queensland with an empty Lindt chocolate wrapper with the words, *I ate chocolates in honour of your birthday.* Ha, ha, ha. Yesterday, I arrived at Katri's by 5.30pm and spent the evening listening to music over a couple of wines. I had a restless night again but got up at 9am after a horrific nightmare in which a young doctor didn't know what he was doing with my blood tests, and the nurses brought the heart paddles as a 'just in case'. It was so scary!

Katri and I went for an hour's walk, with a slight interruption when we found two German Shepherd dogs lost and obviously tired and thirsty. They had name tags and a phone number, so I called the owner and left a message on the answering machine. We left the two girls in the laundry with water and continued our walk in the sunshine. It was nice to see all the country animals enjoying the winter warmth and the green fields were such a feast for the eyes. Later on, our furry guests were picked up by their owner and all was well.

Whilst I kept an eye on the meat and veggie curry, slowly bubbling on top of the fireplace in the old-fashioned way, Katri went to take care of her business in grand Mundaring town. I sat in the sun reading a magazine; it was so peaceful. I had an early shower and cheekily asked Katri if I could use her shampoo.

She replied, 'I have two kinds. Of course you can.'

I smirked at her until she cottoned on that I was joking… no need for shampoo with a bald head! She said I was evil for tricking her… evil laugh… ha, ha, ha…

Sunday 12 June 2011

Yesterday, after a brief shopping trip in Midland, Katri and I visited Visa and Susie before I drove home. Susie said how good I looked, that I looked better now than before the cancer. Of course, I wore my wig and make-up, but I know what she meant. They said my skin was healthier and glowing, and my eyes were clearer, as if I had gone through a detox process. In a way I guess I am. Each time is a breaking down and then a building up process. All the antioxidants and potions I am taking are certainly helping. Susie said it was inspirational hearing me talk and that I would help a lot of other women. I hope to do so.

Tuesday 14 June 2011

What a winter's day. It was a top of 16°C—windy, rainy, gloomy outside but cosy inside. I had my blood tests yesterday to check the levels of my iron and different vitamins and minerals. They're being sent to Perth, so I won't have results yet. I went home for a few hours and decided to watch the DVD Irma gave me: *Answer to Cancer* by Elaine Hollingsworth. The problem with a lot of these DVDs and books is the black and white outlook. On one side some doctors 'pooh, pooh' the natural medicine and naturopathic views on how to treat, for example, cancer. On the other side, some naturopaths think of doctors as dangerous and at the beck and call of big pharmaceutical companies. It is not black and white! It is grey.

My viewpoint is to have a combined effort, where the two sides work to complement each other, giving my body the best chance of living and surviving to a ripe old age. I personally choose not to view chemotherapy as poison but as a way of healing. I view it as a bit like rebooting a computer. First you switch off all systems, then you restart and reboot so that you end up with a new, virus free system. I don't like scare tactics from either side; I am not going to be ruled by fear. I trust my own instincts.

In the late afternoon, I went back to see Dr Gan and I had my usual list of questions and requests. I've decided to go ahead with the portacath, which involves minor surgery under general anaesthetic to insert a port for easier vein access during chemotherapy and the year of intravenous Herceptin infusions. I will feel less anxious (and the nurses will be relieved) not to be poked and prodded every three weeks to find a suitable vein. Dr Gan will refer me to a surgeon in the next few weeks to arrange a day. I will also have a CT scan again in two weeks' time to check on my progress.

Today, I am trying to take it easy, as my cold is still annoying me, and it's my fourth chemo tomorrow. Please, Universe, please help my veins behave and make it easy.

Saturday 18 June 2011

Time to catch up on the past few days... Wednesday started out as 'one of those days' until I turned it around myself. I puked first thing in the morning, probably from a combination of cold phlegm and nerves. Then, juggling making my porridge and putting myself together, I got an upset stomach and didn't quite make it to the toilet in time! I swore and carried on to myself until I realised that I had to calm myself down in order not to continue the day in the same vein (pardon the pun). David was ready on the couch, very wisely keeping out of my way. Just before we were about to leave, it started hailing. I just said, 'Oh well, it doesn't matter if we're late.' They didn't have many booked for that day and, as it turned out, we were right on time.

I wanted to ensure my success in every possible way, so I wore a lot of pink for love, including my fluffy pink hat instead of my wig, and I carried my pink crystal in my pocket for extra healing, love and luck. After settling into my armchair, I assured David he could go. I read a magazine whilst the heat pack did its work on my right hand. I put myself into a calm state and psyched myself into believing that this time it would go smoothly. Poor Marla had got herself into a dither from our last time and, at first, she wasn't going to attempt the insertion of the needle. I said that it was going to be fine this time. I even remember telling her to 'feel the fear and do it anyway'. What a role reversal, patient calming nurse. Marla managed to pull herself together and talk herself into having a go. At 11.22am, we had success!

The only problem we had was the development of a rash and itch on my right arm. They called Dr Gan and consulted him. He prescribed intravenous Phenergan to calm the allergic reaction. In the past I had been taking antihistamine every day, but I'd stopped for a week and I think this is why I got the rash.

The Phenergan made me very drowsy but I didn't want to sleep. I read the same article over and over again, stubborn woman that I am. I was finished by 2pm and David had to support me, as I was unsteady on my feet. I went straight to bed for a couple of hours. For the past few days, I have had the same reactions as before: nausea, fatigue, headache, body aches, stomach pain and cramps. I have, however, managed to do house chores, cook and walk the girls through sheer will power, I think (mind over matter).

Today, Irma and I are going to meet Julz and Shaz for coffee and a movie, *The Bridesmaids*. I can do this. My surgery date is set for 30 June at Fremantle Hospital, with pre-admission appointment on 27 June and more scans and my counselling session on 29 June. Busy, busy me...

Tuesday 21 June 2011

I've got to admit I've been feeling very sorry for myself the last few days. Unfortunately, having a cold on top of the chemotherapy has really knocked me about. I woke up this morning feeling okay from sleep but then threw up from the phlegm, which led to bile. Yuck! Then all day I've had severe diarrhoea. I don't know if it's the after-effects of chemo or the amount of black current and raspberry juice I've been drinking for their high vitamin C. Mentally, I've been feeling low as well and forcing myself to do a few chores and cooking. We managed a light walk with the girls last night, and I also meditated to try and help myself. I am catching a few sun rays in between the clouds and watching nature to make me feel better.

I know I should start clearing the house and sorting through the office. I simply find it too much at present, but I do feel guilty for not getting on with it. Please, Universe and Lord, help me get better and stronger so that next week's operation goes all okay. Surround me with white light and love and protection. Please don't let fear spiral me down to the dark abyss. Love not fear.

Good girl... Irma came over and we sat outside to chat for a bit. I then suggested a walk by the beach. We did half an hour and, apart from the millions of gnats around, it was lovely to be in clean and fresh air. I'm going to join Irma and Khan for a trip to Perth tomorrow; it'll do me wonders to be amongst the living.

Wednesday 22 June 2011

Yes, we had a great day in Perth. The day was a sunny and glorious 21°C. The three of us strolled to the Bell Tower and had a cuppa at Bells Café in the sunshine... aaahhh... Khan climbed all the way up the Bell Tower. Lots more walking and shopping and eating. Although exhausted by the time we caught the train home, I felt better for having the outing and not feeling so trapped at home.

Thursday 23 June 2011

What a lovely start to the day. I woke up at 5am to go to the loo (that's not the lovely part, ha, ha, ha). When I went back to bed, David and I clasped our hands together and held hands whilst snoozing for another half an hour until David had to get up to go to work. It was a special moment for me and for us. We are healing.

I went on the treadmill for half an hour, before making delicious pancakes for breakfast. Bugger, the same tooth that I had a filling put in less than two months ago has partly fallen out. I'm blaming it on the chemo weakening my teeth.

I started going through some paperwork and I found ticket stubs from going to see the medium James Van Praagh. Having the freedom to see shows that interest me reminded me how much David has provided for me. 'Thank you for allowing me to see and do so much,' I said to him tonight. It felt good to acknowledge his contribution to my happiness.

Saturday 25 June 2011

It was a lucky day yesterday. I got a dentist appointment for 3pm in Mandurah, so I went via our house and the colour bond roof was up, yippee. I took photos to show David later. The dentist ended up being no charge, as it was the same filling. As it was raining, I decided to go to Mandurah Forum for a snack and coffee. The only upsetting part to the day was driving back in the storm with poor visibility and seeing a dog that had been run over. It was in pieces—so horrific and so sad to see. Poor owners! It shook me up all night and the image is burned into my memory.

Today, I kidnapped Irma and Khan and took them to see the house for the first time. They were very impressed. We then drove sightseeing around Pinjarra. It was another nice 'jolly' and I am feeling more normal again.

Tuesday 28 June 2011

Katri came over on Sunday and we went to Point Peron for an hour and a half walk, collecting seashells. We then decided we deserved a major feast at the Boat Ramp Café. We both indulged in humungous hamburgers with the lot. No need for dinner after that.

Yesterday was an extremely tiring day. I had to go to Fremantle Hospital for my pre-admission appointment. The parking at the hospital was not free ($3 for the first half an hour and then 50 cents after, what a bloody rip-off). I was there for four and a half hours and it cost me fifteen dollars! I had to keep going back to put more money in, as I wasn't expecting to be there that long.

Anyway, I first saw a nurse who took my blood pressure, my height and weight. She also performed an ECG to check my heart function. Thank God it was all okay. I waited an hour and then saw the anaesthetist. I then waited an hour and had blood tests. Once again, I waited an hour before I finally saw the doctor. I drove back in peak hour traffic. By the time I reached home, I was thoroughly tired and grumpy after such a stressful day involving one and a half hours of driving and four and a half hours at the hospital. David bought a cooked chicken, wraps and salad, which helped me feel better. I am not me when I am hungry.

I understand the Infusaport better. It is a small square with a silicone centre that sits just below the skin, which attaches to a tube that connects to a major vein in the chest, near the collarbone area. It will be visible as a bump, but I don't care as long as it works all okay. I got the go ahead for Thursday. The anaesthetist said that, apart from the cancer, I was fit and healthy, and he didn't foresee any complications.

When I said that I had HER2+ cancer, the doctor, replied, 'Oh good, we have medicine for that.' Okay, not the response I was expecting.

Today, I have been a domestic Goddess. I spent hours chopping, cooking and mashing eleven different veggies to make shepherd's pie. I also made blueberry muffins—more comfort food. We're good for the next few days. I washed all the clothes and dishes (can't wait for a dishwasher in the new house), and cleaned the house. It all smelt so good, domestic and welcoming for David. I felt proud of my achievements. Tomorrow is another day of CT scans and counselling.

Wednesday 29 June 2011

Aaarrrggghhh... After only five hours sleep, I had breakfast at 7am. I got to Medical Imaging at 9am and drank three bottles of barium solution, a thick, white and yucky drink. Next to me, an older woman was struggling to drink the stuff; she was complaining and asking why we had to do it. I resigned myself to it and just drank the glug like a good girl.

Then the 'fun' started. The nurse had to put the cannula in for the dye infusion and tried twice with no luck. She eventually called in a doctor, who then used an ultrasound machine to locate a better vein, although deeper in my arm. He gave me a local anaesthetic to numb my arm, so he could probe with a longer needle. It took him a few goes himself! I prayed for help and tried to visualise myself watching the waterfall and the baby kookaburra from our holiday down south. Finally, all systems go and the actual CT scan only took fifteen minutes. I got the same metallic taste in my mouth and the funny 'wetting your pants' feeling from the infusion. Then, off with the cannula, out the door and home by midday. I was so traumatised by the experience that I went to the shop to pick up a few items, including chocolate.

After talking to both David and Irma, I felt a bit better and went to my counselling appointment at 1pm. I was understandably so stressed out about this entire week that we mostly talked about that. The sorbitol in the barium solution gave me 'the trots' all afternoon long. Well, at least I'll be clear for surgery tomorrow. Anyway, I've got to scrub myself with antiseptic shower foam and then have a light dinner. I have to fast from midnight, wake up at 5am, shower again and stop fluids by 6am. I have to be there by 6.30am.

Please, Universe… white light, white light, gold light, pink light and green light… The antiseptic foam was so strong with the bathroom door closed and the heater on that I started coughing so much I vomited! That started a blinding headache; just what I needed. I took a sleeping tablet at 9pm and finally fell asleep at 11pm.

Thursday 30 June 2011

After all of that! They say patience is a virtue and if that's the case, I must be an angel. After waking up at 5am, we arrived at Fremantle Hospital at 6.15am. David stayed with me in the Day Surgery unit until 7am. At 7.15am, I changed into my gown, undies and pressure stockings, and lay in my bed waiting. At 8.15am, the doctors came around and said there was a chance that my surgery would be cancelled due to the complicated nature of the surgery prior to mine. They still made me wait without water or food (reading magazines, listening to music and snoozing) until 3.30pm when they came to confirm the cancellation!

They said they would reschedule to next week or the week after.

I said no, as I have chemotherapy next week and then my trip to Kalbarri with Katri the week after. So we settled for three weeks' time. David and everyone else were understandably angry at what I'd gone through. My emotions ranged from frustration, feeling fed up with it all and then resignation. Finally, I took it all philosophically. It forced me to rest all day long, albeit without nutrition or hydration. The other patient was obviously more urgently in need of surgery than I. I didn't want to be operated on by an exhausted surgeon. Sigh.

We arrived home and I enjoyed a coffee and a muffin. They had given me a sandwich in hospital, but I started choking on it and couldn't eat it. Later, I went on the treadmill for half an hour and, later still, I had a proper meal. I had gone twenty hours without food whilst waiting for the surgery! I will try and have some fun over the next three days to prepare myself for next week's chemo again.

Sunday 3 July 2011

On Friday, David and I had breakfast at Dome Café Pinjarra and checked out our house again. More progress. They were in the process of mixing the concrete for the inside walls. Yay. I noticed that with all the rain we've had in the last month, the fields are beautiful and green. In fact, some of the pastures were flooded. What a difference from the summer drought when everything looked dead. Another lesson there... nature always recovers.

I invited Irma over for drinks with me and I drank for the first time in three weeks. We stayed up until 2.30am talking and David couldn't believe that we could talk that long (from 6.30pm until 2.30am). That's sisters and women for you, eh? We had fun and I will miss her when she leaves for Queensland in early August.

Monday 4 July 2011

Overall, a positive day today. My bloods were taken in the morning with no problems, and I waited at the hospital until my appointment with Dr Gan in the early afternoon. I saw Maxine and told her about the debacle at Fremantle Hospital. She said that Rockingham Hospital is now doing the surgeries for Infusaport insertions. However, Dr Gan recommends that I still have it at Fremantle because of having Von Willebrand's Disease. The results of my blood tests: my vitamin and mineral levels are good overall. I am no longer anaemic, but my vitamin B12 levels are too high and I have to cut back. My vitamin D is on the lower end of normal. The results of my CT scans: no major change, no new spots or growths, and the two suspicious lymph nodes from earlier scans have both decreased in size, so the chemotherapy is working. Yippee! The CT scan also showed my armpit scar tissue as quite thick and Dr Gan felt it to make sure he couldn't feel any lumps there.

I also asked him if I could have my tooth drilled and fixed properly, as I'd had such trouble with the filling staying in. He said okay as long as it wasn't major dental work, which isn't allowed during chemo due to having such low immunity. Afterwards, Dr Gan, Marla and I went down to the pharmacy to collect the tablets prescribed for my next round of chemo as well as steroids to help with fluid retention, nausea and body aches.

Lunch was a yummy Hawaiian baked potato and salad. After a quick stop at home, I drove back to the Mandurah dentist yet again— same bugger of a filling that keeps falling out. Hopefully, it will be third time lucky. My back tooth is very decayed and needs to be extracted, but it can't be done during chemo or radiotherapy, so the dentist anaesthetised my gum, mouth and tongue (well, it felt like it) and drilled the tooth out. After the first white filling fell out again, she decided to use amalgam, as it is the only thing strong enough to adhere to a decayed tooth. On the positive, she didn't charge me anything. I think that after three trips to see her she felt sorry for me. Prior to my appointment, I found a book on crystals called *Crystal Basics*. I am hoping to study more on the healing power of crystals; it's a topic I find fascinating.

I was home by 6pm, tired after such a day. The numbness in my mouth took hours to dissipate and I couldn't eat solids, as I wanted to give it the best chance to set properly this time. I need to take time out and rest again tomorrow, in preparation for Wednesday's four hours of chemotherapy plus the Herceptin infusion.

Tuesday 5 July 2011

What a fantastic day. I went for a half hour walk on the beach with my music. As soon as I started walking, I saw an osprey flying above me, confirming I was doing the healthy thing. It was a cold and windy 15°C, but the sun was shining. Then I had a coffee with Julz and John. I talked and I talked and I talked. (Could it be the steroids the doctor prescribed?) Afterwards, I went to see Irma and I talked and talked and talked again. I feel like I'm on speed, not that I have ever tried it.

I bought a magazine for tomorrow. It has the cover of a television personality fighting for her life with cancer. Why is it always fighting or a battle with cancer? It's such a negative spin on things... I prefer to think of it as loving myself through cancer: nurturing, caring, surviving, living and loving. On the television show *The Biggest Loser USA*, I heard a famous boxer say, 'P.O.W.E.R stands for Prepare. Overcome. Win. Every. Round.' This can be applied to chemotherapy and my journey as well.

Irma told me about Prahnic healing: using breath, colour healing and crystals to enhance my Reiki. I feel as though that's where I'm heading with my Reiki in the future. I see myself performing Reiki on clients using the ancient power of crystal healing. It is thousands of years old. Okay, Sorja, calm down now. Eat and relax. David called me this morning saying, 'Hello, Beautiful, I just wanted to start your day with saying I love you.' How sweet. I have to allow myself to just 'be' and not always 'do'…

Friday 8 July 2011

On Wednesday, I was at chemo from 10.30am until 4pm. I tried using Emla cream to numb my hand but unfortunately, I underestimated the amount I needed to use. Nor did I know which vein they would use… so two nurses and two painful attempts. I bit my lip to stop myself from crying out. I also squirted a lot of blood and made a mess for them to clean up. Anyhow, I decided to lie in a bed instead of the armchair, as I hadn't slept a wink the night before due to the steroids and my nerves.

This was my first time with both Docetaxel and Herceptin, so they had to monitor my blood pressure and temperature regularly. Thankfully, they were perfect each time. Apart from hot flushes, some pain at the injection site and a few heart thumps, I was okay. I read my magazine, listened to music and chatted to my nurse Megan before resting a bit. Each slow release infusion took one and a half hours and I had to wait another hour afterwards to make sure I was fine to go home. I got a lovely hot meal of roast beef and vegetables instead of sandwiches, which I thoroughly enjoyed. I was also given a nail and mouth care package to minimise the side effects of mouth ulcers and nail changes.

David picked me up after 4pm and I felt okay. At home, I watered my plants, showered and stayed up, feeling tired but still affected by the steroids; they give you alertness and energy. The nurse said that it was fine to take a sleeping tablet, so I did, and I was glad to sleep at least nine hours. I didn't get up until 11am on Thursday. The medication has helped with keeping the nausea away, but I noticed I had very itchy, red hands; headaches; and fluid retention as my main side effects. Taking painkillers also caused the usual dreaded constipation. I am sure these side effects will pass soon enough. Apart from light chores and taking the girls for a short walk, I have been resting as I am meant to do.

Today, I slept until 11.30am. Wow! Obviously, my body needs it, so I'm not feeling guilty. I am currently sitting in the outside sunshine and being distracted by the antics of the birds again. I do so love birds and animals.

I had dreams last night. *I found a huge green feather.* This is a very good omen for healing and faith. *I was also 'taken over' by a huge reddish snake that slid into my mouth and went through all my body parts: my heart, my intestines, absolutely everywhere! It felt like it was healing me from the inside and awakening my life force or Kundalini energy. I was scared but I also trusted it and said, 'I let go. I lovingly accept this healing.' It then slid back out of my mouth, taking away the 'yuck' from my body.* What a powerful dream! I believe I am being cured.

Irma told me about Pa being admitted to hospital after drinking three bottles of spirits during another alcohol bender! He hit his head and ribs on the side of the bed and table. Ma frantically called Irma, begging her to help by calling the Queensland hospital from here. What set Pa off was the fact that our uncle (Pa's brother) had been cremated and not buried like the rest of the family. I am sad to hear Pa taking it so to heart; he has always maintained that for him, there is no life after death, that you die and cease to exist. So why does it matter how your body is disposed, whether it's buried or cremated? Personally, I would like to be cremated even though Pa would hate to hear that. Well, I plan to be alive for a lot longer than Pa, so maybe when he passes over, he will understand that it doesn't really matter...

Irma didn't want to upset me by telling me all of this, but I was surprisingly able to let go of this latest drama. I have to for my own healing. As much as I love them, my parents have kept repeating the same patterns of behaviour over and over for the past thirty years. Any bad news... reach for the bottle and try and obliterate their feelings, emotions and thoughts. It's the same cycle of self-destruction and slow suicide. We kids have to hear it over and over. We've exhausted our own reserves of strength trying to help them want to live. They let themselves be ruled by fear, not love. It is sad and heartbreaking. It's teaching me not to follow in their footsteps. I think of the lost potential. They are nice people, hurt people, damaged bodies, humans, lost and afraid of dying but, more importantly, afraid of really living! I have enough toxicity in my life at the moment and I don't accept anymore. I'm being assertive. I'll be forty-five this year, and it's time to take ownership of my life, my choices and my decisions, so help me, God and Universe.

Saturday 9 July 2011

Last night, I dreamt *A yellow snake came out of my mouth! Fear! I had to feel it all the way and let it out, right to the tail end of the snake. Feel the fear but let it all go...*

Monday 11 July 2011

I cannot lie. I feel like I've been to hell and back these past few days. Oh My God, the pain! I've never begged for help from God and the Universe so much as the last few days. The constipation was so severe it felt like I was ripping in two as the body wanted to purge and get rid of the toxicity and chemo. Yet the cramps and spasms didn't produce results, just excruciating pain! I was up most nights rocking on the toilet seat and crying out, 'Please help me. I don't know what to do!' I felt so alone and afraid, and the fear magnified my pain and my panic attacks. I took all manner of magnesium, fluids and laxatives, and I doubted my own ability to get through the latest challenge.

My body, muscles and joints ached, crippling me so that I could hardly walk or stand for long periods. David and the girls were helpless to do anything as they looked on in worry. David asked whether I should go to the Emergency Department, but I was stubborn and said that it would pass. I didn't want to take any more codeine for the pain, so Irma recommended herbal pain relief tablets.

Finally, on the day I saw an eagle fly over our back yard again, I went to sleep or semi-sleep and performed Reiki and crystal healing on myself for hours. I woke up and, because I was half asleep and calm from the music, I was able to let go in peace rather than crippling fear. What a relief to just be able to empty my bowels. Life's simple pleasures, eh? Since then, I have been able to go okay, and I've taken painkillers as the muscle and joint pain lingers. I had a hot bath yesterday and it helped a little. David also bought me extra heat packs to put on my knees, back, legs and stomach. David did not rest much this weekend from worrying about me. I'm going away to Kalbarri with Katri for a week, and I pray that David will get some rest and 'time out' from my troubles.

A song is playing on the radio by Chumbawamba titled 'I Get Knocked Down'. Absolutely! However, never give up. I've had three nights of hot baths with Epsom salts, heat packs, painkillers… now the flipside: diarrhoea. Oh, joy.

Wednesday 13 July 2011 (6.11pm)

This is so difficult to write. We had to put our beloved Misha to sleep less than an hour ago (at approximately 5.25pm). I am at Katri's and David had to go to the vets by himself and give the vet permission to end Misha's pain.

She hadn't been herself for a few days. Misha was sick on Monday night. She vomited up her dinner and had a very restless night, panting rapidly and unable to lie down or settle at all. Yesterday, we could hardly get her to move on her own. She was 'out of it', and her eyes did not look normal at all. Misha also kept right away from me for days. I am positive she was distancing herself from me, her mother. When David got home, I said that we should take her to the vets because I thought she may have had a stroke. The vet took bloods and asked us to bring her back today for intravenous infusion of fluids, as her kidneys showed dehydration and anaemia. David took her there early in the morning after seeing I was in a deep sleep for the first time in weeks and not wanting to disturb me.

As I brushed Misha before the vet visit yesterday, I kept telling her that I loved her. A part of me was thinking, *Am I brushing her so she looks good when she dies?* Misha normally hates being brushed but she just stood there accepting it.

They infused her with fluids all day long, and I really thought she was going to come through it all okay, ever the optimist that I am. Katri came to pick me up at lunchtime and we left after 1pm. David kept calling me with progress reports. I thought that my Spirit Guides would warn me or tell me in advance and because they hadn't, I believed that Misha would survive this crisis, and that it would be okay for me to go to the hills with Katri before embarking on our Kalbarri trip.

After lunch in Midland, we were nearly at Katri's when David rang me in tears at about 4pm. Misha's organs—liver, kidneys et cetera—had shut down, and she had a fever of over 40°C. There was a possibility that she had cancer as well, and she was too far gone to save. The humane thing to do was to allow her to go, to let go, let God.

A girlfriend rang me this morning for the first time in months, and she mentioned their problems with their dog and the hard choice to be made. She said that it was better knowing you have loved a dog and looked after it well for ten to fifteen years, rather than prolonging its life when it is in pain and ready to go. The Universe was trying to tell us it was time to make that decision.

I believe that Misha chose to go when I wasn't there, that she knew I couldn't cope with being at the vet clinic when they euthanised her. I needed David to be strong for me. I apologised to him for having to do it on his own. I know no-one blames me. I feel like I've just gone through so much the last couple of months; it is hard to keep going on and being strong. I couldn't be strong for David, not at this point in time. I feel exceptionally vulnerable at the moment and, for the first time in months, I have been crying for hours and hours. Grief has hit me hard.

I was sitting outside on Katri's veranda, asking for a sign that Misha was okay right about the time she was euthanised, when a pack of dogs started howling. They sounded just like a pack of wolves! I always talked to Misha about her being my little wolf. That was my sign and confirmation. It's as though they'd collected her and taken her to the Spirit World. Katri heard them from the kitchen too. We both got chills and freaked out, as Katri had never heard such howling from her neighbourhood. I am going to miss you my little Munchkin, my *soulmate*. I will see you again when it is my time to cross over. In the meantime, please come to me in my dreams. I love you always and forever.

I spoke to David afterwards. He said that he patted her for about twenty minutes, although she was unconscious and not aware of him physically anyway. David said that she briefly looked at the clock around 5.30pm, her usual dinnertime. The vet would have argued with us strongly had we told her to prolong her life. She said that Misha had had a good, long life for over thirteen and a half years.

This year has been so full of death, tragedy and natural disasters… enough! Cheyenne must have known that something was wrong with Misha, as she'd kept on looking puzzled and acted like a bully towards Misha. We kept telling her off for stealing Misha's food, but now she is without her mother/sister/best friend. I hope we won't all become too depressed by our huge loss. Rest in peace, Misha. No more pain for you; go and play with our other pets on the other side.

Thursday 14 July 2011

Last night, after a few wines and a sleeping tablet, I finally drifted off to sleep after 1.30am, crying, crying and crying. I remember having a dream. *I exclaimed, 'Is that you, Misha?' She looked so different, so fluffy with fur* (her coat was very sparse due to old age for the past few years). *I cuddled her soft body and felt so much love.* Katri and I got up at 6.30am and left by 8am. It took us five hours to reach Geraldton where we had lunch for an hour. Along the way we had a lot of spiritual messages from Misha. Just as I told Katri that I had prayed for Nero, our male poodle from our childhood and early adulthood, to come and collect Misha, a huge eagle flew directly overhead. We got goose bumps all over. Each time I thought of Misha's Spirit soaring, we saw either an eagle or a hawk (three eagles and two hawks in all). At one of our stops, Dongara, we even saw a sign that read, *Native Wolves*. Wow, thanks for that, my little wolf.

It was a glorious sunny 25ºC for our trip and the views were magnificent. David told me to try and have a good time on our holiday because Misha would want me to. As I showered this morning, I had that very same thought, and when I reached for a towel to dry myself, a white feather fell at my feet. Thank you, Spirit.

Katri and I shed tears, but we also laughed a fair bit today. It was as if we both knew how precious it is to live when we can. I even managed the long drive—five hours to Geraldton and then one and a half hours to Kalbarri—without crippling pain. I feel as though Misha took some of my physical pain away as her gift to me. Thank you, Misha; I am grateful. We even joked a little. While we ate fish and chips in Geraldton, the wind blew the wig into my ear and I thought that it was a bug. Katri was quick to quip, 'It was an earwig.'

We just laughed and laughed.

We arrived at our holiday unit in Kalbarri after 4pm, unpacked, went to the shops and then settled for the evening. David rang and he sounded okay. He told me that he'd bought Cheyenne a bone and also taken her for a walk to the park. She was confused about not having Misha there to herd as per usual. Apparently, Cheyenne has been searching the house for her over and over, and that is so heartbreaking to hear.

David took a card to the vet to thank her for her help and support. He also settled the vet bill. They don't expect you to do it at the time of the traumatic event. We are having Misha cremated, and then we will organise a lovely urn and memorabilia, or a collage of photos with a plaque. The process of organising all of that is going to be emotional for us, over and over again.

Irma texted in the evening and I told her about the dogs howling. She said that she heard howling yesterday evening as well. How spooky! All three of us sisters hearing the same thing but miles apart.

My heart has been acting up today. I think it's because I feel so broken-hearted. I know I have to keep going, and I know that along with my Guardian Angels, Spirit Guides, relatives and Spirit Animals, there is now Munchkin giving me her spiritual strength when her physical strength was depleted. The latest photos showed her looking so tired. I have to respect her wishes to move forward, although it doesn't make this any easier to bear.

Friday 15 July 2011

I had a horrid night. The energy of this place was restless and scary, and I guess it was a full moon also. I grieved for hours. I was in physical pain with fever, chills and back pain, but I finally fell asleep sometime after 3am. I woke up at 9am and was glad it was morning, after that kind of night! Katri and I spent most of the day exploring Kalbarri's town centre as well as the lookouts and scenery. After beef nachos for lunch, we continued our criss-crossing of the town. It was a lovely 23°C day and, although I had a good day with regards to pain, I kept remembering that Misha is gone. This will hurt for a long time, as there is such a space left our lives.

David rang me twice, sounding lost and upset, and second guessing our decision. The X-ray done by the vet showed an enlarged liver and kidneys, and spots on her lungs. Misha was in pain; now she is at peace and running around with our other dogs that have passed over the years. We'll just have to appreciate Cheyenne now and treasure the time we have left with her.

I've been sensing that Kalbarri is an ancient site with a brutal history. This was confirmed today when we found signs explaining the history of the place.

Sunday 17 July 2011

Yesterday was another gloriously warm, sunny day, and we took the opportunity to drive to the Kalbarri National Park and do a few of the shorter walks. The scenery was stunning, truly 'God's country'. The wildflowers were starting to bloom; we saw primarily yellows, purples, pinks, oranges, reds and whites. It's not full wildflower season as yet, but we saw a taste of what it will be like in a month or so. I can visualise how the Murchison River would look framed by the majestic cliffs and clumps of flowers dotted along, as if the 'man upstairs' had randomly dropped a variety of seedlings from the sky.

We visited a few lookouts called The Loop, Nature's Window, Z Bend, Hawk's Head and Ross Graham. We would have easily walked a few kilometres, and my back and legs felt tired and weak by the end of the day, especially with a lot of walking up and down stairs added in as well. Hmmm... not quite what the oncologist recommended when telling me to 'take it easy'. I'm obviously a rebel.

I don't want to just lie down and rest. It felt good to be out in the fresh air and sunshine, and to do normal things like sightsee as a tourist. No-one could tell that I was going through chemo as I looked like everyone else amongst the numerous tourists we saw throughout our day.

As I waited to take a photo at Nature's Window, two young European men before us were taking photos. One of them took a small yellow rubber duck and placed it onto the rock in front of the 'window'. I was taken aback because I'm the duck (my nickname is Duck). It felt like a sign from the Universe that I was doing the right thing in continuing to live, and also that Misha was giving me her blessing.

I dreamt of Misha again last night. *Misha came to both David and I, she looked like she used to when she was a young adult about two or three years old, with her dark fur and a dark face. I patted her soft fur again and I really felt it; it was so beautiful.*

David told me yesterday that he rang Pat, the Keeshond breeder we bought Misha from, to tell her the sad news. Evidently, Misha was the second of that litter to go in the same week. Knowing that she has her brother or sister with her in spirit brings solace to me. The average age Keeshonds live is fourteen; at thirteen years and seven months, Misha nearly made it.

This morning, we had a cooked brekkie of bacon, egg, tomato, mushrooms and toast at our unit. We both read our magazines peacefully, whilst it rained outside. Later on in the arvo, we had a scrumptious coffee. I had rhubarb and apple crumble with ice-cream and Katri had almond and orange cake. Then we went for a look at Eagle Gorge and Mushroom Rock Lookout. My wig nearly flew off and would have glided down the cliffs, so we came back. I exchanged my wig for my pink hat, scarf and gloves, and off we went again. We took lots of photos of the gorgeous wildflowers. Tonight, we are making the most of our last night here by eating leftovers with our wine and watching television, hee hee hee...

Monday 18 July 2011

Another restless night without much sleep. I cried and cried and cried again for over an hour whilst listening to my music. I grieved for Misha but also my own struggles, my fatigue and this whole year. We got up at 6.30am and left by 8.30am, arriving back at Katri's place at 3.30pm. We again saw numerous eagles on our drive; I love seeing them. Tomorrow morning is time for my 'simulation' at the Radiology Department at Royal Perth Hospital.

Tuesday 19 July 2011

Thank God I slept at least eight hours, as I was exhausted. I got up at 7.30am, and Katri and I caught the 9.30 train from Midland to the city. At the simulation, I took off my top half and lay on my back on a very hard metal bed, which was narrow and uncomfortable. Luckily, it was only for half an hour. They placed me into position with both elbows on arm rests raised above my head. They had to adjust it a little and kept commenting on how tall I am. Dr Zissiafis came to mark my breast with an oil based pen before two other females (assistants or nurses or technicians, I wasn't sure) took various measurements—arm to chest, chin to chest et cetera—for positioning purposes during radiation therapy. They traced the lines onto tracing paper and then gave me three tiny black tattoos in a triangle formation, basically three sharp needles or pin pricks. The one in the middle of my chest, between my breasts, hurt for a while and took a bit of time to stop bleeding due to my Von Willebrand's.

Afterwards, a nurse spoke to both Katri and me about how to look after my skin as well as the side effects of radiotherapy, such as fatigue. All in all, we were only there for one hour. We walked into the city to indulge in coffee and blueberry slice as a reward. After that, we went to the Blue Buddha New Age shop. We both ended up buying sixteen new crystals and stones for healing and other physical, emotional, mental and spiritual properties (our bag of goodies).

I received a call from Fremantle Hospital cancelling my operation, which had been scheduled for Thursday, due to the doctors all going to a conference. Hours later the clerk rang me back after the surgeon had consulted with Dr Gan and rescheduled it for next Tuesday, the day before my chemo. Just great... but at least this time I don't have to be there until 11.30am. Is this third time lucky?

I am sitting on Katri's back veranda, catching the day's last rays of sunshine. Misha has been gone a week tomorrow. David has been talking about how depressed Cheyenne is and asking whether we should get another companion for her and for us. I can't make that decision as yet. I need more time. Give me more time. I need all my strength to get through surgery, chemo and five weeks of radiotherapy.

Thursday 21 July 2011

Yesterday, Katri and I drove to Wembley Radiation Oncology for my CT scan—the planning stage for radiation. The Universe made us take a wrong turn which ended up being an easier route to where we needed to go. We arrived early, so we had a coffee and a snack (hmmm... common theme here). The scan was performed by two men—no women in sight. It was an interesting experience having two men look down on me on the metal bed, tracing my breast and marking me and measuring me! They spoke calmly to me in order to be non-threatening and put me at ease through the whole process. They must see hundreds, maybe thousands, of women and their breasts of all shapes and sizes. It was quick and painless, so we were able to get back to my place by 3pm.

Cheyenne was so happy to see me but kept looking behind me to see if Misha was with me, as if I had taken her on holiday with me. Once Cheyenne realised that, no, I didn't have Munchkin, she started whining and crying out loud. I've never heard her vocalise like that before! She was grieving as much as we were, crying just like we were. When Katri left, I broke down for an hour, balling my eyes out and telling Cheyenne that Misha wasn't coming back.

I slowly unpacked, showered and tried to compose myself for when David arrived home from work. When he did, we hugged tightly and talked about Misha. We both broke down and cried together. We knew that we had done the right thing; still, our lives have been left with a huge hole that will be so difficult to fill. It took me ages to go to sleep. I kept on expecting Misha to come by my side as usual, and I swear I heard her breathe as if she was sleeping next to me.

Today, I had a hard time concentrating on anything. I did manage a few errands even though my stomach was upset all day long again. Tomorrow morning, Misha's ashes will be delivered while I am alone with Cheyenne, as David will be at work.

Friday 22 July 2011

Misha came home at 9.30am. It was hard to believe that our beloved

Munchkin, Goober, Gooberguts, Munchkarella, Mish or Hoover was now in a felt bag with a 'Misha Reese' label on it. What broke me down (after paying $209) was the other plastic bag containing lockets of her hair, so recognizably hers.

I cried and cried on and off most of the day. I tried to distract myself with watching TV and reading, but my mind kept on wandering. Our family was incomplete. I know that she is in a better place and I am just feeling sorry for myself. I let Cheyenne smell Misha's hair and ashes, and she was visibly upset. I wanted Cheyenne to truly understand that her companion would not return—physically anyway. I tried to cheer her up by giving her a treat to chew on; I know this was another form of distraction from her pain. I can empathise as I have done nothing but slip back into unhealthy habits, trying to fill up my void with food and wine. I know that's not the long-term solution for me. I need to get fit and healthy to keep going on. Misha would want me to keep on living and loving life. I keep hearing and relating to the lyrics of a song in my head: 'Broken Wings' by Mr. Mister.

Cheyenne has been staring into mid-air in the kitchen and by the couch as if she sees something. They do say that animals can see spirits. I bet she is seeing Misha. I had put the ashes and fur on the dining table, but David had to put them out of sight, as I was constantly getting emotional—grief sucks!

Monday 25 July 2011

It's pouring outside with rain and pouring inside with my tears. I just came back from blood tests and an oncologist appointment. I got shocking news. I thought that this Wednesday was to be my last chemotherapy, but no, this Docetaxel treatment cycle is four times not two as I had been informed in the first appointment with Dr Redfern in Perth months ago. I just lost it and burst into tears while I was with Marla. I had already told Dr Gan and Marla about the loss of Misha and the extreme amount of pain I had with the last round of chemo. I think Marla was shocked to see me break down so much, as all the medical staff always say how good I look and how strong I appear to be. Not at this point in time. How much more can I take? My bloods were okay, just slight anaemia again. My chemo will go ahead on Wednesday even though I have my surgery tomorrow.

On Saturday, David took Cheyenne for her blood tests to check on her Phenobarbital levels—her epilepsy drug—and what dosage Cheyenne required. Rachel, the same vet who had euthanised Misha, admired Cheyenne's luscious fur. She also said that Misha's blood tests had confirmed that her liver enzymes were off the chart, suggesting she only had maybe a day left and we'd done the right thing in putting her to sleep. This is some consolation to David and me. We drove to check on our house and admired the white walls, ceilings, windows and doors. In the late afternoon, we went to see the last instalment of *Harry Potter* in 3D. We tried to have a little fun and escape our grief.

On Sunday, I went, as David put it, 'mental'. I undertook a major house clean, including dusting, which I hate. I was sick of looking at such disarray, and I worked off some of my anger at the world. Hours and hours later, I cooked dinner and finally collapsed from exhaustion. Late in the evening, Irma and Khan came over to stay for the final week before their move back to Queensland.

This morning I was amazed at how many different birds I saw on my way to have blood taken: pelicans, cockatoos, parrots, kookaburras, galahs and more. I thought this was strange enough until I came home between my bloods and my oncologist appointment. Sitting on the ground, next to our door, was a yellow canary! *WTF?* I asked myself. *How strange and bizarre. A canary?* I looked up what it meant in my *Signposts* book by Denise Linn, and it read, *A canary represents music, harmony, joy, and the lightness of a small bird.*

Okay, I am not in the right frame of mind right now, but maybe later that canary appearing will make sense to me. Maybe that's the point. I've been dragged down to the depths of despair, pain, grief and loss. Somehow, my Spirit Guides are telling me to keep going and not to give up, although a part of me so wants to. I pray that there is great joy ahead of me to rival the great pain I have endured. Please, Dear God and Universe, help me be strong.

I caught the canary quite easily with a towel and bucket, and placed it into a cardboard box with holes for breathing and air flow. I lined the box with newspaper and even added a small container of water. I placed a towel over the top and, so far, the canary has been very calm and quiet. It must belong to someone though I don't have a clue what to do to find the owner. My brain is frazzled and my emotions are too raw; I can't think clearly, so I'll wait for David and Irma to come and help later today.

We found a perfect container for Misha's ashes. On their last trip here, Ma and Pa gave us two large, natural, hollow wooden gourds with carved out lids that were souvenirs from the Northern Territory. They have a lovely texture, colour and shine. The smaller of the two gourds holds her ashes nicely, and we'll keep the larger one for when it's Cheyenne's turn to go over the rainbow bridge to doggy heaven. I've placed lots of photos of Misha around it, and both David and I feel at peace with our decision. We actually had the idea at the same time. I was looking at the gourds and David said, 'I wonder...' So it was meant to be.

Wednesday 27 July 2011

Back to the canary story… one of our neighbours has canaries and David went to ask them if they had lost one, but no, they had all seventeen of their canaries and didn't seem keen to get another one. David spoke to another neighbour, a young mum and her young daughter, and they were delighted to take on the beautiful yellow and orange canary to add to their three finches. I hope it will be happy. I don't feel that I was meant to keep him or her; it was a symbolic message from the Universe to smile. I'm catching a few sun rays this morning before another storm front hits later today and I hear a canary singing again.

Cheyenne has been avoiding Misha's doggy bed even when we had to wash her bed cover. She lay on the carpet or by the door instead. It's as if she saw Misha occupying the bed still and couldn't lie on top of her. Who knows? Maybe she did see her sister there.

Yesterday, third time lucky with my surgery. I washed myself with that 'lovely' disinfectant and had the bathroom door open so it didn't overpower me. No coughing or choking this time. I had taken a sleeping tablet the night before and had at least five hours of sleep. Because I was booked for afternoon surgery, I was able to eat a light brekkie and coffee. Yippee. We arrived at Fremantle Hospital by 10.45am, David dropped me off because there was no point in him coming in and waiting with me. I was early anyway as my arrival time was booked for 11.30am. I was able to go into my cubicle and read, listen to my music and clutch my pink rose quartz crystal. In fact, I had held it in my hand all night long, praying for strength and love.

At midday, a friendly nurse got me ready with the usual forms, blood pressure and temperature checks. After that another kind lady, the anaesthetist, came to chat and set up my IV cannula for my DDVAP (Desmopressin for my Von Willebrand's). I had tried Emla cream, but it wasn't very effective this time around, so she used a local anaesthetic to numb my arm and hand before attempting to insert the cannula. Yes, it took a couple of different attempts again and yes, I am bruised. The blood came out quickly, making a mess on the floor and bed blanket. 'Not to worry,' she said. 'It'll clean up.'

They hooked up the DDAVP by 12.15pm, to infuse over a period of forty minutes slow release. It all happened relatively fast, as I was first in line for afternoon surgery with Mr Bond. I had to go to the loo before surgery, and the damn long gown once again dipped into the toilet bowl. I had to walk back with a dripping gown (how embarrassing) and ask for a replacement. The orderly was there already and patiently waited whilst the nurse helped me. I think he took pity on me after seeing my bald head on the trolley bed. He made jokes all the way to the operating theatres one level up and then the theatre nurses took over. They were still getting ready and it was 1pm by now. I waited and got more and more nervous. My heart thumped so quickly and loudly to my ears, and I think I was getting myself into a state of panic. I wondered whether I was going to die in surgery and if my fortitude was strong enough to keep me going on this life journey. I did some calming breathing techniques: breathe in for a count of six, hold for four, and then breathe out for another count of six. Then, I pictured all the family I still wanted to see and live for, and I prayed for my Spirit Guides, Guardians Angels and Archangels to help me. I slowly felt a white dome around me and I calmed down. By the time the anaesthetist and student came to check on me, I was even able to make a little joke. The student was responsible for administering the oxygen and I said, 'Good, I need to breathe.'

The anaesthetist joined in and said that as long as the student didn't have a lighter, I would be okay. Ha, ha, ha. Pretty soon after that, the surgeon was ready (I didn't even meet him or see his face, the elusive Mr Bond). I was wheeled into the theatre and one of them couldn't figure out how to lower my bed in order for me to slide over to the operating table. I said, 'Oh, the lever is at the foot of the bed and you pump it with your foot.' I then joked, 'See, I have done this before.'

They all laughed. They explained where I had to put my arm and placed the monitors on my chest; it was all old news to me. How sad is that? The doctor said I would have a scar on my chest, and the port and the scar would be visible if I wore low cut tops. I wasn't fazed. I replied that I am covered in scars, so what was one more? Just before they injected me with the anaesthetic, I kept silently chanting to myself, *I choose to live. I'm not finished with my life and I'm not done yet!*

At 1.22pm (I was watching the clock), I slowly slipped away. I have had numerous surgeries and been knocked out under anaesthetic multiple times as well. I have never recalled anything from the times I have been unconscious or under anaesthetic—until now. I saw Misha! We weren't in the operating theatre; it was just Misha and I surrounded by white fluffiness, similar to clouds but definitely not clouds. She was facing me and we held each other's gaze. Misha looked to be in her prime, about three or four years old with a thick, healthy fur coat in her gorgeous dark colours. She communicated to me telepathically, sending me lots of love and courage, and telling me not to give up, as though egging me on. Her tail wagged with joy, and she gave me her blessing to get another puppy for company and continued healing. It was truly a miracle and I remember it vividly and clearly.

Funny how instead of seeing a human like my great-grandmother, or uncles or cousin or friends, my Spirit Guides knew that I most connect to my animals and especially my beautiful Misha. It was the best choice for me and I needed that message.

I woke up in recovery about 2.30pm, and one of the first things I saw, to the left of my bed, was a pin board full of doggy photos. I asked the nurse what it was, and she replied that they were photos of the pets belonging to the staff there. What confirmation for me. Misha, thank you from the bottom of my heart. I love you.

A quick chest X-ray confirmed that everything was in place, and that my lung hadn't been pierced. Thankfully, all was okay. Then, as I was alert, they wheeled me back to the Day Surgery ward. I had an extra cannula in my poor right arm, definitely a pin cushion yet again, but at least they poked and prodded whilst I was unconscious. The right side of my chest has the PowerPort in it. I pleaded my case to get a PowerPort, so that I can have an easier time with future CT scans, chemo and Herceptin infusions. The nurses can then feel for the three points in a triangle formation to locate where to access the port opening.

One hour prior to surgery, I had asked about it again and the doctor said they were relatively new on the market and hard to come by but if I wanted, he could ring around Radiology and see if they could get one for me. I think they all felt sorry for me, as my operation had been cancelled so many times and I was going through chemotherapy. I had pleaded with the Universe to provide me with some good news and when they gave me the brochure on the PowerPort, I knew my prayers were answered. They also left the needle in so that today's chemo would be easier for the nurses and me, as the wound site is very swollen and sore.

When I got back into the ward, I couldn't help but start crying again after seeing Misha. The two women next to me—an older mother and her daughter who looked about fifty—were aware but left me to my private grief. My emotions have been all over the place lately, from not being able to cry for months to now crying every day! Tears are healing...

David collected me at about 4.30pm, but we waited until I was steady on my feet, my BP and temperature were okay and I was able to eat, drink and go to the toilet.

David and I had an argument yesterday morning, which was not good at all. He was hurt when I told Irma I needed some joy in my life after all of this grief, that a puppy would give me a purpose to get up in the morning, and I needed someone to need me and to focus on instead of just my illness and pain. He said, 'What am I? Chopped liver?'

I tried to explain that he was working all of the time; he was a grown man and self-sufficient. Cheyenne has always been shy and more independent. Misha was with me all the time as a loving companion and friend. I love David and I love Cheyenne and I love my family. We did apologise to each other afterwards, and I understand we have both been under a helluva lot of stress. We do love each other, and we'll get through all of this one day at a time.

I feel more at peace after my experience with Misha during surgery. I have her blessing and, after much discussion, David understands my needs better. We found a place in Mt Lawley that isn't a puppy farm and top breeders supply them with all kinds of puppies. If I feel okay on Sunday, we'll go for a drive with Irma and Khan.

Anyway, I've got to get ready for round six in the boxing ring.

I'm now a Super Duck as I have a PowerPort. Katri texted, *Hey, Super Duck, I hope you write all this down about the three point power et cetera for your book, cos many (people) at work admire your strength and humour and your book will be well read.*

I woke up this morning with a message in my head. They are not my words, but words of wisdom from one of my Spirit Guides: *Why whatever It is, special simplicity brings heart.*

Friday 29 July 2011

We went via the chemist—to collect the many painkillers and anti-nausea medication needed to get me through—and David dropped me off at Rockingham Hospital just before 2pm. It was easier with the needle left in, as all they had to do was flush it out and then start the Docetaxel (one hour) and then saline flush, followed by Herceptin (forty-five minutes) and flush plus anti-nausea injection. I was done by 5pm. They took the needle out but left part of the clamp or plug in to let the wound heal for five to seven days and ward against infection. I'll have it all removed on Monday, apart from the PowerPort under the skin, of course. I was drowsy, so I listened to my music for most of the chemo time. First night not too bad... I was able to go to the toilet, yippee.

Yesterday, I pottered around the house a little before going with Irma to get the script from the hospital and then to the shops. I wasn't in pain last night; I just couldn't sleep. The Tramadol made me physically comfortable, but my mind was alert and kept on coming up with weird and wacky thoughts that were almost hallucinogenic. I gave myself Reiki healing; I used crystal therapy and finally fell sleep after 5.30am for about five hours.

Today, I'm having a slow day by watching TV and sitting outside a little, trying not to over-exert myself to worsen my condition and upset my muscles. I've taken my creatine and amino acids muscle recovery drink, magnesium oxide and natural anti-inflammatories to hopefully counter any developing pains. I must keep positive and keep going, no matter what.

Sunday 31 July 2011

I spent most of yesterday relaxing and eating. The weather was pretty wild with howling winds and rain, definitely not a day to be outside. I had a relaxing hot bath to alleviate some of my knee and joint pain, with candles and American Indian music playing. I swear some of the shadows against the walls looked like buffalos, wolves, and eagles... or was it the Tramadol? Knowing they'll be leaving soon, Irma and I stayed up late talking. I took painkillers to help me sleep and I dreamt of puppies again; that's three nights in a row.

This morning, I managed to catch two hours in the sun with the wind blustering around me, and I actually enjoyed the taste of my coffee, yippee. In my thoughts, I talked to Misha, asking her to give me a sign by arranging the perfect puppy to be there at Mt Lawley if it was meant to be. After another storm, it became calm and sunny as soon as Irma, Khan and I started our drive to Perth. David had just returned from checking on our house and found it to be at the lock up stage, all boarded up so he couldn't investigate much.

As soon as Irma started the car, the song playing on the radio was 'Werewolves of London' by Warren Zevon, with the sound of a howling wolf. Also on our drive, an eagle soared past us overhead. I felt Misha had sent me those signs, and I felt at peace with our decision to visit this puppy place.

It was a smooth run, not much Sunday traffic, and we got there after 2pm. I explained what I was looking for to a young man. I needed a loving friend after having just lost my faithful companion. He showed me the puppies they currently had and photos of the ones coming in the next week or so. Irma and Khan were already distracted by a particular pen full of puppies, especially one young girl who showed a lot of spirit and character.

I asked one of the women there about the size of a Schmoodle, and she said that they grew to a medium sized dog. I wanted a lap dog. She listened as I explained about my year of breast cancer treatments and my hope for a dog to lay on my stomach, one that would help me heal, to motivate me to get up out of bed and get on with living. She replied that a puppy would certainly do that. She then took me back to where Irma and Khan were admiring those cute little 'ratbags'. Long story short, we *all* fell in love with the same feisty young girl that Irma and Khan had admired—at nine weeks old, she is a cross between a poodle and a King Charles Cavalier Spaniel or a Chihuahua (they were not 100% sure who the father was). I'd left home with my 'joy and fun' crystal which is mostly mottled black and white in my jeans pocket and, waddyaknow, the girl puppy was the only one that was mottled black, white, and a bit of apricot like my crystal rock—a bit spooky once again.

Once I put on a clean shirt and cleaned my hands with antibacterial gel, I was able to cuddle the cute bundle of joy. She snuggled straight into my left breast and armpit! Already a little healer. Irma took a few photos of us together. She was very calm, alert and didn't fidget in my arms at all (also, no peeing on me which is always a good sign). Later, we observed her going to the toilet on the newspaper. She also easily handled a match against two members of the puppy gang, with no sign of fear in her eyes.

Definitely a fighter. Feminine but not a pushover. I liked her spark and spirit and she looked straight into my eyes as if to say, *Well, waddayathink?*

It was as if she was trying to show off all of her tricks: look I can go to the toilet on a newspaper, look I can eat my fill, look I'm a fighter, look how cute I am, look I'm cuddly, look I snuggle into your arms—right on cue as if she had a script from Misha. I didn't have to struggle much with a decision, so I paid $200 as a deposit and there's a further $1,000 to be paid upon collection. We'll be given a half hour talk on puppy care when we pick her up later this week.

We had Maccas afterwards and our heads were still spinning with the lightning speed of how things evolved. The sun shone all the way home and then, as soon as we got back, it poured with rain. David was shocked at the price of the puppy but not by my quick decision. Everyone knows what an animal lover I am, especially when it comes to dogs. Now to think of a name for her. I want something feminine but strong, maybe American Indian? Hmmm... this knowledge will come... My pain is bearable; I think it helps to have a new focus, a happy addition to the family. I've already laughed more today than in weeks, just by seeing her antics. This is good medicine. I wake up in the night thinking, *Thank you for my healing.*

Monday 1 August 2011

David rang with the news that our tax return was in, so yippee, puppy picking up time. No need to wait a week. We went via Rockingham Hospital to get my stitches out. They were a bit concerned over the red rash that had appeared on my neck and chest over the last few days. I've taken antihistamines and I've put steroidal cream on it now. They said to observe it over the next few days and keep them informed.

The traffic to the city was okay and by the time Irma, Khan and I got there, they had finished washing her and were blow-drying her fluffy puppy fur. I paid the balance and bought the compulsory puppy pack containing food and worming tablets. We also found her a gorgeous bright pink collar and lead. We listened to the puppy information talk and then had to go to their recommended vet for a clean bill of health. This was a free check as part of the package. By the time we drove home in peak hour traffic, she was fast asleep in the back seat with Khan.

Within minutes of getting home, David arrived as well. We introduced her to both David and Cheyenne. Cheyenne did really well. She was a bit perplexed but very gentle and showed some amazing foot work to avoid treading on the little rummin. I fed her, she pooped outside and the two of them had a bit of a rougher play session. Now, at 7pm, she is napping. I can't keep calling her 'she' or 'her'... name?

Tuesday 2 August 2011

Ugh... the puppy was sick all night long, vomiting mucous! Probably too much stress for her. Needless to say, not much sleep for me, as Cheyenne was restless all night too and wouldn't settle. I cleaned up puppy poo, wee and vomit, and tried to ignore how exhausted I was. I've also had gut cramps and diarrhoea most of today. I have a slight fever too. My rash is not better. I have to keep an eye out for infection and keep the nurses informed. Today, Irma packed and did some last minute errands whilst puppy slept most of the day. I brushed Cheyenne and Khan vacuumed the fur balls away as the puppy kept chewing on them.

I've thought of a name... Krystal... as in Crystal Healing, my little healer. It's a good feminine name but strong too. David is okay with it and Irma likes it. I called the Mt Lawley pet store and they said she may need to settle for a few days—for us to at least keep her hydrated, as she hasn't eaten anything since yesterday afternoon. White Light Krystal... Please, Universe, and please, Misha.

Thursday 4 August 2011

What a gorgeous day outside. It may be cool but it is sunny and not windy. Both girls are sleeping outside. We'll take Cheyenne for a walk later so that she still feels special and loved. Krystal is on her blankie in her basket, happily snoozing in the sunshine.

Yesterday was a very traumatic and emotional day for me. Krystal has had restless nights so neither David nor I have slept much. We both heard Irma and Khan get ready to leave. When the taxi came at 5am, we hugged each other and said farewell. It was all very quick as we were still half asleep. They forgot to pat Cheyenne goodbye and she looked forlorn.

I spent most of the day frantically cleaning the house and washing tonnes of laundry, including blankets and doonas. Krystal was having diarrhoea (like me) and wasn't eating anything, so I took her to Port Kennedy Veterinary Hospital at 11am. I saw Dr Gary and unfortunately it was the first time I had been there since Misha's death; it was even in the same room! David had told me which room he'd said goodbye to Misha in, so I was aware. The vet asked how I had been. I assumed he knew about Misha, but no, I had to explain and that just did me in. I couldn't stop crying as I told him about my breast cancer, the year of treatments and what a hard year it's been. The poor man didn't know how to comfort me. Dr Gary said how sorry he was for our loss and he remembered Misha as such a happy girl, always with a smile on her face when he had seen her in the past.

In between tears, I explained what was wrong with Krystal and he suspected GIT, a gastrointestinal upset. He gave her some antibiotics and special food to help settle her stomach. I kept crying in the waiting room whilst he got the antibiotics ready and the receptionist comforted me. She had her dog put to sleep three weeks ago, too, so she could understand my grief, explaining how hard it was for her to come back to work.

Luckily, the medicine has worked. Krystal is now eating and playing and attacking Cheyenne and us. She has already made us laugh a lot. I actually heard David giggle for the first time in ages. I've had an upset stomach for three days, but I know that it'll pass too. I've been too busy with the puppy to worry too much about myself; I'm just getting on with tasks. I'll get to sleep eventually. Earlier today, Patricia, from Care Options came to assess whether I'm a candidate for assistance for transport to my radiotherapy appointments as well as some domestic assistance. She just rang and said yes. They will contact me later on to discuss arrangements and payment. Phew, help is at hand. What a relief.

Sunday 7 August 2011

David had to work yesterday, but Katri and Nikiita visited for the day. We sat outside in the sunshine and played with Cheyenne and Krystal. We left Nikiita to puppy-sit whilst we went to the shops for lunch and to get my Somac from the chemist. In the afternoon, we had fun looking at old film footage from when the kids were so small and cute, and which included footage of our fur babies.

I left David to do puppy duty overnight so that I could get some much needed sleep, and I did. I slept for ten hours. We had brekkie outside and then went to a pet shop with Krystal. We bought her a couple of new toys and a carry crate. She settled into it straight away and slept for the whole trip to South Yunderup and back. Our house was locked up, but we saw our new front door as well as the inside doors and shelves. It's looking really good. The rest of the arvo was spent reading my magazine outside before I had to take another nap. I've had a headache all day and have felt like I'm getting a cold. David is exhausted. He's gone to bed early and I'm on duty tonight.

Tuesday 9 August 2011

I sleep when puppy sleeps, just to get some rest. I've caught a cold and have had a fever for the last three days—I'm keeping it down with painkillers. I'm watching a lot of TV, completing house chores and sitting outside with the girls in the fresh air. Krystal has been with us one week already and is still a fussy eater. According to the vet, we've got to show some tough love. Apparently, puppies won't starve themselves, though cats will.

My fingers have swollen to the size of fat sausages and they are very painful! I feel fluid retention in my body and the scales show weight gain too. I'd better watch what I drink and eat, and try to exercise some more. It is so hard when I feel so tired and feverish. At least we took Cheyenne for a walk today. Come on, Sorja. I can do this.

Thursday 11 August 2011

I feel so much better. I slept last night thanks to two glasses of wine, carbohydrates and a sleeping tablet. Krystal also behaved herself and slept in three-hour stints. I let her sleep in the bed with me (spoiling her I know) and at one point, it was so funny. I've been using the breast cancer support pillow to press against my PowerPort scars which are still a bit sore after two weeks. Being half-asleep, I thought I grabbed my pillow but grabbed Krystal instead! I heard an indignant 'ooophph' and I realised my mistake. No harm done. It gave me the giggles though. David didn't snore either, so there we were, the three of us in bed, with pillows in between so that David wouldn't squash Krystal in his sleep. He is a heavy sleeper whereas I'm a light sleeper.

Wednesday was a day of people calling me; I received a call from Visa, Care Options, Lynn, Irma, and several from David. I went to visit Marg and Lynn at Sea Sirens for an hour, with Krystal in her travel cage. David took over puppy care once he got home and I went to do food shopping. One and a half hours later my legs were exhausted, and I was a bit cranky from lack of sleep and overtiredness.

It's another gorgeous arvo, a sunny 20°C. The birds are very active, and I see doves busy building their nests for egg-laying time. Spring is definitely in the air. Although the nights are still cold, the days are getting longer and I am feeling more optimistic again. Krystal is eating and playing like a normal puppy and isn't so lethargic anymore.

Irma says that Ma is up to her usual drunken antics and depressing her no end. Otherwise, Khan likes his new school, it is easy to get to the Bundaberg central city area from their unit, and they are close to all amenities. I told her to hang in there. Ma and Pa will return to Orford soon enough. Pa has the patience of a saint, still loving Ma after all of these years of emotional abuse. I guess we never truly understand what goes on between a married couple behind closed doors and, yes, I understand there are two sides of the story...

Ma has definitely suffered brain damage due to continued and excessive alcohol consumption and abuse. Often, she imagines events that are true in her own mind but are false memories. Sadly, she sees most people in a negative light. Angry liver = angry person. Red liver = red rage. I pray that Ma will find peace in her life and experience joy instead of hatred. We learn our greatest lessons from our immediate families... I keep reminding myself to observe, to learn, to understand, to forgive, to love and to not repeat history, not only from Ma and Pa's mistakes but also to learn from my own.

Saturday 13 August 2011

Yesterday was a blur from lack of sleep and energy. Today was better because David didn't have to work. He was able to take Krystal from the room at 7am and let me go back to sleep for an extra three hours. Later in the day, David went to get Krystal a smaller collar, a new bowl and another chew toy. Boy, those razor-sharp puppy teeth are a killer on our hands and fingers.

Whilst he was gone, I had a goal in mind: to wash Krystal as she was decidedly 'wafty' with her puppy pee smell. Not a nice way to wake up when her body is plastered against my face and neck! It took me forty-five minutes to wash her, rinse her twice, towel dry her (and the ensuing 'rougher' game she made of it), blow dry her and finally to comb her. Krystal was fairly calm in the warm water but what a nutcase when we were all finished! She went ballistic around the living room, attacked all of her toys and looked like she was possessed by a Demon. Wow, all that from being clean. I can't say that I go crazy like that after my shower; I think I would frighten David if I did.

We could learn a lot from a puppy: the joy, the spontaneity, the getting up to mischief, the unconditional love even if having just being scolded, finding fun in little things, such as a used-up toilet paper roll. Forget expensive toys; a corner of a rug or a blanket provides so much more of a challenge (if you get away with it). Each day is a new adventure, for example, grabbing hold of big sister Cheyenne's tail with your teeth and not letting go until either flung off, or the fur comes off in your mouth... wow... to be a puppy! It's a full moon and I usually charge up my crystals outside under the light of the full moon. I texted Irma and Katri cheekily saying that I should put Krystal outside to charge up too, although I don't think she has run out of healing energy yet.

I've certainly got my wish of having a lap dog. Krystal climbs onto my lap when she is tired and has had enough for the time being. It's like having a little heat pack on my lap or at my feet. It is very soothing. Thank you, Krystal.

Sunday 14 August 2011

I had a good day today. I slept in until 9.30am and after brekkie I watched Krystal enjoying herself with her slippery slide—the lid of the bore water outside. David took a huge amount of tree limbs and garden rubbish to the tip and I raked the leaves into the bin. Phew. I also went for a walk on the beach for the first time in weeks. It was a blustery half an hour but worth it. After the rest of the house chores and cooking, I feel tired but proud of all I have accomplished today.

Krystal sounds like a cat sometimes when she almost meows for her food. At least she is eating now and playing with Cheyenne. She has developed a habit of grabbing hold of Cheyenne's tail and hanging on for dear life whilst Ratbag walks around. I laughed so much and it feels so good for my Soul. Krystal ended up with tufts of Cheyenne's hair and Cheyenne looked a bit put out. At least she growls when Krystal hurts her too much. Tomorrow, it's back to my blood tests and my oncologist appointment. I have to leave Krystal here with Cheyenne, probably howling away unless Ratbag teaches her what to do when Mummy is away. Krystal has to get used to being left at home.

Tuesday 16 August 2011

Well, three times yesterday and twice today, I've left the girls in the living room and kitchen/dining room area. I was thankful and grateful that they were both still alive and okay each time I returned home, and that there was no major destruction or 'accidents' in the house.

My bloods showed anaemia still, so it's lucky I made beef stroganoff with lots of good red meat and iron. I verified with Dr Gan that I only have two more doses of chemo and then one year of Herceptin, and he said, 'Yes.' I told him of my concerns over my breathing and the heaviness in my chest, so he listened to my lungs and heart. He said it all sounded okay. I'm due for another heart scan in five weeks' time, just in case.

Later, I went to the chemist and then on to the post office to pick up a package full of 'goodies' that Irma had ordered for me: blueberry punch, alpha lipoiec acid, Traumeel tablets and green and white tea capsules. I feel the difference when I have run out of my health potions, and I've felt more rundown and tired in the past two weeks since not taking my blueberry punch.

I had my fourth counselling session today. I explained all that has happened over the last month: my surgery, Misha's passing, the extra chemo sessions and getting Krystal. Phew! She told me how strong I am in recognising my own needs and being able to separate the physical from the emotional, mental and spiritual, and that not everyone can do that. I told her about my goal of writing a book. She said that I am very articulate, and my words could help other women who could relate to them but have difficulty analysing their thoughts and feelings to the degree that I do. I hope so... I want to normalise my experience, for example, that it's okay to have an 'accident' in your undies if you don't make it to the toilet in time. Chemo does such things to your bowels and it's not always controllable. I am patient with Krystal's pees and poos on the carpet, so why not with my own 'accidents'? It's nothing to be ashamed of and, as David says, 'It is what it is.'

The counsellor said that she is amazed by me and my strength. I replied, 'Thank you.' However, it's hard to believe when you're on your own at home, when you are feeling vulnerable, alone, in pain and lonely. I know that I come across as a secure and strong person. I've had to because of all that's happened in my nearly forty-five years. I am learning that it's okay to show my insecurity, vulnerability, humanness, and to show my emotions and cry in public. It is not a sign of weakness but is, in fact, a sign of courage to show all of me.

Bottling up emotion has caused too much toxicity in my body, and I'm trying to learn from the past. I'm allowing myself to feel and reveal my emotions, to acknowledge them and then to let go of them. I think the reason, or one of my 'defining moments in life', as to why I haven't allowed myself to cry as often as I want to over the years, is due to the fact that my Dad made fun of me when I was seven years old. I cried crocodile tears and he copied me, making me realise how silly I looked faking tears! I think that I took that on board and attached it to all kinds of tears, the real ones as well as the fake. So now I am trying to undo that belief system and know that tears can be very cathartic and a physical release, a feeling of *God, I'm glad that is out of me.*

I took my steroids in preparation for chemo tomorrow. Boy, do they leave a funny taste in your mouth and a funny feeling in your tummy, as well as an increase in your appetite. Roll on and keep on keeping on...

Thursday 18 August 2011

Wow, I didn't think this year would go by so fast. Yesterday's number seven chemo went smoothly. I decided to shock the nurses by wearing my red wig there for the first time. They all loved it and gave me a new name: Veronica Vixen. Ha, ha, ha. One hour prior to chemo, I put an Emla patch on my PowerPort site and it worked well. I felt a slight pain and jab and a giving in. Megan was then able to extract blood from it no problems and check the flow. Pre-med and then the Docetaxel took one hour, a flush, Herceptin half an hour, a flush with Heparin and then a half an hour wait to see if I was okay.

I was talking to them about the fact that cuts don't heal as quickly and I would have a few more scars to add to my collection. I also commented that I was forty-five next month and I had a right to my scars for my age, as they were signs of the life I have lived. Megan was shocked because she thought I looked about thirty-five or so. It made my day. It's our Finnish background and our skin, as our entire family look younger than we actually are. Maxine commented how well I was doing with my rounds of chemo and how good I looked. That's lovely to know, as they see so many people and I know she was being genuine. I asked about my fever episodes last time and she scolded me for not going into hospital. She said I was a very lucky woman, as a fever continuing for days may have meant a virus and could have been fatal in my condition. My stubbornness could have killed me! Okay, lesson learned. Never again ignore the warning signs. The painkillers masked the fever but did not combat the virus.

I've been really lucky with my nails, thank God. A lot of people, mostly men in the nurse's experiences, have had nasty side effects with Docetaxel, for example, their nails going black and falling off and being extremely sore. Ouch! I've been very religious in applying the nail hardener as per the instructions. I've also kept up with my calcium, magnesium and zinc. Maxine also told me that a good trick was to apply black nail polish as well to keep the nails hard. I've never worn black nail polish before; it's a bit Gothic for me. I can't see men applying it either...

The steroids kept me awake last night, although David and the girls slept on peacefully. Never mind, I'll sleep eventually. Despite a lack of sleep, I've had a lot of energy today thanks to steroids, blueberry punch and iron. I've washed the dishes, the laundry, and my wig, which looked ragged after I was drenched in the rain the other day. I've picked up doggy poops, played with the pooches, read in the sunshine... aaahhh.... I've sent a lot of texts to friends and family, and received a few phone calls too. My next heart scan is now booked for 29 August, this time at Palmyra. Geez, these medical appointments are all over the place, and I'm driving here, there and everywhere. We'll take Cheyenne for a short walk when David gets home. I'll collapse later for sure. I feel okay though. I've managed to go to the toilet fine and I feel quite calm. Thank you for my healing and thank you for my strength.

Sunday 21 August 2011

Right at this moment, I feel truly blessed and happy to be alive. I've had a delicious cup of coffee and pannari (a type of Finnish pancake) while sitting outside with the sun warming my joints and muscles. A pair of pelicans flew overhead in the clear blue sky, and Cheyenne and Krystal just had the time of their lives having a 'rougher' play session. My goodness, that little one can run. Our backyard is large and they just went around and around and around. It made me dizzy just to watch them. They had such a happy look on their faces, and it made me laugh and laugh. Genuine belly laughter and it was so good for me to hear it coming from my Soul instead of grief and sorrow. Thank you.

Krystal has now collapsed at my feet on my dirty slippers. Oh, how she loves those dirty, smelly slippers. She sticks her small head inside them and you can see bliss on her face... aaah... Mummy's feet smell... I should wash them but why deprive her of that comfort? In fact, I suspect little Krystal has a foot fetish. She loves Daddy's sandals, Mummy's sandshoes, socks and, of course, nibbling and licking at our toes... hmmm... I wonder if she'll grow out of it?

I feel better after a decent night's sleep. Thank you, David, for taking over puppy duty last night so that I could get some deep sleep for the first time in a week or so. David is napping now as he's got a headache. Working six days a week combined with the stress of everything has caught up with him. After he wakes up, we'll go check on our house again. I haven't been for two weeks. The house is locked up but we'll peek through the windows.

On Friday, I even managed a couple of hours of weeding and gardening. That shocked everyone, I think. I feel more positive this time round. I do have some pain in my knees but it's not as debilitating. I took my healing magnesium and essential oils bath last night, with candlelight and Il Divo music to keep me company. I am appreciating the little things in life more, that's for sure. In that way, all of this has been a blessing. I used to complain about such stupid, meaningless things. I honestly think I looked for things to nag about, possibly out of sheer boredom. This challenge puts everything into perspective. I'm no saint and I'll never be one; however, each day I can change and learn something new or something old that needed to be remembered and treasured.

Yesterday, Krystal and I were outside and she walked towards me 'proud as punch', holding something in her little mouth. I didn't have my glasses on and I thought it was a twig. When I put my glasses on, it was definitely not a twig; it was a very long and wriggling earthworm. She looked so satisfied with her 'hunt' and walked tall with pride at a huge 1.8kg. I almost didn't want to take the worm away from her, but I felt sorry for the poor worm. This reminds us to be proud of our little and big accomplishments in life. I do feel proud of how I have coped these last seven months. What a ride! I know that I've got a way to go but 'onwards and upwards' and 'it's the journey not the destination'.

Hey, my hair is starting to grow. I have more than 5mm now, maybe even 10mm in some places. After my last chemo, it should happily start thriving again, so a few more months of wigs and then hair just in time for spring or summer. Short hair will be 'in' again. I'm looking forward to that. I've been allowing my scalp to breathe in the sun; it feels good without the compression of a wig, hat or scarf. No matter how loose they are, it still feels like a band across the forehead. Freedom for the scalp!

Chapter 23

No Judgement-Life's Lessons

Sunday 28 August 2011

It's been one week since I wrote in this journal. I've got a good excuse, not that I need one. Well, I guess the Universe wanted me to experience another 'little' hiccup! I'm writing this from Rockingham Hospital Medical Unit Ward (Room 8). I hadn't felt well for days and my PowerPort wound site had still not healed fully. A couple of stitches came out on Tuesday and the open wound must've got infected. I had a few days of feeling out of sorts, all grumpy and snappish, and my fever started spiking again. I tried to bombard myself with all the natural anti-inflammatories—olive leaf, colloidal silver, Arnica and Traumeel—but it wasn't enough.

Still, I fooled myself into believing I was okay to go to Katri's for the weekend as David had arranged to have Saturday, Sunday and Monday off. So, on Friday, I packed while also doing puppy duty and was ready to go once David got home. At 3.30pm, I visited the nurses in the chemo unit to get their expert opinion on my wound site. They told me not to be so complacent, that it was my life at stake and that the wound site looked very swollen, angry and sore! They directed me to go straight to the Emergency Department.

Reluctantly, I took their advice. I'd been a stubborn fool again. (I know, no judgements!) Instead of listening to my body's warning signs over the days, I had just continued with weeding the garden and doing the usual cooking and house chores. This is hard to physically write as my writing hand has a cannula and bandage on it. I just had another dose of the IV antibiotics pushed through and it is sore now.

At ED, I showed them my chemo card, 'Medical Alert Febrile Neutropenia' as well as my PowerPort cards. I waited for nearly an hour before they put me in an isolation room, as I was at risk of exposure to other viruses, and ED is, of course, full of sick people. Unfortunately, due to the suspicion of my PowerPort being infected, they could not use that to withdraw blood samples—heavy sigh. Once again, the lady doctor took four attempts to find a useable vein and the pain was lip-bitingly bad.

As the evening progressed, I kept David posted on my progress. I realised that it was not going to be a quick process of seeing the doctor, getting a script for antibiotics and being sent home. One nurse with prior Chemo Ward experience attempted to access my PowerPort to withdraw a blood sample. I say attempted because she missed the right spot and ooohhh, it hurt! Obviously, this stirred up the wound site even more. How foolish of her.

At about 8pm, I called David to bring me a few things for the night, and he arrived in time for my transfer to the Short Stay Unit. My first night was in a private room. I didn't sleep, though, as they took my 'obs' every few hours and administered rounds of antibiotics and other medications. The sound of a poor woman nearby being sick also kept me awake. On Friday night, the male nurse made a mistake and ran my 11.30pm antibiotics through too quickly. It stung and hurt so much. He had put the drip on and left, and it was the next female nurse who observed his mistake. She said that it shouldn't have gone through that quickly. That's how people die, through mistakes and forgetfulness. He had said he preferred the ED, as there was more excitement and more to do there. How negligent of him not to pay attention to the patients he *did* have! An hour later, I had incredible chills and shakes; my body was fighting hard. Later still, at about 4am, the fever spiked yet again, up to 38°C. After I was given heated blankets by the concerned female nurse, I finally dozed fitfully for two hours.

My little nephew Khan sent me a beautiful text that read, *Hey Sorja, I heard... Eek! Don't worry, ur strong and good :-D love u! :-D happy sunshine B-) :-D from Khan B-)*. How gorgeous, and yes it helped.

On Saturday, I was admitted to the Medical Unit Ward and given another private isolation room. For a hospital, it really is quite pleasant. I'm trying to look at the positives still; this has once again forced me to rest and not do. I have a window in this room and I can draw the blinds right up to watch the blue sky, the sun and wildlife. I've been watching pelicans in the sky, cockatoos and parrots eating on the ground, white butterflies, dragonflies hunting, pigeons, and I even saw my trusted eagle. Mother Nature is with me and wants me to stay positive. I even observed a spider unsuccessfully attempt to pounce on a few bugs flying close to its web. Everybody's got to eat, right? Speaking of which, the food has been high quality in this hospital, and I have been pleasantly surprised by the lunches and dinners.

Last night, I asked for a sleeping tablet and, thank the Lord, I slept. Two nights without sleep was not helping my recovery at all. It has been constant rounds of taking my obs and giving me numerous and different types of IV antibiotics. Today, I was told it is definitely a staph infection again, and they've taken swabs to ensure it's not one that is antibiotic resistant. I'm feeling so much better now. The wound is healing and crusting up. It's no longer hot to the touch or sore to push down on in contrast to how sore it was yesterday. But still no going home for this pup yet... They are bombarding me with antibiotics to ensure it doesn't come back.

Tomorrow, Katri is coming to pick me up and take me to my heart scan in Palmyra, and then they want me back here for another dose or two. I'm hoping they'll let me go home afterwards. Please? I've been reading my book, listening to music and David came by today to bring me more clothes, vanities and this journal so I could catch up. I miss my home, my man and my girls. Krystal must be wondering where on earth can Mum be?

Oh yeah, earlier this week David and I went to have an onsite meeting with the Dale Alcock supervisor prior to the tiling being done. Wow, what progress. The bath is in, the sinks are in, the kitchen counter-top is up and it all looked great. He said that they've made such excellent progress, it should be complete by approximately 5 October. Yikes, we've got to start packing... Come on body, heal thyself. I've got lots to do.

Krystal had her twelve-week booster shot on Thursday evening. She now weighs a healthy 2.2kg. She is a gannet just like Misha was and she hoovers, too.

Sometimes Krystal reminds me of Nero (our black poodle from years ago) when she runs around like a mad dog. At other times, she acts like Misha, then just as herself. We can't take her to the park until her sixteenth week and final booster to combat against parvovirus. However, we have enrolled her in puppy preschool for four weeks on a Monday night starting a week from tomorrow. Now, that should be fun.

Monday 29 August 2011

Well, the hits just keep on coming! Last night, the cannula they'd used for three days had to be re-sited. A couple of doctors, and several attempts, later, a nice (and good eye-candy) young male doctor finally succeeded. However, this put my rounds of IV antibiotics behind schedule. My 6pm was pushed back to 8pm, my 8pm pushed back to midnight, my 10pm pushed back to 1am. The Temazepam helped me sleep for four hours, then the next round of antibiotics at 6am. My poor arm and hand are so bruised, swollen and sore.

I was woken up at 7.40am and I rushed to get ready for Katri and David's arrival after 8am. David brought Krystal in the car and I got to see her, yippee. Katri and I drove to Palmyra in good time. We had to wait a bit for my injection and then another half an hour before my heart scan. It took two goes, as the first time my stomach was too close to the heart and interfered with the reading. Two goes in an uncomfortable position flat on my back, arms above my head, holding still for eleven minutes each time. Finally, Katri and I could drive back. We bought Red Rooster for lunch and stopped off at home. Sneaky I know, but it was so nice to be out of the hospital for a while, in fresh air and 22°C sunshine. We sat outside and chatted whilst we ate and watched the girls play. I then packed a few more items to take with me to the hospital. Katri came into the room briefly and also bought me a magazine to read.

Soon afterwards, I was visited by the doctors from the Infectious Diseases (ID) Department. They've been able to identify the particular staph infection I have and can adjust my antibiotics to better suit the strain of virus. Unfortunately, they want me to have the PowerPort removed surgically at Fremantle Hospital as soon as it can be arranged. What's more frightening is that they are concerned that the virus could have done some damage to my heart! They want me to undergo some procedure where, under sedation, the doctor places a tube down my oesophagus and gets as close to my heart area as possible. The doctor will then perform some kind of scan or internal ultrasound to check my heart valves. It's called TOE, a trans-oesophageal echocardiogram. The female doctor from the Infectious Diseases Department listened to my heart and said she heard a murmur. It was imperative that it be checked out through that procedure. The female doctor also said chemo next week would have to be postponed, as they cannot do it when an infection is present in my bloodstream. I will need a couple more weeks of antibiotics at least. She checked other indications for possible damage to my heart, signs in my eyes and my nails. It was a very serious talk and after laughing with Katri a lot today, it was another 'slap in the face'. What a wake-up call. This is serious!

After they left, I had a bit of a cry. I felt overwhelmed by the constant knocks. My cannula had stopped working again, and this time it took two doctors and one nurse a couple of attempts. I am so sick of being a pin cushion. The gentle, handsome doctor was again able to succeed in a different spot. Ouch!

After dinner, I texted everyone with an update and asked for their positive thoughts and prayers. I received an avalanche of encouraging messages. Irma replied that Pa had a dream last night and he saw that I will be okay. That's huge coming from Pa. My friend Lynn texted to remind me to *remember even after the darkest of nights, morning always comes. We send our thoughts for your well-being and peace on golden wings of love.* I felt comforted by the beautiful words and the knowledge that I have a team of 'Earth Angels' praying for my healing.

David came by later and we discussed my next few days. I will be transferred to Fremantle Hospital by ambulance. I can't go with David, as it's against hospital policy. David was sweet and brought me chocolate for my pain. I deserve a tonne of chocolate after all this crappy news and events! I hired a TV for the night to keep my mind off things even though the rounds of antibiotics have continued.

I called the chemo ward and talked to Maxine to let her know about all of this, but she had just been informed. She said she'll visit me tomorrow. I asked the cute ICU doctor if they had many patients with veins like mine and he replied, 'No, not many. Very few in fact.'

Oh great, I'm a bloody individual.

Oh yes, I had a very ditzy nurse tell me about her mother's battle with cancer. Sadly, her mum battled for a year, went through radiotherapy, which caused her a lot of fatigue, pulled through, lived another year and then died. Seriously, is that helpful to tell someone going through cancer treatment?

Wednesday 31 August 2011

The last day of winter, woo hoo. Well, yesterday before lunch, I was transferred by Patient Transfer to the Fremantle Emergency Department. We waited for quite a bit for a room; however, the male and female ambulance drivers chatted with me to help pass the time. What a difference in hospitals: Rockingham is relatively new and clean looking, while Fremantle Hospital is dated, old and dirty. The ED was full of people in cubicles, rooms and in hallways on trolleys. It was a shocking sight.

Eventually, I was allocated a paediatric room with pictures of cartoon animals. I ended up being there for four hours with plenty of time spent waiting, followed by lots of doctors and nurses poking and prodding me, and getting urine and blood samples. My veins kept collapsing over and over (usual fun and games), and it made a bloody mess of my dressing gown. I asked David to bring my other clean one plus some other items when he visited later.

At 5pm, I was wheeled to Ward V6, Room 4, Bed 8. It was a two-person room, no more private room, sniff. This room doesn't have a toilet or shower; we have to use the communal ones in the hallway, which are not always clean. When I visited the loo last night, there was urine all over the floor and the toilet seat! I guess they're not too concerned about my immune system being compromised. This morning, there was an adult incontinence pad full of faeces on that same floor. How disgusting! Needless to say, I didn't use that toilet until it was cleaned.

I am sharing the room with a morbidly obese woman who has injured her knee. My bad luck is that she can't sleep without having noise, so she leaves the TV on all night long. She also has sleep apnoea and snores. Unfortunately for me, it is so loud that I can't sleep. Even with a sleeping tablet, I could not sleep. I tried to clamp down the headphones to drown out her noise with my music, but all I achieved was a bit of dozing and earache from the pressure of the earpieces.

I'm not getting any rest at all, as she is talking my ear off. I've been polite and chatted back, and then had to assertively say that I wanted to watch my favourite TV shows. My darling David has visited me every day. I am so tired and I miss being home.

After fasting from midnight, I was taken to the Cardiac Department and the TOE was performed at 9am this morning. I first had to gargle a jelly looking substance for a minute and then swallow it. Yuck. The doctor sprayed the back of my throat with local anaesthetic, which brought tears to my eyes. I was given twilight sedation and I needed lots, as I was too aware. I felt a probe going through the mouthguard and down my throat. I gagged over and over, and I think some fluid came up. Anyway, it was not pleasant at all, but it was all over after twenty minutes, and I was taken to the recovery room. They changed my hospital gown, as I had made a mess of it with my spitting up. After that, I took the opportunity to nap for one and a half hours in the peace and quiet.

At 11.30am, I was back in my bed with a raging headache and sore throat. I was able to eat lunch, which made me feel a bit better. Since then, there's been another vein change—I've lost count of how many veins have become flat or non-viable—and more antibiotics, two different types via IV. I enjoyed my shower and David was there waiting when I got out, which was a nice surprise.

Another night of listening to groaning and complaining and snoring (and I'm not talking about me). I have never heard anyone complain so much or want attention constantly. At least I'm not like that, I hope. Even the doctor was impressed at how I just kept quiet when it took him three goes to get a cannula in again. Don't get me wrong, it hurt like hell. I was resigned and fed up by it all, but there's no choice, as they need to continue the antibiotics every few hours, for either the next two or six weeks. I'm praying for two weeks.

As for the TOE results, it was mostly good news at first look. Only a thickening of one valve. Whether from aging or from the infection, they won't be sure until the 'top dog' specialist looks at it tomorrow morning. So the next step is the surgical removal of the port in the next two days and a peripherally inserted cannula (PICC) line to be put in for the infusion of my antibiotics, chemo et cetera. The doctors are having a meeting in the morning to discuss my case and the best treatment options for me. My oncologist, Dr Gan, is to be present too. Dear Universe, dear God, please help me, and help my care team come up with the best plan for me. I repeat, I am not done yet!

Thursday 1 September 2011

The first day of spring, and I love spring. I had another night of disrupted sleep from having my IV antibiotics at 11.30pm and then at 1.30am. I managed a quick sleep with my eye patch mask, ear plugs, and a sleeping tablet, as well as my dressing gown over my face and my head. My roommate turned down the volume of the TV when I asked but then left her light on. She even made phone calls in the middle of the night and then at 6am. I don't swear much, but how f...... rude! What disrespect to me and other patients, eh? This was after I repeatedly helped her to get this and that out of her bag because she wasn't mobile. When she asked me to wet her face cloth, I had to say an emphatic no (it was already used). She knew I had cancer and was in hospital because of an infection, yet she assumed that her case was more important. Obviously, I'm not happy. Lack of sleep for so many days leaves me feeling very grumpy and short-tempered.

My fever spiked a little and I'm not surprised. I've had brekkie, it's 9am and they've told me to fast from now on as the operation may be tonight. I'm going to go outside on the balcony for a bit of fresh air before my antibiotics at midday. I've been in hospital for one week already. Wow. This was not what I was expecting at all... heavy sigh... keep on smiling, *sisukas* Sorja. (Finnish for courageous.) My Guardian Angels will always look after me and guide me. I surround myself with the white light of protection.

Oh, thank you, Universe. I spoke to one of the lovely older nurses and explained my lack of rest. She was so kind to arrange a transfer for me into the next room with a quiet little old lady as my roommate. The nurse had seen me outside on the balcony and asked if I was okay. She was concerned about me, as I looked so white in the face from stress, lack of sleep and pain. I was worried about what my existing roommate would think of the move, so we did it discreetly whilst she was busy on the phone again. This is so much better, and I feel that I will get some rest and sleep here. Thank you, Universe, for listening to my plea.

I've been seen by the surgeon, the Infectious Diseases (ID) doctors and the consultants. So far, all systems are a go; my PowerPort is to come out. Hopefully, a new cannula and a PICC line will be put in whilst I'm under tomorrow. Onwards and upwards eh?

Friday 2 September 2011

Phew... surgery... the removal of the port actually happened. There was a chance of cancellation, even after I'd been given the Desmopressin for my Von Willebrand's Disease. It was all a bit of a kafuffle due to a lack of communication between the nurses and doctors at handover. It really highlighted the problems encountered in a hospital. I showered and gowned up in a sexy, broken hospital gown and disposable undies. Then an ECG was performed and a saline drip put in. When the orderly came to take me to theatre at 3.30pm, I was supposed to have had my DDAVP but hadn't! This resulted in a lot of mad running around by the nurses and the decision to administer it in the prep room prior to theatre. Then the solution of DDAVP from the pharmacy was sent to ED and not the ward or theatre. Seriously! There were a lot of frustrated surgeons, doctors and nurses just waiting, waiting and waiting (oh, and me). After that, there was a possibility of an emergency surgery taking priority over mine which was fair enough. By this stage, I had to pee, so had to do so in a bed pan, which is very awkward let me tell you, but I was beyond embarrassment and hey, when you got to go, you got to go!

Finally, the DDAVP arrived. The doctors gave the nod to infuse it, which resulted in my usual headache, flushing and fluid retention. Yet again, the possibility of the emergency surgery reared its ugly head and I was wheeled into recovery whilst the doctors debated the whole situation. Another half hour of suspense on my part and some furious praying. Enough torture, please dear God. Then at 5pm, it was all systems a go again. I was wheeled in. I scuttled over independently onto the operation table (déjà vu), was given some oxygen and then sedation but not total anaesthesia. I was exhausted and fell asleep. The surgeon and doctors were surprised that I fell into a deep sleep, as the sedation was twilight only, but oh, how I loved and needed that rest even if it was only for half an hour.

Once in recovery, I woke up fairly quickly. I was alert (the nap certainly helped) and was able to have a cup of tea and a biscuit to help bring my blood sugar levels up. I stayed there until 6.30pm before being taken back to my ward. There followed the usual round of obs and IV antibiotics. I watched TV, had some tasteless sandwiches as I had missed my ordered dinner, and I was so tired that I napped at 9pm. Antibiotics at midnight again, a sleeping tablet and with the quiet room (yippee!) I slept for five hours. I had my antibiotics at 5.30am and then breakfast at 8am.

The doctors just did their rounds and after my PICC line is inserted, I may be able to go home. Yay. I will need four to six weeks of antibiotics still, but I will have some kind of attachment to my PICC line to administer the antibiotics every day 24/7. A Hospital in the

Home nurse will come to my place every day to readminister them and check on my progress. The Infectious Diseases Department at Rockingham Hospital will monitor my weekly progress when I visit them every Wednesday. As for my chemo, that's a no go until my infection has cleared. But I may be able to go to my radiotherapy course of five weeks and then finish my chemo. I will need to speak to Dr Gan about all of that on Monday.

The TOE showed a thickening of a valve in my heart, but the specialist believes it's more likely a degenerative part of aging rather than caused by the infection. So that's good news in a way.

OMG. What a week this has been. I'm so looking forward to going home. I can recover better at home: fresh air, sunshine, love and care. I am exhausted and my face shows it, what with my puffy eyes, black circles under my eyes, my pale skin and puffy body from fluid retention. I feel my nearly forty-five years, that's for sure.

I found a live cricket under my slippers and suitcase in hospital, which means good luck. Well, I am definitely in need of some good luck for a change.

Sunday 4 September 2011

I was too traumatised to write in this journal after the experience of having the PICC on Friday. The PICC nurse came in at 1.30pm and the procedure took about forty-five minutes altogether, with a lot of that time being set-up time. She did it in my bed on the ward. It had to be a sterile environment, so she took every possible measure to make it so. She used an ultrasound machine to locate a good deep vein in my right inner arm, about an inch from my elbow joint area. Once it was located, she injected local anaesthetic to numb the area (yikes it stung). After that, all I felt was the needle go in, her pushing the tube in higher up my vein, a tugging and pulling feeling without being painful. I didn't look down much because *when* I made the mistake to look down, I saw a lot of blood as a result of my having Von Willebrand's and I felt faint. She was kind and tried to distract me by chatting the whole time.

She said that a PICC line could stay in place for up to a year provided good hygiene was maintained and an infection didn't set in. Please God, let it be so. Afterwards, I felt very stressed by the whole experience and a little in shock after seeing the mess the blood made. I felt my heart thumping very fast and my blood pressure being all out of kilter. I stayed in bed and calmed myself down with a cup of tea and some mindless TV.

The next step was to wait patiently for the X-ray Department to check that it was inserted correctly, and then the Hospital in the Home (HITH) nurse could attach my antibiotics bottle to the PICC line. The bottle looks like a baby bottle with a balloon inside it full of antibiotics.

The nurses in the ward knew that I was anxious and eager to go home. They were doing their best to hurry the process along, but the X-ray Department was so backed up that it wasn't until 6pm that an orderly wheeled me down. By then, David had arrived with a change of clothes for me, and we still didn't know if I could go home or not. Luckily the HITH nurse had agreed to stay back even though her shift had finished. She knew that being a Friday night, if I didn't get to go home soon then I would have to stay the weekend. Nooooooo...

Boy, there were a lot of impatient and angry people in the waiting cubicle at X-ray. There was only one radiographer on duty and she was run off her feet. I felt so sorry for her. A man next to me complained about the wait and when I was called in before him, he said, 'How come she gets to go in when she arrived after me?' It was all about priority cases and I was determined to not justify to him, a total stranger, why I was going in before him. Couldn't he see that I had a scarf on and was bald underneath? Hello, there is a reason for everything. I have to stop justifying myself and my needs to other patients like my ex-roommate. I deserve to be helped and I deserve tender loving care.

At about 6.45pm I was back on the ward and the HITH nurse came in. They had reviewed the X-ray and the PICC was all good. The antibiotics bottle was attached, and I was given a blue bum bag to keep it in so that I could move freely. The Flucloxacillin is released through the PICC line into my bloodstream on a slow release 24/7. The bottle, or antibiotics balloon, lasts for twenty-four hours, so it only needs changing once a day. It is safe and won't let air in if the nurse is unable to come before the twenty-four hours is up.

David and I eagerly packed my stuff. David took it down to the car, I got my instructions about HITH, said my thankyous and goodbyes to the nurses, and gleefully went down the lift to the car. On the forty-minute drive home, David chatted and I did my best to act normal even though I still felt sick about the whole day. I was grateful to be going home, but I knew I wasn't one hundred per cent and I had to be careful. It was such a joy to see my girls again. Krystal has grown so much in just over a week and was a healthy 2.4kg.

I pretty much collapsed on the couch for a bit, before unpacking and trying to shower with all of my attachments: the PICC line and AB drip bottle. I was glad David took Krystal with him into the other bedroom, as I desperately needed some sleep.

It was interesting sleeping with my bag and bottle. I think I'll call it *Bob* from now on. Bob, the antibiotics bottle and bag (so much easier)... Bob didn't get in the way too much, as I never sleep on my stomach anyway. Basically, Bob moved when I moved.

Yesterday, Saturday, I rested and watched TV most of the day as my body really needed it. The lovely HITH nurse came at about 11am to change Bob and to look at my dressings. Today, I woke up about 8am after a good night's sleep and felt so much better. I even managed to do the dishes and a bit of laundry. Katri came over at 10.30am and we talked for hours. The nurse couldn't come until 1pm. She changed Bob and both the PICC and port dressings.

At 2pm, Katri, David and I bought take away lunch and then drove to take another look at our house. The tiles are finished, some rendering has been done, the oven is installed, doors are stained, and light fixtures and speakers are up in the home theatre room. It all looks fantastic. It's going to be such a stunning house when it's done, if I do say so myself. We discussed landscaping ideas and took a look around other houses for possibilities and ideas. After we got home at 4pm, Katri left and I went to sit in the sun and write this recap of the past few days. I feel better and yes, the sunshine, the sleep and the love have helped.

David's had a week off and has decided to take this week off too. He is not feeling well today, a bit under the weather. I'm not surprised with the level of stress he's been under the past week, the past month, in fact the past year. Poor Darling. I feel sorry for him and the kind of wife he chose in this lifetime. What a challenge to be a carer! I try to be as independent as possible for my sake as well as his. I don't want the chance of never having a decent sex life again due to him viewing me as a patient rather than as a wife and lover.

Days prior to my hospitalisation, David and I had an argument again. I yelled, 'Do you want me to die? It would be so much easier for you if I did!'

I think it shocked me as much as him and I burst out crying. I just wanted him to talk about us as a couple and not talk about the house all the time. David replied that it was easier for him to focus on the house because what was happening to me was too hard for him to think about. He said, 'Don't *ever* say that again, about dying!'

He added that the house was for us and wouldn't mean a thing to him without me there. I needed to hear that and I need to also understand that men react differently to women. We talk, they plan. Well, I'd better put my shower sleeve on and do my best. At least I don't have to worry about getting my hair clean, ha, ha, ha...

Tuesday 6 September 2011

I am now sitting in my camp chair in the sun eating hazelnut chocolate. My taste buds have been back to normal for one week and I'm feeling grateful to be here. A song from this year's Eurovision is playing on my mind: 'I Am Still Alive' by TWiiNS from Slovakia.

Yesterday was a busy day. We went to PathWest for my blood tests at 9am. The nurse there couldn't use my PICC line so prodded my poor hand again and used a vein in my knuckle, for heaven's sake! Give me a break. Then I went to the HITH office for my Bob change. The nurse said that next time they could take the blood test there using the PICC line, as trying to save my veins was the whole point.

David and I had a coffee at the hospital café whilst we waited for my next appointment. At 11.30am we went to see Dr Albert Gan's stand in whilst he was on holidays. Anyway, whatever this oncologist's name was, it was a bloody waste of time to see him. He had not read my file or notes, and knew absolutely nothing about the past few weeks, so I had to fill him in. Seriously! He then said that he wasn't willing to make any decisions regarding my chemo and that I would have to wait and see Dr Gan next Monday.

I asked him about my blood test results from the morning. Thankfully, my liver and kidneys were fine, and my white blood cell count was good, but my red blood cell count showed I was anaemic still (it was 94, down from 99 last time). A blood transfusion would be required if it dipped down to 90. To avoid that I'd better get stronger iron tablets and eat a better diet. He didn't say that; I am being proactive.

After a brief visit home to feed Krystal and ourselves (a yummy beef burger with the lot), we went to Bunnings to find a hand held shower because it has been extremely hard to keep my chest area and my right arm dry while showering. We then visited the pharmacy for a whole heap of tablets, followed by a caffeine hit to keep us going.

I was absolutely spent by the evening and my feet hurt with a continual pins and needles sensation. I showered, which was so much easier with the hand held shower, and rested by watching evening TV shows. I kept falling asleep towards the end of one program, a definite signal for me to go to bed.

Today, David took me to the HITH office at 11am, after returning from sorting a few things out at work. My Bob had been empty for two hours. It had infused more quickly for some reason, but the nurse said that it was okay and didn't matter. Oh, Irma told me to record how I explained what Bob, the antibiotics bottle, looked like. I said to her, 'It's like a used condom when it's nearly empty, inside a baby bottle that you carry in a bum bag'. Therefore, it's a used condom inside a baby bottle in a bum bag. We laughed and laughed over the phone. When it's full, it's an oblong balloon inside a baby bottle.

My chest wound from the removal of the PowerPort is still oozing a bit. It's been five days but for some reason it hasn't quite stopped bleeding. They are keeping a close eye on it. As for the PICC line, it's working great. My arm feels sore and bruised, but it's not too bad.

I've gained a few kilos in the past two weeks, but I still believe that some of that is fluid retention. My fingers and toes looked like fat sausages when I came out of the hospital after eight days of intravenous saline solution. They're better now and I feel that with all of my tablets and 'potions and lotions', my body will return to 'normal' soon. I have to 'fess up' to doing some serious emotional eating lately. It was my one pleasure and joy to indulge my taste buds with chocolate and 'feel good' food. Even during my hospital stay, I asked David to bring me chocolate for my evening munchies attack and why not? After all the torture I have gone through, and am still going through, I refuse to feel guilty.

I do miss my treadmill and other exercises. All in good time, Sorja. Walking is great for now. David and I walked for a short while today. After clinic, we went to a few shopping centres and furniture stores to look at stuff for our new house. We ate a lovely Indian meat curry for lunch. This afternoon, I received a gorgeous bunch of flowers from a friend I haven't heard from for months. It is absolutely beautiful with such a range of colours; I will enjoy them for days maybe even weeks. I am blessed with caring friends and family.

Wednesday 7 September 2011

Looks like Bob and I are going to be joined at the hip (literally) for a few more weeks. The doctor from Infectious Diseases gave me a date when the antibiotics can stop: 30 September. Well, at least that's a good birthday present to look forward to. In the meantime, HITH is to continue until the thirtieth, and I'm to have another heart scan soon. The doctor said that there is no reason why the chemo can't go ahead next week. It will be up to Dr Gan on Monday. If so, they will unhook the antibiotics for the duration of the chemo (three and a half hours) and then hook me up again. I've been understandably grumpy and feeling fed up. Feel it and then let go of it, Sorja!

David and I went for a calming walk on the beach. We then washed Krystal—such an endeavour. She's lovely and fluffy and clean again, for a day at least. Her puppy antics in the soil will soon take care of that cleanliness.

Thursday 8 September 2011

Super busy day. I woke up early and got dressed up for a change; it felt good and normal. We took Cheyenne for her grooming day. After coffee (of course), we went to get my Bob changed at the hospital. I saw Megan there and, as she had been on holidays, she didn't know about my unlucky port infection. Megan informed me that it's very unusual to get an infection in the port, only about a one per cent chance! I'm the exception not the rule once again. Just fantastic (not).

After looking at more furniture stores, we collected a new and clean Cheyenne and a happy re-union followed (well, on Krystal's side anyway, as Cheyenne was tired after her big day). We left them to it and departed for our drive to South Yunderup to see our landscape artist gardener. It was a quick meeting, but I think he got the idea and will come up with a design for us in the next few weeks.

Phew. Home to a cup of tea outside whilst David went to get taco ingredients. I was just too spent. Like I said, I tire easily nowadays and being dragged from one store to another is draining even when not sick. I can rest when David returns to work next week. At the moment, I feel the need to be supportive of his dreams for the house, furniture and landscape designs. It has been too much of a focus on me and my medical appointments, and it is draining for both of us. Don't get me wrong, I am excited about our house and looking forward to the future.

Friday 9 September 2011

For the past two nights, I have had dreams of still being in hospital and attached to machines. In fact, I've been so disoriented that I haven't known where I am: home or hospital? I was busting to go to the toilet, but I thought I was connected to a machine in hospital and couldn't move. It was frightening and I had to switch the bedside light on to see where I was. It was only then that I realised I could move, that it was only Bob attached to me and it was safe to go to my toilet. Post-traumatic stress for sure, as my mind keeps playing scenes out over and over again.

I just had to stop writing as I burst out crying. I am so *tired* of all these medical appointments and procedures. They have taken over my life for the whole year and I don't feel like I've had a break. I know I have to keep going on and not give up. It would be so easy to do, to stop fighting. As you can tell, I'm at a low point at the moment and that's okay.

I have heard of women holding it together for the whole duration of their cancer treatment and then having a mental breakdown once they're healed physically. I am conscious that this is not just physical but that the emotional, mental and spiritual are equally important.

I'm starting to get a phobia about the mail delivered to the mailbox. Silly I know. However, receiving letters from the hospital or specialist clinics with future appointments tends to make you wary of the postman's delivery. Of course, it's nice to get cards, flowers and pressies from family and friends, too, so it's not all bad. Today, I received a letter from Heartswest about an appointment on 22 September for an echocardiogram. My father is in the process of having these heart tests himself and now his youngest daughter is undergoing similar tests at the same time. Dad is in his mid-seventies and I'm nearly forty-five. Life is weird sometimes with its patterns and synchronicity.

Monday 12 September 2011

Yesterday the HITH nurse came before lunch to remove the stitches from my chest port scar. The skin had started to heal around the stitches, pulling the skin tight, so she had to cut the stitches and tug away small bits at a time. It wasn't too painful. It decided to bleed a bit from the middle section but hopefully that will heal quickly enough. I'll still have a bandage on it for a few more days.

I lay like a lounge lizard for most of the glorious day and I even dozed in the sun. Ahh, pure bliss. Remember, there are no rules! In the evening, I started going through the office and the tonnes of paperwork gathered over five years. I managed a couple of hours before I got a headache from it all. It was a good start and enough for one day.

Today, I went into Rockingham Hospital for my 'usual' Bob change. Once a week, they take bloods from my PICC line to check my liver and kidney function as well as the level of infection in my blood to make sure it's going down. I had a nice chat with the lady ID doctor who I saw when I was at Rockingham Hospital as an inpatient. She said that it was better to be safe than sorry by having the full five weeks of antibiotics. Perhaps it would even help fight infection and protect me during my last round of chemo. I'm seeing Dr Gan at 5pm today. Please let him have some good news for me, either no more chemo or the last one on Wednesday with my radiotherapy to continue on same date given.

Irma said, *Maybe your Soul loves to live on the edge.*

I got upset and angry with her, especially because when I received that text from her on Friday, I had been crying over the continued tests and procedures! My Soul may have chosen this journey, but my physical body just wants a break. I feel like it's the typical 'pot calling the kettle black'. My sister continues recurring patterns of self-defeating behaviour but expecting a different result. Anyway, her text said she was so tired of trying to make everything right. I texted back to say I didn't expect her to fix things, just that I wanted to keep her in the loop.

I don't expect my family, husband or friends to fix me or to come up with miracles or solutions; I want their support and understanding. This journey is mine and I make my own choices and decisions. Sometimes they are good and beneficial. Other times, they are not so good and, in hindsight, a detriment to my overall health and recovery. I own my own choices and I'm learning from them each day.

I'm learning not to always take negative comments to heart and to *not* seethe silently. I am finally growing up and standing up for myself. It's hard being the youngest of five children, as I'm so used to accepting my siblings' words without challenging them. Now I have had enough of not talking back. I have the right to my own opinions and words. Strangers listen to my 'words of wisdom' with respect, so why can't my own husband and family? With age comes wisdom. Well, I hope so…

Oh, I've noticed a strange thing: my fuzz of hair is growing back dark. I've been blonde my whole life and now dark hair! What the? Oh well, let's see what happens over the next few months… In saying that, I had been a dark-haired newborn according to my parents and then my hair lightened over time. Another confirmation that I am *reborn*.

Tuesday 13 September 2011

I went to see Dr Gan at 5pm yesterday and finally got to see him at 5.45pm. I caught him up on the past month and he looked at my blood results. He agreed with the ID doctors that I could go ahead with my last chemo, as my liver and kidneys are doing fine and the infection markers are going down. He confirmed that the pins and needles and dead feeling in my feet has to do with the Docetaxel and that it may last for up to six months after chemo. No. I'm going to do all that I can to boost my recovery and circulation. My heart function test at Palmyra weeks ago was fine, which is good news. I'm sure the echocardiogram will be fine too.

I rushed home, took a quick call from Irma and all is okay on that front. Forgiven and forgotten. You know, family… I had a quick snack, and then David and I were off to Krystal's first class at puppy school. The class ran from 7pm to 8pm, and she whimpered a lot as she was tired and wanted to sleep. However, she was a star pupil. Krystal picked up on the commands quickly, just as I knew she would, proud mother that I am. When let loose, she even went systematically from left to right to say hello to the four other puppies there. It was very impressive, as the other puppies didn't do that. What a smart girl. The treats helped motivate her to perform the commands sit, calm, come, look and stay. We have to keep practising every day and also come up with a trick she can perform at the graduation at the end of the four weeks (how cute). I've been teaching her 'fetch' anyway, so that will do.

Today, I slept in with the help of a sleeping tablet, went to the hospital for a Bob change and then tidied up the house so that it would be easier for the cleaner. The domestic help is provided by the Cancer Council for up to eleven hours in total. When she came at 12.30pm, she was a whirlwind of an Italian woman. In the one and a half hours she was here, I ended up doing as much as she did. I moved chairs (she asked me to), mats and doggy beds as well as washing the dishes and so forth. By trying to keep up with her, I felt out of breath by the time she left. I thought this was supposed to make it easier for me?

The cleaner said that we had too much stuff and we needed to simplify (yes, I agree), and that the dust had to be removed (once again, I agree). She also said there was too much dog hair; it was bad for my health and it would be better to have the dogs outside and ban them from most of the rooms! *No*, I did not agree with that one. Our dogs are our children and play an important role in healing me. I nodded to avoid further remonstrations by a total stranger, but I am *not* going to banish my girls from the house. No bloody way. Yes to vacuuming more often; however, a lot of people just *do not* understand the fatigue caused from having treatment. The simplest of tasks feel hard; the mind is willing, but the body is lagging. Oh well, it's my life and our house and I am doing the best that I can. It does feel good to have a clean house so that I can just have chemo and focus on getting better for the next week or so.

Anyway, the cleaner's words stung, so after she left, I had a strong coffee. A short time later, I continued with the dusting. It's these Dexamethasone tablets; they always make me hyper for the first few days. I was still going when David got home at 6pm, and he became upset with me for not resting before chemo. I told him I couldn't. Also, I felt a bit put out by what the cleaner said, so I got 'my A into G.' As I write this, it's now after 10.30pm. I still feel jittery and somehow have to calm down. I think I'll need another sleeping tablet tonight.

Thursday 15 September 2011

Wednesday was another full-on kind of day. I had clinic at 9.30am for a dressing and Bob change. The ID doctors said that my blood work looked good and it was okay to do chemo. Afterwards, I spent three hours catching up with my friend Julie at Jamaica Blue, Rockingham Shopping Centre. We hadn't seen each other for nine weeks and a lot has happened for both of us. John and Julie's European trip sounded like a lot more fun than my sequence of setbacks and medical dramas. I ended up buying a takeaway salad and rushing to my chemo appointment. I was fifteen minutes late, out of breath and light-headed from not eating, just drinking coffee and talking one hundred miles an hour. Blame it on the Dexamethasone.

Another chemo lady came up to me and chatted away. I was too polite to say, 'Hey, I'm sorry but I really need to calm down and eat.' Luckily, Marla came to my rescue and said the other patient was okay to go home. Phew! I lay on the bed and got hooked up. Bob was put on hold whilst the chemo went through the PICC line. All went smoothly in just over two hours. As I've had three lots of this combination of chemo drugs, they could put it through quicker. This was my last chemo. Yahoo! Only Herceptin from now on—every three weeks, still intravenously, for one year. Hopefully, it's going to be less invasive and with fewer side effects. Thank you for my healing.

When hubby picked me up at 4.15pm, he showed me some photos of our newly painted house from his quick trip there. The colour choices look great and I'm happy. With the garage doors in and everything painted, the outside looks complete.

I stayed up until 1am as I was way too hyperactive again. My night was restless as usual. I got up to feed puppy Krystal brekkie and then went back to bed. The HITH nurse came at 10am and I was still in my PJ's, but it didn't really matter. She knows what I went through yesterday. It's drizzling rain outside, so a perfect low-key kind of day to mostly rest.

The Universe is truly kind. I confirmed my transport to my radiotherapy sessions with Care Options and asked about the price. She called me back and reduced it even more for the month I'll need their services. How kind is that? Very supportive of our circumstances.

At 5pm, I gave myself my last Neulasta injection to help fight cold and flu infections and I accidentally hit a blood vessel. It bled a little and is bruised. It was the first time this has happened in all the times I've done it. Now, I'll just go with the flow. There's the usual side effects from chemo but it helps knowing it's the last time.

Saturday 17 September 2011

I had a fair amount of energy yesterday. I was able to do the usual household chores and prepare a healthy pear and marinated chicken salad with pine nuts. By the evening, I had a splitting headache, so off I went to bed about 9pm, which is unusual because David is normally the first to go to bed. I tried to drink a glass of wine but had to pour half of it away, as it was acidic to my taste buds and to my stomach. Oh well, never mind.

Today, I had my 'usual' HITH at 10am. They are all so kind, lovely, helpful and comforting. I washed my wig, as all that hairspray I used makes it cacky after a while.

Krystal continues to both amuse me and frustrate me—when she pees and poos inside. Despite this, her training is going really well; what a clever cookie she is. Today, she had one of her spastic run around sessions in the living room. All of a sudden, she jumped up lengthwise, like a jungle cat, and landed in my lap on the couch. That was the first time she could jump up, although she's jumped down before. Krystal looked wild-eyed, chest heaving but very proud of herself as her wriggly body all too obviously showed. She was all over me as if saying, *Did you see that? Huh? Huh?*

How could you tell her off for that? I could learn a lot from her… I should be wriggling my body with pride after enduring eight rounds of gruelling chemotherapy! Did you see that? Huh? Huh?

Krystal has grown a lot; she's 3kg now and a lot longer. Also, she is fifteen weeks old today. I still miss Misha every day and regularly look at her photos. However, she is in a good place with all the other dogs I have loved before—and still love. I know Misha approves of the laughter and joy Krystal produces inside of me.

Wow, the pelicans are flying in perfect unison and formation, just gliding high in the sky—so free I envy them.

Tuesday 20 September 2011

Hmmm... Let's see... On Sunday, we visited our house, had coffee and pancakes at Dome Café Pinjarra and a brief walk along the suspension bridge and the riverside. On Monday, a HITH nurse took bloods from my PICC line. My blood pressure and pulse were high, but I think that was because I hadn't met her before and I was nervous. I sorted through a few more office folders and it feels good to get rid of stuff. David took Krystal to puppy school because by the evening my temperature was up again and I had a splitting headache. Krystal did well again, although she's having a hard time in learning 'lie down'. Oh well, who's perfect?

Today, I had excruciating back and kidney pain, so it limited me just a little bit. I still managed the laundry, dishes, picking up doggy doos and even cooked a shepherd's pie. Not bad considering it's only one week after chemo and I'm in pain. Well done, Sorja.

I started reading a novel; it's been so nice to just be and read in the partially sunny day. Krystal amused me by dragging a huge tree limb probably six times her size and happily chewing on the palm fruit flavoured branch. She even got Cheyenne interested in it and that's saying a lot for geriatric Ratbag. Cheyenne got confused last night and couldn't see in the dark. I heard a banging noise and switched on my torch, only to see Cheyenne in the corner of the room, baffled as to where the open door was. Poor Ratbag. The years are showing on her too.

Wednesday 21 September 2011

I had a restless night, lots of dreams and nightmares. I had my clinic at 10am, so I got ready early. At the HITH clinic, there was a bit of a fright. The code red alarm went off; apparently the hospital mortuary had a fire scare. We sat and waited for the firemen to arrive and give the all clear to the whole hospital. My ID doctor chatted to me and asked how I was feeling.

'Not too bad,' I replied.

For a moment, I even forgot that I'd undergone chemo last week until he mentioned it. That's great; I'm not focused on it!

Apparently, my ID marker was five last week. Ideally, the result should be zero, as that is normal, and this week it has crept back to twenty-five or so. It could be due to chemo, the Dexamethasone or the Neulasta injection. We'll see what next Monday's results are (please be zero). He told me to keep an eye on my temperature and the chest wound site. I still have a dressing over it, as it hasn't completely sealed yet, even after three weeks. Come on body and skin, you can do it. Although the wound was tender, at least when he pressed on it *really hard*, it didn't bring up blood or anything else nasty, so that's positive. My blood pressure, temperature and my pulse were all good, phew!

After my PICC dressing was changed, and Bob of course, I went to Rockingham for a much-needed coffee (and cake—maybe not needed but wanted). A few more errands and then home to check on my girls. After three hours alone inside, no drama, all present and accounted for, no mess inside, just two happy-to-see-me dogs.

Krystal is funny, and so possessive of her toys. When Cheyenne grabs one, Krystal distracts her by licking Cheyenne's face. Cheyenne drops the toy and voila, Krystal has repossessed the toy. She even collects all her toys around her so that Cheyenne can't get them. Hmmm... what about sharing? It is hilarious to observe though.

I've been humming all day long. Although I have an upset tummy and my fingernails are very tender and fragile, it is a great sign that I've been singing and humming tunes, isn't it? I think so.

Friday 23 September 2011

Goodness, my emotions are all over the place! From humming to then crying. I was so emotional on Wednesday night, so worried about everything. I worried about my echocardiogram and so forth. I cried a few tears when I was on my own. I tried to talk to David about my fears but he could not help me. I think he is so overwhelmed at the moment, not only with everything going on for me but also a heavy work load supervising three work crews at the one time.

After HITH on Thursday, I went for my echocardiogram. As it turned out, I had nothing to worry about. A female ultrasound technician took me in, I changed into a gown and the ultrasound took about half an hour. I had to lie on my left side, have two heart monitor stickers put on my chest and then lie still until she told me to scoot over. Occasionally, I heard snippets of sound: my heart beating or blood travelling through the valves, chambers and blood vessels. It was quite interesting. I felt relatively calm throughout the whole procedure. I happily left and went home. The girls had behaved. I stayed outside for the remaining daylight hours and thoroughly enjoyed reading my novel. I could have continued sorting through paperwork but life's too short. Enjoy it while you can, eh?

Today was another lazy day. I slept in. The HITH nurse came at 1pm. In the evening, I took Krystal to the vet for her sixteen-week vaccination, the last one. Now we wait for two weeks until she's clear to go to the park, yippee. Ratbag will be happy having her company at the park. David worked late again. Sometimes I feel so lonely. This journey is taken alone most of the time.

Tuesday 27 September 2011

Even though I'm not doing much, the days continue to speed past. David worked on Saturday. My HITH nurse changed my PICC dressing again, as it wasn't feeling right. In fact, it was pinching all the time and feeling sore. It had moved from the correct position and was chafing my skin. It was so much better after the dressing change.

Katri visited on Sunday and we decided to look at our house again, followed by lunch at Hog's Breath Café. We also went for a lovely walk at the beach. Yesterday, after a day of watching DVDs (because I can), we took Krystal to her puppy school. Krystal sent this text to Kirsti today:

Hey Aunty Kirsti, Krystal here. I was a star at puppy school last night. I did fifteen 'lie downs' or 'puppy push ups' in one minute when the others could only do four or seven! And I didn't have an 'accident' on the floor like a certain someone. I held it until home. I do have accidents at home, but I don't mean to. Mummy gets annoyed when I drag in rotten veggies from the back fence. I don't know why... Anyway, busy, gotta go chase doves... xo Krystal.

It's Graduation Day at puppy school next Monday. I wonder if they 'fail' any puppy? Surely not. Anyway, Krystal is a star pupil.

Thursday 29 September 2011

I received good news from the ID doctor yesterday. My bloods were back to normal levels, so Bob is officially retiring tomorrow. Yay, yippee and yahoo. The nurse changed my PICC dressing again, so it should be good for another week. I asked the doctor if he had my echocardiogram results and he was kind enough to call HeartsWest and get them to fax the results through to him. He gave me a copy too. How kind. Good news there. My results were all in the normal heart range—what a huge relief. There was no sign of Endocarditis (an infection of the heart), thank God and thank the Universe.

After buying petrol and dropping off the DVDs, I went to check on the pooches and feed Krystal, who is still performing her commands very well. I figured I deserved a treat too, so I went to Jamaica Blue for coffee and a complimentary slice of birthday cheesecake. It was pleasant but kind of lonesome; at least I had my book to read.

In the evening, David and I went to the Austin Cove function, a welcome to new residents of South Yunderup and Phase Two. There were about fifteen of us, staff included, and we were served yummy finger food and wine or beer. It was informative and enjoyable.

Today, I am waiting for the energy to hit me. A multivitamin and two coffees later, I am still waiting. This fatigue and lethargy is a bummer. I need to get 'my A into G', as I plan to do a lot of cleaning, walk on the beach and start packing for my trip to the hills. Yahoo, freedom!

I'm going to the hospital tomorrow at 10am to get Bob detached and become a cordless Duck as my brother said, hee, hee, hee. But I plan to keep the PICC line as long as possible for the Herceptin infusions, due every three weeks starting next Wednesday. I'll leave for Katri's in the arvo, which is when her school holidays start—Katri is a Primary School teacher.

Tomorrow is our sixteenth wedding anniversary and my forty-fifth birthday. We're not doing anything, as all of our finances are wrapped up in the paying of rent, our mortgage, bills, and David is the sole breadwinner. Yesterday, I asked him why he wasn't enthused at all compared to previous years. He said that he was so over 2011 and couldn't wait to move into our new house. A fresh start and a new year. I have to admit that this year has been extremely hard for both of us. However, I find it very depressing to think that the spark he feels is not for me but the new house. I've got to find happiness, contentment, enthusiasm and passion for myself. Not necessarily in a new man but in something in my life. A reason to live and keep living, to find joy in my days, to feel excitement in waking up each day to new possibilities. It's up to me to be happy. It's a choice.

Chapter 24

Onward and Upward

Monday 3 October 2011

Phew, what an action packed few days I've had. I left for the hills once David got home Friday afternoon. I was in the middle of doing the coming year's forecast using my animal Tarot cards, with the main theme being 'self-reliance'. David gave me two of my favourite white wines to take with me, one for my birthday and one for our anniversary.

I found Katri's new rental place with only one missed turn and got there about 6pm. Katri had made a fabulous dinner of Swedish meatballs, baby carrots, broccoli, mashed potato, and gravy with peas and corn in it. We had a few wines and ate and talked and talked.

On Saturday, we went to the Kalamunda markets and Katri bought me a pretty pair of pink earrings. It was a gorgeous, perfect spring day. After lunch, we got back and I did a quick wardrobe change and freshened up, then drove to Visa and Susie's, while Katri worked in her garden. Visa, Susie and I drove down to the dance academy to watch Susie's daughter, Alex, participate in the ballet, *Peter Pan*. I had a bit of a musical chair performance myself as I started at the back, in the seat number I was allocated, but was able to move closer to Visa, Susie, Susie's girlfriend and Susie's parents after intermission. I thoroughly enjoyed the dance, costumes and stage. The dancers ranged from as young as three to about nineteen. The three-year-olds made me laugh; they were so cute in their ballerina outfits or their lion and tiger costumes.

I had a funny moment with Susie's dad. He looked at me and said that I looked great and he loved what I had done with my hair. Without batting an eye, I replied, 'Thank you, but this is a wig. I've lost all of my hair from chemo, but I paid good money for this wig so thank you.'

He stammered something about my face looking good too, but he wouldn't want to go through what I'm going through to look that good. I was proud of how I handled that situation. In the past, I would have been mortified by his comment and the fact that others were listening; this time, I was matter-of-fact and didn't really care if others heard me talk about my chemo and radiotherapy. It's my life.

Afterwards, we went back to their place. Visa, Susie, Alex and I had nibblies and a good chance to catch up on all of our latest news. I got back to Katri's about 9pm. On Sunday, we went back to Visa and Susie's for a coffee and a chat. In the daylight, I was able to see how much work had been completed with the renovations and extension of the house. My brother is a hard worker and very artistic. Such beautiful work with the rammed earth walls and the garden beds. A joint effort with Susie. Later, Katri and I walked to Noble Falls. We ate lunch there and then walked for forty-five minutes, admiring the full creek, the rushing falls and the many and varied wildflowers in full bloom. Aaah, so enriching to the Soul once again. I managed to walk, although I got the usual pins and needles towards the end. At Katri's, I needed to rest for an hour before packing up and driving home, arriving before 6pm. I had the usual greetings from hubby and my pooches with their tails wagging (I mean my girls, not David).

Being at home and knowing what my week entailed, I found my elevated mood plummeting again. When David had gone to bed, I became depressed and emotional watching television. Oh, these rollercoaster moods. Up one minute and down the next. People see me so positive; it is the face I present to the world. If only they saw me when I'm all alone and thinking about my mortality, struggles and fears.

This morning, I had my bloods taken from the PICC Line at the chemo unit. Later, at 3pm, I went back to see Dr Gan. The good news was that my bloods were all good—liver, kidneys, white and red blood cells. Also, I don't have to see him until December, as the Herceptin appointments are all set up for every three weeks. I thought I had another year of Herceptin but I was wrong. Dr Gan said they count the four I've already had with my chemo so only nine months of Herceptin to go. I'll have another full body scan in late November after my radiotherapy is complete. Speaking of which, it all starts tomorrow. I'm driving one hour to Wembley, having the treatment—about half an hour including set up—then coming back another hour. At least I'm only driving this week, as the transport service commences on Monday 10 October. I'm pooped. It's late, so I'd better finish writing and get some rest. PS. Krystal had her puppy school graduation tonight as well. My clever ragamuffin passed with flying colours.

Wednesday 5 October 2011

I leave home around 9.30am to allow for the traffic build-up and the usual road works. My appointments range from 10.30am to 11am so far. The girls either stay inside if it's raining or outside when it's gorgeous and sunny.

I found out yesterday that after five weeks, or twenty-five rounds of radiotherapy, I'm going to have a further five booster sessions directly on the sites where they found the cancer—local treatments of radiotherapy. Six weeks of radiotherapy not five. Heavy Sigh. Good news one day, not so good the next... phooey!

The procedure is that you go there, insert your appointment card in a slot at reception and then wait. A clinician fetches you to go change into your gown; the gown is in a plastic bag with your name written on it in an allocated numbered slot. Then they call you into the treatment room. Yesterday, it was so funny. After I'd put my basket down with my belongings in it, the male radiologist told me to take off my gown (I could keep my jeans and shoes on; I just had to take off my shirt and bra). He then introduced himself and put out his hand to shake my hand. It was amusing for me to stand there half-naked and shake hands with a stranger. I know they are used to seeing breasts every day but still, from my perspective, it was strange.

I was placed into the same position as during the simulation, and pen markings and measurements were done once again. The procedure took about twenty minutes altogether, as they took pictures and scans as well. These aren't done every day though. I felt a slight buzzing feeling but no pain or discomfort, thank God. I visualised a golden beam of light healing me. I think that each day I'm going to picture a different colour. Today, I visualised pink and green to represent love and physical healing. I won't run out of colours or colour combinations. I was tense as a board yesterday but today, I relaxed my fingers, not white knuckled like yesterday. I also pictured Misha looking at me and encouraging me, her tail wagging with love.

I'm taking flower essences to help with my emotions from the stress of the environment and dealing with the drive there and back. I decided to be a bit of a superwoman when I got home yesterday— doing laundry, picking up doggy poops, washing my wig, watering the plants and walking half an hour by the beach. I still had enough energy to do one and a half hours of ironing afterwards. It was lucky David took cooking dinner off my hands, as I was close to collapsing with fatigue.

Today, I'm having a mini break outside after my three hours Wembley trip and before my 2.30pm Herceptin infusion and PICC dressing change. Later, it's time to pack again as I'm going to Katri's straight after my radio tomorrow. We've got the *Queen Tribute Band* concert to go to at Burswood Casino in Perth. It's something to look forward to; it is so important to have my rewards and treats. Got to stop now and have lunch. I've got a splitting headache. I let go. I let God.

Friday 7 October 2011

Busy, busy, busy bee... Smooth run to the city yesterday. I got there in forty-five minutes, had a coffee and my radio, then another smooth forty-five-minute drive to Katri's. I rested a bit whilst Katri baked bread. We went for a lovely half hour walk around the Mt Helena suburb. Then after a shower and dinner, Katri drove us to Burswood Casino for the *Queen Tribute Band* concert. We had luck in finding a parking spot, with time for a glass of wine. What a fantastic show, with over two hours of Queen music. They were great imitators, very realistic and authentic. It was such a fun night.

We got up fairly early today for my 10.15am radio appointment in Wembley. Afterwards we decided to treat ourselves to a trip to

IKEA for coffee and cake, followed by walking around, meatballs for lunch, and more walking around, about four hours in total. Back at Katri's I had to rest as I was so spent. I had a headache again, and I stayed on the bed, in exactly the same position, without moving a muscle, for over half an hour.

Irma texted. Ma and Pa are up to their usual police and hospital routine… sigh. What can we do when they can't help themselves or want to live? Anyhow, got to get ready for the Mount Helena Tavern with Katri, Nikiita, Visa, Susie and Alex.

Sunday 9 October 2011

Friday night turned out okay. We all sat outside talking until an inside table was free for dinner. There was a hilarious moment (for me anyway) when a blowfly landed on my wig, and Susie took a swipe at it and nearly knocked my wig off! I grabbed it and Katri was ready to catch it if it flew off. Susie was mortified, as she had totally forgotten I was wearing a wig. I just laughed and said, 'Be careful.'

I had an image of it landing on top of someone's dinner. Goes to show how much has changed with me. I would have been so embarrassed in the past, but now I just laughed it off. I'm also comfortable not wearing make-up all of the time. I'm letting go of a lot of my hang-ups. The tavern had a good band, but we all were tired so decided to have an early night.

We took it easy on Saturday. So nice not to have to go to treatment over the weekend. I left just after lunch and arrived home to unpack and rest a bit before getting ready for a fundraiser cocktail party. I got all dolled up and it felt good to catch up with some friends there. The party started at 7.30pm, and David and I lasted until 11pm. David and I talked to a few friends, but I felt quite disconnected from a lot of the people there. I find I lack a few social skills, such as chit-chat. At least I made the effort to hug everyone I knew. They all said how great I looked (said with such a tone of surprise) and that I was 'glowing'. I thanked them all and wondered how bad they thought I would look. I know some people who go through chemo and radiation look very drawn, skinny, pale and hollow... I'm very grateful to have kept my shape and a good application of make-up takes care of the pale face. One woman said that if you didn't know I was sick, you wouldn't know. That's the best kind of compliment.

Today, I got up later than normal and spent most of the day catching up on my recorded TV shows. I did a few chores and washed Krystal, who I call 'Snookums'. She came out looking so fluffy that I had to keep cuddling her. Whilst I'm at radiotherapy tomorrow, David and Visa are going to our house for the final inspection. I'm being picked up by the transport company—less stress when I don't have to drive. I've also got to see the radiology oncologist weekly.

Sunday 16 October 2011

Another week notched up. Let's see... I shared my transport with other patients going to their own medical appointments, whether at Fremantle Hospital or Subiaco or Wembley. The downside of relying on Care Options Transport Service is being picked up earlier than I would normally leave and waiting after my appointment, sometimes up to one and a half hours, before being picked up. The cars are only comfortable if there are not too many people. One of the days I was squashed up against the door and window as two morbidly obese people sat in the backseat with me. It was very uncomfortable. They had heavy clothes on even on a hot day and they smelt terrible (I had to breathe through my mouth only). The day is pretty much gone by the time I get home, and then I'm tired from the travel and treatment. So, two weeks down and four to go...

During my radio treatment, I have visualised rainbows and their colours (for I am a rainbow Duck), fairy dust falling down on me, and beams of healing white light or gold and red beams destroying any remaining minute cancer cells. I leave there with a smile rather than a frown. The waiting room is always full of people with long faces; I try not to be like them. Instead, I chat to the staff and technicians, often asking questions about the equipment or the busyness of the centre. I'm getting used to the routine of changing into my gown, positioning myself on the hard treatment bed, letting them mark me with a pen and measure me; have the healing beams, chat, chat and then get back into the change room; remove the pen marks with wet wipes and apply my 100% aloe vera gel; put my clothes, jewellery and wig back on; place my gown back into my slot; get my appointment card back, chat, chat; and wait for my pick up again. It's such a long trip for the set up and then only ten minutes of radiation. I know it's got to be done. I know my Spirit Guides are walking by my side. I saw a hawk today when I was listening to the song 'What a Wonderful World' by Louis Armstrong.

I went for a walk on the beach on one of the days and I felt stronger. I think I can increase my distance a little next time, yay! I still have a lot of pins and needles in my feet and my arms, but I'm sure that will dissipate with time. My poor nails have gone all funny and ugly; two of them have gone green! The hospital pharmacist said that ten per cent of people on the chemo drug Docetaxel get similar nail changes: going yellow, green, black, brittle and sore, maybe even crumbling off. I thought I would be lucky and bypass that reaction but no.

One morning around 5am, I woke up to a 'visitation' from Nero, a young version of our poodle from long ago. Nero came through first, then Irma's dog, Zoe, looking healthy and then Misha in her prime. It was as if they were coming to say hello and wagging their doggy tails in encouragement. I felt much loved by all three of them; it was so beautiful. I even visualised them individually, holding a ray gun and beaming white healing light at specific points in my body. That sounds funny I know but it works for me. I think of it as *getting rid of the yuck!*

I went to a Cancer Council Fundraiser Ladies Night—at the Pink Duck in Rockingham—on Thursday night. Even though the theme was pink for Breast Cancer and we received a pink cocktail upon arrival, I was surprised how little the focus was on cancer awareness. To me, it appeared that the women there were more focused on enjoying time out from their husbands and children, getting tipsy and socialising. That in itself is not a bad thing; however, when I talked to other women about my ongoing treatment for cancer, it was amazing to witness how few of the women wanted to really listen. For a function specific to raising funds and awareness for cancer research and support, I would have expected more of a mention, rather than a 'raise your glass and toast' and the selling of raffle tickets. Oh well, as long as the money has gone to the good cause.

At the fundraiser, I was hurt by some of my friends and acquaintances not feeling relaxed in my presence for long. I wanted to say to them, 'Hey, I'm not contagious you know!' I understand that some people become very uncomfortable, as it brings up their own inner fears about the dreaded C word. I'm still Sorja, even if I wear a wig for now. Maybe they don't know what to say or are afraid of putting their foot in it; I'm not certain. It did make me feel very alone in a room full of about one hundred and fifty women. I was glad to come home where I could be myself, whip my hot wig off, wash off my make-up and jump into my PJs.

On Saturday, Katri and Nikiita visited and were shocked at how much Krystal had grown. We went to Rocky City for lunch and later filled up the outside pool, the pond pool, for Krystal to play in. We had fun throwing stones and sticks into the water and watching her dive for them. Even Cheyenne put her paws in the cool water.

Sunday was a shock to the system when it hit 36ºC. David and I drove to our house. The fence wasn't up but the driveway was complete. I was so tired afterwards. Not sure if it was the heat or fatigue hitting me, but I had to have an afternoon nap, and I actually slept. The doctor did say that the fatigue would hit in the second or third week while the cells in the body are busy trying to recover from the radiation, and the body needs time to build itself up again. My breast is surviving okay, just a little pink so far. I'm being very careful to apply the correct moisturiser every day. I also have to be aware of lymphoedema—avoid fluid build-up by doing the arm exercises recommended by the physio.

Monday 17 October 2011

As I was brushing my teeth this morning, I felt a crunch and spat out a piece of my tooth! No, not the dentist again! It's right against the gum line and the nerve ending is exposed, so unfortunately, the dentist has been booked for Friday. Aaarrrggghhhh! Gimme a break, excuse the pun. It's cloudy today and cooler. I feel tired after my trip and treatment, so I think I'm going for a walk by the beach to wake up.

Friday 21 October 2011

No treatment today as the Radiation Oncology Centre has a machine service for the day, for my machine at least (number two out of the three there). Thank God for that. A three-day break from it all. The Care Options Transport Service is great in one way, not having to drive myself, but—and this is a big but—I get tired of the length of the trips with so many detours. On one of the days, I was picked up before 9am and I didn't get back home until after 2.30pm. We went in an eleven-seater minibus with numerous pick-ups and drop-offs at three different hospitals. I was jammed in the back seat, squashed up against belt buckles and wondering if it all was worth it. I needed a two-hour nap afterwards, as I was a total wreck. Yesterday, we had a morbidly obese man in the back with two of us and, once again, I couldn't move at all for such a long time. It is so bloody frustrating! I've had thirteen radiation treatments so far and I still have seventeen to go. Maybe I need to drive to some of them?

I guess the 'highlight' of my week has been an incident where I fought back. Let's see... it was 11.45am on Wednesday 19 October 2011. I had finished my radiation treatment but had to wait for two other passengers to complete theirs before the driver could take us home. So I decided to eat my apple on the grass, under a tree opposite the centre. I was tired and vague from the drive and my treatment. I didn't notice that an old woman had tripped and fallen down onto her knees about fifteen or twenty metres to the right of me. When I looked up, I saw the old lady under a tree and thought she was having a rest just like me. I continued to eat my apple, oblivious to her plight and attempts to get up. I just looked into space and thought about all of my treatments and so forth. The next thing I know is the screeching sound of tyres and a man in a 4WD pulling up in front of me onto the grass verge. He gets out and starts yelling at me. I'm confused until he says, 'I see you weren't quick to get up and help her!'

He's angry at me as he stalks off to go to the old lady. By this time two other women had rushed to help her as well. I felt the anger well up in me and I screamed back, 'I've just had cancer treatment!'

I felt the need to fight back at the injustice of his abuse, so when he walked back to his 4WD (the old lady was safe and sound), I waited until he was in front of me and, still sitting down, I said, 'Excuse me, Sir, but I've just had cancer treatment myself, so don't be so quick to judge!'

I whipped off my wig to show him my bald head! Oh My God! I think my reaction surprised myself as much as everyone who witnessed the scene, including the man, two other women standing close by and the oncoming traffic in both directions. He looked horrified and muttered, 'I'm sorry.'

He got in his car quick smart and drove off. I didn't see the reaction of the two other women, as I was too upset and busy putting my wig back on. Oh dear, what's happening to me? When I texted my sisters about the whole event/episode/incident/whatever, they were proud of me for teaching him a lesson. I can laugh about it now, but I was so close to tears at the time.

After today's dentist trip and over two hundred dollars later, I drove to our new house to admire it and the new fence. Now it looks like a house and yard with the landscaping still to go. It's a lovely 30°C today. Aah, it feels so good.

Monday 24 October 2011

Last night I had a dream. *Shane, a friend of ours who passed years ago, was being arrogant with me, so I did some Reiki symbols to his face and said, 'Don't mess with me, I have powers!'*

He then smiled and his eyes twinkled. I think Shane approved of my 'wig episode' and standing up for myself.

Saturday was a mad cleaning day and on Sunday, I finally started sorting through some stuff and packing for the move into our own house. Today had a rough start, though. When I called on Friday for my pick up times, I was told 9.45am for Monday. The driver rocks on up at 8.30am. I'm nowhere near ready, so I tell him to go without me and that I'd drive in. I rang the office straight away and said that I wasn't happy at all. Why give me a time to plan for if they aren't accurate? They assured me that it wouldn't happen again. Sure.... you know, it took me forty-five minutes to drive in and then forty-five minutes to drive home. That's so much better than hours.

I've developed a rash on my chest, which I showed the doctor and the female technicians. They said that it was normal during radiotherapy and advised me to use lotions and creams to protect my skin. Afterwards, I went to IKEA for coffee and a slice of cake. I bought a few goodies for home too.

This arvo, I went for a forty-five-minute walk on the beach. It was a gorgeous balmy day with a slight breeze and as I walked, I thought about my year. Phew, I've been through a lot. After tomorrow, I'm halfway through my six-week radiotherapy course. What a long journey I have undertaken. I had a dream about climbing a mountain and that I had to do it by myself. There was not a single hand reaching out to help me.

Wednesday 26 October 2011

That's it! I've had enough of the transport service. The driver is always arriving much earlier than the time given to me by the office girls, I'm squashed up against the door frame and other passengers, and then I have to wait for up to two hours after my radiation treatment for the drive home. If this was a free service, I would understand, but I am paying for this and am certainly not getting my money's worth. It's cheaper to drive in myself. I'm more exhausted from the travel than the actual treatment. So I have decided to cancel the Care Options Transport Service and drive in by myself for the next three weeks. I know it will be tiring, but I feel it's time for me to get back behind the driver's seat and have some control over this experience.

It is said that a car represents your body; therefore, I am taking back control over my car (and my body) by not letting someone else take me to my destination. I keep hearing the tune 'Fight Song' by Rachel Platten in my head. I feel I'm regaining my strength alongside my hair growth. Some American Indian tribes believe that strength lies in their long ponytails. I'm starting to agree. My hair is growing back everywhere and I feel like I'm returning to myself.

Ma and Pa continue to be at war with one another, subjecting us kids to their drama. I think of the story 'The Boy Who Cried Wolf' and wonder if any one of us kids will believe them if a real emergency arises. That's a scary thought. We've become immune to their accusations of physical abuse, sexual abuse and so forth. I honestly don't know who to believe anymore! I've had cancer in my body physically; my parents have cancer in their Souls daily. When will there be peace for them? We all feel helpless, as they refuse to take their own driver seats in their lives...

Sunday 30 October 2011

Wow, this year 2011 is nearly over. Thursday went well with me driving in. Afterwards, I did some weeding and gardening in the front yard. The final inspection for the house went well for David also. Now, just to make the final prestart payment on Wednesday and then schedule a day and time for the handover of keys to our house. The past three days were spent either weeding or packing the house up. I'm proud of all we've achieved so far and I'll continue a bit more each day. I do find it very hard to throw things away though, especially gifts people have given me. We've got so much stuff, and I know I have to find strength within me to clear out some of the clutter. I've been dusting the objects before packing them to make it easier in the new house—no need to pack the dust, eh?

I am disappointed with myself, as my bad habits have crept back in. I've been eating way too much and drinking two or three glasses of wine each night. I understand I'm trying to cope with stress through these unhealthy means, but I'm not doing my body any favours. This week I will do better. I owe it to myself and I'll feel better about myself. I know I've been feeling angrier lately and I'm thinking angry liver equals an angry person. I've even contemplated divorce again. That's how messed up my emotions have been. No rash decisions; I'm going through enough already!

Friday 4 November 2011

What a week... I'm exhausted just thinking about it. Driving every day for at least two hours, radiotherapy and doctor sessions, PICC dressing change on Wednesday, shopping for all of my wonderful tablets I'd run out of but make me feel so much more energetic and alive, food shopping, cooking and housekeeping. I don't know how other people continue to go to work as well as all of this activity.

Today was a very special day. David drove me to my radiotherapy session and then we both went to Dale Alcock Central for our handover. We got our house keys, documents and warranties, and lovely presents too (a large wooden chopping board, a cookbook and a stainless steel oil pourer). We then thanked the staff profusely and complimented them on our whole house building journey with them. David and I drove to our house and I had the honour of opening the door with our own keys for the first time. It was splendid. A few minor details to be fixed but overall an excellent job. We spent over an hour looking through and visualising where to place everything. I texted everyone with our happy news for a lovely change.

I'm trying not to be so hard on myself by remembering the saying by William Shakespeare: *There is nothing either good or bad but thinking makes it so.* I haven't curbed my eating or drinking, although I've been conscious of the need for change. I'm not an evil person; the person I hurt the most is truly myself.

Even today, on such an important day, I was drawn into family drama and politics. It's so hard to remain neutral and not to take sides. I know that it's a part of my own Soul healing to not get so caught up in others' issues and conflicts. It's been a part of my nature, and my professional learning as a counsellor, to mediate between family members; however, I'm learning to step back and look after my own needs for a change. I have to learn to let go of the feelings of guilt and learn how to accept myself unconditionally. I'm able to love Misha, Cheyenne and Krystal—in fact most animals—unconditionally; therefore, why not me?

Mum rang me today as we were in the car heading towards our

house with our new keys. I was excited about this momentous occasion and it was so frustrating to hear her complain about life again. Ma kept focusing on the negative and I tried to tell her to look forward not back. Out of the blue she asked me if she is a good mother! For the first time in my life! I was honest and said that she wasn't a bad person, but she had been nasty to me and us at times and no, she wasn't a good mother all of the time. When I repeated to her what I had said as a young ten-year-old in Finnish, along the lines of 'people have to try', I guess that was the final straw for her. She hung up on me! Oops, this honesty business is getting stronger. I'm speaking more 'home truths' to everyone. Maybe it's a huge part of my healing?

Tuesday 8 November 2011

We've done really well with our move. I've been a mad packing woman for at least a few hours each day and we've made numerous trips to the house with our packed cars. I've got six more radiotherapy sessions to go, one of which is the last of the twenty-five treatments and then five more 'booster sessions' on 'ground zero' where the cancer was found. My poor boobie is red and tender as is as my armpit. The rash on my chest is worse, and I'm applying cortisone cream on top of my aloe vera gel and lotion. My nipple has gone bright red and is so sore, like unbelievably bad sunburn. I keep telling myself that it's not forever and the end of radiation treatment is in sight. Yay.

Two of my nails have broken off halfway—the dead bits from the chemo drugs. I'm trying to keep the others strong with nail polish; however, they still feel very tender to touch. My hair grows every day; it's soft like rabbit fur and still dark, which is strange after being blonde all of my life. Maybe another month and I can go out without my wig. My sleep is still topsy-turvy. Some nights I manage five hours straight whilst other nights I'm up every hour with a very restless body. My stomach continues to be upset every single day... weeks and months on end... I feel sorry for the toilet, myself being a constant visitor. I hope I'm absorbing some of the nutrients from my food, not just passing it straight through. Hang in there, body, please.

Tuesday 15 November 2011

A whirlwind of activity for the past week. As I drove to my treatment last Friday, I was thinking, *I am cured already and this is all just to make sure!* I already knew that the Friday was the eleventh day of the eleventh month of 2011 (11/11/11), but what spooked me out was that I was called in for my radiation at 11.11am. How freaky! I took this as confirmation from the Universe that yes, I am cured. Eleven is a very powerful number in numerology and has played an important role in my life for years, as has the number twenty-two. I took this as an indicator that my thoughts are on the right track.

On Saturday, I spent two hours packing and then drove half an hour to our new house. I spent another four and a half hours cleaning the sawdust from the shelves, lining them with paper and then unpacking the kitchen. I had fun looking out of our kitchen onto the reserve and singing or whistling to the songs on the radio. By the time I got home, David was back from work and had made us nachos.

Sunday had to be a day of rest, as my body was aching from my toes up to my head. I'd banged my head on a wall while packing, and I think it was a message to slow down. Doctor David put his foot down and told me to rest and no arguments, so I haven't... I read outside all day and tried my best not to feel guilty for not continuing with our packing. Yes, I can be so hard on myself at times (often).

Oh, I forgot, on Thursday (10/11/11) I sent a text to my sisters:

I must be getting better. Finished forty-five-minute walk by the beach, the usual, and now looking at some eye candy. Mmmm... Jean clad guy in white shirt, sitting on a fence with biceps bulging nicely... Fitting his jeans nicely too, ha, ha, ha... Yup, that's a good sign that I'm getting better alright.

Ma rang again this week. It felt like Ma was trying to be a better mum after my comments to her, so maybe it sank in? She was trying to make me laugh with her anecdotes. I'm still upset that Mum and Dad totally forgot my birthday this year. I don't mean getting presents, I mean acknowledgment. I have to forgive them and let it go. I haven't had the courage to tell her how upset I was.

Krystal had her operation, spaying and microchip put in, on 7 November and, apart from the first night whimpering in pain, she bounced back after a couple of days. It's amazing how animals just get on with life instead of wallowing in their pain or feeling sorry for themselves like us humans, although I did catch Krystal looking at me accusingly on a few occasions. The hardest part has been trying to keep our little energiser bunny 'quiet, warm and calm' as per the vet's instructions. Huh, she's such an active puppy and goes and goes and goes...

I don't have to worry about my fingernails anymore because they have all peeled off halfway down the nail. This was after taking off my nail polish on Sunday night. They just came off but luckily my fingers aren't too sore. The new nail growth is very strange as it's got ridges like waves all along every toe and fingernail. It's certainly harder to scratch my rash, which is just as well. And picking up small items or opening tabs off things like yoghurt is impossible. I've had to resort to using my teeth.

Sunday night was a horrible night to try and sleep. My PICC line was hurting and felt like a hot poker, which is definitely not normal. My skin under my left breast was blistered and sore, as was a large patch on my collarbone. Yesterday, the radiology doctor gave me gel to put on my blistered wounds and padding for under my breast to prevent chafing. She said that it'll get worse for a week or so and then start to heal. Oh well, I count myself lucky to have got to the end of radiotherapy before experiencing these yucky side effects.

I made my mind up (Oh, Libra, to finally come to a decision) to have my PICC line removed, so after my radiation yesterday, I went to Rockingham Hospital to see the chemo nurses. They listened, and removed the dressing to have a look before consulting with Dr Gan. He was surprised I still had it in after three months, as he had advised me to have it removed after my antibiotics had finished. Julie withdrew it from my arm. The procedure was far less traumatic than when it went in, thank God, and also no blood. Phew. Dr Gan said the nurses could use a smaller needle for Herceptin and both hands could be used as the dose was only a small volume. So, fingers crossed, my right hand can still have breaks in between. The doctor said to 'err on the side of caution' and whip the PICC line out, so now I'm a PICC-less Duck. Yippee, I'm free! No attachments for the first time in months and months. Okay, I've got to get ready for my second last radiation.

Sunday 20 November 2011

Krystal is hyper alert and barking at everything; she thinks she's a ferocious, highly trained guard dog, all 4.6kg of her. Katri calls her

Mop because of her long hair, but I still call her Ragamuffin. Both Cheyenne and Krystal need their summer trim as the weather is getting hotter every day.

Everything went well on Wednesday. I had my last radiotherapy session, said my thank you and farewells and drove off home. My afternoon Herceptin was also successful. I wrapped my left hand in Emla cream and cling wrap one hour prior to my appointment. Julie then applied a heat pack for a few minutes and, hey presto, success with the first needle and no need to hunt for another vein, thank God. I am now free from medical appointments until my full body scan on 29 November, so I have been able to concentrate on packing and cleaning.

Yesterday, Katri and I had a full day visiting our house and finding that the landscaping is almost complete, with only the grass to go. We had a delicious lunch at Redcliffe Barn Restaurant and a brief wander around the suspension bridge and nearby zoo. Of course, we had to have a coffee in Mandurah later on and so we didn't get back until after 4.30pm. David has just left with the ute full of stuff from the shed. I'm psyching myself to tackle the office... heavy sigh... well, it's got to be done...

Chapter 25

Learning To Forgive, To Love, To Hope and To Understand

Friday 25 November 2011

What a good girl I have been. 'Head down, bum up' as the saying goes. I've been working hard every day either sorting or packing or moving loads. My muscles are aching but at least I haven't dwelt on my illness. The big furniture move is tomorrow at 7.30am. Most of the household stuff is at our new place already. As David has been at work, I've had to do the majority of the sorting and packing. (Is that a note of resentment, Sorja?) I'm earning my keep with my productivity just as David is earning our living.

I received a call from a boss at Care Options responding to my feedback form on the transport service and its failings. Of course, he gave me an apology, along with the reasons and explanations about why they were having difficulties.

'I don't normally fill out feedback forms,' I responded, 'but I wanted to be a voice for those people, like the elderly, who can't speak out for themselves.'

I was proud of myself for finding my voice. I've grown a lot through this cancer journey. I'm being more open with my family and friends; I'm speaking from the heart and not the mind. That's a huge shift. I know that I still have a lot of self-discovery to complete, but I have made a start.

Upon going through various files and boxes, I found so many links to my past, including my various jobs and what I learned through each of them. Nothing is wasted, certainly none of the learning; I've gained a wealth of knowledge in the process. I also discovered our love letters to each other and noticed how we spoke to each other eighteen years ago. How we have changed and how real life has changed us. I laughed at David's sense of humour in the letters, and his flirtations made me blush all over again. What happened? Where has it gone? It makes me so sad and upset to realise how serious we have become. Will we rediscover it? I hope so for the sake of our marriage. The passion we had for each other has to be there somewhere under the layers of life's disappointments and challenges. We both have to take responsibility for our part in losing, or misplacing, that sense of wonder in each other, that spark and curiosity.

Monday 5 December 2011

I've been so busy for the past two weeks that I haven't even thought about writing in my journal. The furniture move went well. I stayed at the new house on my own for the first four nights, driving back and forth from the old house to sort out the last bits and pieces. It was a bit spooky with the wind a-howling and the fences a-rattling. I kept the radio on for company as I sorted out the new kitchen and bedroom. David and the girls stayed at the old house, as we didn't have the gates fitted until a week ago. At the old house, David concentrated on the yard—mowing, weeding, edging and cleaning out both sheds—whilst I worked on the inside of the house for a full three and a half days in preparation for the final rental inspection. On the Tuesday, I was grateful that Julie helped us clean the house.

TREE WITH NO LEAVES

I was going to be all proud and refuse the help she kept offering, but once again I've grown and learned to accept assistance. This was the same day of my full body CT scan, and I was already stressed about the medical procedure, drinking the three bottles of barium sulphate, and the cannula for the injection of dye during the scan, so help was what I needed and gratefully accepted. I also had my bloods taken on the Wednesday.

The days have been all about work, work, work... either at the old address or the new one. It was with great relief that I finally handed in the keys to the real estate agent on the Thursday 1 December. Yahoo! Finitio! The next day, they told us how impressed they were, and even half of what we had done would have sufficed. I feel good knowing that the new tenants can move in and not clean one bit. I also feel good that we were able to donate a lot of our old clothes, dishes and knick-knacks, handbags, boots and trinkets to the RSPCA shop for resale. We even donated our old king-size ensemble mattress, microwave, elliptical trainer, BBQ and an old cupboard to a couple starting anew. Boy, we still have a lot of stuff. It's amazing how much two people can accumulate in sixteen years of marriage.

I was absolutely spent by the Friday. I could not do much at all apart from dishes and laundry. I was so sore that my body refused to move. My muscles felt weak, and my body was cut and bruised from moving and cleaning. So I listened to what my body was telling me: it was time to slow down, rest and recover. I read, watched TV and even fell asleep on the couch for two hours in the afternoon. That's how exhausted I was.

The weekend and today have been stinker hot days, 35°C to 37°C. Without air conditioning, it's been hard to unpack and organise the rooms. Like my sisters tell me, we've got all the time in the world to do that, and we're not moving for years again. We'll get there bit by bit. David has had to doggy-proof the back yard so that they can't do the Houdini, that is do a disappearing act. Our lovely new plants are being doggy stomped on, so David has had to put a chicken wire fence across the flower beds. Krystal adapted very well to the new surroundings, however it's only now that Cheyenne has settled down. She was at the old house in Safety Bay for over five and a half years and that's a lot in doggy years.

Since living here, I've seen an eagle, ibis, parrots, wild duck, black cockatoos, galahs, and willy wagtails. Today we saw kangaroos hopping along the reserve facing our backyard. How lovely. It is as though we are in the country without fully being in the countryside.

Today was a special day all round. I had my appointment with Dr Gan for the scan results and my blood test results. Wait for it... The blood tests were all good and my scans showed *No abnormalities detected*. Yippee! Yahoo! I will still have to have the Herceptin every three weeks, including this Wednesday, and Dr Gan wants me to have the heart echocardiogram in January once again. No blood tests required! I asked about my continuing upset stomach, and he didn't think the previous chemo, radio or Herceptin was causing the diarrhoea. However, Irma did say that my stomach and intestines would take a long time to recover from the battering they have endured, and she made a few recommendations about my diet.

I texted all my family and friends with the great news and our new address details. I received so many lovely responses in return and I felt loved indeed. I felt like celebrating with someone, but everyone was at work or living interstate. Sniff... I went to Rockingham City Shopping Centre for a solitary lunch and then completed my errands. Most of this journey has been on my own—the doctors' visits, the treatments and the medical procedures—so it is fitting that I now sit and write in my 'journey' journal about my solitary celebration. Of course, everyone is happy for me, especially my hubby, and I understand that everyone is caught up in their own lives and challenges. Why do I feel like crying? This journey is not complete; I've got to focus on living instead of the threat of dying hanging over my head. What do I want from my life? What now? I've booked to see the counsellor again next week.

Friday 9 December 2011

I had my Herceptin day on Wednesday. I applied Emla cream again and took painkillers one hour prior as instructed. It took three attempts until a successful cannula insertion occurred, with one of the attempts hitting a nerve. I screamed and jumped as the pain was unexpected! The poor nurse was shaken as well. Anyway, the rest of the treatment went well with the aid of a heat pack.

Yesterday, I took the girls for their beauty day and it was Krystal's first one. She must've known something was up, as she howled all the way to Port Kennedy Vets. Whilst they were there, I paid off a layby, visited John and Julie, and then spent a couple of hours at Tall Poppy catching up with Bert and Narelle, where we compared our notes on puppy training.

Krystal is on the couch now and obviously dreaming. Her eyes are half open (very spooky looking) and her little paws are a-twitching. She looks so cute with her hair shaved off for summer, just like Cheyenne, body clipped but face and tail remaining fluffy.

I haven't done much today; I feel kind of flat and that's okay. I drank too much wine last night and that doesn't help my mood. I was feeling depressed about the state of our marriage. I feel we have slumped into a rut and our sex life is stale. Of course, my illness hasn't helped but, in all honesty, it has been stale for years and not just this year. Please, Universe, bring back the passion and physical intimacy in David's and my relationship. Let us be husband and wife in all areas please. Let us both feel good about ourselves and each other. Bring us back to life.

Friday 16 December 2011

It would have been Misha's fourteenth birthday today. I still miss her even though Ragamuffin Krystal has such a big personality. Even now as I'm writing she's trying to get my attention by biting my fingers or snuggling close to me and squealing as if to say, *Hey, focus on me. I'm in the land of the living.* She's been getting into trouble lately by eating rubber door stoppers, drain water covers and basically everything she shouldn't. Krystal then vomits and feels sorry for herself, only to chew on something else a few hours later. Ugh! Unfortunately, even at the age of seven and a half months, she still has accidents inside the house (great, more work for me). On the flipside, I love waking up in the morning with her little body either snuggled up against me or close by on the bed. Even when I'm on the couch during the day, she sometimes climbs on to my stomach and lays there comfortably, well, for her at least. I really feel Misha approves of her.

This week has passed very quickly. David and I have spent time rearranging some of the furniture. I've moved boxes into their respective rooms and am slowly going through them.

On Tuesday I woke up very early and I drove all the way to Perth for the appointment with my breast surgeon. It took one hour to drive there, to find the hospital car park full. I ended up driving to an industrial area and leaving my car next to others in a gravel yard before walking twenty minutes to the hospital. I hoped my car would still be there afterwards.

Mr Fernandez and a female nurse spoke to me about my helluva year. He spoke to me about my CT scan results and was happy that the two spots of concern were gone. He did mention two tiny 4mm spots in my liver, but they could be cysts and weren't of concern. He said that everyone who has a CT scan had some spots in some part of their body and guaranteed me that at the next scan neither they nor any other indeterminate spots would be there. As the saying by Franklin Roosevelt goes, *there's nothing to fear, except fear itself.*

After stripping down and having Mr Fernandez stare, compare and even measure the droop of both breasts, he concluded that my right breast was only one and a half centimetres lower than my left. He didn't recommend surgery and the risks of anaesthesia and possible infection without a guarantee of a good result. He also said that most women have uneven breasts. He said he could move my nipple up one centimetre if I really wanted it, but I decided not to because of my record with staph infections this year.

He gently reminded me that the purpose of the original surgery was to remove the cancer. If I was to see him for cosmetic reasons, he would recommend a breast lift for both breasts. I know I need to be grateful I was able to keep my original breast, only lose about 180g of breast tissue and not need a mastectomy. So I have to resign myself to lopsided boobs. Oh well, as I told him and the nurse, I'm forty-five years old and have been married for over sixteen years. They smiled at that.

The surgeon asked if it was okay to photograph my breasts (not my face) and use them for teaching purposes. Of course I said yes. Anything that can help future doctors and surgeons. I then waited for about fifteen minutes for a hospital photographer (also a man) to take shots of me, both in a bra and without one. What a weird experience. Add it to my many strange moments this year. Posing my breast face on, side on and to the corner of the room. At least the nurse stayed in the room and the male photographer was professional at all times. Mr Fernandez told me I would need another mammogram in February and to see him in March.

Phew, my car was still there. I decided to go to Booragoon Shopping Centre to have lunch and to look at clothes. I felt a bit lost and insecure; I wandered around aimlessly and, as a result, I didn't find any clothes I felt good in.

On Wednesday, a tradesman came to fix our kitchen bench top. I was watching *Dr Oz* and the episode happened to be dealing with a mother and daughter experiencing breast cancer together and then needing a makeover to feel better about themselves. That's how I feel, like I need a confidence booster session. I let the tradie see me without my wig and had already mentioned what a rough year I'd had. I could tell he was listening to the television show whilst working. Somehow, by hearing me open up about my journey, he felt comfortable sharing that his father had died of prostate cancer two years ago without the chance of going through chemotherapy or radiation. In a way, it comforted him knowing his father didn't have to suffer the horrid side effects of chemo and radiotherapies. I believe I was helping him by talking and listening. It reminded me of how I've felt when I've facilitated a successful counselling session with a client in the past. Perhaps I'm being directed back into using my skills as a counsellor.

Thursday 22 December 2011

It always seems like the end of the year goes into fast forward mode. Talking to others, they all feel frazzled by the frantic pace of the weeks before Christmas. Let me see... I had my counselling session with Marie. As usual, I was open about my eventful last few months. I even opened up about the intimacy problems between David and me. It was great to hear and see it from a different perspective. I became more aware and was able to look at our relationship from a different angle. This has helped and we have made progress as a couple. After everything we have been through in the past year, it will take 'baby steps' for us to reconnect physically, as we both feel self-conscious and my body feels different. Time will heal us. Give it time... After all the go-go-go of the past few months, I've felt flat, fatigued and unmotivated. I've done a bit of unpacking and organising rooms, but we still have a way to go. As everyone says, I've been through a helluva lot. It's okay to rest and recover, and to do things slowly.

I spent most of Monday on the computer. For some strange reason, I felt the need to research HER2 positive breast cancer for hours. Why now? I wasn't ready before and now I wanted understanding. I was left even more confused with the contradicting websites and information. I wanted to find out if I was somehow responsible for getting cancer. Also, what I could do to ensure that it doesn't return? I know that it is quite normal to question everything. I ended up with a splitting headache and confusion and fear of the future. In hindsight, it's not a good idea to read too much information. Blaming myself is not helpful or healing. For whatever wrong I perceive myself as having done to myself, I forgive myself.

I did not deserve this 'C'. It was not payback for being unable to have children. It wasn't my fault. I must stop this self-sabotage. I need to take care of myself physically, emotionally, mentally and spiritually. I deserve happiness. I deserve good health. I deserve a long life.

Reading some of the internet websites, I felt guilty for not doing everything some doctor or another suggested, for example, cutting out all caffeine and alcohol, having a perfectly healthy diet, exercising and reducing stress in life. Let's see how they would travel if they were diagnosed with cancer. The most stressful time of your life and you're meant to be some sort of walking and talking angel. Yeah, right! Talk about needing some crutches or coping mechanisms just to get through each day. I'm the first to admit that I'm no angel. Someone commented that I must have been very careful with what I ate and drank through this and I was honest and said, 'No.'

David and I have been way too exhausted to always cook healthy meals, resulting in a lot of takeaway and alcohol this year. I've cooked when I've had the energy and, in fact, I've cooked three times this week. I'm aware that I've had more wine than recommended but, again, no apology to anyone except my own body. I'm addressing the issue (I am a work in progress); 2012 is a brand new year and I am still here.

I haven't gained or lost weight. I'm pretty much the same as I was a year ago. Next year I will do a twelve-week fitness course, run twice a week by the Cancer Council. I'm looking forward to having someone guide me into getting stronger and fitter. It is time. I want to reassess my lifestyle choices and make little changes at a time. No major upheaval—I've had enough of that this year—just slow progress in the way of more vegetables, more movement and more love of self.

My hair continues to grow. It's still dark and soon I can give up my wig. My stomach is still upset on a daily basis. I may have to reduce or eliminate gluten and normal milk and replace it with lactose free milk and other alternatives. Baby steps, Sorja.

David has two weeks holiday as of today. We'll get a lot done around the house together. We've worked well as a team on ideas for our house. We're spending Christmas Eve just the two of us feasting, Christmas Day evening with Julie and John, and Visa, Susie and Katri are coming over on Boxing Day. Lots to look forward to.

Friday 30 December 2011

It all went as planned. On Christmas Eve, we cooked up a feast for the two of us. On Christmas Day, David and I worked hard sorting out the house from early morning until evening. David worked outside and I worked inside on the living room, dining room and the bedroom. We were both exhausted by the time we showered and changed to go to the party. We didn't get there until after 8pm and we stayed until midnight. We were both able to loosen up and talk to more people. I wasn't brave enough to go without my wig. The next morning, Boxing Day, Katri arrived by 9am and we were still cleaning. We chatted whilst I kept on cleaning. Visa, Susie and Alex arrived a couple of hours later. We all had a fun filled day with lots of food, wine and laughter. Just what the doctor ordered, ha, ha, ha.

On Tuesday, I left at 1.30pm to visit Lynn. Another great day. We talked for hours, went for an hour's beach walk, and then talked for hours more. I got home at 8pm to a delicious meal cooked by my hubby. Wednesday was my Herceptin day. Julie was able to use my right hand and was successful with her first attempt. Afterwards I went to Harvey Norman to print off photos of our house and Krystal, to send to Ma, Pa and Irma. Oh, I forgot, I was very brave and decided to go without my wig on both days. Some people looked but not rudely, and it was way too hot to wear any wig (39°C). I sort of combed it over and it looked like a buzz cut.

I had a flustered moment at the photo selection machines in Harvey Norman. I couldn't get the memory card out of my phone and asked for assistance from a male staff member. He asked, 'Don't you have nails?'

'No, I don't,' I replied. 'I've lost them.'

He looked taken aback, observed my hair or lack of it, and inserted the card into the machine next to me. What do you know? Up pops photos I'd taken of me with my bald head and pulling faces! Oh, My God. I was mortified to have those images in a public place for all the world to see... I couldn't complete my order fast enough. I didn't even edit any of the photos, add borders or eliminate red eye; I just wanted to escape the hell out of there. I really needed someone with me to calm me down and stop me getting so flustered and embarrassed. When I collected my photos half an hour later, he didn't even need my name or receipt; he just got them from the stack and wished me a good day. I obviously made an impression he won't forget in a hurry.

We don't have air conditioning, so my lymph nodes have been struggling to cool me down and I've felt heat exhaustion for days. I haven't been getting good sleep because of the hot, humid nights. Yesterday was another stinker of a day. David and I decided to check out a local beach. I made us a picnic lunch and we took a couple of beers as well. We swam a little (yay, no PICC line) and then ate our lunch whilst watching a couple of dolphins playing in the ocean.

My moods have been all over the place: upbeat one moment and down the next and questioning our marriage. We talked for a long time last night. I think it helped to air a few things out and talk about our future, our 2012 goals and so forth. I felt more stable emotionally today but physically faint and lightheaded all day because of the heat.

We still went to Bunnings and Harvey Norman again. David and I ate a late lunch at Hog's Breath Café. When it cooled down in the evening, we were able to do a few chores. It's New Year's Eve tomorrow and, after asking David if it was alright, I've decided to go to Katri's for two nights. David returns to work on Tuesday, so now is the only chance to go, as he can look after our girls and Katri is on holidays.

Wednesday 4 January 2012

Katri and I started early on the champagne on New Year's Eve. We walked to the pub in the dark with our torches (spooky) and got to the pub at 8.30pm. We ordered a bottle of wine and wedges with chilli sauce and sour cream. Katri met up with some of her teacher friends and we joined a few groups. Yippee! 2011 is over and a new year has begun. We walked back a different way through lit streets and got to Katri's after 1am. Of course, it was time for hot milo and cake by then. The next day we watched DVDs, walked for one hour in the late afternoon and then back onto more wine and music. When Katri went to bed, I listened to my iPod and shed a few tears. It was a combination of too much wine, missing Misha and the news that one of Katri and Irma's friends (Louise) died two months ago from breast cancer after a two-and-a-half-year battle.

On Monday, we decided to visit Visa and Susie before I headed home. Their swimming pool was finished, so I *had* to go for a dip and, aah, it was so pleasant... wine, cheese, nibblies and lulling in the cool water on a hot summer's day... pure bliss. I made Visa and Susie laugh with my talk of spiking my hair up with hair wax, or alternatively doing a comb over. I drove home, arriving by 7pm while it was still light outside.

I've decided to have a break from alcohol. It's not good for me physically or emotionally to have it so many days in a row. I've replaced it with tea and sometimes, like tonight, I've done half an hour on my treadmill followed by walking the dogs. Good girl. I can change. Tomorrow, it's another trip to the city for my radiotherapy follow up in the afternoon, but I'll go earlier and meet Katri for coffee and gallivanting before my appointment.

Tuesday 10 January 2012

Well, I lasted six days without alcohol. That's better than nothing. I know I'm drinking due to stress and fear. I've had red spots on my left breast and when I showed them to the doctor on Thursday, she wanted another follow up in two weeks. If the spots are not gone, she wants another biopsy done! My scan was clear, so surely they'll turn out to be heat rash or irritated hair follicles? Anyway, I decided that, instead of having to wear the wig occasionally, I needed a nice hat as an alternative. I was not shy at all and spoke honestly about my cancer and subsequent hair loss to the older shop assistant. I then whipped my wig off (becoming a habit of mine) and asked Katri's opinion as I tried on various hats. The lady looked embarrassed and taken aback, but I was very matter of fact. It was another opportunity to teach people.

On Friday I debated keeping my counselling appointment. It would have been so easy to call up and cancel, and stay at home feeling sorry for myself. Instead, I dressed up in black and white with my matching new black and white striped hat, put on my war paint (make-up) and faced the world with my head held high (higher with the hat, ha ha, ha). I'm glad I went. Marie and I talked for one and a half hours and I felt better. We even brainstormed my desire to run a women's group for other cancer survivors in the future.

On the weekend, I was a busy bee cleaning the house, as the sand is blowing everywhere from the empty blocks of land around us. Monday was time for my repeat echocardiogram (doctors, doctors, doctor's appointments). I saw one of the senior heart specialists and he was very thorough; hence the appointment took longer than the last one in September. I'll get the results from Dr Gan next Monday; however, the cardiologist didn't seem overly worried when I asked him how my heart was doing.

When I returned home, I felt motivated to spend hours sorting out the office and was very proud of myself. In the evening, however, my fears overwhelmed me and I succumbed to wine as a coping mechanism. I put good ole Barbra Streisand music on, grabbed Krystal in my arms and waltzed around the living room. Understandably, hubby-of-mine was worried, and he cautioned me not to drink too much because I would feel worse in the morning. We had a big D & M, and I explained that he couldn't understand how I was feeling, as he wasn't in my shoes... the constant fear of the Grim Reaper grinning at me from the sidelines of my life! One of the Barbra Streisand songs is titled 'Without Your Love'. I mentioned this to David, saying that without my family and friends, I'm not sure I'd still be here after my year from hell. He disagreed and said I was such a fighter that he couldn't see me ever giving up, even without the support of family et cetera. Hmmm... something to think about...

Surprisingly no hangover today. I decided to have a day of rest. I even played Wii Sports which caused me to giggle out loud—wonderful after so long of not allowing myself to play or have fun. As my counsellor said, do things for the pleasure this year. Allow myself to have fun and enjoy my painting, writing, travelling and Reiki for no other reason than pleasure. Not for monetary gain or comparison with others or my own need for perfectionism in everything I do. So okay, that's what I did. Baby steps towards joy, fun and laughter. I don't always have to be so serious.

Chapter 26

Brave Face, Quivering Insides

Saturday 21 January 2012

You know, I haven't been motivated to write in this journal for a couple of weeks and that's okay. So what have I been doing? Apart from the endless ho-hum household chores, the highlight of the past two weeks has been updating my addresses in a new address book. My old one was over ten years old and, in going through it, there were names I didn't even recognise, no memory of them at all. How sad to suffer memory loss. Off with the old and on with the new, eh? I've also been using our treadmill and jogging at least twice a week (good girl trying to counteract the weight gain).

David and I had a fun moment spraying the hose at each other on the lawn to cool down. We've had such heat waves, days and days of them, including today. We just laughed and laughed, and I squealed like a little girl when David hosed me in the face. My lymph node removal (45 of them) has certainly affected my body's ability to regulate my temperature, and I've been suffering a lot without air conditioning in the house. So grateful that Katri has come to the rescue and loaned us the money for two aircon units, one for the bedroom and one for the lounge, to be installed next weekend. Yippee! I've been lying on the couch spraying myself with water and sitting in front of the fan with just my undies on and no bra.

I went to the mall a few times and no-one stared at my short hair.

I'm not wearing my wig anymore. Phew, back to normal in that regard. I made that comment to Marla when I had my appointment with Dr Gan on Monday 16 January, and she said it nearly brought her to tears, that as a nurse she forgets what it's like for us going through cancer and experiencing the small breakthrough events.

My freebie hearing test was all in the normal range, so that's one less thing to worry about. My heart test results were all good and normal, yay. I asked for a second opinion from Dr Gan about the red spots on my breast, and he agreed about the need for a biopsy. This led to more worry on both David's and my parts. In typical doctor fashion he said that if it turned out to be a recurrence of the cancer, they could still do a mastectomy. Like that was reassuring to me! He told me not to cancel my follow-up appointment with Perth Radiation Oncology in Wembley, and to keep him informed about the biopsy.

On Wednesday 18 January, I had my Herceptin day again, my tenth one. I put Emla on my right hand in preparation, but unfortunately it wasn't effective this time as the veins kept on collapsing. Maxine had to go deeper to get it before it collapsed again and boy did it hurt! Well, only two goes this time around. I became all fearful again, thinking the worst about my red spot—close to my nipple—that wouldn't heal. I texted Irma: *I'm tired of my body letting me down when I've been trying my best to keep going on...* The fact is, the image of Misha I saw during my anaesthesia and operation last year keeps haunting me—the way she stared at me and telepathically said, *Don't give up, Mum; you've got to keep on fighting!* Krystal has given me the same look with her puppy eyes, as if to say, *Don't you dare leave me!* I call her Snooks, Snookums or even Snook-de-ville. When she's in trouble it's 'Krystal, No!'

On Thursday, I met Katri in the city and we had coffee and cake before looking at the shops until my 3pm appointment time. The same resident from two weeks ago saw me and again said, 'Yes, we need to biopsy that.'

Luckily, she had to check with Dr Zissidias, my radiation oncologist and the woman in charge of Radiology Oncology. Dr Z came in, examined me and said that we shouldn't jump to conclusions or do a biopsy just yet. She prescribed two weeks of antibiotics in case it was a staph infection instead. Ugh, not again! I told her about my mammogram on 7 February, and she said she would see me the week after as a follow-up as well as giving me the mammogram results. I felt a lot better, as she was so calm and motherly, and didn't appear as worried as the other doctor's knee-jerk reaction to the red rash.

I called David straight away as he was so worried. I knew I needed to reassure him as quickly as possible. He was funny when I got home. He said, 'Thank God it's a staph infection.'

Yeah, that's a lot better than cancer reoccurrence I know.

I've been doing a lot of research on the internet about staph infections, HER2 positive breast cancer and drinking alcohol during treatment. It continues to amaze me how much contradictory 'evidence' is out there and how you end up being just as confused at the end of hours and hours of reading. I know, don't believe everything you read. Too much knowledge can be detrimental to your emotional and mental health. I'll just keep doing the best I can on any given day. It's been a year since all of this began and I'm still here, stumbling along day by day. I've had Flucloxacillin again for two weeks and it's giving me such headaches as a side effect... oh well, as long as the infection clears, eh?

Thursday 26 January 2012

Happy Australia Day. We've sweltered through a week of searing hot days, with temperatures ranging between 36°C and 42°C. I've really struggled with the heat; it's made me extremely short-tempered. The waking up to heat and the continued headaches, and then the same thing at the end of the day. My breast has been hard and tender; I don't think the fluid has been draining properly. My poor hubby has copped some of my acerbic tongue, that's for sure. We went to the beach today (hot, hot, hot sand) and stayed in the water for over an hour. That plus three showers and spraying myself with water over and over again. We also walked the girls to the start of the nearby man-made lake in the evening to try and cool them down, too, as well as hosing them down and using wet towels.

David worked all of last weekend (ten days in a row); at least he now has these four days off to recover. I couldn't go anywhere until Tuesday, as I had no energy or motivation and just existed in the house doing the usual house chores. I picked myself up out of my 'blues', or the 'black dog' as Irma refers to it, and went to the Pinjarra Recreation Centre on Tuesday. I even managed to do twenty laps of the twenty-five-metre pool: breast stroke, freestyle and some pool exercises. It was a lovely three hours in total. I spent a few hours of Wednesday in the cool shopping centre trying my best to escape the heat and let my body breathe for a change. It was a madhouse, as everyone else had the same idea. I bought myself a few beauty products to make myself feel better. I must say my hair is growing back thicker. My eyebrows are the best they've been in decades and my eyelashes are lovely and long. My legs need to be shaved on a weekly basis now (I could've done without the leg hairs growing back so quickly). My hair is still darker than it's ever been, even with sun exposure, but at least I'm not bald anymore. My nails are also recovering slowly but surely.

Even though I've exercised a lot more and I feel myself getting stronger and fitter, my weight still bothers me. Typical woman, worried about being overweight... sigh... I know I have to change my eating habits to complement my exercise routine. Neither one of us has been consistent with our healthier eating plan; we're all talk and no action in that regard. I'm just as guilty as David with the over consumption of goodies and treats. Rather than the occasional treat, we're having daily treats. I think we are still reacting to the stress of the past year by eating and drinking too much.

It's strange that I can fight so hard to stay alive through all of the cancer treatments and complications; however, I haven't fought hard to change my self-defeating habits. Why? It's a slow death instead of a quick one. Poor diet and excess alcohol intake leads to so many other health problems, so why am I doing it?

Saturday 4 February 2012

I went to Katri's on Friday arvo and came back late Sunday. It was a mixed bag of experiences and feelings. I clashed with my niece Nikiita's boyfriend on Friday night and found myself being a ferocious protective aunt. We went to see *Sherlock Holmes II* on Saturday afternoon. Katri had to take Nikiita home before the movie, as she was sick, while I waited at the shopping centre. I had an interesting experience with an Indian man who worked at a health food shop. After I purchased my magnesium orotate, he looked me up and down and then all around me as if seeing my aura.

'Impressive! He said. 'Very Impressive!'

He almost smacked his lips in appreciation. I had to stop myself from bursting out laughing because it was funny but also flattering.

On Sunday, we went to visit Visa and Susie, and I had so much fun playing in the pool like a kid again. Head down in the water doing handstands, twirls, somersaults and what-have-you. I laughed with glee. Katri swam as well and later Visa and Susie joined us before a feast of goodies. Visa noticed an eagle flying overhead and said how unusual to see one, but I wasn't at all surprised. It was my Spirit Guide saying how great it was to see me happy and in the moment (through sending me an eagle).

This past week I've gone swimming again; I did forty laps in forty minutes. Yahoo! I've jogged on the treadmill and my yoga classes have started (every Friday for six weeks). I enjoyed the yoga so much that I even did more than an hour at home today. Physically, I do feel stronger and fitter. I'm learning to make small changes, even if its exercise for now and not a hundred per cent with my eating and drinking. I'm learning to love myself just as I am, for doing what I can and to remember that progress doesn't have to be rapid. Just think about the fable about the tortoise and the hare.

I do love sitting outside, watching the kangaroos in the reserve, listening to my water feature, enjoying the taste of coffee or wine on my lips and tongue, feeling the warmth of the late afternoon sun on my legs and the smell of my freshly brushed and perfumed dogs beside me. I'm appreciating all of my senses in this moment.

This is such an isolating journey and I have to enjoy my own company. I don't feel ready to find a new job yet; the nights are too unpredictable. I've been keeping a record of my food, exercise and sleep patterns. In the past month, I've only had two good nights of sleep. No wonder I have the munchies. My body is trying to get energy from somewhere, unfortunately through the cravings for sugar and carbohydrate laden foods. I've also had daily headaches; this is not a good recipe for the vitality and energy needed for work.

All in good time. Thank God that hubby is keeping us afloat.

This too shall pass... I'm on the home stretch now... Irma and I talked for hours on the phone a couple of nights ago. It was fun. I'll go there for a holiday later this year.

I had a dream. *I was going upwards on a rope, being pulled up past clouds and seeing a bright light coming towards a group of us. I thought that it was a plane. The others on the rope had parachutes strapped to them, but I didn't, so I had to hang on tight to the rope. I had jumped the queue to get on the journey, and it was very scary but also exhilarating!* I wonder if this dream referred to the journey of life in general or my cancer journey. Interesting thought...

Sunday 12 February 2012

What a busy week. Tuesday was my first mammogram since my diagnosis. I had it done at Royal Perth Hospital. There was a bit of a problem, as I forgot to bring my previous X-rays; I blame it on mental fog. They had to chase up the films from Waikiki. Anyway, the right breast handled the squishing okay, but boy did the left breast hurt! Aaargh! The scar tissue was still sore from the radiotherapy. I had to grit my teeth and just endure it. To top things off, they won't give me the results until my doctor's appointment next week. The Breast Clinic is always so busy and the technician isn't the one to compare the films or analyse the results. Why the system makes a woman wait for the results, I don't understand. I mean, I'm already anxious and nervous enough without the added week and a half of extra fear of not knowing. I guess the fact that they haven't called me back for an ultrasound or biopsy is a good sign. Once again, the need for patience, Sorja.

On Wednesday, I had to drop little Krystal off to the vets for dental surgery. Her two baby teeth were solidly pressed against her canines and refused to fall out on their own, so poor Krystal was knocked unconscious and had the two teeth yanked out. I went to catch up with Julie for a couple of hours prior to my Herceptin. Yep, it was that time again. Thankfully, the needle worked the first time. Krystal was not a happy camper when I picked her up in the late afternoon, although the painkillers kept her pretty dopey for the rest of the day. I was dopey too from lack of sleep; too many things have been stressing me out.

Thursday was an extremely emotional day for me. Cheyenne was losing the ability to walk on her back legs, and we thought it was time to make another hard decision, particularly when she wet herself. I was at home alone with my girls, balling my eyes out at how unfair this life is with so much pain, sorrow and challenges. I asked Cheyenne if she was ready to join Misha, and she looked at me bright-eyed and wondering why I was so upset. I had a day filled with fear and panic. I felt myself disintegrating bit by bit, almost having a panic attack. I didn't feel that I could cope with another loss so soon. Luckily, David called our vet and he recommended that we try Cheyenne on a week of the strong painkiller Cartrofen. Within a day, she was able to walk normally and go to the toilet okay. In fact, she seems to be smiling in relief from not having pain. Krystal and Cheyenne have even played chasies again. How my heart rejoiced in seeing her so much better.

On Friday, I went to yoga again. It was so relaxing with the added meditation at the end. I'm trying to do my best and I even sorted out my creative/art room later that day. However, what has made this week extra challenging and difficult has been my stomach and bowels. I believe that the Herceptin is affecting my inner health. I've had constant stomach cramps and toilet runs and, as a result, my haemorrhoids were bleeding. My mind is eager to just get on with it, my tasks I mean, and then my body puts a halt to my activities. It's so damn frustrating! I've stopped drinking wine. I'm drinking healthy juices and taking probiotics, slippery elm and Intestamine. I'm keeping a log (pardon the pun) of my food, drink, toilet, exercise and sleep as I try to understand my body more and make necessary changes. The girls have been following me around the house, watching in concern as I'm bent over in pain. David has just about had enough with all three of his girls having such a rotten week. Well, at least Krystal and Cheyenne are feeling good now. I'll get there... I've given myself Reiki healing energy, crystal therapy healing and said prayers. I cannot give up. Even my dreams are telling me not to leave, that I must continue this vertical challenge—one handhold at a time.

Tuesday 21 February 2012

I have been in no state to write again... No, the mammogram results were good with no suspicious findings, yahoo! There is no need for a follow up for six months and my next mammogram is in a year. Yahoo again! I thought that by finding out such good news, my stomach would miraculously recover. No such luck. I found out my results last Thursday, felt semi-okay on Friday and went to yoga, had a very productive day on Saturday with tonnes of cleaning, sorting out the house and then a Reiki healing session on my friend Lynn in the arvo. I enjoyed catching up on girlie chatter. I even made a birthday cake for David and pasta Bolognese on Friday, not to mention a two hour conversation with Irma. I thought all was on the mend. However, by Saturday night I was back on the toilet repeatedly and then, horror of horrors, at 2am, I was vomiting violently into a bucket! David woke up in alarm at my violent hacking and tried to help. Krystal was crying in panic and Cheyenne was confused by the late-night activity. I didn't get back to bed until after 4am and I felt miserable, hurting all over as well as having the chills. David had to work half a day on Sunday, but I stayed in bed until after 3pm. The last two days haven't been much better. No more vomiting but constant stomach cramps and unable to eat much. I know I wanted to lose weight but not by getting a bout of gastro! As one of my friends texted, *this too shall pass in a few days.*

My poor immune system has not had a chance to get stronger with these constant health setbacks. Come on, give me a break. I feel like screaming in anger, *Enough is enough!* Speaking of anger, it's been the forefront emotion in me recently: anger at the unfairness of it all, anger at my ill health and pain, anger at not being able 'to get on with life' or 'with it all'... As my friend Lynn put it, maybe now that I've received the clear mammogram results—apart from damage done by surgery and radiotherapy—I'm allowing myself to feel the anger about why I had to go through all this in the first place.

Hearing that Ma and Pa are up to their usual abusive behaviour with each other, and other family members having conflict, issues and life dramas, it all seems a bit too much for me at the moment. My usual 'counsellor' persona has rebelled and gone into hiding, silently yelling, *Leave me alone... I'm too raw to help you... Please sort yourselves out. I'm struggling enough with my own feelings let alone the whole family unit!*

Why do I feel like I have to keep the family connected, loving, understanding and peaceful with each other? It's just not possible, is it? I'm the youngest of five children; who appointed me the role of pacifier? I must have assumed it along the way, but you know what? I've changed and that suit no longer fits me. We're all adults and individual Souls on our own particular circus or carnival ride.

Thursday 1 March 2012

I've been too drained to write; it too takes energy. Apart from the usual shopping expeditions and yoga, I attended a meditation and Reiki share session at Carol's—where we take it in turns to give and to receive Reiki healing. It was lovely catching up with Carol and Beryl. They all said that I looked great and my eyes were shining, which is a good sign of my Spirit being strong. I received the following messages:

- Remember to give Reiki to my feet.
- Balance my physical and spiritual.
- My stomach and chest areas are very fragile, so I need to take care of my nutrition and digestion.
- Be gentle and nurturing to myself.
- Allow this gift of time to do what I want to do and not what is expected or should be doing…
- This is a time of energy building.
- I'll know when it is time to focus and move, maybe in a new direction.
- Carol saw great focus and determination and was surprised at how strong my energy was as she didn't think I would be at this point in time.
- Both Angie and Carol spent a long time at my feet and my stomach area.
- I have to watch for headaches.

Yesterday, I had coffee with Julie before my Herceptin and, once again, it was successful with the first vein, phew. Today, I accepted an offer of Reiki by June through the Cancer Council. It was nice to receive for a change; the hardest part was to relax, let go and accept the process. I've got a way to go, according to June, who also focused on my feet, stomach and head areas. Afterwards, I spoke to Christine from the Cancer Council about the possibility of future work, maybe help with a monthly Women's group. She said that she'll keep me in mind if she hears of paid work, not just volunteer work which is plentiful.

Later, I went for a gorgeous forty-five-minute walk along the Mandurah foreshore. I saw a dolphin, pelicans, lots of other diving sea birds and cockatoos in the trees. It was very peaceful and a perfect 28°C.

It is hard to concentrate at the moment, as the Herceptin side effects have kicked in: body aches, migraine and extreme fatigue...

Friday 9 March 2012

Last weekend, I went to keep Katri company. We watched DVDs on Saturday and on Sunday, we went to Visa and Susie's for a swim, snacks and wine. I'm certainly a lot braver with my communication. I spoke to Visa about his rift with Pa. I explained that from Ma and Pa's perspective, they were upset about being mentioned as an after-thought at his wedding. Visa also opened up about how hurt he was that Pa never defended his own son against Ma's drunken accusations and lies. I tried to present all sides of the conflict, recognising that Ma and Pa don't know any better. I explained the brain damage caused by alcoholism and suggested we can learn what not to do.

This odyssey through cancer has certainly changed me; I am now able to discuss true feelings more openly. I even told my brother that I loved him, which is not a usual part of our conversations. The members of our family have never been able to say 'I love you' easily or frequently. I certainly surprised him by patting his hair, clasping both of his cheeks and saying, 'Love you, bro.'

He looked taken aback and took a while to reciprocate. That was okay. I totally understood.

In fact, the weekend was all about mending bridges and reconnecting with family. David rang his mother in the USA. Katri and Irma have also been able to forgive each other and reconnect, phew. Pa and Visa talked for a long time, and Visa, Katri and I had a long D & M discussing our family. I came home on Monday after a trip to the cinema with Katri, exhausted but happy about our Soul group progress. My heart felt full and at peace. I spend too much time worrying about family conflict and it's not a healthy occupation to have.

This week I've gone to yoga, with the last session today, and I practised yoga at home. I also went swimming again and completed forty laps of the twenty-five-metre pool. One kilometre of swimming, well done, Sorja. I've felt weary and yet not slept well at all, with many restless nights. Yesterday, I felt as though I was walking in a fog and that a barrier separated me from everyone else even though I had slept for a change. I even had a hard time communicating with the shop keepers; it was like being enveloped in cotton wool and it was such a strange sensation. I wonder if that is quite normal considering the continuation of my treatment with Herceptin. I've had twelve doses of it and I think it may have an accumulating effect. Lately, I've had a few episodes of my heart pinching; I'll mention it to my doctor when I see him next.

Thank God (or my sister Katri for lending us money) for this air conditioning. We've had a heatwave lasting five days of 38°C and higher. I think David and I will take the girls for a dip in the man-made lake tonight.

Hey, I actually painted at 10.30pm last night. I suddenly got the urge to be creative. I know I have been neglecting that part of me for such a long time. For the past year, I was too consumed by the negative aspects of cancer and didn't allow myself to feel the joy of painting. Was I punishing myself? Denying myself something I love doing because I felt self-hatred? Now that I'm starting to love myself and forgiving myself for being human, I'm giving myself permission to experience happiness and to love again. I keep hearing these words in my head: *To every question, the answer is love.*

Self-hatred of my body, my mind and spirit is what got me to this state; therefore, if I'm to really heal and be whole, and become the person I'm meant to be, the answer is self-love. Loving all of me, scars and all. They say that scars are a roadmap to your life; well, what a life I've had! I have scars from my appendectomy, laparotomy, laparoscopies, hysterectomy, oophorectomy, lumpectomy, breast reconstruction and axillary clearance, and of course my PowerPort scar. When someone complains about a little scar, I laugh inside and have to bite my tongue from listing my numerous and large-scale scars. As you can see, I'm still working on the 'loving all of me' concept.

Sunday 11 March 2012

I just woke up to another night filled with dreams and nightmares. However, as I was brushing my teeth, I thought about the book I'm going to write and publish. I came up with the title—*Tree With No Leaves*—over a decade ago, but I have decided to add the subtitle, *A Life Lived Through Infertility, IVF and Breast Cancer.*

I'm in the middle of painting a tree trunk; it's not a 'normal' looking tree. The colours are more alive and vibrant than any tree you see out in nature. I am that tree. My journey through this physical life has slowly chopped away pieces of me. Like a barren and bare tree, I've learned to live without these leaves. Yet I am still here, standing tall and proud. The core of me is strong and sturdy like the trunk of the tree. My life force still pulses beneath the layers of bark and shines through, revealing a multitude of colours.

Occasionally, I read back on what I've written in my journals. It's amazing how much you forget about what you've gone through. The human body is an incredible machine. Time certainly does heal, for example, my nails. Katri looked at them the other day and commented that 'they're normal'. Yay, progress!

Chapter 27
Counsellor, Counsel Thyself!

Tuesday 20 March 2012

A week of highs and lows, just like a lifetime... On Sunday 11 March, I finally got up the courage to call my interstate friends Samantha and Robyn. This whole isolation shakes your confidence and you don't feel that you can interact socially; you worry the words might come out all muddled. So you take a deep breath, with the knowledge that your friends will understand if you have a few brain lapses or jumbled sentences... As usual, my fear of sounding like a fool was unjustified yet again. Different friends fulfil different needs and I found the two conversations varied a lot. I felt that I had overcome another milestone, one of reaching out to my friends instead of handling all of this on my own.

The next day, I covered forty laps in the pool again and still managed to be a house cleaning fiend on Tuesday. On Thursday, it was the dreaded CT full body scan time again and, funnily enough, the 700ml of Barium Sulphate Oral Suspension didn't taste as bad. OMG, could it be that I'm getting used to it? This was my fourth time, after all. I went straight into the scanning room and the nurse cannulated me there. I had my blood order form from Dr Gan, so I asked the nurse if she could also take my bloods before the scan (kill two birds with one stone... what a horrid expression, eh?). At first, she was hesitant, but as I pleaded my case and she saw how little and deep my veins were, she agreed. Luckily, a male orderly was happy to fetch the vials for the blood. I was impressed with the nurse's method of spending time feeling for my veins with her fingertips and being sure before attempting to use the needle. It took a few minutes but she was successful the first time around. What a relief. The scan proceeded as normal, with the injection of the X-ray contrast medium given midway through; I experienced the usual metallic taste and hot feeling in the bladder area. It did feel like I was given it twice though. Possibly it didn't work the first time? After it was all done, I felt sick in the stomach and had to have a hot chocolate in the hospital café. I waited near a toilet as a precaution. After another hour, I drove home feeling yucky and headachy. The evening and night were not comfortable for me, but I knew the feelings would pass.

As a reward the next day, Friday, I went to the Mandurah foreshore and spent a magnificent day walking around whilst drinking my take-away coffee and then visiting the art supply shop. That evening included a marathon telephone conversation with Katri and later Irma. The past weekend was lovely. David didn't work, so we spent a lot of quality time together, relaxing and laughing on Saturday and exploring a nearby nature reserve on Sunday. We walked and talked sporadically, mostly enjoying the glorious sunshine, water birds, the ocean breeze and the peace of it all. It was very calming and relaxing. We ate lunch out and then I felt weary and needed a nap at home. I give myself permission to snooze when I need to. I was so invigorated by my nap that I had to make us pancakes with blueberries and syrup, ha, ha, ha…

I was very grateful for having such a peaceful weekend. It helped me prepare for Monday's appointment with Dr Gan. The beginning of the consult was excellent with the good news that my bloods—

liver, kidneys and cancer markers—were normal, and the full body CT scan showed no reoccurrence of the Big C or Little C. After normal discussion about the side effects, such as my heart pinching after the last Herceptin, Dr Gan ordered another heart echo in five weeks' time.

My doctor then proceeded to put all his notes and test order forms aside. He sat directly opposite me, looking very serious. Of course, I grew concerned when he said, 'There is something else that I wanted to discuss with you...'

I thought, *Aaarrgghh... what now?*

He was worried that one year of Herceptin wouldn't be enough. His concerns are that out of the 45 lymph nodes, 44 were cancerous. The two in my chest and collarbone areas had been inoperable but responded to the chemotherapy, so it was very likely that they were cancerous as well. Also, HER2 (Human Epidermal Growth Factor Receptor 2) is not hormone responsive and, therefore, hormone targeted therapy like Tamoxifen is not applicable. Systemic treatments vary, so Herceptin is my 'drug of choice'. It's standard and normal to have Herceptin to treat such an invasive and aggressive form of breast cancer.

Dr Gan suggested the continuation of Herceptin treatment for *one additional year!* This is after my supposed last (eighteenth) dose on 4 July this year. It was meant to be my Independence Day. He asked what I thought about it. I was in shock and, as a result, all calm and matter of fact. I said, 'What about my veins? Do you think they will handle it?' Instead, I wanted to scream, 'No, don't do this to me! I've had enough!'

Dr Gan will consult Dr Redfern, the head of Perth Oncology, and wants to see me after my heart scan in six weeks' time to tell me the course of action. I thought about the celebratory holiday to Queensland I had planned for July: my reward for the completion of the marathon of surgeries, chemotherapies, radiotherapies and Herceptin. Now, the possibility that I would have another full year on top of it all was all a bit too much to take in!

I held it together whilst I went for an ice cream at the Rockingham foreshore and read in the park, surrounded by people. However, once I got home (purchasing a bottle of anaesthetic—i.e. wine—along the way), I lost it! I cried about the lack of control over any of this. Here I was thinking I could see the end of the journey and WHAM, out of the blue, another mountain to climb! I tried to 'just get on with it' by doing the usual and necessary chores. I felt like a robot going through a pre-programmed set of tasks to complete. Upon talking to Irma, we tried to focus on the positives—the cancer hadn't returned; I am feeling stronger, fitter and recovering quicker from the treatments; and who said that I couldn't still go on the holiday to Queensland in between the Herceptin treatments?

When hubby arrived home, he gave me a big hug and words of comfort. He also said that for purely selfish reasons, if I had to go through another year of Herceptin and that made a difference to me being able to stay here with him forever, then he agreed with Dr Gan. I guess given the choice of ensuring a positive outcome with continued Herceptin or the risk of the cancer returning, and having to go through surgery, chemo and radiotherapies all over again, I'll choose Herceptin.

It's a waiting game once again to see what Dr Redfern says. Today, I've had a sleep in, accomplished forty-five minutes of yoga and sat outside writing in this journal for two and a half hours. Time to cook dinner soon and it's Herceptin day tomorrow.

Wednesday 28 March 2012

The Herceptin went okay. Two goes and a bit of bruising but all done. I did feel very fatigued that night. Usual chores completed so that I could have the weekend free to spend with Katri. David and Visa went on their camping trip to Lane Poole Reserve for two nights. Krystal had her grooming day on Friday with a local groomer. Oh, how funny she looked all naked—Krystal that is, not the groomer, ha, ha, ha. I even finished *my painting for the front cover of my book*. Katri was impressed by the painting. She said it looks beautiful and I agree. I keep looking at it with pride.

Katri and I had an enjoyable weekend. We walked around the reserve by the ocean, enjoying bird watching. Saturday evening was spent outside admiring the sky turning gorgeous colours of purples, pinks, blues and yellows whilst the black swans flew overhead to roost on the lake for the night. The kangaroos came to show off in front of us, doing their usual kangaroo stuff like boxing, hopping and eating. We played music, rang Irma, and partook in wine accompanied by a delicious vegetable, cheese, dip, ciabatta bread platter. On Sunday, we walked at Mandurah Forum and then along the foreshore before enjoying some churros and coffee.

I've definitely noticed some major emotional eating and drinking over the past week, since Dr Gan told me about the possibility of one extra year on Herceptin. I may act calm and collected on the surface, but the truth is being pushed down by food and drink. Instead of letting myself ball my eyes out the healthy way, I've reverted back to old methods of coping. Still a lot to learn in this life. On the bright side, I have performed Reiki self-healing energy, meditated and enjoyed yoga. I've also pampered myself with a face mask and given myself foot massages, so not all bad... I even started to google airfares to the Gold Coast and it felt so good to make travel plans.

On Tuesday 27 March 2012, I actually started typing out my book from all of my handwritten journals and diaries! Yahoo! It's a beginning and I know I will allow myself time, however long it takes. It is a positive direction and a step towards the goal of publishing my book. It *will* get published; I am positive of it. I have a good feeling about it all.

Thursday 29 March 2012

Okay, bad mistake... I researched information about Herceptin on the net, particularly the duration of treatment. In one HER2 cancer support forum, I read about one woman with metastatic breast cancer who had been on Herceptin for over five years! What? I know it's a miracle drug, but it's still a drug in your system and it still has side effects. Sure my stomach has improved in the last few weeks with my own introduction of IBS support and Inner Health, but my poor nose keeps sniffling and dripping a clear fluid despite antihistamine use. Its inner membranes are so red, sore and peeling. I'm embarrassed by my constant sniffling as though I've been snorting cocaine or something. I'm probably driving people nuts, or is it just my own self-consciousness?

Another observation... I'd forgotten how tickly hair can be. I keep thinking I've got bugs on my forehead, but it is just the new and longer hair strands tickling me. I'm not complaining about it, as I feel so normal walking to the shops now, especially as it's still warm and I've got a short 'do'. I think I need to get out of this house and be with friends because I'm getting too morbid on my own.

Thursday 5 April 2012

What can I say? I'm trying to keep my spirits up by painting and writing. I even went to an art demo of new art products on Tuesday. I've exercised in our home gym, done yoga and continued giving myself Reiki healing. I've watched DVDs, mostly comedies and romances. Yet I still feel flat. I've made sure that whilst hubby is at work, I've 'earned my keep' by shopping, cooking and cleaning—being the Domestic Goddess. In a way, I'm trying to justify my existence on this earth, that I'm worthwhile and of value.

I've been reading my old journals for my book. It feels like someone else has written those words of hope and optimism. The IVF journal is bringing countless memories to the surface. I know that it is cathartic and will help with my healing; the counsellor in me is encouraging me to continue working through these emotions. The going is *tough*, though, and a part of me wants to stop and bury it all back down again. Why go through all of that emotional pain all over again? The other part of me is saying, *Keep going. You know you're strong and you need to let go of a lot of emotional baggage to be able to move forward in life.* I have to be patient with myself and allow myself to *feel* whatever emotion my past words evoke...

Damn it! I'm sick of feeling sorry for myself. Now is the time to reclaim my power.

Thursday 12 April 2012

Life goes on. Emotions all over the place—from the determination to get fitter, to having a heart to heart with David, to gallivanting with Katri in Perth, and then anger at my hand that's bruised from four attempts to get a vein for my Herceptin infusion. My mind is so busy that it has a hard time shutting down and resting, and then I'm crabby from being tired.

As I read my past journals, I have a hard time believing all of the procedures I've undergone. The other day I was in a silly mood and started listing them to David, almost like a poem or rap song. He smiled at first but then, as I kept going on, he said it wasn't funny! I replied that I had to laugh; otherwise, I would just curl up in a foetal position and sink into severe depression. It went something like this: appendectomy, renalscopy, gastroscopy, colonoscopy, laparoscopy, laparotomy, hysterectomy, bilateral oophorectomy, lumpectomy—in fact procedures ending in Y's—chemotherapy and radiotherapy. I've had lots of other procedures and treatments, such as axillary clearance of lymph nodes, but I don't think they end in 'y'. This is my dark humour. Irma said that humans are resilient and that sometimes we have to laugh it off to remain sane and keep going. How true. I am making peace with myself.

Tuesday 24 April 2012

I had a dream last night about jumping into murky and muddy water. My mouth was full of the sludgy water. Many books suggest water represents your emotions. Certainly, taking the flower essences Irma sent me and being off my progesterone cream have stirred up such a range of emotions. I've laughed, I've cried, I've felt furious and angry and let my mouth fly with words, and then felt empty and flat afterwards. I don't even know how I'm going to wake up each morning, whether emotionally stable or off-kilter. It's probably for the best if I stay at home for a few days now...

On Saturday morning 21 April, Katri and I drove down to Yallingup and Busselton for the weekend. We went to the maze at Yallingup, and it took us one hour to find all four towers in the right sequence, with the assistance of other tourists, including a young girl with her family and some other guys. Katri was reluctant to go at first, but we had a ball playing like little kids in the maze. Darling David had booked our overnight accommodation at Martin Fields Beach Resort. It was a lovely B & B in Wonnerup, just outside Busselton. There were wetlands around the B & B and we saw so many different types of birdlife—eagles, hawks, pelicans, ducks, swans, egrets, parrots, cockatoos, galahs and little sparrows. We enjoyed wine on the balcony in the afternoon sunlight before heading off to a delicious dinner at a restaurant close by (yummy chicken parmigiana, mashed potatoes, salad and garlic bread). On Sunday, after a continental and cooked breakfast, we had heaps of energy to not only go for a forty minute beach walk but also later to complete the Busselton Jetty Walk, which is one kilometre one way and it took us one hour return. What an accomplishment!

After all the hours of driving on my part over the two days, and all of the walking, I collapsed when we got back to my place. It was an hour before I could even unpack or do anything else besides greeting hubby and pooches, and saying 'bye to Katri.

Sunday night was horrid and I was very restless. Having Cheyenne poo inside the house three times, and needing to clean up after her, certainly didn't help me get back to sleep each time. Therefore, I was even more tired and cranky yesterday. I rushed to Rockingham Hospital for my quarterly heart echo test as well as an ECG this time. The technician was determined to get the clearest pictures possible and therefore dug into my left ribs whilst I held my breath. He spent longer this time due to my mentioning the heart pinching episodes. Normally, I don't feel much with the echo, but this time I'm bruised and sore in my left breast and ribs. They do have to be thorough, so no blame, just *ouch*; it's still tender to touch today. I'll find out the results when I see Dr Gan next Monday.

I had a better sleep last night, though lots of dreams. In one of them, *I was talking to a man, a doctor I didn't recognise, and he was saying that, unfortunately, there was no cure, just ongoing preventative treatments. He also said that 'negativity could bring back the cancer but positivity would repel it'.* When I woke up, I wrote down these words: It's important to work from a base of gratitude not guarantees. That makes sense. There are no guarantees in life, but feelings of positivity and gratitude for what I do have in my life can help me lead a happier 'rest-of-my-life', however long that may be...

Tuesday 1 May 2012

Yikes, time-a-flying... where's the rush? I'm watching a willy wagtail bathing in our bird bath, and he's having the time of his life, chattering away in a monologue only he can understand.

Last Thursday, I went for my blood tests at PathWest in Mandurah instead of Rockingham Hospital. They were very kind and patient. It took two of the ladies four attempts to get a decent blood supply for the vials required. At one point, one of them hit a major nerve. I jumped and screamed as what felt like an electric, painful current ran from the top of my arm all the way down to my fingertips. I broke out in a clammy sweat and had to calm down before another attempt was made. The woman had to settle herself down as well. In an attempt at humour, she commented that the jugular vein in my neck looked good and perhaps they should put a tourniquet around it and draw blood from there! Ha, ha, ha. Sick humour again. They asked me when I was due for more blood tests, and the cheeky one said that she'd have a lunch break if she saw me coming...

Hmmm… talk about making me feel welcome.

We had a fun Saturday night. Well, for me that was from 3pm until 12.30am and David joined the party in the evening. It's nice to let your hair down (now that I have hair) and giggle with your girlfriends. Of course, there were some awkward moments for me when they made comments like 'Isn't it great now that you're over the worst?' or 'Now that you've finished treatment…'

I had to bite my tongue and stop myself from snapping out, *Are you kidding me? I'm not finished treatment and there is still plenty of crap I'm going through!* Better to be polite, smile and gently correct a few misconceptions…

Yesterday, I had my follow-up with Dr Gan. My bloods (liver, kidneys, cancer markers, full blood count and magnesium) were all okay. However, the heart tests—transthoracic echocardiogram and left ventricle ejection fraction (LVEF), which measures how well your heart can pump blood—showed a drop in the functioning of the heart muscle. The LVEF measurement had dropped from sixty-six to fifty per cent. He asked me if I had noticed extra breathlessness or difficulty exercising. I said that I still walked and did yoga but hadn't run on the treadmill lately. I had noticed light-headedness, though. My iron count was good, so it wasn't anaemia related.

He wanted to discuss my report with the cardiologist before continuing with my Herceptin treatment. We may have to postpone for six weeks to allow my heart to recover. Dr Gan hasn't had the opportunity to discuss the extension of my treatment with Dr Redfern but still strongly advised that we complete an extra year due to the aggressive nature of this cancer. We've got until 4 July to decide. If they decide I need a six-week recovery period, he would like me to get another echo done in about five weeks.

I noticed my patient file on his desk and, OMG, it's as thick as a bible! Well, I guess paperwork adds up, especially over a year. When I spoke to Irma later yesterday, I guess the enormity of all I've gone through got to us. We were almost laughing hysterically when I recounted the latest, i.e. the decrease in my heart functioning.

My cup runneth over, so to speak! On the bright side, it would be nice to avoid my torture sessions for a few weeks and give my veins a break.

Wednesday 2 May 2012

Bugger! No break for me. Herceptin to continue even though the heart test showed reduced function. Dr Gan has decided to continue my treatment with very close monitoring. I've booked another echo for 7 June. Soldiering on, Duckdat. That's one of my nicknames…

Friday 4 May 2012

I've been doing a lot of gentle exercise, such as yoga and walking at the nature reserve. Today, I had a lot of errands to run before my Herceptin. As a result, I was all warmed up, my hands were red-hot and the veins were bulging nicely. Maxine had success the first go. It helped that I was also very hydrated. I think that sometimes nurses forget that I am not their work colleague when talking to me. They use a lot of medical jargon and talk about the latest research, advances and targeted therapies. I usually nod and try to keep up with the conversation but, honestly, it's so hard to even concentrate on simple conversations sometimes, let alone complicated medical language. I understand that they all mean well and are trying to keep me positive and optimistic.

I returned *Life After Cancer*, a CD and DVD I had borrowed, and

Maxine asked me whether I'd found them helpful. I replied that yes, they were mostly good, but I got depressed when a whole section was devoted to getting your affairs in order, such as wills and finances. That did not encourage an optimistic outlook on the rest of my life...

I cheered myself up by booking flights to Queensland. I leave on the red-eye flight on 4 July and come back on the twenty-fourth... a nice three week getaway to Gold Coast and Bundaberg, yay.

Saturday 12 May 2012

I've certainly noticed increased breathlessness and light-headedness lately even when completing simple tasks such as washing the dishes. I have been drinking lots of nettle tea to help. Sometimes it feels like someone is sitting on my chest. Despite these sensations, I'm determined to keep on with my gentle exercise and housework, and just rest when I need to. The other day, I was all fired up with energy and I did an hour's gym workout with band work, walking on the treadmill and sit-ups. That night, I had heart pain and heart pinching, so it probably wasn't a smart move on my part. It's so bloody frustrating when I want to get fit but am limited in what I can do at the moment. I keep telling myself that it won't be forever.

Thursday was a beautiful, joyful day and I am grateful. I went for my Reiki session at the Cancer Council, and it was such peaceful, motherly and healing energy that I received. It was very appropriate, as Mum had sent me some money for my air tickets. Later, I went for a long walk by the Mandurah foreshore and called Ma and Pa to thank them.

As I sat on the park bench by the ocean talking to Ma, two playful dolphins came right up to me, or as close as the water allowed them to, and joyfully frolicked in front of me. It was truly amazing and it felt like they were happy that Mum and I were reconnecting and talking as a mother and daughter should. I mentioned the dolphins to Mum and she agreed that it was a good sign from the Universe. For me, it was a healing of my heart as well as a healing of parental issues.

This reminds me of another fantastic experience I had about a week and a half ago. I was standing outside, watching two hawks flying and hunting in the evening sky. I stood on our backyard lawn and, for some reason, I put both arms up in the air, my palms facing upwards. To my utter surprise and wonder, the two hawks flew to me and one hovered above my left hand and the other above my right hand! I was silently talking to them and thanking the Universe for my healing. Wow! It was a bit spooky but amazing at the same time. Our prayers and calls for help are heard. I know that I've always had an affinity with animals and this felt like confirmation of the fact. Other people might think me crazy but I really don't care.

Earlier today, I was thinking about a message I received from my Spirit Guides during Thursday's Reiki session. The message was that I don't need to fight, as in fight to keep going all of the time. I'm always in fight mode rather than flight mode when dealing with stressful events and situations in my life. My great-grandmother, who communicated with me through telepathy, told me to be gentle with myself and others, and to accept love. I fought back tears, as I didn't want to break down in front of June, the Reiki Master. I did notice that she kept on wanting to hug me after the Reiki session.

I also received the message to stop being such a hermit and closing my heart to people. I needed to contact people and visit friends. June said that she felt a cold area around my heart during the Reiki. I'm so not surprised by that! I do believe in the mind and body connection, and it's a reminder to allow other people closer to me, to stop putting up an emotional wall. My automatic response lately has been showing people how tough and resilient I am. That's one of my biggest lessons in this life: to allow connections with people, not just animals.

I had a fun evening on Thursday to top off my day spent smiling (such a nice change). I painted for four hours. I'm getting right into abstract paintings lately and it's been bliss.

Today was a glorious autumn day, sunny and mild. I took it easy to counteract having caught a cold. I sat next to our water feature, writing then resting. David and I went to a Japanese Restaurant for dinner as a treat for the both of us. During dinner, darling hubby commented that he wanted to look into my beautiful blue eyes and see them smile rather than looking like I'm in pain all of the time. Ooohhh, how sad! True but sad...

Tuesday 22 May 2012

The days are cooler, the nights are growing colder and the daylight hours are shortening, which is always depressing to me. I try to catch a few sunrays and vitamin D during the day to stimulate the feel good hormones. David and I have been out a few times for breakfast, lunch or dinner. It's a nice change to be out of the house.

I've been increasingly breathless and feeling faint. I nearly fainted doing food shopping, and sometimes it's been a struggle to get enough oxygen into me. Even doing simple tasks like washing the dishes gets me all breathless as if I've run a marathon. I called the Chemo Ward nurses and told them of my concerns. Marla spoke to Dr Gan yesterday and, after explaining my symptoms, we have decided to skip this round of Herceptin. I'll have my echo on 7 June and see Dr Gan on the eleventh. I hope this nearly six-week break from Herceptin will give my heart muscles a good chance to recover. I'm doing light yoga and walks still but resting when I feel breathless. I don't want to cark it from the actual cancer treatment by having a heart attack. At least they listened to me; I was assertive that this doesn't feel normal or right to me. Again, listen to your own body. Pay attention to its whispers and signs. It's frustrating not being able to do a lot at the moment; my mind is strong and willing, but I have to be patient with my body.

Wednesday 30 May 2012

Nearly the official start of winter. I can't complain, as it's sunny and a gorgeous 25°C. Exactly a week ago I had such a social day. Julie and I had coffee and chatted for one and a half hours, and then I caught up with the girls at Health Kick. Later, I bumped into Beryl from meditation. We stood in Rockingham Shopping Centre chatting for forty-five minutes. It was a fantastic spiritual conversation, reaffirming my beliefs about why my Soul has chosen all of this. It was tough standing up, talking non-stop, and I had to sit and catch my breath for quite a while afterwards. I then continued with my errands and decided to go to Tall Poppy to order our hang tracks, perlons and hooks. Another hour of talking with Marg and Bert, and boy, was I ready to go home and be quiet for the rest of the evening.

I've commenced a new project. I've printed out numerous photos of Misha and Cheyenne, family photos from my fortieth birthday, Visa and Susie's wedding and Pa's seventieth birthday. I'm making up collages and then having them all framed in three separate frames. It's been fun and nostalgic to look at the stages of life: from Misha and Cheyenne as puppies to how tired Cheyenne is looking now; and also how we have all aged. Of course, it's a natural progression of life.

I've been taking quite a few solitary walks at the nature reserve, the Bunt near the canals. Yesterday, I did the loop twice; it took me one hour and fifteen minutes. I was very lucky; not only did I come across the usual birdlife but also, as I was thinking *It's great to be alive*, I saw an eagle perched on a tree limb about fifteen metres away. I had my binoculars, so I got a close up look at him or her. It only got startled when another woman walked past it from the opposite direction.

On the weekend, David and I had a real conversation, not just about daily events. We snuggled in bed with the lights out and really talked. We agreed that we had both been so absorbed by the cancer treatments, the house, David's stressful job and our fur babies that we had forgotten about us as a couple. Sitting watching TV together was not 'connecting' or being intimate. With my body changes and my libido dropping from normal to almost non-existent, it certainly doesn't help. David is encountering such high levels of stress at work and then worrying about me; that doesn't lead to a high sex drive either.

I think we've both been trying hard to keep each other's spirits up, yet we've lost *us* somewhere along the way. It's understandable, of course, and we recognise that there is no blame attached. Now we are going to take baby steps to reconnect, starting with just snuggling, hugging, kissing and caressing each other. There is no pressure for either of us to perform, just to be with each other. *Fear has ruled us for far too long; it's time to give love a chance.*

TREE WITH NO LEAVES

Sunday 3 June 2012

Must be something in the air. Winter has set in with lots of rain, dark early and general feelings of discontent along with the changing weather. I even had an argument with hubby; it ended up being a misunderstanding on both our parts... heavy sigh. I went to Katri's for the long weekend, as David had a few days off and could look after the girls. We had a great time collecting firewood for a bonfire. I was finally able to burn my box full of paperwork—too much to shred and too personal to recycle. I got a bit puffed out but the end result was worth it; it was nice to sit outside in the evening staring at the burning logs. It was also a break from the house chores and the routine. My book is coming along nicely, so I didn't feel guilty having a break from typing. Not that I really should feel guilty. Such pressure I put on myself all the time.

Friday 8 June 2012

From laughter to tears in quick succession... I came back early on Monday after David rang to say that Cheyenne—our loveable 12 years and 4 month old German Shepperd—had had another epileptic seizure. This time it was more violent and lasted far longer. He said that she was curled up so tightly and her mouth was locked in a snarling expression. Afterwards, Cheyenne took about four hours to recover fully. David said she kept banging into walls and chairs as her legs were so weak. We came to the exceedingly difficult and heart-breaking decision that it was time. David made the call on Monday, and on Tuesday morning 5 June, the vet told us that 6pm was the best time to take her in.

Thank God that the last day of Cheyenne's physical life was a glorious, sunny 24°C, and she could enjoy it laying down on the grass in the backyard. We tried to make it a memorable day for her and for us. I gave her a raw hide treat that kept her happy and occupied for an hour. Krystal and Cheyenne had a few 'rougher' play sessions and I threw the toys for them outside. Cheyenne kept looking at David and I all day, which was very unusual. I didn't want to spend the entire day dwelling on the evening's appointment, so I went into 'mad' cleaning mode for four hours. David joined in as it was a distraction from our thoughts and fragile emotions. We did break down a few times and second-guessed our decision when we saw her playing and so very much alive. It would have been so easy to cancel the appointment, but it would have been for the wrong reasons. It would have been selfish, and we would have had to face it all over again—very soon judging by Cheyenne's deterioration. I took a few photos to add to my already large collection, and tried to keep busy, busy, busy!

As it happened, it was a full moon. I thought that it was an appropriate time to release my ratbag Cheyenne to join her wolf pack—all the beloved dogs that have gone to doggy heaven before her—and I knew she would be so happy to see Misha again. I can't believe I'm losing both my girls within eleven months. Life punches you hard in the heart, doesn't it?

At 5.20pm, we got ready to go. I picked Krystal up and placed her face against Cheyenne's to say goodbye, but of course Krystal didn't understand. It looked as if Cheyenne *did* understand. Even the night before—as I had been looking at her and talking to her about her beautiful ears and her fluffy tail—Cheyenne who was mostly an independent and sometimes aloof girl, had stood up from where she was lying, walked over and squeezed herself between the coffee table and the couch to lay down next to me so that I could pat her head. I just dissolved into tears. It was as if she was saying, *It's okay*

TREE WITH NO LEAVES

Mummy, I understand.

David lifted Cheyenne into the back seat of my car and, as we drove away, we heard Krystal yelping and crying inside the house, as she wanted to come with us. During the half an hour drive to Port Kennedy Veterinary Hospital, Cheyenne gazed out the window at the pastures and passing scenery as if memorising them. At one point she slipped and couldn't pull herself back up; we had to stop the car and make her comfortable on the seat again. This was definitely another sign for us. A couple of days earlier, I had put country music CDs into the CD player in my car, and the songs were playing randomly. Both David and I broke down crying as the song 'The Beaches of Cheyenne' by Garth Brooks came on. Our beloved Cheyenne loved the beach but hadn't been strong enough to go for years. Another sign... We arrived at the vets just before 6pm, and David stood outside on the grass with Cheyenne while I went to sign the permission paperwork; it gave him a private moment to hug her and say goodbye. I burst out crying as soon as the receptionist looked at me, and she realised I was Mrs Reese and the paperwork was for Cheyenne. She asked for payment (very insensitive we thought), so David and I swapped places because he had his wallet. I stood and hugged Cheyenne and apologised for being impatient with her sometimes. I told her I loved her as much as I loved Misha. Oh, I'm balling my eyes out writing this and reliving the moment.

This all happened between 6pm and 6.20pm. We took her in to the room together, although I had to go and compose myself in the toilet for a bit. The vet nurse took Cheyenne away to put a cannula into her neck. We had told the vet that we didn't want a prolonged goodbye, as we had been saying it for two days. Rachael, the same vet Misha had last year, came into the room once we had Cheyenne back. We sat her on a blankie on the floor, and Rachael and I sat with her and kept caressing her.

David stood behind the metal table, absolutely broken-hearted. Rachael said it was okay for me to feed Cheyenne a few liver treats to distract her whilst she euthanised her. I kept saying 'I love you' as tears flooded my eyes. It was so quick. One minute she was sitting eating her treat and the next she lay down with our help. I was distressed, as I couldn't get her sore leg from under her to straighten it more comfortably. Rachael helped me. She said that we had done the right thing and hadn't waited too long, when there would have been no quality of life left. As we spoke, she listened for a heartbeat; she must have heard a slight one and so she added a little more of the drug. I knelt so that I could see Cheyenne's eyes and they were blank. No spark there anymore… I knew that she was gone. The vet confirmed it.

I continued to caress her with love and felt how warm she was. I prayed that Misha had come to collect her and greet her on the other side. The vet said our pets were lucky to have us as parents because we took such good care of them. She also said that most German Shepherds live to about nine or ten years of age, so twelve years and four months was brilliant. I did most of the talking, as I could see that David was so overwrought. After a few more minutes, I sensed that he wanted to get away from that room, so I kissed Cheyenne one last time and we left, thanking Rachael once again. I briefly saw a man look at me sympathetically as we left the front reception. He was patting his dog and probably thought of having to go through something similar in the future. David and I hugged each other and sobbed in our grief outside. The drive home was emotionally difficult.

Krystal was very subdued when we got home and sensed something was terribly wrong. She didn't eat her dinner. I proceeded to drink a lot of wine and found it hard to concentrate on anything. I did manage to text my family: *Ratbag Cheyenne is at peace with Munchkin Misha and the rest of the wolf pack now. David and I are devastated. No more pain for her though.*

Krystal cried and looked lost all evening. She kept sitting by the front door waiting for Cheyenne, which made my heart break and hurt. I talked to her in between my bouts of tears. It's amazing how many tears I have cried; it seems like a never-ending bucket.

That night I had another amazing dream. *Two people, a woman and a man, came to collect Cheyenne. She looked confused like 'What happened?' The man and the woman put a lead on Cheyenne and led her away gently and with a lot of love. Ahead of them, I saw Misha and a few other dogs free and waiting to greet Cheyenne. Misha was jumping in eagerness!* It was beautiful and I feel very privileged to have been shown that. It gives me a lot of comfort to know that she was welcomed like that and with so much love.

Today, Cheyenne's physical body will have been collected for cremation by the same company that cared for Misha last year. The weather has turned nasty since Wednesday and Cheyenne would have hated it. I went for my blood tests—three nurses and five attempts—and my heart echo yesterday. The cold and the rain have been suiting my mood. Krystal is still crying and looking for Cheyenne. I guess time will heal all of us so that we can continue to live our lives. I received a lovely email from my nephew Trent on Tuesday 5 June : *Oh wow... Humm thats bit sad... Wonderful big doggie, im sure shes so glad she had you guys to share her life with and no doubt you already know she'l be with you and help you with her love forever. Im white lighting with you n david—Sunskate.*

Monday 11 June 2012

We've had some severe weather the last few days; I guess the weather has reflected my own stormy emotions. We lost power. In fact, hundreds of thousands of people were affected all across Western Australia. I've felt like I've lost power for a while. The feelings of sadness, despair and sorrow have hung around me for the past week. Last night, in particular, I had some very disturbing and dark thoughts about my life. Not healthy at all! The wine I drank certainly didn't help, as it made me even more morbid and angry. I'm not doing myself any favours by such self-destructive behaviour and habit. The naked pain I witnessed on David's face last Tuesday as we said farewell to Cheyenne haunts me. I'd hate to cause him even more grief by my actions causing an early and untimely death. Imagining how my death would cause such pain for my family and friends, I realise I can't continue to be so selfish. I have to take responsibility for my actions and learn to take better care of myself.

Today, I saw Dr Gan for the results of my heart echo and blood tests. The echo showed the same result as the last time, no worsening but no improvement. My bloods were good: my liver, kidneys, white and red blood count, and cancer markers were all in the normal range. My Herceptin is to continue on Wednesday this week. Dr Gan managed to get a hold of Dr Redfern and they are in agreement. Herceptin is to continue for another year until July 2013. At least he said that there's no need to do my bloods so often now, only every few months. Yeah, good news.

I asked about theories of why I developed HER2 breast cancer. He said he couldn't pinpoint it to one thing, that a number of factors play a hand in breast cancer. For me, these include not having had children, having a total hysterectomy at age forty, going through early menopause, hormones such as oestrogen in the fat cells, lifestyle and so forth. I'm still struggling, even after all this time, with questions such as why me? What did I do so wrong? I have to make peace with myself and accept it, regardless of how it all began. I guess we'll never really know if the doctors don't even know. He did say something that stuck: at this stage it was important for me to keep a calm mind. Yes, calm thoughts do lead to lowered stress levels and, in turn, to a peaceful and calm body. I've been through so much in my life and it has made me a strong and resilient person. My heart is strong and it will keep beating! I know that I will receive a lot of help and support from the spiritual side. Little things such as painting my nails and having my hair cut (first one in over a year and three months—what a milestone) will help me get into a more positive frame of mind. Remember the Finnish concept *Sisu—to never give up; persevere and have a strong will.*

Friday 15 June 2012

You know, I've got to admit I'm a little drunk as I write this. How much is a human being supposed to stand? I've dealt with the raw pain of loss this week. Today, I received the delivery of Cheyenne's ashes and locks of her tail hair (the triad of colours from dark brown/black to beige to white); a couple of days ago, we found out some low life got a hold of our credit card details and clocked up over $700 of debt on TAB online betting and recharging their mobile phone; and now some drunk or drugged out driver has slammed into my husband's ute and then taken off! A hit and run. Honestly, what is this world coming to?

I'm tired. Not just because I've not slept well lately. The tiredness I'm talking about is more than a few nights' restless sleep. I'm tired more than from a few nights, more than from a week, even more than from one month. I'm tired from this past year. In fact, I'm tired from this last decade.

Every time I convince myself that I have to keep going on, keep fighting strong, I get hit sideways by something totally unexpected. Surely I didn't sign on for all of this when I chose to incarnate into this body and this life? My mind plays the song 'Why Worry' by Dire Straits. Universe, please hear my plea! Enough sorrow, enough pain, enough tough love—ENOUGH! I don't know if I'm strong enough to continue wanting to live if life is nothing but continual challenge and disappointment, physical and emotional pain. Don't get me wrong, I do want to live. I want to love. I desire life. I crave happiness. I'm addicted to rainbows, the full moon and rain drops on leaves. I love the courtship of wildlife, their games and their play. I constantly seek beauty in all its forms.

The interactions of total strangers fascinate me. I walk through a shopping mall and I get the strangest sensation of knowing everyone. Like we are all connected somehow. It sounds crazy I know. I see the tiredness in so many people. Like we are all 'in it for the long haul'... how did it get this way? I know that we're not supposed to be running around grinning like Cheshire cats all of the time, but why are so many of us so sad? Tiny spasms of joy and pleasure intermingle with a swamp of learning, accepting, judging, drowning and persevering. Is this only my reality or can anyone out there relate?

Saturday 16 June 2012

This morning, I woke up to these words in my head: *I'm not done yet!* I also had a dream. *I was driving my car through a fog. I couldn't see the road in front of me, no matter how fast the windshield wipers were going. It was a wet, dark road and I had to slow down in order to be safe. I had to take care.* I guess that was another message for me.

We had a better day today. Better frame of mind and yes, the sleep helped. David and I spent a few hours at Mandurah Forum getting new mobile phones and having lunch. We even bought a bright pink doggy jacket plus new toys for Krystal. She loved the toys but wasn't that keen on wearing the jacket. Going for a walk soon took her mind off wearing that strange attachment and, oh, how cute she looked. It was so sad when I let Krystal smell Cheyenne's ashes and locks of hair yesterday. She became excited, jumping up and down, and trying to grab the bag of hair from me. Krystal then went to the front door whimpering and waiting for Cheyenne to return. I just cried and cried, and tried to explain that Ratbag wasn't coming back. I had to distract both of us by giving her a treat and making a coffee for me. Time. Time to heal. Time to celebrate Cheyenne's long and happy life instead of dwelling on her passing.

Sunday 17 June 2012

I had a good day today. Katri came for a day trip. It was a wonderful sunny day, so we made the most of it by being outside. We took Krystal for a walk and later we went to Pinjarra for another walk and lunch. David had a chance to relax at home after another exhausting week and the dramatic hit and run episode.

Friday 22 June 2012

The Universe certainly finds a way to get our attention when we are choosing unwisely how we live this life. I have to go back to Monday this past week. I'd had a good day. I did forty-five minutes of yoga before dressing Krystal in her bright pink jacket and heading out for a lovely evening walk of about forty minutes duration, taking photos with my new phone. Sounds ideal, huh? Then why did I once again choose to drink a bottle of wine over the course of the evening and into the night? I guess I felt an overwhelming feeling of loneliness, sadness and tiredness of this life path. I did make sure to eat something and drink my herbal tea before bed. I also took my normal magnesium, calcium and glucosamine tablets. As I still had a headache after lots of water, I took two headache tablets with a calmative component in them, and then off to bed I went.

I woke up just after 3am busting to go to the toilet. David and Krystal were sound asleep. As I sat doing my business, I felt a rush of heat go right through me. I became clammy and sweaty, and started to tremble. Next, I felt nauseous and thought I might keel over right there and then. I became very breathless and started to panic. I finished in the toilet, struggled out to the bathroom and quickly tried to cool myself off. I took my dressing gown and nightie off as I was burning up by this stage. My heartbeat was very slow and I felt as though I was dying. There was no pain, just a sense of separating from my body. I lay on the bathroom floor (déjà vu from years ago in 1997 when I collapsed due to the ovarian abscess) and raised my legs onto a stool. I felt worse. I knew this was serious. It felt like I had a choice then and there. Do you want to live or do you want to die? The choice is yours. I was petrified!

From somewhere deep inside of me, I found the strength to fight back and not give in to the sensation of leaving my body. I slowly pulled myself upright, reached the sink and splashed cold water on my face and chest. I drank some tap water. My heart was struggling and I fought to take deep breaths of air into my lungs. I also mentally talked myself out of panicking. I dragged myself back into bed, grabbed my protection crystals and lay down, dropping my clothes on the floor next to me for when I cooled down. I then did some serious praying. *Please let me live. I'm not ready to die. Please help me and protect me,* I said silently over and over again. For one and a half hours, I lay there afraid to go to sleep in case I didn't wake up!

David and Krystal did not wake up and I didn't want to wake them. Why? I didn't want David to panic and call an ambulance... why? I was embarrassed! I was embarrassed that I had brought this on myself. It had been less than a week since I'd had my Herceptin; I'd drunk a bottle of wine and had had two painkillers, obviously a lethal combination. I thought I was safe because I'd gotten away with it in the past. However, the continued infusion of Herceptin combined with the wine drinking had obviously weakened my heart.

When David got up for work at 4.45am, I didn't let on that I was awake. I was still very shaken by my near-death experience, and I didn't want him to worry all day at work or not go at all. Stupid I know, but that's how I reacted at the time. I finally fell asleep for a few hours from sheer exhaustion. I was cautious all day on Tuesday, as I still felt weak. I made a pot of stinging nettle tea, which is good for the heart, lungs and stomach. I didn't dare do anything taxing—no exercise, just a calm day.

Talk about having the fright of my life, or a slap in the face. No more binge drinking, Sorja! And no more taking such a risk with my life! I texted Irma and we had a long talk about it all when she rang later that evening. I also confessed everything to David when he got home from work. Understandably, he was upset and angry at me for not waking him up. As he said, it's better to be embarrassed and alive rather than proud and dead! I promised to never do it again and to wake him up if ever I needed help.

Since then, no alcohol whatsoever. I've been taking very good care of myself—Reiki, yoga, Pilates, walks with Krystal, lots of herbal teas and good cooking. My sleep is disjointed, but I get it in spurts and I've been dreaming lots. Major life lessons, eh? I'm forgiving myself and doing the best I can to become healthier and stronger every day. I still feel breathless at times, but I'm working through my limitations.

Monday 2 July 2012

I was proud to have an eleven day break from any alcohol. Since then I've allowed myself some wine in moderation but am definitely not adding any painkillers into the mix. I've been open and honest, and told others of my foolishness in the hope they may also look into their less-than-safe habits and take stock of their lives. The teacher in me is coming out.

I've continued to take walks with Krystal on the sunny days as well as the cooler, winterish ones. On Sunday last week, David and I had a yummy cooked breakfast at Dwellingup before completing a one and a half hour bush walk. There were so many trees down from the recent storms that some of the walk involved a bit of bush-bashing and climbing over tree limbs. I really enjoyed the walk even though we had to take a few breathers when my heart felt as though it was going to push out of my chest.

I have finished typing out the IVF chapters of my life. It feels good to have accomplished that despite my health limitations. I painted a little, but my inner critic kept pointing out what looked wrong, so I didn't enjoy it as much as usual. How do you stop the negative voice we all have inside our heads? By telling it to shut up—easy to say, hard to do!

TREE WITH NO LEAVES

Krystal had her beauty day on Thursday and, instead of a winter cut, she got clipped again, her summer groom... oops, a bit of miscommunication. She was indignant (Krystal, not the groomer) and snuggled under our quilt at night between David and me. On Saturday, after a busy day shopping with David, I ran a hot bath with the whole works: candles, calming music and a glass of wine. Our bath is lovely and deep, and it felt wonderful to just be and relax. I'd forgotten that getting out of the bath would be a bit of a struggle. Such a slippery surface with the bath oils and no handlebar to pull myself out. I didn't want to call out to David to yank me out of the bathtub, so I tried to get on my knees... splash... I tried to use my left arm for leverage. Too weak... splash... I tried to push against the bottom of the bathtub... splash... oh dear! Finally, I pulled the plug out, let the water drain out and then success... sigh. I felt weak and my heart was fluttery after getting dressed. I didn't have the water that hot! I lay down on the bed, and drank water and my herbal tea.

Yesterday, we went to Visa and Susie's place. The insurance company had decided to total David's ute, so we were buying my brother's old ute from him. It was a glorious 21ºC, and we had a tasty lunch and chat with them. Katri came over as well. Krystal came along for a play date with Visa and Susie's two dogs, and she slept well after such a social day. She still misses Cheyenne and is insecure on her own. I'm sure we'll get another puppy later this year to keep her company when we're not at home.

I'm very excited and counting the days until my flight to Queensland. I've been slowly doing my preparations and will start packing tonight. Tomorrow, I'll bake a cake for the chemotherapy nurses and staff for all of their support in the past year and a bit. We're busy getting quotes for the liquid limestone for the backyard and spray-on paint for the driveway. David started his holidays today and is busily working on his ute.

I have my Herceptin scheduled for 11am on Wednesday. I did that so I can come home, finish packing, have a shower and rest before my midnight flight. David will take me to the airport, which is an hour's drive away. I hope all will go well for all of us, that we'll have a happy holiday and lots of fun.

Tuesday 31 July 2012

I've been avoiding writing in this journal for a month. Like picking at a scab that's just starting to heal, I've been afraid to reopen old wounds and relive the past month. I know I have to as part of my healing journey. They say your parents are the most influential people in your life as you grow from childhood into adulthood. I haven't mentioned my parents to a great extent in my journals. This is because it hurts my heart to think about what and who they have become. For the past thirty years, I have watched as my loving and confident parents have turned into strangers I often have a hard time loving. You see, they are both alcoholics. Alcoholism is just as devastating a disease as cancer. It erodes your self-worth and self-esteem. It can make you act like a different person, sometimes hurtful to others, even your loved ones.

My father is what you would call a quiet drunk who loses himself to bottles of spirit. I have watched in pain as he's transitioned from a strong and funny man to a stooped, often suicidal and demented old man. It saddens me to see his spirit suffering and his desire to quit life. My mother had a hard upbringing and it has ruled her life. My mother is often volcanic and in fight mode. She is not a quiet drunk. It's as if she becomes possessed by an evil spirit. I know that sounds crazy, but I cannot recognize her as my mother when she is in one of her alcoholic rages. The evilness that spits out of her mouth is horrific to observe, especially when it's targeted at me, her own daughter! Even writing this I feel my heart start to race at the remembered horrors and the words that are left imprinted on my Soul.

Our whole family—my three sisters and my brother—have all been affected by the destructiveness of the cycles of alcoholic parents. We've each tried to help in our own way over the years. Unfortunately, as most people know, you cannot help those who won't help themselves. Bit by bit we've withdrawn from our parents, realising that we have to focus on our own lives and hopefully learn from their mistakes. All we can do is try to let go of the hurt, forgive them and love the parts of them we *can* love. For me, I learned a huge lesson in my latest encounter with my parents. I learned that responding in anger and hatred to the nasty words hurled at me only made me feel horrible. I'd descend to my mother's dark level. It was only with thoughts of love and light that the situation changed for the better. I realised that I was handing over my own power to them 'on a plate' and retreating into my own head space. I was reverting back to being a vulnerable five-year-old, a white-haired child crying out for love at a time in my life I felt the need for it most.

For the first two weeks of my holiday in Queensland, I suffered from a particularly nasty strain of influenza. I even lost my voice for three days. Thinking back, it's no wonder I lost my voice at the same time as seeing my parents again after more than a year. *Voice is power.* I had lost my own power. Temporarily! My voice was just starting to come back when my mother and I had an argument. Through me screaming 'Do you want me to die?' and 'I hate you!' and the subsequent uncontrollable, heart-wrenching sobs, I lost the little voice I had.

I am proud of myself for being able to say that all of my life I just wanted love and support from my parents. I wanted a 'normal' life and 'normal' parents. Is there such a thing? When my parents are sober, I'm able to really *see* them. They look like other retired, travelling grey nomads in their mid-seventies. Once they have recovered from their latest binge drinking, they either act all sheepish or pretend that nothing happened. The ambulance rides or police interventions are but a distant memory, or conveniently turned around as reinvented stories to tell their few and far between friends and acquaintances. They give you some money to 'buy something nice', a kiss on the cheek and a hug, and off they go. They don't realise that they have left far more than that: bitter memories, extra emotional baggage and a dying hope that things will change one day.

I went on my trip to Queensland with the intention of reconnecting with family and friends, and I did that. I had some wonderful conversations with my sisters, my brother-in-law and my nephews. Sure, not everything went according to plan. Best laid plans and all that.

Unfortunately, the Herceptin's side-effects of chills, aches, and fatigue kicked in on the flight to Gold Coast. In hindsight, not the best idea I've had to save money by flying at night. The plane was small and squishy, especially for such a tall woman as I am. The passenger next to me was a woman in her twenties holding a coughing and spluttering toddler. We swapped stories and it turns out she was waiting for a heart transplant. She was travelling with her mother and two young children. We all have our own life stories, don't we? No-one gets off lightly. Each of us faces challenges that are physical, emotional, mental or spiritual in nature.

Some highlights of my trip were spending quality time with two of my nephews, Jarrin and Kailum, and Jarrin's girlfriend, Morgan, at Pacific Fair Shopping Centre; walking over two hours in a feast of flora and fauna at the Gold Coast Botanical Gardens with Kirsti, Irma and Khan; and a spending spree at Harbour Town.

Kirsti, Irma and I caught up for lunch with our good friends Robyn and Gary, who were on holiday from Tasmania. The hours of talking probably contributed to me losing my voice the next day. It was lovely to see them, though, and the hugs were appreciated.

Irma, Khan and I drove five hours north from the Gold Coast up to Bundaberg for our reunion with Ma and Pa. Friday 13 July was the first anniversary of our beloved Misha's passing. Oh, how I miss you. It was also D-Day for my altercation with Ma.

I loved exploring Bundaberg. We walked along the various beaches, reserves and a river. We also went to the cinema to see *Brave*. Irma and I laughed the loudest in the cinema. What's wrong with people these days? Even after what we've gone through, we can still see the funny side of life and be 'tickled pink' by cartoon characters. It was such a treat to talk until 2am with Irma face-to-face rather than through phone calls.

I appreciated the loving words of support from my elder sisters and texts from friends. I may not have had the support of my parents, but I certainly get support from others in my life, and for that I am so grateful.

On Monday 16 July, after days of stress due to my parents, I suffered a heart episode, or rather a panic attack, at my sister's place of work, Natural Magic. It was very scary, as I couldn't catch my breath at all and made horrible rasping sounds. Lucky for me, my sister knew how to calm me down and help me breathe. I drank my stinging nettle tea and took my Traumeel tablets. I rested for a long time and then Irma gave me a Bowen Therapy session.

The following day, Tuesday, I had a horror experience of having a molar tooth pulled out at a Bundaberg dentist. I had put it off for ages; the tooth had been repaired and filled on several occasions in the past but had worn away and needed to come out. On top of everything else, I'd had a jaw and toothache for over a month, and I couldn't deal with it any longer. It was unwise for me to have the anaesthetic with adrenalin because of my heart, so the dentist could only give me three doses of local anaesthetic, which were short-lived in duration. The result? I felt most of it! I was a good patient according to them, but the tooth was stubborn. I'm not normally scared of the dentist, but this is one trip I'll find hard to forget in a hurry. Afterwards, I had to sit for an hour to calm down and make sure all was okay; luckily Irma was with me in the waiting room. That night I wrote these words: *Help Me God! Let Me Live! No More Pain and Horror!* Thankfully, during the night I dreamt of a happy Misha, and a smiling and regal Cheyenne, helping me from the Spirit World. Cheyenne appeared first as a puppy then later in her prime. I miss them both.

On Friday 20 July, we had a fantastic day. Irma, Khan and I went on a day trip to Agnes Waters and Town of 1770, about one and half hours from Bundaberg. What gorgeous weather, so nice and warm. We walked on the beach, up scenic tracks to lookouts and later drove to see the fancy houses on the hills. Wow, what views. We laughed all day long; it was much needed. I found two colourful kaftans for summer. We made the most of it and didn't get back to Bundaberg until 7pm. This day was definitely the highlight of my holiday. A day full of sunshine and butterflies. We also saw three eagles, and an unusual looking kangaroo grazing on someone's front yard. A magical moment was when we saw a pure white horse standing close to a fence in a forest of trees, just staring at us as we drove past. White horses are symbolic for me and it was just what I needed to keep going on in this life. I thought I was hallucinating because it was in such a bizarre place, but Irma and Khan both confirmed they had seen it too, and we all got goose bumps! Irma and I finished the day off by drinking a few wines and giggles until 1am. What a hoot! Thank you for my laughter and healing. I'm learning to be joyful in my own creativeness.

On Sunday 22 July, I had a serene and enjoyable late afternoon walk by myself, collecting my thoughts at Baldwin Swamp, Bundaberg. I took some amazing close-up photos of a family of swans: mum, dad and five kids. Peace at last. I was ready to go home after a supply of homeopaths, flower essences and another Bowen Therapy session from Irma. Three weeks of holiday gone just like that.

Chapter 28

Rediscovering Creativity

Tuesday 7 August 2012

I've now been on Herceptin for over a year. My treatment on Wednesday 25 July was my eighteenth dose of Herceptin. I have come to a conscious decision not to write so much about the treatment episodes. By this stage, everyone knows that either my veins behave or they don't. I have side effects, but I refuse to focus on them all of the time. I pray and hope to live, and choose to stop dwelling on the possibility of death. We all die someday after all. Yes, this road is long but hey, I'm still here and many cancer patients aren't. *I'm a Survivor!*

I'm going to concentrate on what brings me happiness and joy. I know when I push myself too hard with physical activities, like major cleaning for hours, I suffer for it. So, lesson to be learned... take it easy, Sorja. It is okay to not always show the world how strong and tough you are. Balance is the key... I am a Libra after all.

I've enjoyed spending time with my hubby and Krystal, who was beside herself in seeing Mummy again. David spent most of his one-month holiday completing projects on his ute, my car, both inside and outside of the house. Busy husband-of-mine and yes, it all looks great. I've had coffee and lunches with my friends, and it's been so nice to have sanity and normalcy again in my life.

I'm back to yoga and walking at the reserve and lakes with Krystal.

I'm grateful to be home and I see it with unclouded eyes. We are very lucky. I've painted my acrylic paintings and written again. I am rediscovering my creativity and loving it. It is very healing and cleansing. I feel better than I have in weeks. Rest and being by myself again has helped to recharge my batteries. I value peace and quiet, and I love watching the waterbirds, parrots, white cockatoos, native pigeons and doves. On occasion, a hawk hovers and then swoops down to catch an unsuspecting lizard or frog in the reserve. *Love is the key to all the locks on your heart. I'm breaking those locks one at a time. My heart is open to loving and being loved.* Speaking of hearts, I've got my heart echo again tomorrow; all will be well.

Wednesday 22 August 2012

Why is it that we humans feel the need to blow our own trumpets? We talk about our accomplishments and our breakthroughs to others, and wait for the expected pat on the back. I do this all the time. I think what we are really trying to do is convince ourselves that we are good enough. We are worthy. We are loveable.

I hear myself talk to my family, friends and acquaintances about my treatment milestones or my growth as a human being, for example, what I have learned about my own strength and perseverance. A part of me stands back and waits with bated breath and anticipation for words of affirmation and encouragement from them. The lyrics from Whitney Houston's song 'Greatest Love of All' are so true. It takes such self-love to stop waiting for other people's approval, to be able to look at yourself in the mirror and say, *Hey, do you know what? You are a glorious, breath-taking, awe-inspiring and shining light. You are loved because you are you. It is enough that you approve.* Full stop. No more questioning. No more begging,

Please love me. Look what I have done and can do.

I know there is a fine line between self-love and gloating. One is quiet and self-possessed; the other is loud and in-your-face. I'm learning how to become melodious like a flute or a bird, rather than trumpeting like an elephant to anyone in my range of vision. My aim is to politely listen to opinions and then let my inner guidance decide whether to take it on board or not. The choice is always mine.

How ironic. Just writing these words, I noticed two idiots riding their trail motorbikes in the restricted reserve, scattering the wildlife out of their way. I ran outside and yelled at them to get out of the reserve! Okay, so I trumpeted! I never said I was perfect, did I? Ha, ha, ha. I must have looked quite formidable standing tall, with my finger pointed in their direction because not long after, they turned and rode their trail motorbikes out quick smart. I guess not all loud trumpets are bad, eh?

Tuesday 28 August 2012

I woke up to a dream. *I was hanging from a ledge of a cliff top, with a huge drop to a murky river full of fallen logs and rocks. I couldn't use my arms to lift myself up, as they felt weak, so instead I had to rely on the strength of my legs to save me. I swung my left leg up and, using my muscles, I managed to swing my body to safety.* The fact that my left arm is hurting me may have played a part in the dream, but I also believe that my higher self is telling me to use whatever strengths I possess when confronting difficulties or challenges.

The other weekend, I got right into the spring gardening and weeding, as it was perfect weather for it. I wasn't at all aware that a shrub I was leaning over was covered in ants. As my left armpit is still numb from the surgery, it took a while to realise that numerous ants were biting me! I finally felt some stings as they travelled down my arm and my leg. After squealing like a pig, I ran inside to strip, apply some Stingose gel and get rid of the few remaining ant carcases. Now, I don't know if it was the stings or that a couple of veins were traumatised during my Herceptin (two veins 'blew'), but whatever the reason, my left wrist, forearm and bicep—in fact the whole arm—has been throbbing for over a week now. I've put anti-inflammatory cream on every day and tried to massage it, but it's so tender to touch. I don't want to develop lymphoedema, so I have to be careful. I called and left a message with the physiotherapist I saw last year. I want to see her about my arm, of course, but also the fact that my radiation oncologist pointed out that my breast still looks slightly red and has some fluid build-up. She recommended speaking to a physiotherapist, who would be able to show me how to properly do lymphatic drainage massage, especially with summer approaching.

Recently, I've been to a few social gatherings and have had fun whilst there. I've come to realise that I'm very sensitive to other people's energies. I thought it was because of the cancer and subsequent treatments; however, even as a small child, I hated being in large groups and always ended up with a headache. I recall fighting my parents when dragged into shopping centres, shows or fairs. To this day, I can handle an hour or two, but then I feel the need to escape fast. The busy-ness, the stress, the noise and a thousand energy waves just get to me, and I guess that after forty-five nearly forty-six years, it won't change. I find I need to have time out to recharge my batteries after 'close encounters'. The best way is to sit outside and just observe nature, or listen to calm music, or walk in the reserve or near water, or to paint or enjoy other crafts. I also want to surround myself with people who have soothing energies to help build me up, not to tear me down. It's already hard enough to lift myself up, like in my dream, without having to spend my energy reserves on either mediating between family members or justifying my actions, beliefs and goals.

I feel like I'm growing up. I'm learning to speak my own mind and not the mind I thought was expected of me by others. Sometimes that involves saying things that others don't agree with and that's okay. I have always been cautious and mindful of not hurting other people's feelings. As a result, I have not been truthful to myself or, in fact, been myself. I'm not talking about blurting out every thought that crosses my mind. What I mean is just... to say what I mean without being mean. I need to speak up if someone treats me like a child, and not hold on to the resentment so that it churns me up inside. I know I have lost some of my confidence as a direct result of the past few years; however, I'm determined to gain it all back and some. Afterall, I used to be comfortable speaking in public to groups during my career as a training officer as well as a group facilitator and counsellor for Serenity Lodge (Drug and Alcohol Rehabilitation Centre). Therefore, it is all there still; the skills may be a bit rusty, but they're not buried forever!

I've enrolled in the six-week yoga classes—for the second time, running every Friday and sponsored by the Cancer Council. The first class was last week. I remember going to yoga five months ago and being very self-conscious about my short hair. I looked around the group of thirteen and noticed how each of us was at a different stage of healing. There was a woman with a turban on and I could relate. There was a woman with new hair growth but very short and I could relate. There was a woman with a PICC line and I could relate. I realised how far I had come in just observing them and listening to them talk about the chemotherapy side effects. I haven't been standing still so to speak. I have taken many steps forward in my recovery and that makes me feel proud. I am grateful for this gentle reminder.

Chapter 29

The Dreaded Four-Letter Word FEAR Versus Its Opponent LOVE

Friday 31 August 2012

It's my forty-sixth birthday in one month's time. I am grateful to be able to celebrate it. There was a time I thought I wouldn't reach my forty-fifth let alone my forty-sixth birthday. Last night, I had a dream in which I had a happy look on my face and was saying, *I'm alive, I'm alive, I'm alive*. David and I are happy to be having a party to celebrate our house warming, my birthday, our wedding anniversary and spring. Today is the last day of winter and it's bucketing down at the moment. I hope the sun smiles for us on 30 September, the day of our party.

I haven't had anyone call me back from the Physiotherapy Department, so I've decided to google 'lymphatic drainage massage on the arm' on YouTube. I found many helpful short demonstrations. My arm has been sore for two weeks now, so the massage is particularly important to reduce the slight swelling and discomfort. I realised that not all of it was due to the lymph nodes. I believe that I've actually sprained my wrist while lifting Krystal, so there are two separate issues, i.e. the sprain and the lymph fluid building up.

It's amazing how quickly you can panic and jump to the wrong conclusions, such as *Oh, no, is the cancer back?* Often, it is a simple matter of thinking back to what you may have done and relate the pain to something you have experienced in the past. For example, I have sprained my wrist before, so I can identify with the same pain, the inability to put weight down on the wrist and the associated pain when twisting it. I have to be aware of my body, take responsibility for it and not always rely on others. I have to learn self-management techniques.

I've thought a lot about FEAR versus LOVE. The other night my brain came up with its own definition of the two words by breaking the letters down into acronyms...

F = FOREIGN

E = ENERGY

A = ACTIVATING

R = RESPONSE

When you are gripped by fear, it's as if a foreign energy takes over you, which activates a response inside of you, such as breathlessness, heart palpitations, breaking into a sweat, eyes dilating and so forth. However, on the flipside...

L = LIBERATING

O = OPENESS

V = VENDING

E = EQUALITY

When you are enveloped in feelings of love, there is a sense of freedom and an open heart, which allows you to give out that joy and nurture unconditionally.

Friday 7 September 2012

What a busy week again and I've needed today to just *be* to recover. Oh, to have an abundance of energy again. It was Herceptin week, so I guess I need to give myself a break and be gentle with myself. I saw Emma, my physiotherapist, in Perth yesterday. We spent the first hour talking about my past year. I apologised for talking her ear off and she had a lovely reply. 'You are more than just your arm.'

How comforting to have a friendly and caring person to listen and offer some good suggestions, for example, to go back to swimming a little or doing exercises in the supportive environment of the water. I complained about not being able to do the same amount of exercise as in the past, hence gaining weight. She said that I didn't look overweight to her, but I may have to concentrate on just maintaining for now and not gaining any more.

It's natural to feel frustrated by changes out of our control, but I know I've got to stop feeling sorry for myself and accept that it's only temporary. I'll continue with my walking and my yoga, and I'm going to go back to the pool. I'll also see what other gym equipment I can use at home: walking on my treadmill, using my bands and lifting light hand weights. I must stop using my continuing treatment as an excuse for not trying alternatives. Okay, that's my own pep talk.

My emotions have been haywire all week. One minute, I'm up and singing, the next I'm down and defeatist. I've even felt intense anger over the chronic episodes of pain. The Herceptin wasn't too bad this time, but my left arm continues to throb and is still slightly swollen. Emma took measurements which confirmed my suspicions of fluid build-up. She suspected that I had some cording happening, too, which explains the pain. I will see her next week for physio and to be shown the correct way to handle it in the future, i.e. learning self-management techniques as well as how to recognise and prevent lymphoedema. I'm also going to be fitted for a pressure sleeve to use when I'm highly active, or I notice my arm or wrist swelling at any time. I clarified with her about whether I was able to go into a sauna, spa or hot tub in the future. Basically, it's not advised to go in anything higher than my own body temperature, so no sauna or spa, but a bath is okay if I don't have it too hot. Another sucky thing to hear, taking away some of life's pleasures. Heavy triple sigh.

Isn't it funny how you can have feelings of guilt for feeling angry? Like it's acceptable to feel some emotions but not others? All feelings and emotions just are—I mean, there's nothing to feel guilty about, you just have to go with the flow. If that means you act a bit bipolar at times, so what? Of course, those unfortunate Souls around you may bear the brunt of your acidic tongue once in a while… Hopefully they love you enough to forgive you and ultimately understand the pressure of living inside your head with thoughts about the Big C and your own mortality. It's like a pressure cooker or, at times, a slow cooker. *It's okay to feel angry sometimes as long as you don't live in the anger.*

Sunday 16 September 2012

Right at this moment in time, I feel happy. The weather is perfect, 25ºC and the sky is cloudless with a beautiful palette of blues. I spent yesterday working hard outside and inside the house, preparing for our party in two weeks' time. Today, my body 'doth protest' so I'm taking it slower and that's okay. I keep being side-tracked from the book I'm currently reading outside under the umbrella. The sun hasn't had a chance to scorch the green grass to a beige colour, so my eyes are drawn to the soothing reserve and the activity within it. A lone kangaroo pauses in the blanket of yellow flowers before bounding off down to the creek. A white butterfly flies erratically in search of a safe place to settle. It's not just the sights that are so distracting to me; it's the varied calls and songs of the birds as well. As I write this, to my delight, a kookaburra chortles in the background.

Thankfully, the feelings of anger have subsided so that they're not consuming me anymore. Thoughts of forgiveness have been plaguing me lately. I dreamt of my mother last night. *Mum had made me an apron with many little pockets. Inside the pockets were many little presents. At first, I didn't want to accept it until Irma said that Mum had spent a lot of time preparing it all for me. I put the apron on and found the gifts inside. I then reluctantly hugged my mother. At first, I only meant to give a quick hug, but then we stayed together hugging for a long time. She was the mother that I used to know, the loving and kind mother.* When I woke up, I knew that I had to let go of my anger against her and forgive her. I also need to hold on to the memories that brought me comfort, joy and love.

I feel lighter. At a Reiki session on Thursday, I felt a heaviness against my chest as though someone was sitting on me, spiritually and physically! I believe it was the negative energy stuck to me from the experience with my parents on my Queensland holiday. I've been silently chanting to myself, *I let go. I let God.*

I've tried to get the balance between working and playing right. I get into these frenetic modes of operation where I have to complete all of the tasks I've set myself for that day. As a result, I overdo it and feel exhausted and flat the next day. Then there's my perfectionist tendency, where I've got to get it just right. Ugh! It's so frustrating being me sometimes. I'm aware of my cycles and patterns of behaviour, and I'm endeavouring to bring about change as a direct result of my awareness. Awareness is not enough if you sincerely want to make changes in your life. Action is required. It may be a 'two steps forward and one step back' approach but I'm okay with that. It's still progress, eh?

Ooohhh, pretty! (I got side-tracked again.) The wind is caressing the tall grass in the reserve and making waves of movement. It's very hypnotic...

Chapter 30

What's in a Word?

Monday 15 October 2012

I've taken a break from journaling for one month. Instead, I focused on living life day to day. Some days have been spent in doing everyday tasks and chores. Other days I've allowed myself to enjoy painting or reading in the sun. I've continued with my yoga and walking in the reserve or around our suburb. I'd love to start a more vigorous exercise routine, but my left wrist is still swollen and has ached every day for the past two months. My physiotherapist, Emma, told me to halt the lymph drainage massage until we knew what was causing the pain, as doing the massage made my wrist throb even more. She recommended I see my GP and perhaps get a referral for an X-ray and ultrasound.

The party on 30 September was a success. David and I had worked incredibly hard to get our house spotlessly clean as well as being welcoming to all of our guests. We had about twenty-five people altogether and the day was a gorgeous 27°C. I spent the day doing the 'hostess' thing, making sure everyone was happy and getting enough to eat and drink. Deciding to be myself, I deliberately wore a bright, multi-coloured caftan shirt with black leggings. I looked like an artist and it's about time too. I gave the 'grand tour' of the house to everyone who was interested, and I must say I felt like a tour guide giving the same speech over and over.

It was fun, though, and I felt proud of our house. Our hard work had paid off. At one point one of our new neighbours said to me, 'You look like a vibrant couple, you and David.'

'Yes, we are!' I replied cheekily.

It's funny because we so haven't felt like a vibrant couple for many years, but I think it's never too late to change. Considering I'd only had two hours of sleep the night before because of a migraine, I think, if I do say so myself, I did brilliantly most of the day and only started to tire and wear down towards the evening. By this stage most people had gone home (we started at midday). It's funny—weeks of preparation for an event that lasts hours. Anyway, it was the first party or get-together at our new place, the first of many I'm sure.

I love spring, but I don't love spring gnats, mozzies and the other bugs that come out of hiding once the sun goes down, and commit suicide on your face, their bodies sometimes getting stuck on your make-up. Hopefully, the citronella I just lit will give me a bit of peace here outside. Krystal just had one of her moments where, out of the blue, she decides to have a race, chased by or chasing an imaginary friend around and around the backyard. It is so funny to watch. All being well, she will soon have a flesh and blood four-legged friend to play with. I think David and I are ready to get another dog. We'll never forget Misha and Cheyenne, and we continue to love them. It doesn't mean that there isn't room in our hearts and lives for new doggy children.

I've been spending hours and hours typing out my book—this book. I was so afraid of how I would react in reliving my life through typing out my journals. It has been cathartic. I had pushed down so many memories and emotions over the years, buried them deep down inside of me. I thought it was the best thing to do, to close it all off. What I now realise is that I hardened myself, encasing myself in a layer of concrete so that the world didn't see how hurt I was. This concrete surface didn't let other people too close, or to know the real me. I mistakenly thought that my vulnerability was a sign of weakness and that I had to put up a front of being tough and invincible. *Vulnerability is not a sign of weakness.* On the contrary, showing your true self to others is a sign of incredible strength. I feel that this cancer forced me to put a sledgehammer to that concrete wall and break it down bit by bit. Writing about it so openly will allow me to breathe freely without building another concrete wall over my heart. I'm hoping that by doing so, other people will avoid repeating my mistakes, and instead show their true colours to those around them.

I saw my GP on Wednesday 10 October, the first time since she gave us the diagnosis of cancer last year. I apologised for not coming to see her earlier, but she said that there was no need. She has been kept updated by my team of professionals, and is very much aware of all I have gone through this past year and nine months. I had a list of things I wanted to discuss with her: my wrist (X-ray and ultrasound); renewal of scripts; a request for a bone density test or bone scan—Osteodensitometry test—to rule out osteoporosis developing; and also blood tests to check out my cholesterol, glucose, thyroid, and full blood count. I'm going to have the blood test done when I have my other bloods done for Dr Gan at the end of this month. We also had a brief chat about my 'journey' and the insights I've gained. It's nice to have a doctor know me better, even if it is as a result of having seen her for the past decade.

Today, I had an appointment at Rockingham Hospital at the Occupational Therapy Department. My physiotherapist, Emma, and

Dr Gan had referred me there to be fitted for a pressure sleeve for my left arm. The occupational therapist was friendly, and we spoke about what I've gone through and am still going through. I was measured up for a pressure garment and was told it would be made and sent from Melbourne. It is a preventative for fluid build-up and I will need to use it, for example, when I exercise more strenuously. I was amused to be told that I could order it in a range of colours, and she pulled out a colour chart for both the sleeve and the thread. Evidently, most people choose to go neutral and select the skin tone or nude/beige. She said that she had only ordered a few other pale colours, and no-one had been brave enough to go for a brighter colour. Well, I thought it was time. I said I was an artist and loved bright colours. If I have to wear the damn thing, it may as well be pretty, eh? I selected a lovely royal blue for the material and a hot pink as a contrast for the stitching. If the royal blue isn't available, my second choice is a bright purple. We are both eager to see what comes back in a few weeks' time.

You know, it's so easy to think negatively about this world and the people in it. If you focus on the daily news, and thought that wars, road accidents, natural disasters, robberies and murders made up our lives, why would any one of us bother getting up in the mornings? I've found such lovely, caring individuals, especially those working in the medical field. There are so many good people out there who aren't mentioned in the daily news. The volunteers at hospitals are often kind, older people who have come to realise that volunteering their time not only benefits the patients and visitors, but also makes them feel useful in society and good about themselves. I choose to believe that good people far outweigh bad people in this world of ours.

In the past few weeks I've been chanting to myself, *Thank you for my healing, thank you for my good health, thank you for my joy, thank you for my laughter and thank you for my happiness.* Any time I have seen a first star of the night, I've made a wish. Any time I have seen a rainbow, I've made a wish. Any time I have found a ladybug, I've made a wish. It may seem childish to some people but it gives me comfort. Where's the harm in that?

Saturday 20 October 2012

Wednesday was a really low day for me. I felt truly defeated and discouraged about life. I picked up my bone densitometry results from Perth Radiological Clinic in Rockingham prior to my Herceptin (three weeks comes around very quickly). Of course, I opened up the envelope and read the report. The numbers didn't mean much to me, but the conclusion did. It read: *indicates low bone density or osteopenia* and that *there is a mild increase in fracture risk*. I felt shattered (no pun intended). I drove to a park to eat my lunch and google more information about osteopenia. It's not as bad as osteoporosis, thank God; however, I have to make some lifestyle changes so that down the track I don't develop osteoporosis. I already take vitamin D, calcium and magnesium, and I do weight-bearing exercises like walking, but I'm sure there are other things that I can do.

By the time I got to my Herceptin, I was so down, thinking, *What else am I supposed to suffer through?* I spoke to Maxine, and she said that I was being too hard on myself, that I was doing the best I could in very difficult circumstances. She said that I had been so brave and strong throughout everything. I replied that I would pick myself up again and bounce back as I always did. I still felt like bursting out crying there at the Chemotherapy Ward; however, I held my tears in through the treatment, and the drive home. I finally allowed myself to cry once I was sitting in the backyard with a coffee and cake in front of me. Krystal didn't know what to do and ran away from me in confusion about why Mummy was so sad.

In my research I found many factors that could have contributed to my osteopenia.

1. Early menopause due to my total hysterectomy at 40 and the subsequent decline in hormones.
2. Family history—my sister was diagnosed with osteopenia over three years ago and my mother has very brittle bones—osteoporosis.
3. My cancer treatment—both chemotherapy and radiation can weaken bones.
4. Diet—alcohol and caffeine can leach calcium away from the bones.

I have come to accept that the majority of factors listed above have been out of my control and I have to stop blaming myself—a bad habit of mine I'm trying to outgrow. When I was crying, I looked up at the sky and silently prayed for help, as I felt my will to keep going fading. I was so fed up with bad news!

Even the news that David brought home that afternoon—the purchase of two tickets for Katri and I to *The Truth About Love Tour* by Pink at the Perth Arena Saturday 29 June next year—failed to cheer me up. Next June seems like such a long time away and I feel bad and miserable now. I guess I allowed myself to wallow in self-pity that day and the next morning also. The usual Herceptin side-effects had kicked in and contributed to my defeatist attitude.

I was busily engaging in emotional eating—coffee and pancakes at Dome Café Pinjarra—and texting interstate friends on Thursday afternoon when I received a call from the Cancer Council. At first, I had difficulty hearing in the busy venue, and then I heard the words Cancer Council. My heart dropped and I thought, *No, not more bad news!* To my utter shock and delight, the lady on the other end of the phone continued with words that were music to my ears. The Cancer Council competition I'd entered in August/September to *Win a pamper weekend, compliments of Parmelia Hilton Perth* for two people... you guessed it, I had WON! The luxury pamper weekend includes: *Two nights in a stunning King Suite, with chocolates on arrival, valet parking and a sensational buffet breakfast in The Globe Restaurant each morning. Relax in the pool and gym or watch ten free Foxtel channels in your room. This fantastic package is valued at $1350.*

Wow! I had to fight back tears in the middle of Dome Café. This time they were tears of happiness, not grief and sorrow. I was so accustomed to bad news that I was taken totally by surprise. The Cancer Council representative said that she would pass on my details to the Parmelia Hilton and they would contact me regarding the voucher. I truly believe that the Universe, my Spirit Guides and loved ones who have passed on to the afterlife had witnessed how unhappy I was and how close I was to giving up. So they decided to give me this gift to keep me persevering. A bit like, *Here, have this pamper weekend as encouragement to keep going on and as a reward for all that has passed.* I must say that this has come at a perfect time and I am very grateful. I am also looking forward to receiving the voucher and making arrangements for our stay.

Sunday 28 October 2012

Like I said I would, I picked myself up, dusted myself off, as well as the negativity, and continued onward. David and I decided it was time for us to plan a camping trip again. With that in mind, we went for a day trip to Lane Poole Reserve last Sunday for a picnic and to check out campsites. We took Krystal with us, and she was very confused about the whole event but soon had fun sniffing out the new environment. The day was fun and we are definitely booking a campsite for next month.

I had my ultrasound and X-ray on my wrist on Monday. There was no obvious fracture, but a full report will be sent to my GP. I'll just have to be patient yet again. It's still bothering me, but I refuse to give in to the pain. I've been wearing my wrist brace whenever I need extra support.

David took my old bicycle for a service and I tested it out on Thursday. Note to self, don't go bike riding in the middle of the day with the sun beating down and a need to swat flies the whole time. I was proud of myself riding for half an hour against the odds, or should I say against the wind and the mob of flies. Next time I'll plan it a bit better, probably best to go in the morning.

This weekend has been brilliant. We went to a fun party on Saturday, where I laughed so much I had tears in my eyes and had to catch my breath. It was so heartwarming to see David bursting into genuine laughter and joking around with the other guys. God knows we deserve some happiness and joy in our lives.

Today, we went back to Lane Poole Reserve to double-check the campsite number we had in mind out of those still available. We decided to leave Krystal at home, much to her outrage. We walked around and, after a drink and nibblies, I decided I wanted to dip into the creek. It was a hot and humid day and I wanted to make the most of it. We found a perfect sandy entrance to the creek and I gingerly lowered myself down into the icy water. David watched in amusement as I shrieked out 'Eee, eee, eeeee...' After a few moments, my body got used to the cold and I began to really enjoy myself. I lay there in the water, listening to the birds, and watching the sky and treetops. I felt very grateful and at peace to be alive. I wanted to savour the moment and hold it in my heart memory so that I could draw on it in my darkest moments.

Tuesday 30 October 2012

I had to draw on that heart memory a lot quicker than I thought. All I can say is that yesterday was a horror kind of day. It started out nice enough, although a bit early for my liking. As I was booked into my CT scan (it's been seven months since my last one), I had to stop eating solids and milk products by 6am. I ate a health bar and drank a coffee at 5.30am so that I wouldn't be starving by my appointment time. I leisurely got ready to drive to the hospital by 8.15am for my appointment at 9am. Purchasing a magazine in the gift shop, I chatted with a woman in a turban who was getting ready for her chemo appointment. I said I needed to escape into some celebrity gossip whilst drinking my white glug barium sulphate. She replied that we could swap and I could go to her chemo. There eventuated a conversation about 'already been there and done that'. As it turned out, she also has HER2 positive breast cancer and has started on Herceptin, with this being her last chemo. I was flattered when she said how great I looked and that I obviously took care of myself. I reassured her that hair does grow back and tugged at my ever growing thicker hair. We briefly talked about the Herceptin debate, one year versus two years, and then off we went to our own appointments, each wishing the other good luck. The gift shop lady was privy to our whole conversation, and I guess it must have been interesting for her to see us talking so matter-of-factly about our cancer journeys.

I drank my gluggy solution without grimacing or complaining; I'm so used to it by now. At 10.15am the nurse took me back to the 'torture chamber'. I changed into a hospital gown and bravely waited for the usual 'fun' to begin. The nurse tried a few times to cannulate me and thought the one she put in would work. When I was settled into the CT scanner machine and raised my arms to the appropriate position, the needle hurt and wouldn't flush. So back to the seat for another try... no go. She decided to call the doctor. He tried a few times... no go. He asked me if I was cold. Well, of course I was cold! I was sitting there in just a hospital gown with the air conditioning making me even colder. Frustrated, he told the nurse to get me blankets and a heat pack, and that it was a waste of time if the patient was freezing. I had already mentioned that the chemo nurses always gave me a heat pack first, but would they listen? No, not until four failed attempts of finding a vein.

The doctor left for ten minutes, letting me warm up and calm down. Upon returning, he decided to take me to the ultrasound machine to help locate a deeper vein. Okay, it looked like success at last. Back to the CT room to be hooked up. The nurse manager wisely decided to stay next to me after the tracking and positioning had been completed by the machine. When it was time to inject me with the dye, the nurse raised my right arm upright against the machine in order to see clearly, and make sure the cannula would hold for the pressure of the dye. Within a few seconds, it was obvious something was wrong, as the dye and my blood poured down my arm! The nurse manager banged on the machine. 'Stop! Stop!' she yelled to the controller behind the window.

I was numb from shock and stayed still as they cleaned me up, changed the dressing over the cannula and tried to figure out what was wrong. To their anger and disgust, they discovered that the doctor had not tightened the cannula cap completely. The pressure of the machine had made it 'spring a leak'. After tightening the cap, they tried again, but the vein had blown and was no longer viable. They were muttering that doctors did that all of the time and I replied, 'You should tell them so they learn from their mistakes.'

After changing my gown, back we went to the ultrasound room. I was just following the nurse in automatic-mode and trying not to scream. The sheepish doctor returned and was obviously sweating from his forehead (at least one of us was warm). Sixth time lucky perhaps? Back into the machine for the third time and we had to start from scratch, as it had been so long that the computer had refreshed its screen. Finally! Success!

I felt relieved and sick, not only from the barium solution and the dye but also from the level of stress. The nurses joked that I would run out of the hospital after all of that, and I just smiled weakly. The nurse suggested that next time I tell them about warming me up first. What? Hadn't I done that? Seriously! Obviously, I'll have to *demand* a heat pack, blankets and the ultrasound machine. Blaming the patient is a low blow.

I think my body just shut down for the rest of the day. The usual diarrhoea from the barium sulphate didn't occur. I just went home to bed so as to shut out the horror of the day. My mind keeps playing out that scene over and over again... my arm dripping with sticky dye solution mixed with my own blood.

I'm writing this all down now, even though my arm is black and blue with bruises, because I want it out of my system and onto paper. I had nightmares last night and it's no wonder. Today, I'm trying to stay calm and look for the pockets of happiness around me. I have to keep being brave and strong because I have to go back there tomorrow for another heart echo as well as having more blood taken (for Dr Gan and Dr Moore). I'll also be collecting my bright purple sleeve from the occupational therapist as well.

I received a call from the Parmelia Hilton today, confirming my win of the pamper package for two. I told her it was a Godsend after my last two years of hell. They will send us a voucher, which is valid for a year. Okay, time to stop dwelling and relax.

Chapter 31

Cycles and Patterns

Monday 5 November 2012

Time and again, I pick myself up from that sinking feeling, that dark pit of emotions. It would be all too easy to just dwell there, but some stubborn streak in me refuses to give in or give up. I'm sure the majority of cancer patients can relate to the mixed bag of emotions that this experience provides us on a weekly basis. Last Wednesday, I was a trembling mess prior to my bloods being taken. Thankfully, it wasn't the same ordeal as on the Monday. The heart echo was a lot easier and even the technician mentioned that it was not difficult to get the readings this time. Friday's appointment with my GP went just as smoothly. We had a good conversation about everything and my blood results were good. The X-ray and ultrasound of the wrist showed no obvious damage, so most likely it's just a nasty sprain or strain that is taking a long time to heal. She didn't recommend I go on any other medication for my osteopenia, just that I ensure an adequate intake of vitamin D and calcium.

On Saturday 3 November, I participated in the Cancer Council's *Relay For Life Survivors Walk* in Mandurah. The weather was absolutely atrocious and yet the Rushton Park Oval was full of eager participants for the Relay For Life. I said yes to participating because it's time for me to think of myself as a SURVIVOR. Through the waves of rain, people of all ages registered their teams for the 24-hour relay. As I had never been to this event before, I was initially confused by the many tents dotted along the outside of the oval, the banners bearing team names and the wonderful costumes people wore. After speaking to Christine—a Cancer Council Coordinator—it all finally clicked in my mind... oh, light bulb moment... they're raising funds for the Cancer Council. I had thought that it was only a Survivors and Carers Walk.

I registered and received a 'Survivor' pin, and a lovely purple sash to drape over my shoulder. We also placed our pink or purple handprint onto a Survivor's banner to be held at the front of our procession. It was unfortunate that the loud rain and wind drowned out the speakers even though they spoke into a microphone. A few people spoke about their own cancer journey, but I could not hear their voices above the thundery storm. Most of us huddled under the cover of the roof of a building, wearing disposable rain ponchos, until the worst of the storm passed. Some brave people stood in the oval despite the downpour and I hoped that they had a change of clothing in their tents.

It's strange how the rain stopped just long enough for us, the Survivors and Carers, to do our lap of honour to commence the relay. It's as if the Universe paused for us out of kindness. I walked beside Christine and, together with the rest of the Survivors and their Carers, we slowly but surely walked around the oval. The other teams stood beside their tents and applauded us loudly as we walked past them. I was surprised that I had to hold back tears at the amount of community support and genuine caring emanating from everyone. I didn't expect to feel so emotional. After our lap, the sky opened up again, just in time for us to head into the tent for our morning tea—and what a sumptuous morning tea it was. I spoke to a few people at our table. One man proudly declared that he was five years cancer free and asked each of us how long we had been Survivors. Two women responded that they were less than a year. When he asked me, I said I was still having treatment but I was a Survivor. You betcha!

Today was time to see Dr Gan again. Of course, I was so anxious about the CT scan results that I didn't sleep again. It's easy to say, *Don't worry*, or *Don't think about it*. But it's human nature to fear and to worry, and to think, *What if?* Thank God everything was fine. The CT scan was clear, bloods all good and heart echo reading was better at sixty-eight per cent. Yay! The cardiovascular support supplements I am taking are definitely working. What a huge relief. I don't have to see him until February next year; no more bloods or echoes until then. Phew. Only Herceptin to deal with for the next three months.

In fact, the only 'bad' news is that I've gained weight. I've done a lot of emotional eating lately and the results show on the scales. I know what I need to do. I have all the knowledge and skills from my Jenny Craig and Betty Baxter days of being a weight loss consultant. I texted Irma: *Been saying to myself would I rather be plump and cancer free or thin and cancer ridden? No contest!* No contest indeed. I'm grateful for feeling stronger than I have in a long while. I no longer get breathless and gasp for air when walking or doing simple tasks. Today, I power walked with Krystal at the reserve against strong winds and I was fine. Luckily, Krystal was attached to her leash or she would have blown away.

I heard a kookaburra this morning at 4.30am when I couldn't sleep, and I thought, *Yes, I need to laugh more*. Well, I guess the Universe thought so as well. After my doctor's appointment, I bought a coffee and a muffin. As I stared into space and enjoyed my cuppa, an old man started a conversation with me. At first it was about his free coffee and then about his grandchildren. All nice and innocent. I was polite and smiled and chatted back. It got a bit disconcerting, however, when he looked at my feet in my sandals and blurted out, 'I have a foot fetish!' Okay… Then he said, 'You have nice feet and you obviously take care of them.'

Okay… So how did I to respond to that?

'Thank you', I replied, whilst laughing silently. I thought, *please don't go any further about my feet and possibly what you would you like to do with them.* Anyway, he left shortly afterwards and I sighed in relief. It's good to have a sense of humour and not take everything so damn seriously.

Thursday 22 November 2012

The weeks flow on, one after the other, and I often wake up not quite certain what day it is. I've kept myself busy with the usual house chores, weeding and gardening, and getting into a better exercise routine. The other day I went on the treadmill and managed to jog slowly. Today, I am proud to have completed forty laps at the swimming pool in Pinjarra; some of the laps I walked and lunged. My left arm has been sore for over three months now, but I'm determined not to let that stop me from trying. I don't want to use it as an excuse for not doing anything. During my last Herceptin infusion, I let them use my left hand because my right arm had been black and blue with bruises for three weeks. However, that turned out to be a mistake. For whatever reason, the left arm became swollen and very painful. It's hard to describe but it feels like broken shards of glass under the skin from my inner wrist to the top of the elbow area. I think the lymph nodes are too traumatised to work properly, leading to fluid build-up. To avoid the inflammation, I need to only allow Herceptin infusions in my right arm from now on.

The cool water of the pool felt good on the arm and I have been using ice packs against my skin for the past two weeks. I have to make peace with the fact that my body has changed, and some of the things I was able to do in the past, I may not be able to do again. I have to be mindful of my arm and do my best to support it, be gentle with myself, wear the pressure sleeve when I can and do lymph drainage massage.

We left for our camping trip on Friday 16 November, eager to just get away for a few days to 'chillax'. Of course, we packed for an army rather than the two of us and Krystal. We had a relatively fight-free time setting up our tent, camp kitchen, camp shower and bug-free enclosure in which to eat our meals. Krystal was bemused by the whole set-up and whimpered incessantly, which tested our patience big-time. After more than two hours of setting up, we gratefully escaped the flies into our human enclosure and enjoyed a beer in salute to our efforts.

We had hoped for a temperature in the mid-twenties for our weekend trip but, as luck would have it, it ended up being hot. Unfortunately, I can't cope with the heat anymore and my poor left arm just looked bloated. I raised it on a pillow and kept on icing it for pain relief. By mid-afternoon, we decided to sink ourselves into the river to cool down. Krystal eagerly followed us into the icy river and took to the water like the water doggy she's meant to be; poodles and spaniels are water loving breeds. Afterwards, she wasn't too impressed and stood there shivering like a skinny rat, as we'd had her clipped just the day before.

I was sitting on the sandy shore in shallow water when I noticed movement under the water. I thought it was river debris until I saw a claw! The more we looked, the more we spotted the crayfish swimming and walking under water. Luckily, hubby didn't get an unpleasant surprise, as the rock he was sitting on also hosted a crayfish directly under his 'family jewels'.

The first night's sleep was very disturbed for me. Firstly, the blow-up mattress was not comfortable for my throbbing arm. Secondly, other campsite members decided to party until 1am and thirdly, David snored away next to me until I huffed and puffed in frustration and woke him up. The gentleman that he is, he got up and went to the other tent, our bug-free zone, and tried to rest there. I felt guilty until I heard his snores emanating from a couple of metres away instead of right next to me (oh, how sound carries in the bush). In with the ear plugs and, failing that, I listened to my music for hours. At about 5am, David came in shivering with cold and to, I quote, 'warm me up'. Krystal, or Snooks as we call her, was not budging from her spot between us under the blankets. It was nice having her lean against my lower back like a hot water bottle. I finally drifted off to sleep for about three hours.

On Saturday, we read our magazines, went for another swim to cool down and watched the blue wrens and red-tailed black cockatoos fly past. It's not a camping trip without toasting marshmallows in the fire, so even though I was full from tacos, I managed to successfully toast five marshmallows for dessert. I was so bone-weary that I showered early and was in bed by 10pm. Thankfully, after swallowing a sleeping tablet, and with David propped up on three pillows to prevent snoring, I finally enjoyed a quiet night's sleep.

It's amazing how much laundry piles up after only a couple of days away, eh? All the blankets and pillows had to be washed due to the smoky smell of the campfire. I think I have to avoid camping in summer from now on; wintertime will have to do. One of those things I have to come to terms with. Yes, it sucks big-time, but at least I'm still alive to enjoy the outdoors. So put things into perspective, Sorja. I still picture David and myself buying a campervan or caravan in the future and travelling around Australia. You've got to hold onto your dreams and make plans despite your fears.

Thursday 29 November 2012

What a doozie of a week. Last Saturday, I drove one hour south to Bunbury for the free information forum, 'Living Well Beyond Breast Cancer'. This was proudly sponsored by the Breast Cancer Network Australia and the Australian Government. I arrived early and, after collecting my name badge, I walked around the information stands, picking up some useful brochures and pamphlets to read at home. They were on interesting topics such as reducing your risk of lymphoedema, depression and breast cancer, breast cancer pathology, and breast cancer and sexual wellbeing.

We were also given a 'show bag' (ha, ha, ha) of other information, contacts, lip balm and a note pad. I was astounded by the number of people there for the forum. I later found out that three hundred of us filled the room and they had to cut off the number of attendees due to the venue capacity. Apparently, they could have easily hosted five hundred because of the amount of interest expressed. This goes to show the great demand and need for more of these forums, and more frequently, too, as the last one here was four years ago. It's sad to see how many people are affected by breast cancer and it was a bit overwhelming for me.

My first impression was how welcoming they made it for us, from the pink cut outs of ladies pasted on the walls, showing us the direction to go, to the information stands, and then the scrumptious morning tea for us to partake in. The ballroom was a sea of pink shirts, pink scarves, pink head wear, make-up and jewellery. The hundreds of people came in all shapes and sizes and age groups. The majority of attendees were women; however, a few brave male partners tagged along in support, or were dragged there by their wives and girlfriends, or—who is to know—maybe they themselves were survivors of breast cancer.

I sat in the front row so that I had a clear view of the speakers. I must have looked like a journalist or a reporter as my pen flew over my notepad throughout the speeches. I noticed that a few women next to me glanced over at me writing down notes so furiously (not in anger) and probably wondered why I was doing so. I didn't see others making use of their notepads. To tell you the truth, I was interested and found the forum highly informative. The speakers included the CEO of Breast Cancer Network of Australia (BCNA), a professor of surgical oncology (breast surgeon), a psycho-social expert and a McGrath breast care nurse.

The hotel provided us with a delicious, carb-laden lunch between the sessions, and the forum concluded at 3pm. There was ample opportunity to ask questions throughout the day and I felt sorry for some of the experts, as some of the attendees appeared to be bent on grilling them or catching them out somehow. I observed as one of the speakers grew redder in the face and obviously had to 'bite her tongue' at some of the more aggressive questions and remarks. Some questions just don't have answers. Cancer is still a huge puzzle; the 'experts' are human after all, and don't necessarily know everything.

I found out that in 2012, there are now over 73,000 members of BCNA. Distressingly, there are thirty-eight women diagnosed per day here in Australia, and in Western Australia four women are diagnosed each day. That's just horrific to hear. I knew I wasn't alone in going through this, but the number is staggering! What about in the whole world? Scary thought, eh?

The *comforting* thought was that in the audience, there were women who had been diagnosed ten years ago, and even twenty years ago, and are still around, 'alive and kicking,' so-to-speak. I listened to the psychological, emotional, social and practical impact that the diagnosis of cancer has on an individual, and the way relationships may change with friends and family as well as our intimate relationships with our partners. I learned the importance of breathing properly and deeply, and the way it affects how well our lymph system removes toxins from our bodies. I know that I often breathe shallowly or hold my breath, and that is something I am consciously working on now.

I was reassured to hear that I can return to the full and active life I led prior to my diagnosis, as long as I do so gradually and build my strength back up slowly but surely. Yoga and Tai Chi are particularly beneficial to combat lymphoedema and my swimming breaststroke is also a good move on my part. Trusting in your body again takes time, so I have to persevere, practise patience and allow time for healing to take place.

I was fascinated to hear that breast cancer is not a new disease. In fact, the condition was described in old artefacts dating back thousands of years, for example, on papyrus. Cancer is now the most common disease in Australian society, ahead of heart disease. Other topics discussed were menopause, weight gain, fatigue and using exercise to combat fatigue, body image and accepting the 'new you', long-term pain, sexuality and loss of bone density due to chemotherapy and menopause. It was said that we don't have to live life in fear. Hmmm... easy to say, practically impossible to do.

Evidently, if you have a defective immune system, the cancer grows faster. I'm definitely on the right track building mine up through the immune boosting, natural therapies I have been taking these past two years. I guess what frightened me was the talk about interval cancers, i.e. the ones that develop in between mammograms and scans. A man in the audience spoke about the mammograms giving him and his wife a false sense of security when they read 'all clear'. He stressed the importance of 'never taking the eye off the ball' and continuing self-examinations. Sadly, they trusted the 'all clear' and found out that the cancer had reoccurred well before the next scheduled mammogram. *Take note: do your breast self-examinations! Notice any change and speak to your doctor.*

To add insult to injury, I heard that every child a woman has reduces her likelihood of developing breast cancer by ten per cent. Thank you. I would have had children if I could have... another shot to the heart! Did I put a cross against the children box and a tick next to the breast cancer box when the menu of life was given to me?

The clinical sexologist who spoke at the forum was very amusing and delivered vital relationship information in a non-threatening manner. She spoke about the way sex and sensuality encompass a kaleidoscope of feelings and activities. Touch and connectedness make a relationship more meaningful. An intimate bond does matter; however, partners often experience a ripple effect as a result of what their wives or girlfriends are going through, which in turn leads to a decrease in their own libido. It is natural and normal to fear hurting a loved one, and be unsure about how to proceed with sexual intimacy. Often it is challenging to regain a sense of normality and a number of factors play a hand in this: *self-esteem*—self-worth, self-confidence and self-respect; and *body-esteem*—image of self and making peace with your changed body. As a couple, celebrating the good in life is vital for the relationship too. It is crucial to say words of love and appreciation for each other every day, and to explore new ways of being together. In turn, this leads to avenues of deepening your level of intimacy and being able to experience pleasure once more. For women, the mind plays a huge role in her own sexuality and feelings of desire; therefore, words of love, comfort, caring and support act as an aphrodisiac... men, take note.

Phew! After such a full day of absorbing all the information, not to mention the energies of hundreds of people, I felt weary. No surprise there. Before I left (I let the hordes of people leave before me), I spoke to the CEO of BCNA and the breast surgeon about the extent of the lymph nodes—forty-five of them—I'd had removed and asked if they'd heard of that many removed before.

'No, that's a bit excessive,' said the CEO of BCNA, adding that the usual was from ten to forty.

The surgeon said that although it was very unusual, she had once removed fifty-eight lymph nodes from one side of a woman. I know it sounds bad, but I felt better about someone else having more lymph nodes removed than I did, like I wasn't particularly unique. I was on autopilot the whole drive home, my mind no longer capable of storing any more information for that day. I had done enough.

On Monday 26 November, I was invited to a Christmas party for the Breast Cancer Care Support Groups, which was held at Nedlands Yacht Club. I received an email from Cathie Smith—one of the Breast

Cancer Care WA (BCCWA) counsellors and group facilitators—about both the Mandurah support group and the Christmas party. A minibus picked us up from meeting points in Mandurah and Rockingham. The day involved meeting and chatting with other survivors of breast cancer. At the venue, we were greeted by waiters bearing champagne, and the club was very festive in all its Christmas decorations and table settings. A lot of effort had gone into the entire day, and it was enriching to spend time with other women travelling a similar, but not identical, path to my own. The day consisted of a lot of food, wine, Christmas gifts, group photos, a fashion parade, Santa arriving on a Harley Davidson, raffles and other party games. When the dessert and an array of confectionary came out, we eagerly lined up like a bunch of schoolgirls waiting impatiently for the sugar-hit. I guess the healthy lifestyle choices were put on hold for the duration of the day. Oh well, never mind.

We were all at different stages of treatment, some going through chemotherapy, others radiotherapy, and the lucky ones having finished all treatment; however, it was obvious that we were all determined to 'let our hair down' and enjoy ourselves. What camaraderie! That joyous atmosphere is priceless, albeit found through our unexpected common bond. I met some remarkable women and I look forward to attending the Mandurah Angels support group. It's time for me to come out of my shell and stop being such a hermit crab. I am not alone.

Monday 3 December 2012

I believe that *cancer* is the least discriminating entity in the world. It doesn't care if you are:

- married or single

- female or male
- seven or seventy
- heterosexual or gay or lesbian or bisexual
- religious or atheist
- Caucasian or Indigenous or whatever ethnicity
- employed or unemployed
- a supermodel or ordinary looking
- famous or not
- tall or short
- slim, fit or fat
- vegan or a meat eater
- rich or poor
- a neat-freak or a hoarder
- a mother or a father or childless
- a teetotaller or a drunk
- human or a domestic animal.

My belief is that cancer just doesn't care and is not really interested in the surface package. It snickers with glee and contempt at the human imposed rules of what to do and what not to do. I believe what cancer really hates is LOVE. Self-love and love from others, as well as love for others. It doesn't understand love and therefore runs away when bombarded by these alien waves of emotion. So the cure for this abnormality is *one hundred per cent love*! Love yourself to the point that this entity feels repelled, bombarded, suffocated and unwelcome... it can no longer coexist in such an atmosphere.

Friday 14 December 2012

I've rediscovered *gratitude*. I am so grateful to be alive nearly two years down the track from my diagnosis. I've really felt good for the past week. I'm over the cold and tummy bug I caught a couple of weeks ago and I have a lot more energy. Due to this renewed feeling of energy and strength in my body, I've got right back into my exercises with no excuses. I've been proud of myself for fast walking or jogging on the treadmill three times this week, as well as doing some strength training exercises such as band work and using my abdominal machine. Krystal has been overjoyed at getting more doggy walks, too, and she seems to psychically know when we are about to 'go walkies' even if I haven't made a move towards her leash. She comes up to me, tap taps me on my thigh with her little paws and says, 'Ee, ee, ee, ee, ee... ' That translates as 'Let's go now, I'm ready.'

The more confident I feel in my physical strength, the more it converts to confidence in my interactions with others. I've noticed that this week in particular I have been able to be myself and say what I mean, and it feels good. I've chatted more naturally to neighbours, strangers at shops, my father, my sisters and my husband. My self-esteem and confidence are definitely improving, although there's always room for growth and expansion to another level. I've accepted invitations socially as well, for example, free tickets from BCCWA to see the ballet *Nutcracker*. I'm at a point where I've been able to read up about HER2 positive breast cancer on the internet without totally 'losing the plot' and curling up in a ball under the bed covers. I even hired out the DVD *Living Proof* with Harry Connick Jr playing the role of Dr Dennis Slamon, who fought so hard to get Herceptin approved to treat HER2 positive breast cancer. Sure, the film made me cry a lot, yet I found it inspirational too. I did shake my head at the glossing over of side effects of Herceptin. Huh, no side effects? Are you kidding me? The HER2 support group website tells of hundreds, maybe thousands, of women experiencing the same side effects I have, and most of them had Herceptin for a year; I'm into my second year. The most common side effects listed were constant sniffling, runny nose, nose sores, diarrhoea, fatigue, flu-like symptoms, joint pain and nausea. I was interested to read about unwanted weight gain, particularly in the stomach area. Women who had always been active and slim complained about gaining an extra tyre around their waist during their Herceptin... Hmmm... maybe that's why I've got two tyres now. Oh well, I'll never know unless I continue to exercise and watch what I eat and drink (maybe not just 'watch' what I eat but actually not eat and drink as much, ha, ha, ha). I've certainly felt more alive by eating more protein, drinking protein shakes with fruit and low fat lactose free milk, and I've slept better by being more active and not just a couch chip (the term couch potato has been taken, ha, ha, ha).

My own sense of humour is coming back bit by bit, even if I'm the only one laughing at times. David and I put up our Christmas decorations this year, for the first time in years, and we'll be getting some presents as well. Last year, neither one of us felt like celebrating and I'm so happy to feel different this year. There's a lot to celebrate, eh?

Which reminds me... a group of us Survivors were asked to put our birthdates down on a 'birthday list' a few weeks ago at the Mandurah Angels support group. I noticed the older woman next to me only put her date as the day and month, leaving the year blank. A few others chose to do so as well. I spoke up and asked, 'Why?'

Putting down your birth year is a good thing and there's nothing wrong with showing how old you are. It means you are a *survivor of life* and turning older is great; we can celebrate another birthday being alive! I'm proud to be forty-six, and I look forward to having my forty-seventh, forty-eighth, forty-ninth and fiftieth birthdays—

and many more after that. There's no shame in age. Women in particular need to get over the embarrassment and stop hiding their real age, or even lying about it. Come on... there are worse things in life, eh?

The year 2012 is coming to an end but I'm not. I know I still have many treatments of Herceptin ahead of me, other tests and the annual mammogram and ultrasound. Who knows what the future will bring to any one of us, so there's no use in fearing the worst or wasting precious energy on such negative and unproductive thoughts. I truly feel that the worst is behind me. I don't know why, but I feel like, *Phew, I did it!* I've crossed that chasm a hand hold at a time. At times, I've had support, at other times I've crawled alone. The wide-open drop beneath my feet has been deeper and longer than I ever imagined. It has been the scariest experience of my life, and I've often held my breath at the magnitude of my journey through cancer. It's now time for me to run and to keep running. I won't let anyone drag me down or backwards anymore! I'm keeping this newfound wisdom, and I'm willing to help others find their way out of their own individual black hole. I thank God, I thank the Universe, and I thank my Spirit Guides and Spiritual Helpers (humans and animals) for helping me through my own personal struggles and fighting my own Demons.

Chapter 32

The Paint Strokes of My Life

Wednesday 20 February 2013

I saw Dr Gan on Monday and his words were, 'I am so happy with your progress.'

My mammogram and ultrasound were both fine, my bloods are good and my heart scan results are stable. *I am so happy with my progress.* I've got back into swimming laps at the pool on top of my yoga, treadmill and gym workouts. I've redone my business cards and circulated my Reiki brochures to the support group women, neighbours and the hospital. I feel stronger and fitter, and I am getting a natural high from my activity and exercise rather than an artificial high from food and wine. Our new addition to the family will be picked up very soon... a Maltese x Shitzu puppy, a friend and sister for Krystal. I've just thought of a name for her. I'm going to name her Xena, my little warrior princess. I'm going to be surrounded by the healing energy of Krystal and the female warrior energy of Xena; it makes sense, as I'm moving into my time of strength in this life.

Monday 22 July 2013

My life at present, two and a half years since being diagnosed... I am here, alive and happier than I have felt in a long, long time. I was given the wonderful news that I'm in remission from the cancer a month ago on Monday 24 June 2013.

Of course, there have been a few hiccups along the way these past few months, which meant that I skipped my last three doses of Herceptin. That's okay, as I had thirty-two doses of Herceptin altogether, quite enough, thank you! I've continued to have a few issues with my heart, such as dizzy spells, low heartbeat, vertigo and low blood pressure. I am hopeful that the longer I go without any more treatment, my heart and so forth will recover on its own, given time to do so. As a precaution, I have been referred to see a cardiologist and am waitlisted. My oncologist was very happy with the results of my latest scans and bloods. David was with me at that appointment when I asked Dr Gan, 'So, can I say that I am officially in remission?'

'Yes', Dr Gan replied. 'Your scans were all good and no more treatment, so yes, you are in remission.'

David and I sighed loudly. I felt a huge weight lift from my shoulders and I burst into song spontaneously (okay, not at the doctor's but at home over the next few days, ha, ha, ha).

Earlier this year, I volunteered to take over the role of facilitator of our breast cancer support group (Mandurah Angels) from my friend Jane Nikora. Over the past five months, I have been able to put my knowledge and skills to good use. At the beginning of this cancer journey, I said that I wanted to run a women's support group, and look, here I am doing just that as co-facilitator with Cathie Smith—a BCCWA counsellor. Isn't it fantastic? I'm going to Sydney in two weeks' time to a Breast Cancer Network of Australia (BCNA) summit for a few days. BCNA is flying group facilitators over for the event, and I am sure I will learn a lot, as well as connecting with other women who have taken on the often challenging role of leading a group. I'm extending my stay for an extra four days to stay with my dear friend Samantha and her hubby John who I haven't seen in ten years. I can't wait!

I'm learning to balance work with play. David and I went to see the Cirque Du Soleil production of *OVO* last month (Friday 14 June) in Perth. What a spectacular show! In addition, the Saturday (29 June) after I received the great news of being in remission, Katri and I went to see Pink's *The Truth About Love Tour* at the Perth Arena. It was appropriately timed and I was able to celebrate being alive. Music can be so uplifting, healing and entertaining.

I'm learning to listen to the cues my body sends me. For example, my left hand and arm hurt when I have done too much and my lymph nodes aren't coping. The solution is to prop my arm on a pillow and do some drainage massage. I have learned how much I enjoy meditation and it has become a regular daily habit. I am proud to have established this new routine, and I crave meditation when I have not been able to do it for some reason. I still choose to give myself Reiki healing energy when I feel the need, and *receive answers to my own questions when I am in a state of relaxation as opposed to stress and anxiety.* I am learning not to use alcohol as an emotional crutch and also to open my heart to others through my words and actions. For so long, I was in an anxious, fearful state and often did not recognise when something or someone was not a threat to me. I believe that anyone who goes through cancer or a major life-threatening illness gets so caught up in the fight or flight stress response that they lose trust in life. I'm learning not to fear people as much, allowing the real me, Sorja, to shine through.

As I am a Libra and 'To Balance' is my motto and goal, I have been thinking about ways I can aim to be in balance, breaking it down to the physical, emotional, mental and spiritual...

- *Physical*—physical expression through my artwork (paintings, drawings, sketches and so forth) and physical care of self and others.

- *Emotional*—emotional expression as support group facilitator, and as a counsellor, connecting with people and expressing my emotions openly to family and friends.

- *Mental*—mental expression through my writing of books, my poetry and challenging myself with new experiences.

- *Spiritual*—spiritual expression through Reiki and meditation and just 'being'.

I appreciate life and I understand that only I can choose to be happy. We all have choices and I am responsible for finding avenues of having my needs met. Sure, life doesn't always go exactly to plan. I have learned that I can help others with the knowledge and experience of what I have gone through, but I must be sensitive as to how I communicate with them (still learning this). We all have our life paths and we react to major life events differently. Often through our own upbringing, we are conditioned to believe in human limitations, and it's only ourselves who can determine how much we can handle. *We are stronger than what we think*, and I don't only mean physically. I welcome laughter, joy, happiness and fun into my life. May they find you in the most unexpected of places.

Tuesday 4 March 2014

Way back in October 2013, I finally had all of my tests done with the cardiologist at Fremantle Hospital. The results were all good, with just a few things to remain aware of. I have postural hypertension which explains my vertigo and dizziness at times. I also have a minor hole in my heart; apparently forty per cent of people have them.

As for now, in March 2014, I believe that *happiness resides within us*. I can honestly say that the past few months have been the happiest of my life. I have come to learn that it is safe for me to be the real Sorja, and to accept that some people will be confronted and perhaps drift away, and that's okay. We are all connected in some way or another. We need certain people in our lives for short periods of time and others our whole lives. I have made many new friends to replace those I've lost.

I am now living the life I always wanted to live. I am painting in my unique, individual way, and you know what? People are loving my art, buying my paintings and even commissioning me to do a painting for them. How cool is that?

After one year of being the facilitator of our breast cancer support group (Mandurah Angels), I stepped down from my voluntary position in order to follow my dream of running an art therapy group for survivors of breast cancer as well as their female family and friends. At this present time, I am holding the Art Therapy Workshop once a month and the feedback has been amazing. Instead of the focus always being on breast cancer, I try and encourage participants to use creative art therapy as a way to explore thoughts and feelings, and to find meaning to life experiences. In a relaxed atmosphere, with calming background music, we are free to connect with ourselves and share within a supportive group.

It's been three years since my diagnosis, and I am able to wake up in the morning and not have 'cancer' as the first thought in my mind. I have to let it go, as it is no longer a part of my life, thank you.

I am finally participating in the twelve week *Life Now* gym program after many postponements due to my heart strength, and I'm loving seeing the strength return to my body and muscles. All in all, I breathe more easily and no longer suffer from panic attacks from feeling fearful of life and my responsibilities. I enjoy my life now, and I can see how I have been the major instrument in creating this life for me, not to take away from the one hundred per cent support from David, my *anchor and grounding force* throughout this journey.

I have been given another chance, so I am following my dreams, my desires and my authentic truth. The flow on effect from this is that I am an open-hearted person and people can see how happy and well I am. Relationships improve, not only with family and friends, but with total strangers as well. The ripple effect is jaw-dropping to witness at times. I am so glad I didn't give up on myself and that I persevered through all of my life challenges thus far. I would have missed out on all these blessings now! I would have missed out on feeling happy, fulfilled and whole. That sounds funny considering how many body parts I have lost along the way, but it doesn't really matter. *I am whole.* My Soul is singing in the background and twinkling away behind my eyes. I hear people comment how bright and clear my eyes are and I grin.

Chapter 33

Make a Wish on a Ladybug

I joined the world of social media in 2013. I hesitated for the longest of times, not sure if it would be a blessing or a curse. Of course, it can be both; however, what a way it is to remember memories and words written by you as another form of self-expression. When I discontinued writing in my journals, I expressed myself through the medium of Facebook. Now, as I write the final two chapters of my book, it has been of great benefit to find old Facebook posts and photos as a timeline of my life.

On Saturday 16 and Sunday 17 August 2014, I ran a weekend retreat in Dwellingup called *Sorja's Arty Weekend Getaway*, which was attended by nineteen women. It took many months of organisation but how proud I felt with everything falling into place. I organised a combination of art therapy activities, story time, a Saturday evening 'Come dressed as your wild woman' theme party, and a walking meditation. With the help of many of the women, all meals were prepared, and Jenny Willis took photos to capture the experience (thank you). And what fun we had having a campfire sing-a-long. Many, many fond memories of this time and a group of women supporting each other...

Towards the end of 2014, I felt the need to re-create my image. The first drastic change, and shock to my family, friends and even my own hairdresser, was to go from a natural blonde to black hair!

It suited me well and brought out my blue-grey eyes; however, if I let more than three weeks go by without redoing the roots of my hair, I looked like I was going bald again. I actually sustained this black hair for ten months; what an achievement, ha, ha, ha... After losing my hair from chemotherapy, I've never been afraid to experiment with other colours and styles, and that is a blessing.

The second drastic physical change had to do with my skin on the right side of my chest as a result of the PowerPort/Infusaport. If I wore a top that revealed that area, people stared at the scar and it really upset me. I knew that they didn't do it to be rude; it was just an automatic reaction and human curiosity.

On 17 November 2014, I bravely took a before photo of my skin and scar prior to going to a tattoo parlour and letting the artist create a beautiful tattoo over the scar. These are my words that accompanied my Facebook post and before and after photos: *I did it! This is another step in regaining my personal power. The before and after photos clearly show why I did it... Last night I relived what that Infusaport scar represented. The port got infected five weeks after implantation (used to give chemotherapy), I spent eight days in hospital followed by six weeks of intravenous antibiotics 24/7 (nurse visited me at home every day for six weeks) because the infection could have killed me! Now I can let that go. I chose a butterfly, which represents 'new beginnings, rebirth and transformation'. The ladybird or ladybug (in the centre of the tattoo and the indent of skin) is a great symbol of good luck. Gotta say I'm feeling pretty emotional now...*

After many responses to my Facebook post, I also commented: *Thank you everyone. For some reason I've been bawling my eyes out for an hour now... it's like I'm re-writing my history. So many bad* memories coming to the surface! I'm listening to Josh Groban singing 'Remember When it Rained'. And to answer your question, yes it bloody well hurt! I put my Emla cream on at 11am (to numb the area), they rang me to say it was postponed until 1pm, so I put a bit more on, and then he didn't start the tattoo until 1.30pm. The Emla wore off by 2pm! Tattoo took two hours to complete. Hey, the pain was worth it! Replacing a nasty scar with beauty... Now I can wear low cut tops and dresses again, yippee!

In 2014, I also wrote down a few of my own quotes into my *Wellbeing Affirmation Diary 2014*:

- My happiness is in my hands and my heart.
- I breathe fresh air into my Life.
- I am busy in moderation.
- I spin words, I paint pictures.
- Time for a fresh rearrange in my Life.
- Like this Sauvignon Blanc, I am best served young and lightly chilled.
- Keep calm and laugh like a lunatic.
- Sorja is just a Sorja.
- My goal in this life is to make people feel > more than, rather than < less than.
- Our human condition is not to be perfect; otherwise, we would not be on this Earth plane, if not to learn!
- Pain is a manifestation of Inner Turmoil.

Thursday 4 December 2014

As the end of another year approaches, it is natural to take time and reflect on your life. I have been sorting through a lot of memorabilia lately and reliving my life through my own words in my journals. I've laughed at some of the treasures I have kept: old tickets, photos, newspaper clippings of me, poems and short stories I have written since my teens. I have to say that the last forty-eight years of my life have certainly not been mundane… challenging yes, boring absolutely not! Very much looking forward to what the rest of my long life has in store for me. I'd better get a bigger memorabilia box.

We all get bogged down by everyday work, chores, tasks and our 'to do lists'. My wish for my family, friends and acquaintances is that you look at the big picture. Isn't it wonderful to be alive? What an adventure it all is! You never really know what's around the corner; blessings are often hidden within the challenges, love often overpowers fear and finding your own power brings joy to your Soul! I can honestly say that I am proud of myself, for always giving it a go, sorting through my experiences in life and finding the positive slant to my story. I am grateful.

Chapter 34
Conclusion of Book, Not My Life

What is life if not a compilation of births, deaths and marriages? At the end of December 2014, new beginnings were made with the beautiful wedding of our nephew Jarrin and his lovely bride, Morgan. David and I took the opportunity to also have a longer stay in Queensland to catch up with family and sightsee for a few weeks.

Speaking of marriages, my very own was at risk of disintegrating in February 2015; in fact, David and I had a brief trial separation due to a lack of trust in our relationship. People respond to hardship, grief and fear in many different ways, and sometimes resort to unhealthy avenues in an attempt to make themselves feel better. Coping mechanisms are not always in the best interest of the marriage or partnership. Speaking for myself, it was important and crucial to look at the big picture of someone trying to stay strong for far too long; in this case, that someone was my husband. Help was found and achieved through going outside of ourselves, and seeking professional help and guidance. We needed to rebuild our relationship step by step... rediscover the reason we fell in love in the first place, going on dates again, and not taking each other for granted. We acknowledged the hurt caused, and I had to learn how to forgive and let go, and remember the steps travelled together as a couple. As much as this period in my marriage was achingly difficult, we have grown from the experience as a couple and have had many romantic dates, getaways and even cruises after this challenge.

Monday 14 March 2016

One happy woman! I don't have to see my oncologist for one whole year. 'You're our miracle woman,' were his words to me. Yup! I will keep doing what I'm doing because it's obviously working.

Monday 6 June 2016

Another surgery in store for me, not my breast but my left foot. You would think that after all this time, I'd be used to the nerves, uncertainty and trepidation. After all, it's almost a comical song or a character from a soap opera; you witness their life story and roll your eyes at the continued drama. Alas, not from where I stand. I'm not yet fifty years old and my list of surgical procedures is just ridiculous, so numerous that I'm sure I will forget a few. Let me try anyway:

- wrist surgery—removal of a large ganglion
- appendectomy and peritonitis
- laparoscopy and cyst removal
- laparotomy—removal of benign ovarian tumour/abscess and peritonitis
- In Vitro Fertilisation (IVF) and multiple surgical procedures
- total hysterectomy and bilateral oophorectomy
- breast cancer—removal of cancer, breast reconstruction and axillary clearance of cancerous lymph nodes in left armpit
- infusaport (PowerPort) and PICC line for chemotherapy and infusion of antibiotics.

Oh yes, that's without mentioning other past procedures such as renalscopy, gastroscopy, colonoscopy, endoscopy, TOE and more. Well, I guess foot surgery is a first for me. I have to have a ganglion and multiple bone spurs removed from the top of my left foot, as these have been causing me pain for a long time, due to the location and its rubbing against shoes. My foot will be in a cast for two weeks, I have to stay in bed (non-weight bearing) for at least two weeks, and after that a moon boot, crutches and physiotherapy. I am waitlisted for surgery through the public hospital system, so it's about waiting for now. Permission given to roll your eyes with me, you won't be alone! All together now, *Please, Universe, give this Soul a break, I think Sorja has earned it!*

Saturday 24 September 2016

Way back at the end of 2015, I sent out invitations to family and friends to help celebrate my reaching the fabulous milestone of fifty years of age on the Saturday before my actual birthday. *Hallelujah!* The majority of those invited had been kept in the dark about a second celebration. For many months, a select few had been assisting us to organise secret plans, to unfold on the evening. Oh, what a fantastic night, one that will remain special for the rest of my life. This is what I wrote on Facebook on the evening of Saturday 24 September 2016:

Secret can now be revealed. David and I just renewed our wedding vows in front of over fifty loved ones (family and friends) at my fiftieth birthday party! Surprise!

As a special keepsake, my friend and wedding celebrant Jayne Dilley suggested I paint a tree on a small canvas for the occasion. All of our guests marked their presence at the 'Renewal of Our Vows' ceremony by dipping their finger or thumb into little pots of paint and pressing them against the branches to create different coloured leaves upon my tree. My tree was no longer barren.

It was an emotional night in many ways: the surprises along the way; the presence of so many of my family and friends; the dancing to music; and the food and drink, laughter and tears. Jayne (A Day Your Way Ceremonies) is an incredibly special lady whose love for being a celebrant shows from the initial plans to the big day. The renewal of our vows on our twenty-first wedding anniversary was magical, thanks to all of the beautiful touches Jayne added.

Later on, I posted, *Yes it's 3am and yes I'm the last one awake. My loved ones are sound asleep, I am at peace and I have tidied everything around the house (in typical can't let go control Sorja style). I am so very grateful for the blessed day and night I have just lived. Photos will follow once my beautiful professional photographer and friend Jenny Willis supplies me with the evidence of the night. So thankful for the yummy food by Eden's Catering much appreciated by everyone. I meant to say this to everyone after my OMG cake organised by my lovely husband (seriously, he managed to get the same cake decorator, Marguerite Cakes, who made the cake for Prince Charles' sixtieth birthday in Australia!), but I was so stunned! So... this is what I meant to say... Through my life's journey I have learned to be my authentic self. The fact that I have so many of you here tonight to celebrate means the world to me, and confirms that you accept me just as I am. I am very blessed to be here, to be fifty. I feel very loved and I thank you from the bottom of my heart. I look forward to opening all of my prezzies later, much later today. Sincerest thank you to everyone, much love.*

Darling David gave Marguerite Cakes a photo of one of the acrylic artworks I had painted and, as an artist herself, she recreated the colours and image as best she could onto my birthday cake. That cake is something I will never forget, and it was so delicious. Luckily, even after everyone had eaten a piece, there were leftovers for a long time afterwards.

Saturday 22 October 2016

Healing the feeling, feeling the healing. In every photo I have from childhood, I am the tallest. When I was eleven or twelve, and a foreigner from Finland, I was so tall that I towered over every girl and boy my age. At thirteen or fourteen, the cruel kids in Queensland called me Santa Claus because of how white my hair and skin was. At fifteen, and now living in Tasmania, I was mistaken for my older sister's mother because I was tall, an Australian size 14 and wearing a bulky sweater. These memories are like brands, from so long ago, yet they feel so fresh. At sixteen, I got into Hobart Wrest Point Casino because I looked like I was at least eighteen. Irma and I pretended to be the same age—yet not twins! The footballers chatting us up certainly caught us out on my lie; how embarrassing.

At eighteen, I worked for the State Government Public Service and decided to do something about my weight. In an attempt to fit in, I tried to hide my weight loss shopping bags from my workmates... but they noticed. I was a five foot eleven inches tall young woman, a size 14 to16, yet made to feel abnormal by the 'professionals'. And so continued the self-hatred of my body and my identity. Such a sad spiral. I managed to lose fifteen kilos and kept it off until I went travelling around Europe—all those foods to sample and, let's admit it, gorge on. At nineteen and twenty, I was at my heaviest, an Australian size 16. As I travelled around Europe, I was alternatively ridiculed for my size (I caught a young American man viciously mimicking my walk and talk at a youth hostel—another branded memory) and admired and lusted after by many Italian and Greek men... bless them. In Finland, aged twenty, I worked hard, I worked out, I ate less, and I succeeded in becoming a skinny size 12 for my return to Australia and my twenty-first birthday party. Oh, how the compliments flowed, yet I was the same 'me'. At twenty-three and twenty-four, alas the weight crept back up to a size 16, and my female Dutch flatmate in Melbourne denied me the pleasure of going out with 'the gang' because I didn't fit the part—petite that is—what an arrow to my heart! Denied to join in because of my height and size. She actually told me that I would be more comfortable at home, solidifying my belief that size matters. So the yo-yo continued: losing weight, gaining weight, the fight against the bulk but also the fight against societal expectations. Over the years... an Australian size 12, 14, 16, 14, 12, 10, 12, 14, 16, 14... You know, underneath it all I was still Sorja, whatever clothes I wore.

In my twenty-one-year marriage to David, I have slid through the scale of size 10 to size 16 and yet he loves me no matter what label I wear. At fifty years of age, I am a size 14 and you know what? I accept that I am 180cm's tall, nearly six foot and a size 14—and that is perfect! Don't always listen to the professionals and experts. It's how you feel in your own skin. Look in the mirror and say, *I am enough. I am beautiful. I am worthy.* By the age of fifty or more, we've earned 'our stripes'. We've endured our own personal wars. I know I crave peace from my own body battles. I am enough. I am beautiful. I am worthy.

As I think about births, deaths and marriages, there have been a few births into our family (I am a great-aunt now) but far too many deaths. In the past few years, I have farewelled many loved ones, and too many to cancer! I want to name just a few; these beloved individuals have appeared in my dreams, and made it clear that it is okay to speak their names in the context of this book. With love, honour and remembrance: Penelope Mary Elizabeth Shepherd (28/01/66 – 08/09/15), Lindrene Esther Olivia Roberts, also known as Lou Lou (27/10/51 – 15/09/15), Andrew Robert Jackson (24/12/69 – 27/05/16) and Yvonne Weckmann (17/05/66 – 09/08/17).

I have been to many funerals and my tears have flowed. I have also asked why I have survived when they did not? My answer came to me in deep meditation. We had all agreed to belong to a cancer group—our common 'Cancer Pact'. Many belonged to this group and we would, as a group, affect many, many people. As a Survivor of cancer, I would continue to teach on behalf of them. In turn, they would continue to learn through my life journey, vicariously but lovingly. I feel their presence often; I felt some of them at my fiftieth birthday party and they created the most gorgeous rainbow over us as we celebrated. Sometimes when I'm struggling or fearful, in the words of a song, or the sight of an eagle or white cockatoo (or their feathers), they let me know that they are with me, even if I'm driving alone in my car. *I know I am not alone.*

February 2017 was an extremely hard time for me and my family. I finally had my foot surgery on Monday 13 February. All went well, thank God. I spent two weeks in a plaster cast, bedridden but able to endure through lots of shows on my iPad, art therapy, reading and visits from friends. We hired a wheelchair to help me zip through the house to the kitchen. We had another cancer scare with our fur baby Xena, who had a growth on her lip! After surgery to remove the growth, the two of us were a sorry sight on the bed, me with my plaster cast and Xena in her bucket collar to prevent her from further injuring herself. Luckily, it was a benign growth. Thank God and the Universe.

TREE WITH NO LEAVES

On Sunday 26 February, I received the heartbreaking news that my dad, my Pa had suffered a heart attack at home in Tasmania. Can you imagine how hard it is for me to write about this? My mother and father had both been sober. By this point in time, they had not been drinking any alcohol for one and a half years. How proud we all were. My mother performed CPR for a long time before the ambulance arrived. Later, the helicopter flew beloved Pa from Orford to Hobart. Over numerous hours, many, many hands kept bringing Pa back to life. How helpless I felt being so far away in Western Australia, unable to travel due to my foot and the possible risks of flying. Only a month earlier, on Wednesday 4 January, I had farewelled my Ma and Pa at Orford after spending two and a half weeks with Katri, Irma, Khan and my parents for Christmas and New Year. Those memories are imprinted on my mind and I hope also on my siblings' minds. When I hugged my Pa, I had a strong feeling that it would be for the last time physically.

On Monday 27 February 2017, I went to have my cast removed, was given a moon boot and shown how to walk using my crutches. With my friend Sharyn, I bravely went through the process of speaking with my orthopaedic surgeon to find out how everything was going. Inside, I was screaming that my father was in ICU, barely with us but kept alive by machines. I was keeping a brave face because that is what is expected by society, eh? How I wanted to scream and cry, but I didn't...

Later that night, as I spoke with Irma in Queensland, we both cried copiously. Two of my sisters, my brother and my brother-in-law had made arrangements to fly to Tasmania to be there, not only for Pa but also for Ma. As Irma and I spoke, something strange happened in our conversation—twice. At this point in time, my father was on life support and hooked up to so many man-made life-prolonging apparatuses… Some of you may find this hard to believe, but twice my sister and I were suddenly disconnected from our phone conversation. In Queensland, Irma didn't hear anything when we were disconnected; on the other hand, I heard very clearly my father breathing mechanically! I heard, oh so clearly, the ventilator (myself in Western Australia, my father in Tasmania). I also heard (so hard to write these words; I am crying as I do) my Pa saying to switch him off! He was no longer there in his body, had not been there since his heart attack on Sunday. He had jumped out and was watching it all from outside of his body. He was apologising to my Ma about the trauma surrounding his death… He was communicating these words directly into my head, telepathically. Needless to say, I was an absolute mess when I reconnected with Irma, and I shouted to her that he wanted to be switched off.

On Tuesday 28 February 2017, before my brother Visa, sisters Kirsti and Irma, and brother-in-law Steve could arrive, a doctor from Royal Hobart Hospital ICU rang Mum to say that there was no indication of life. They asked for her permission to switch life support off. The official record of death is Tuesday 28 February; however deep in my Soul, I know that Pa left his body on Sunday 26 February, at age seventy-nine.

I wasn't able to attend my father's funeral the following week; however, I was honoured to be asked to write a eulogy. I touched upon his essence, his love of nature, his sense of humour and being a gentle man. Irma spoke my words to those assembled at the funeral service and that gives me a sense of comfort. Pa understands why I couldn't be there and, in his way, he wanted to spare his youngest daughter some pain from a pain-filled life.

Monday 20 March 2017

At my annual check-up, my current oncologist—Dr Tim Clay—told me that without mentioning my name, he uses my story to tell his patients about this miracle woman he knows who is here against the odds. I said that I don't mind because it's a good story and I love to encourage people not to give up. A timely reminder to remember that I am stronger than what I think at times.

Wednesday 31 May 2017

What a funny emotion grief is. Not funny ha, ha, ha, but funny in the way that it's so unpredictable. There are no formulae even though many academics and psychologists have tried to come up with the stages of grief. Personally, I think it is so dry—and yet grief is anything but dry. I have shed copious amounts of tears, foolhardily thinking, *Phew, that's done then; I'm over that phase of grief.* Revisiting a memory from years gone by, the emotions are just as fresh, just as real. Drawing on my years of studying and being a counsellor, I think the truth is that feelings never expire. As humans, we can tap into a time and place and relive how we felt on that day. Healing occurs each and every time we allow ourselves to feel, whether about the past, present or future. It's the release of pent-up emotion that helps, so that it doesn't stagnate in our cells and cause us physical mischief.

Friday 28 July 2017

I was bullied for being different from the moment I arrived in Australia from Finland at the age of five. I tried my hardest to fit in. All the way through primary school and high school on the Gold Coast, Queensland. It never quite worked. I couldn't squeeze myself into the box they all wanted to put me in. In fact, I distinctly remember nearly coming to physical blows with two young girls on the volley ball court (funny how I still remember their names from when I was thirteen).

'You really love yourself, don't you?' one of them asked.

Being pertinent, and having had enough, I replied, 'Oh, yes!'

And I started kissing my own forearm to piss them off. It worked! Little did they know I was covering up my low self-esteem and self-confidence. Ever since then, I've spent many years moulding myself to different scenarios and groups, never quite 'hitting the mark'—well, in my mind anyway.

What is so wrong with coming to a point of accepting yourself, flaws and all? Isn't that what we as Souls are here to learn? To go against the tide sometimes... to find our authentic selves despite the opinions of others? Yes, it can be a lonely road at times. I have been called weird, strange and different throughout my life. That's okay; I'd rather those adjectives than being labelled boring. The shy five-year-old in me is still grappling with the fifty-year-old... can I be myself and be loved? Is it okay? Am I okay? Am I enough? My fifty-year-old self is replying to my five-year-old self, 'Oh sweetie, keep being you. Those who want to stay in your life will and those who don't... they were there for a reason and a season and now let them go...'

Friday 13 October 2017

My eldest sister, Kirsti, travelled from Queensland to Tasmania to support our Ma on 10 September (again after many trips). Ma was inconsolable after the death of her life partner of so many years. *The grief is bruising, and memorable long after the colours of the bruises fade away.* Earlier in the year, Mum and Kirsti sorted out the clothes to give away to charity and what keepsakes to hold on to. I love and honour the strength of both Kirsti and my mother. Unfortunately, grief often acts like the Grim Reaper, leading us to act out and cling to what brings us momentary comfort. For my mother, it led to her breaking her sobriety after one and a half years. No blame, no judgement, only understanding...

From far away, I felt my family in Tasmania celebrate what would have been my father's eightieth birthday on 10 October. Visa, Susie, Kirsti and Ma honoured Pa by laying a plaque at his grave. I had input into some of the words with my brother, once again, I am so grateful for being a part of it all.

Oftentimes, life is so unpredictable. Kirsti left Orford on Thursday 12 October to return to her family in Queensland. Visa and Susie left the following morning. What truly happened with Ma after they all left, only Ma can tell—if she could remember it. What we do know is that the local nurse (a scheduled visit) found Ma unconscious, having hit her head on the slates under the fireplace at her home. We thank God that this lady found her at lunchtime on that Friday and was able to call an ambulance; it's unbearable to think about the alternative. As a result of a brain bleed (extensive bilateral subdural haematomas), Mum underwent emergency brain surgery at Royal Hobart Hospital.

Many months of hospitalisation and rehabilitation were required. Kirsti, Irma and I flew to Tasmania on numerous occasions to help and support Mum as much as humanly possible. This is what I posted on Facebook to my family and friends on Monday 4 December 2017:

I know I've been quiet about Ma lately... I haven't found the words to express how I've been feeling and not known what to say. Truth be told, life isn't always kind. I know we all like happily-ever-after endings after a time of sorrow and hardship—especially for our family this year—sometimes, or should I say oftentimes, it's beyond our control what happens with our loved ones. We feel powerless, we may try to push things to happen because we feel frustrated, we struggle to realise that not every event, situation or outcome is in fact in our hands, and we release our pent up breath and try to let go—to trust that 'everything is in divine order'... Ma has been in hospital nearly two months now!

Ma is not the Ma of old. In fact, the sad truth is that Ma is old and even sadder is the realisation for us that Ma is living in her reality of dementia—an ever changing existence in her mind. A fluctuation of moods, time zones, memories and thought processes. If only a person could be happy in this world of dementia then it wouldn't appear so sad to witness or hear about... I'm not sure I would like to spend time in that world. Anyway, time for me to soak my 'young' bones in a hot bath and enjoy my candles and music—to pause for a moment.

Thursday 25 January 2018

Find Your Feet, Find Your Fight (written 25 January—posted on 29 January):

Life has knocked my family like an unexpected foul play or 'hitting below the belt'... In terms of boxing, since our Pa died, as a family unit, we have gone into defensive guard mode. We have bobbed and weaved, parried and blocked and clinched... On occasion we have had to resort to jabs, uppercuts, hooks and cross just to keep going on... We have fought for our mother. We have fought *amongst ourselves and against each other... However, now in more news of heartbreak and sad tidings... We as a Unity of Blood, we can choose, through our love for each other, to support, lean upon and be leaned upon—that is what family is all about.*

The news that led me to writing this was the discovery that my eldest sister, Kirsti, had just been diagnosed with oesophageal cancer.

On Monday 19 February 2018, I flew to Tasmania to help Irma with the most difficult challenge of packing up Mum from her nursing home. On Friday 23 February, the three of us then flew from Hobart to Maroochydore, Queensland via Melbourne. That journey could be another book in itself! All joking aside, I don't know how we managed it all: the luggage (suitcases, Mum's wheelchair and her walker), an entire day of travel, with Ma being strapped to her airline seat for hours on end due to a lack of strength in her back. We were all in pain once we finally arrived at her new nursing home. What an absolute trooper Ma was. Luckily, she was able to take medication for pain and to help her sleep.

After a few days of visiting and making sure all was okay, Irma and I drove down to the Gold Coast to support Kirsti and her husband Steve. On Tuesday 27 February 2018, the day before the first anniversary of Pa's death, Kirsti underwent a massive five-hour surgery to remove the cancer from her oesophagus and stomach. We all knew Pa was there with us, supporting us from the other side. Kirsti stayed in hospital for ten days and amazed everyone with her strength and determination. After a week, Irma and I drove back up to the Sunshine Coast, and we visited Ma every day until my flight home to Perth on Thursday 8 March.

Sunday 25 March 2018

Following our epic family challenges, it's taken me over two weeks of being home to return to some kind of even keel. I'm the first to admit that I was off balance; being a Libra, I tend to tilt my scales a bit. Exhaustion, sensitivity and self-doubt led me to question whether I had done enough to help others and whether I am a Reiki *Master* (I qualified as a Reiki Master in 2015). I had forgotten that, like a sponge, I inadvertently absorbed some of the feelings, emotions and fears of those I had provided Reiki healing to and supported as best I could. I've given myself time to sleep, rest, watch nature outside, walk our girls, binge on Netflix, read romance, listen to music, make a new batch of flower essences, enjoy relaxing baths and—joy of joys—paint. Now, on this Sunday afternoon, housework and chores are done, and I'm reflecting on the past year: Pa passing on, Ma living in her world of dementia, and big sister courageously tackling her challenge with cancer, the many interstate trips I have made, my continued visits with another new oncologist, grief and loss of friendships. Really, it's no wonder the wind was knocked out of me. My own erratic behaviour—impulsive decisions and then changes of mind—has calmed somewhat. As long as I continue to learn from my actions and forgive myself for not mastering my emotions, then I grow as a Soul living an earthly existence. I'll let go of the pressure to be someone I'm not, and continue to be me.

Friday 8 June 2018

The last chapter, number thirty-four of my book is called Conclusion of Book, Not My Life. I have finished writing and typing over twenty years of my life. I have wanted to write the last pages of this chapter for many months. I have struggled because I wanted my book to end like a fairy tale, just like my middle name ('Satu' means fairy tale in Finnish). However, life is rarely like a fairy tale, is it? I have also come to realise the totally irrational fear that finishing my book, my life's work, would somehow mean that I was done, my story complete... I have so many stories and books in me that await my embrace: fiction, poetry, children's stories and even romance novels. My imagination runs riot in my dreams—many, many stories yet to be told. I am not done yet.

Thursday 14 June 2018

There are many happy occasions to look forward to: more travelling, weddings to attend, and births of new family members. Realistically, there are more funerals to attend in the future, too. The little pockets of happiness we find in life allow us to endure the dips of sadness. My creativity and sense of humour, combined with the ability to persevere and persist, will keep me on this Earth plane for as long as I am needed.

I thank each one of you for travelling alongside me through my words. I no longer feel like a tree with no leaves; I feel very full and alive with *life*.

Contact the Author

If you resonated with my book and found my words helpful, I welcome your thoughts.

I encourage the sharing of experiences and support of one another.

Please email the author of *Tree With No Leaves* to the address below:

sorja.author@bigpond.com

www.ingramcontent.com/pod-product-compliance
Lightning Source LLC
Chambersburg PA
CBHW040239010526
44107CB00065B/2805